CANADIAN LEGISLATURES 1992

ISSUES, STRUCTURES AND COSTS

ROBERT J. FLEMING

GLOBAL PRESS

To my grandchildren,
Nicolas, Philippe and Amélie,
who are the future.

ISBN: 0-7715-3980-0

Publishing Director: Susan Yates
Editor: Warren Fisher

Global Press
A Division of Canada Publishing Corporation
164 Commander Boulevard
Agincourt, Ontario
M1S 3C7

Jacket and Text Design: Brant Cowie/ArtPlus

Printed in Canada by The Bryant Press

LET US TEACH OURSELVES, and others, that politics should be an expression of a desire to contribute to the happiness of the community, rather than a need to cheat or rape the community.

Let us teach ourselves, and others, that politics cannot only be an art of the possible, especially if this means an art of speculations, calculations, intrigues, secret deals and pragmatic manouevering, but that it can even be an art of the impossible, namely, the art to improve ourselves and the world.

President Vaclav Havel
Czechoslovakia
1990 New Year's Address

Contents

Part Four: The American Counterpart

Appendix

Acknowledgements

THE HARD work, personal interest and enthusiasm of many people made possible the publication of this, the Tenth Edition of *Canadian Legislatures*. In order to provide the latest information on the various facets of the administration and management of the Senate, House of Commons and Canada's legislatures, it is necessary to obtain a large volume of information for assessment, analysis, checking and re-checking, within a very short period of time. To those who have been a part of this process, and also to those who were involved in the preparation of articles, and the monographs for the *Canadian Legislatures* Roundtable on Government and its Institutions, my appreciative thanks.

The first discussions about the Roundtable took place last July on a cottage porch overlooking the St. Lawrence River when John Hallward, Neil McKentry and I (like many Canadians) were talking about the future of the country. The result was a series of short articles by Louis Applebaum, John Robert Colombo, Jean de Grandpré, Bill Dimma, Barbara Eastman, Paul Fox, Reva Gerstein, Peter Hanson, Eric Jackman, John Mallory, Susan McCorquodale, John Meisel, Fraser Mustard, Knowlton Nash, Chris Ondaatje, Tim Reid and David Taras. Their contribution to this edition is significant.

Donald MacDonald has provided yeoman service in his analysis of 1988 election costs in Canada and the United States, as have David Docherty—a former Ontario Legislative Intern, who with associate Paul Holmes, reviews election statistics since 1988. They are joined by Michael Adams and Jordan Levitin of Environics Research Group who present the findings of their poll for *Canadian Legislatures* on third party advertising as it affected the 1988 federal election.

Many other people who have provided assistance, support and encouragement come to mind: Gordon Barnhart, Mary Dickerson, Marilyn Domagalski, Basil Entwistle, Patrick Fafard, Jerry Goodis, Brian Hay, Tom Jurenka, Brian Land, Tom Mitchinson, Binx Remnant, Doug Schauerte and Erik Spicer.

The original impetus for this book was provided through my association, starting twenty years ago, with Dalton Camp and Douglas Fisher who with the late Farquhar Oliver constituted the Ontario Commission on the Legislature (The Camp Commission). I am grateful for their friendship over the years and their contribution to this edition of *Canadian Legislatures*. I also extend thanks to William Pound, Executive Director of the National Conference of State Legislatures for his help in preparing the U.S. material, and to Rich Jones for his overview of administrative arrangements in U.S. state legislatures.

Those who have helped *Canadian Legislatures* assemble information in the Senate, House of Commons and the provinces and territories are: John McCrea (House of Commons), Gordon Lovelace and Frances Bertrand (Senate), Elizabeth Murphy (Newfoundland), Charles MacKay (Prince Edward Island), Don Hubley (Nova Scotia), Diane Taylor Myles (New Brunswick), Gilles Angers (Quebec), Gayle Laws (Ontario), Bev Bosiak

(Manitoba), Linda Kaminski (Saskatchewan), Jackie Breault and Kathy Bruce-Kavanagh (Alberta), Ian Fraser (British Columbia), Sandy Kim Harris (Northwest Territories) and Jane Steele (Yukon). Their important role in the preparation of this book is recognized, and I salute them.

I would also like to thank the Jackman Foundation and the Churchill Society for the Advancement of Parliamentary Democracy for the assistance which they have rendered in the past in helping to establish *Canadian Legislatures* as a permanent publication.

Through the good offices of friends Eunice Thorne and Ed Matheson of Amersand Communications Services Inc. in Ottawa, I was put in touch with Susan Yates, Publishing Director of Global Press, who was courageous enough to take on this project. Her ability to always be cool under fire is impressive, as is her penchant for clarity and thoroughness. Warren Fisher has carried an enormous load with equal good humour; he never misses a beat. Both Warren and Susan are supported by Eileen Brett, who is equally enthusiastic. Heartfelt thanks.

An undertaking of this magnitude would not have been possible without the support and ideas of my wife, Patsy, as well as our son, John, and his family. I do thank them all for their patience and understanding in the face of deadline after deadline.

Introduction

CANADIAN LEGISLATURES was begun in 1979 in response to a need to find out how the House of Commons and the ten provincial and territorial legislatures handled their general administrative arrangements, including indemnities, salaries, allowances and services for their elected members. At the time, I was Administrator of the Ontario Legislature and this type of information was almost impossible to obtain.

The first edition of what was then entitled *A Comparative Study of Administrative Structures of Canadian Legislatures* consisted of 32 typewritten pages, cerlox bound.

In 1992, although it retains its original purpose, *Canadian Legislatures* hardly resembles its early prototype. What began as an attempt to provide information about the structures and costs of Canadian legislatures has grown into a major project of national information gathering and sharing, geared to making the operation of Canada's political institutions more understandable to those both inside and outside the system. Now our research includes the Senate, and for broad, comparative purposes, the 50 U.S. state legislatures have been added as well. From time to time, legislatures from overseas have also been included. An analysis of the so-called "new" Supreme Soviet of the former U.S.S.R., largely a product of the reforms brought by former President Mikahil Gorbachev, was scheduled to appear in this issue of *Canadian Legislatures*, but events in what is now the Confederation of Independent States made that impossible: it no longer exists.

In 1992, there are 1 065 members elected to the House of Commons and the provincial and territorial legislatures. Between them they are responsible for a 1992 total operating budget of $585 million. In 1982, just a decade ago, that same figure stood at $263 million. Collectively, and often singly, legislatures are burgeoning institutions.

It would be impossible to produce *Canadian Legislatures* without considering the "operating environment" of legislative institutions as well as reporting on their administration and management. The subject matter is simple, but the traditions, culture and attitudes, together with day-to-day practices which have tended to develop in a kaleidoscopic manner, are extremely complex, and must always be taken into account. More than anything else, it is these "ill-defined" forces that have determined just how Canadian legislatures are administered.

Politics, as presently practiced in Canada, seems to have developed a reputation for devouring good people. It is clear that a great deal of the responsibility for this rests with the political culture which has particularly developed in the past decade. It seems impossible for the individual elected member, no matter how well-motivated or well-intentioned at the outset, to rise above the expected "norm" for the party man or woman. That norm in 1992, as may be seen from some of the articles in this book, seems divisive, petty and strangely at odds with the greater national challenges confronting politicians. Unfortunately, this has carried over into how our legislatures are administered, and their associated costs.

Denis Vaugeois, a historian from Laval University, and former member of the Quebec National Assembly, in his 1982 report entitled, "The National Assembly in Evolution", sounded a prophetic note for the whole legislative community in Canada. He attempted to put his finger on the pulse of the legislature as an institution of government, which should not be perceived, as he put it, "purely in terms of raw political power. Another power must appear: that of the House as a whole, and of its members without regard to their place at the right or left of the Speaker. This power is perceived when the House votes unanimously at times of crisis, displaying signs of life and action. The people recognize then the supreme authority."

In Canada, our elected members are working diligently, often enthusiastically, and usually under difficult circumstances brought about by separation from families, pressures from constituents, the frustration of not having "real power" (at least not in the ordinary sense of the word), the inflexibility of the partisan party system itself, and the need to get re-elected.

Unlike the United States, where there is a large cadre of people in the private sector who have had substantial political and/or government experience and move back and forth between sectors, Canada doesn't have this tradition. Nevertheless, there are a growing number of Canadians who at one time or another have served in government, or been associated with government in some way. They have "been there" and are ready to contribute their ideas and expertise as "citizen diplomats".

We invited some of them to submit their best thinking to *Canadian Legislatures*, hence the special section, A *Canadian Legislatures* Roundtable on Government and Its Institutions.

Knowlton Nash, veteran CBC television anchor and reporter, writes about giving the public "more ice time" in the political process. Speaking about the need for openness everywhere in governmental institutions, he says "The loss of public confidence in politicians in Canada is unparalleled and so, too, is the challenge in retrieving that confidence. But retrieval is essential if Canada is to survive."

Jean de Grandpré, a respected figure in the Canadian business world ventures forth to give his views on how the Senate should be reformed, and Tim Reid, President of the Canadian Chamber of Commerce and a former member of the Ontario Legislature writes about the need to train prospective leaders to be bridge-crossers. "There are too many solitudes between those who argue public policy issues in Canada and, in the end, it makes for bad policy. Here I refer not to the public arguments among partisan (party) politicians but to a much deeper division. And that is isolation from one another of our leaders in the different worlds of business, the public service, labour, academia, social agencies and politics."

Reva Gerstein, well-known psychologist and public-spirited Canadian, picks up on the same theme, "Key players who 'kindle' the flames of change must be civil servants, legislators and the public at large, energized by responsible media and committed leadership," and Louis Applebaum who served as Chairman of the Federal Culture Policy Review Committee, and co-authored the Applebaum/Hebert Report in 1982 points out that, "While we busily search for ways to reform our political system or procedures, we cannot escape an issue that is perhaps more vital, viz: what do we Canadians believe, what do we stand for and are ready to do battle for."

Political practitioners, Hershell Ezrin, Douglas Fisher, and Dalton Camp each of whom have had considerable experience at various levels of politics and government write in this edition on themes related to injecting new life into the established political parties, a subject which concerns them enormously. As Ezrin points out, "The road to parliamentary and political revival should start with a focus on the individual elected member. It is ironic that in the haste to improve the system, we focus on democratizing the Senate, at best a chamber of sober reflection, rather than revitalizing the most accountable institution, the House of Commons."

In attempting to assess the growth of Canadian legislatures in the past decade in terms of structures and costs, we examine in the the following pages a large number of elements relating to members' indemnities, salaries, tax-free allowances, services, and general administrative issues as they apply to most legislatures.

Perhaps more than anything else, our analyses show that if, as we are told in the article by Michael Adams, the restoration of the public's faith in government largely hinges on their perception of politicians, political institutions and processes, then a great deal of work is required to clarify and straighten out some of the problems associated with the costs and management of these institutions.

This review, at times, may emphasize how things are done in the Ontario Legislature more than some others, partly because information from that legislature is, for the most part, in the public domain, and because I spent considerable time at Queen's Park in a "hands-on" capacity. I believe that drawing on my experience there enriches the depth of the analyses; it is not intended to single out the Ontario Legislature for special comment, nor to make the book a "central Canada" document.

Some across-the-board conclusions emerge as a result of endeavoring to obtain a "bird's eye view" of legislature operations in Canada:

- Legislators are paid relatively well, when their basic indemnity and tax-free allowance (which in nearly all jurisdictions is being treated as "salary") are taken into account. This is reflected in the Table "1991 Actual Earnings", on Page 76, and does not include any other per diems, or tax-free emoluments they may receive.

- At a time when taxpayers are demanding openness in government, Boards of Internal Economy are, for the most part, reluctant to make public the individual expenditures of elected members.

- The intense partisanship of our brand of parliamentary democracy places tremendous pressure on some caucuses to get as much as they can in terms of funding from the Legislature, so that they're not placed at a disadvantage either in terms of remaining in power, or trying to win an election. This is distorting "orderly" growth in some legislatures.

- There is an urgent need to establish bodies outside the legislature to review all matters relating to indemnities, salaries, allowances, pensions, etc., so that fairness and wise management of the public purse may prevail.

This book catalogues facts and figures and makes recommendations as to how some areas of legislature management and administration might be handled in the future. We do this because we believe in those who have been elected, we believe in political parties, and in the integrity of the political system in Canada. If changes are to take place in the way things are done, however, it will have to begin from within the system. It is urgent for Canada that this process begin.

Robert J. Fleming
March, 1992

PART ONE

Political Commentary

CHAPTER ONE

The Impact of Advocacy Advertising: A Case Study of the 1988 Election Campaign

BY MICHAEL ADAMS AND JORDAN A. LEVITIN

Michael Adams is President and Jordan A. Levitin is a Senior Associate of Environics Research Group Limited. Environics, one of Canada's leading polling firms, is well known for its surveys on national issues. This analysis by Mr. Adams and Mr. Levitin is based on a survey conducted for Canadian Legislatures.

THE CANADIAN political culture has changed dramatically in the course of the last two decades. Technological, demographic and lifestyle changes are transforming the way Canadians view the political process. We are a less ideological and increasingly pragmatic people and our decisions today are more likely to be driven by information than by instinct or loyalty to a political party.

Institutions, governments and private corporations face intense daily scrutiny, rising expectations and seemingly contradictory signals from the public. We have become a more critical and skeptical people thanks in part to the media, particularly television, which has made Canadians one of the best informed societies in history.

At the same time, there are those who say that the Canadian electoral process is under duress and that it is time to take stock of what is happening. As Canadians debate the pros and cons of their style of democratic government and look ahead to the next federal election which could come as early as the fall of 1992, they would do well to reflect on the unprecedented level of third party involvement in the 1988 federal election campaign. For example, it caused many Canadians to seriously question the role and influence of advocacy advertising in the modern democratic process.

Advocacy advertising is advertising that promotes a particular point of view on an issue by groups other than political parties. Over the past decade, for instance, the tobacco and pharmaceutical companies have launched impressive campaigns either supporting or opposing government legislation that would affect their industries. All manner of professional and public interest groups are making increasingly sophisticated efforts to influence public opinion in an era when public opinion is having a greater impact on government policies and regulations.

To what extent are Canadians aware of advocacy advertising? How does the public evaluate this form of advertising? Does it engage their imagination and their support? Do they believe that access to this particular kind of public forum is fair and equitable? If not, should advocacy advertising be banned during political campaigns or even between elections?

To examine public attitudes on this issue, Environics surveyed Canadians four months after the November 1988 federal election. This survey was based on in-home personal interviews conducted between March 7 and 28, 1989 among a modified probability sample of 2 005 adults.

The poll results indicate that Canadians are often not aware that they are being exposed to advocacy advertising. Only one-third (33%) recalled having seen or heard such advertising. Almost half (48%) said they had not seen these ads and two in ten (20%) could not remember.

Among those who recall having seen advocacy advertising, the largest proportion cite abortion as the subject of the ads they saw (26%, including 14% who specified pro-life ads and 2% who mentioned pro-choice advertisements). Environmental issues (8%) and free trade were also mentioned (5%).

Questions about the quality of the ads elicited evaluations that are comparable to those found for other kinds of advertising. Majorities considered them interesting (57%) and informative (59%), but a much smaller proportion (36%) said the ads were believable. Significant proportions expressed no opinion.

Although 36% may seem like a low level of believability, it is comparable to other surveys of believability for product advertising. For example, a December 1989 Environics survey of attitudes toward advertising that dealt with health and nutrition found that approximately two-thirds thought these ads were informative, but only one-third judged them trustworthy.

Canadians were somewhat equivocal when asked if they approve of advocacy advertising. A slight majority (51%) said they do approve, and only about half as many (25%) expressed outright disapproval. But a large proportion—24%—offered no opinion.

Regarding questions of fairness and control, the poll results indicated that Canadians do question the accessibility of advocacy advertising, but they do not favour its banning. Clearly, fairness of access was not a factor for most Canadians when they were asked if this kind of advertising should or should not be allowed.

Only three Canadians in ten (30%) said they believe all groups have an equal opportunity to publicize their views. A majority (55%) agreed that some groups have an unfair advantage when it comes to promoting their point of view through the media.

Nevertheless, although more Canadians thought advocacy advertising should be banned during election campaigns (33%) than during non-campaign periods (19%), majorities opposed the suggestion that these ads should be suppressed, either during campaigns (56%) or at any other time (71%).

Better-educated Canadians were more likely than others to perceive an unfair advantage (from 41% of those with less than nine years of schooling to 66% of those with post-secondary education). At the same time, better-educated Canadians were also far more likely than others to say that advocacy ads should be allowed during elections (from 45% of those with less than nine years of schooling to 70% of those with a university degree) and in non-campaign periods (from 62% of those with less than nine years of schooling to 81% of those with a university degree). Similarly, members of the younger age groups were more likely to perceive unfairness, but less likely to support the banning of ads.

Supporters of the federal New Democratic Party (64%) were more likely than either Liberals (54%) or Conservatives (55%) to perceive unfair access to the media. Union members (63%) also expressed a high degree of concern. There was little variation, however, among these groups in terms of approving advocacy ads, either during or between campaign periods.

The 1988 Election and the Free Trade Debate: A Case Study

In October 1983, all three political parties unanimously endorsed amendments to the federal Elections Act prohibiting third-party advertising that supported or opposed a party or candidate during a federal election unless the advertiser has authorization. Transgressions were punishable by a $5 000 fine or up to five years in jail.

These provisions were successfully challenged in the courts, however, when an Alberta judge ruled in

1984 that they violated the freedom of expression guaranteed under the Canadian Charter of Rights and Freedoms. The Conservatives, who won the 1984 election, never appealed the ruling.

By the 1988 federal election campaign, the lobby groups had built their war-chests and planned their strategies. In some targeted ridings, Campaign Life attempted to make abortion the issue. Many others were concerned with the Canada-U.S. free trade agreement. Some, like the Canadian Alliance for Trade and Job Opportunities, were attempting to counter what they perceived to be a "left-liberal" bias in the media by taking their messages directly to the public.

It is clear from the spending estimates of such groups as the pro free trade Alliance, the National Citizens' Coalition, the Alberta government, the Business Council on National Issues, the Canadian Federation of Independent Business, the Pro-Canada Network, the Canadian Manufacturers Association and dozens of smaller groups, that opponents of the free trade deal could not match the budgets of such pro free trade organizations.

An Environics survey conducted among a representative sample of 1 500 Canadian adults in December 1988 (just after the federal election) found that only 37% of Canadian voters said they had firmly made up their minds at the time the election writ was issued on October 1. Another thirteen percent reported that they had decided during the first three weeks of the campaign. This means that half of the electorate made up their minds after the leaders' debates and during the period of intense advertising by the parties and the pro and anti free trade forces.

The survey indicated that, in comparison to the paid advertising of the other two parties, the ads commissioned by the federal Progressive Conservative Party were the most memorable. Pluralities also considered the Conservatives' ads were more informative (27%) and had the greatest influence on the way people voted (48%). The influence of these ads—many of which questioned Opposition Leader John Turner's credibility on the free trade issue— was also reflected in the finding that the proportion who said the Liberals had the most truthful advertising (12%) was only about half those who said the same of the Conservatives (24%) or the New Democrats (23%).

The survey also found that advertising by pro and anti free trade groups and the televised leaders' debates were more important than other factors in helping voters make up their minds. Almost three in ten considered advocacy advertising (27%) and the leaders' debates (27%) very important. Fewer than half as many gave the same importance to party advertising (13%), to candidates' literature delivered to their homes (11%) or to political polls (11%).

The results of the March 1989 survey confirm that third-party advertising during the 1988 federal election played a significant role in that campaign. They may, in fact, help to explain the remarkable Tory recovery following the leaders' debates.

Our survey found that recall of advocacy advertising relating to free trade was higher than that for advocacy advertising in general. Just under six in ten Canadians recalled having seen advertising by business groups in favour of free trade (59%) and by groups other than political parties opposed to free trade (56%). These figures are significantly higher than the one-third who could recall advocacy advertising in general.

Recall of pro free trade ads was highest in Toronto and Saskatchewan (64% each) and lowest in Atlantic Canada (51%). Recall was higher among better-educated Canadians (from 46% of those with less than nine years of schooling to 70% of those with a university degree).

Recall of anti free trade ads was highest in Saskatchewan (69%) and British Columbia (63%), and lowest in Quebec (48%). Recall of these ads was also higher among better-educated Canadians (from 42% of those with less than nine years of schooling to 63% of those with a university degree).

The survey also found that most Canadians agreed free trade advocacy advertising had had some impact on the November 1988 election vote. Four in ten (40%) believed that pro and anti free trade advertising had a major impact on the way people voted in that election and another three in ten (29%) said a minor impact. Only eighteen percent said the advertising had no impact. Quebeckers (49%) were the most likely to suggest that the advertising had a major impact.

A significant minority of Canadians (31%) said their own vote had been affected by the ads, and within this group, almost half (14%) said that the advertising had had a major impact on their vote. However, the majority of Canadians (59%) insisted that advocacy ads on free trade had had no impact on their final decision.

There were notable linguistic variations in response to this question: francophones (37%) were more likely than anglophones (29%) to say the ads had had a personal impact. Admission of influence also tended to increase among better-educated Canadians (from 22% of those with less than nine years of schooling to 33% of those with more than 14 years).

Equal proportions of the partisans of all three federal parties admitted that advocacy advertising had had an impact on the way they voted. One-third of those who would vote Liberal (35%), Conservative (32%) or NDP (31%) admitted to at least some influence.

It is instructive to look at the way in which third-party advertising during the November 1988 election functioned as an important factor in the Conservative victory. Following John Turner's impressive performance during the televised debates, the Tories trailed the Liberals by six points. On election day, the Tories had surged back to an eleven point lead.

Central to an understanding of this remarkable recovery is an awareness of the dominance of the free trade issue during the latter half of the campaign. The March 1989 survey showed that approximately equal proportions of supporters of all three parties admitted to being influenced by pro or anti free trade advertising. However, the ads reinforced the dominance of the free trade issue and induced the electorate to vote as if the election were a referendum on the agreement.

Although a majority of Canadians were against the agreement—51 % according to a November 3-8 Environics poll—opponents split their vote between the two opposition parties. The minority who were in favour of the agreement (39%) had no choice but to vote Conservative. The impact of advocacy advertising on a significant segment of the electorate may have made the difference between a Tory minority and the Tory majority needed to ensure the subsequent passage of the free trade legislation.

The 1988 election is historically important in that its outcome was so influenced by a single issue. The apparent success of advocacy advertising in 1988 and the since-acquired right to deduct advocacy contributions from taxable income suggest that third-party intervention, both during and between election campaigns, will become more widespread in the future unless regulations that will be upheld in the courts dictate otherwise.

Approval of Advertising: 1989

Approve	51%
Disapprove	25%
No Answer	24%

Assessment of Advertising: 1989

Informative	59%
Interesting	57%
Believable	36%

Impact of Advertising: 1989

Major Impact	40%
Minor Impact	29%
No Impact	18%
No Answer	13%

Should Advertising be Allowed? 1989

	During Campaigns	At Other Times
Yes	56%	71%
No	33%	19%

CHAPTER TWO

Political Parties: Change or Face the Consequences

HERSHELL EZRIN

Hershell Ezrin has had considerable experience in federal and provincial government as a member of the Canadian Forgein Service, Executive Director of the Canadian Unity Information Office and Principal Secretary to former Ontario Premier David Peterson. He is currently Senior Vice-President for Corporate and Public Affairs for the Molson Companies, and is a director of several public interest bodies, including the Public Policy Forum.

GOVERNMENT AT all levels today are in desperate need to "stand and deliver". Their ongoing inability to produce results has undermined public confidence in government. Extended overexposure of the failings of both individual politicians and the system has also damaged their capacity to provide moral leadership, new direction and innovative programs at a time of significant change and uncertainty. To reverse these trends, we need to nourish and revitalize the elected members of Parliament who are the democratic roots of government, and focus on strengthening effectiveness, not simply accountability.

In the historical Parliamentary model, one of a political party's most important tasks was to broker competing interests; compromises were forged, rooted in principle and taking into account geographical considerations as well as single interest issues. Parties helped nourish a Parliament which

could, and did, act to resolve issues; party affiliation was a sine qua non for the public to participate in decisions.

Today, individual empowerment and bureaucratic complexities have overwhelmed this time-honoured process. While issues have become more global in cause and effect, individuals seek a greater role in influencing their resolution. Meanwhile, each level of senior government, overwhelmed by debt and ever-increasing demands on resource, seeks to push responsibility for issues to the layer of government below. This, in turn, questions the very purpose of the nation state and its structures; "not in my back yard" has become an everyday political credo.

The response of the old line parties to the change in process in Canada has been to bury their heads in the sand. Despite lip service to reform, there is little commitment to rethink how they operate and to whom they appeal. Worse still, these parties have lost their ideological compass, as they restlessly hope to appeal to the changeable moods of every constituent.

Politics at every level seems process-oriented, symbolically driven. Tough decisions have been replaced by values statements; accountability for results has been substituted by consultation models; measurable achievements have been downgraded in favour of the ever-present public opinion polls. The political expedience of icon politics has become both the focus and cause of public complaint and media attention.

The public perception of the loss of effectiveness of the governing process has coloured a sense of little value gained for money spent.

The public has grown more frustrated and cynical about government, fueled by its inability to address issues effectively. This despair is compounded by the spiraling costs of inefficient expenditure programs, outrage at the systematic abuse of the perks of office, the hypocrisy of shifting positions and incoherent ideologies, the sometimes pointless adversarial nature of the system and the seeming failure of anyone in authority to carry forward the public's position.

Politicians and their parties are frequently their own worst enemies in generating these types of reactions. Question Period, the daily broadcast of the clowning of Parliament, is less an exercise in accountability, of checks and balances against an unbridled majority, than a second-rate dramatic presentation of the theatre of the absurd. It is certainly not answer period. Candidate selection races, with their dubious lists of portable electors and soap opera-like chicanery, reek of hypocrisy while often failing to deliver the "right" candidates. The carefully crafted government message of the day, with obligatory photo opportunity, is more a reflection of perception than reality.

The malaise which animates the public's disdain for politicians and the process also infects those within the system. Parliamentarians of all backgrounds and stripes feel frustrated because they do not seem able to make a difference; yet, they, their families and immediate associates, are subject to an unparalleled intensity of public scrutiny, for which few legislative achievements can compensate. In the name of a higher moral imperialism, motives are regularly impugned, actions discredited. The

spectre of conflict of interest creates a paralysis of action, and triggers an indecently wasteful process of studying issues to death.

A series of other factors also conspire to constrain their ability to act as our democratic representatives. Members are accountable to everyone—but responsible for little. The ceaseless demand for public consultation and participation, coupled with new individual protections afforded by the Charter of Rights and Freedoms, confines their ability to act.

By contrast, the proliferation of extra-parliamentary, single-interest pressure groups, accountable to few but with the satisfaction of a direct impact on specific issues, provide a real competitive challenge to the established parties for limited human and financial resources and media attention. These single interest groups set the news agenda today as effectively as political parties did a generation ago.

The instantaneously wired society, and the relentlessly broadcast measurement of public opinion, increasingly force leaders to follow rather than create agendas, to manage rather than shape opinions. While the public cries out for leadership, it measures the quality of leadership by a standard of popular opinion.

Little wonder then about the growing difficulty to recruit candidates for each election from a broad spectrum of backgrounds for the "sham" of elected office. Nor is it a surprise that it is more difficult to retain their interests, talents and experience after they leave office. The very same structural impediments undermining the popularity of the old-line parties will ultimately harm the capacity of the fast-growing political protest movements, as their representatives are co-opted and tainted by the existing system.

If we in politics have seen the enemy, and it is us (POGO), much still can be done to redress the problem. But the changes require a coherent, holistic approach which starts with the role of government.

The Canadian national political experiment, nurturing a small and varied population with several distinctive societies on a large land mass, is unique and admired by many, even if Canadians lead the self-doubt about its capacity to survive. It encourages diversity and equality of treatment in many basic facets of life.

While government is not the engine of prosperity, it is also not a necessary evil whose influence needs to be restrained in all circumstances except helping the less fortunate. As such, its structures need not be condemned to be flash frozen in some immutable political state, dictated by forces from a prior era, without a sense of evolution or adaptation.

Canada's persistent identity challenge has led its government in recent years to seek to restate the political institutions through a series of constitutional redefinition exercises. This macro-approach which has also been focussed on rectifying the political malaise has not achieved its goals. Parliament and its members are held in lower esteem, if possible, than a decade ago. Few admit to admiring their politicians; fewer still would ever contemplate becoming one.

The focus today revolves around new means of representation through structural reform, through accountability rather than effectiveness. Current proposals range from a new House of the Provinces, a Triple E Senate, more institutionalized First Ministers' Conferences to major devolution of powers to the provincial levels. Layered on these reformist empowerment notions are proposals to recognize qualitatively a different Canada consisting of from two to several distinct societies, and governed under an amorphous social charter, designed to make us feel good about what we stand for, even if we lack the tools to achieve those goals.

In one grand step, we seek to redefine what Canada will be. The foundation is based on tapping into public opinions which, in turn, are influenced by competing eight-second sound bites, nationwide focus groups and constituent assemblies, a veritable heritage of a generation of introspective navel-gazing and bleating.

One enduring Canadian principle has been that politics is the art of the possible. This statement remains less an indictment of vision than a recognition of needs. Leadership must include understanding and a capacity for explanation. A distinguishing feature of many of the current structural proposals is their complexity and subtlety. But if the public does not easily comprehend who is serving it, and consequently to whom it can turn, how, in a democracy, can the institutions created serve the public's needs?

In the interests of both effective execution and results from our Parliamentary process, more modest approaches may ironically offer greater hope. They are rooted in theories currently being em-

braced by a range of public and private sector managements. The empowerment of individuals, the de-layering of the decision-making process of organizations and the quest for total quality are concrete goals which can make a difference to the vitality of our political system.

The road to parliamentary and political revival should start with a focus on the individual elected member. It is ironic that in the haste to improve the system, we focus on democratizing the Senate, at best a chamber of sober second reflection, rather than revitalizing the most accountable institution, the House of Commons.

Empowerment of each elected member is at the very root of the reform needed. Combined with other mechanisms to enhance timely public consultation, such action will have a natural and salutary impact on their recruitment, motivation and credibility.

Simply put, we need a hybrid system of representation rooted in a revitalized House of Commons, evolving from British tradition but accepting the influence of North American practices. Members of Parliament should be freed from party discipline on all policy votes, with the exception of confidence measures, including overall budget votes. The free vote can serve a number of important purposes.

- It reinforces a simple point of effective contact for the public. Successful members are already effective advocates of local constituent needs. By enhancing the relevance of the role of each backbencher on national and regional issues, it serves to reemphasize the role of Parliament and the need and value of contact between constituents and their elected representatives.

- It reinforces the important brokerage function at a Parliamentary level, which in turn permits greater consideration of competing issues and the need for compromise, and an accountability unavailable to single interest groups.

- It permits greater sensitivity to issues of local concern, not an insignificant issue in the era of "not in my back yard" politics.

- It returns substance to the political debate, because no single MP or MPP can hide behind the excuse of a Parliamentary Whip. What each candidate stands for before an election has a new meaning and importance. It would replace a system of unnecessary party shackles which now serve to undermine public confidence.

- By requiring Ministers to seek support from colleagues on all sides of the House, especially for issues not reflected in election platforms, it undercuts the role of shadowy unelected political advisors.
- By raising the esteem in which members are held, it can encourage more persons to run for political office because they can be seen to make a difference.
- The give and take of a minority House is believed to better serve the public interest. However, by maintaining the British tradition of cabinet solidarity and support on confidence votes, we can protect the capacity of government to act quickly and with a sense of purpose, often lost in other systems.
- The freedom accorded parliamentarians in many legislative affairs could be effectively carried to a confirmation process for selected appointees. Nowhere is the soft underbelly of the current Parliamentary process more exposed than in the selection and approval of patronage appointees. The perfunctory and mundane review of many aspirants to appointments (eg., Ontario process) sheds little light, positive or negative, on their capabilities and the approach they might take. Yet this is information vitally important as members of judicial and quasi-judicial bodies take on additional tasks (such as the Charter of Rights). By participating in a more thorough review with the right to reject unworthy candidates, members could strengthen both their own credibility and that of the individuals selected.

Parliamentary precedence acknowledges the principle of free votes on a range of issues from moral ones to private members' bills. Provided members undertook to support their respective parties on confidence matters, including budgets, the implementation of such a program could be achieved through a simple announcement by each party.

In itself, this reform may not give sufficient grounds to encourage a groundswell of participation. After all, the abuse heaped upon the process has tarred many politicians. Much of that abuse revolves around the failure of government to make a difference. The ability of politicians to have access to public opinions and to vote freely on many policy issues may help address that aspect of the problem.

By contrast, reforming the Senate, another option, requires the congruence of a number of conflicting agendas. Should it represent the provincial perspective, interest groups, aboriginals? Making it equal, elected and effective is not acceptable to the largest provinces. The complexity of this task mitigates against its easy acceptance.

Empowering members is not a new suggestion. It forms a prominent part of the political dogma of the fast-rising political protest movements. What makes it so radical from the current parties' perspectives is that it requires a form of power-sharing which our increasingly leader-oriented politics has found uncomfortable to accept.

Yet, this empowerment is at the very core of successful initiatives in North America and abroad to increase the productivity and quality of individual business pursuits. It focuses on achievement as well as process. To dismiss this notion because of the company it keeps is neither sensible nor in keeping with what politicians should be skilled at doing, namely adopting good ideas as their own.

Giving parliamentarians the right to have a real impact on the process may deal with one element of public frustration and help to improve the system's credibility. However, if we strengthen the role of MPs without striving for participation by the best individuals, the system will continue to function ineffectively.

Different kinds of inducements are required to encourage initial political participation. We must also change public perceptions of the selection and funding support process, which have engendered a suspicion of sleaziness about politics and discouraged some candidates from throwing their name into the ring.

Many adult Canadians can recall the spectacle of recent candidate selection meetings which saw bussed-in delegates, underage or non-citizen voters, recruitment of unsavory supporters and controversial funding support. On numerous occasions, the candidate accused of receiving such support has been parachuted into a constituency race by the central party office or leader. To safeguard the candidate's nomination and to ensure the party leader does not lose face, the end goal justifies any means in "anything goes" campaigning. About the only thing absent in the selection process is a discussion of substantive matters.

This system has undermined the public trust of political parties, and denigrated individual candidates. Real abuses of authority in these campaigns raise significant barriers of entry to newcomers to the political process and help maintain a closed-shop atmosphere. Few prospective candidates are willing to face such additional challenges, even if they are prepared to take the initial steps to subject their families and themselves to the toll which any campaign exacts.

The political parties' response to their bad press is simply to throw up more barriers such as minimum membership times and a nest of special rules. All this serves to limit participation and exclude ever more potential candidates.

Yet, parties need an ongoing infusion of new talent. Members' personal circumstances change. New issues arise. If Parliament is to be more representative, parties need to reflect the broader trends in the community, and actively recruit rather than forcing talented newcomers to seek ghettoized support in a few ridings. The challenge is to protect democratic practice while encouraging involvement.

There is a better way to secure the commitment of a broader cross-section of Canadians to the process. But it requires some substantial changes in the way we nominate and elect our representatives.

One way to open up the process is to add an additional ten percent of seats to Parliament to be filled by proportional representation votes cast in a general election. Each party could nominate a slate of candidates. These slates, approved by the parties in their own fashion, might reflect an effort to shore up a regional or community's specific lack of representation or to add a star candidate to the roster. A party which believed it had an insufficient number of women candidates running, for example, could give women a priority on its slate.

Since the candidates selected by popular vote would be accountable in Parliament, they should not be considered different by their colleagues. The number would also not constitute a significant bloc in any one party thereby eliminating concerns about changing the balance of regional representation. We would provide access for "star" candidates to Parliament, while avoiding some of the more degrading and ignominious fights to ensure their participation. Some voters might even judge parties on how well they filled positions within their own control. Voters who felt they were under-represented in a "first past the post" system could still have an opportunity to get representation within a gov-

ernment party, in the most significant national body, the House of Commons.

In this age of neo-puritanism, the funding of the political process, the politicians' abuse of perks and the endless allegations of conflict of interest have also offended many public sensibilities and dissuaded participation. Even here, some reform is possible, though much change is required.

Members have to be paid proper salaries; to do otherwise, given the vicissitudes of regular elections, is to encourage the creative extension of perks as salary enhancements. If running any important business is well remunerated, why not pay properly those whom we expect to manage our nation's affairs?

We must also avoid the temptation of maintaining a class of professional politicians. While some critics might reflect we have had enough amateurs in place in politics, experience suggests we need more politicians with broader and varied experience if Parliament is to be more relevant. A Parliament made up of teachers and lawyers is no more representative of the public interest than one made up of any other specific interest group. To attract certain candidates, we need lower financial barriers and higher levels of public purse support. This could be tied to electoral performance to ensure that there was a reward tied to effort and success; it would, however eliminate odious suggestions of bought politicians. But to avoid any cronyism, limits should also be placed on the number of terms any member can serve. Forced interchange with the outside real world is a necessary requirement.

To encourage more interchange, we also have to address the regulations affecting prospective members. Current conflict of interest legislation prohibits many from seeking the higher public office unless they divest of their life's work. In some cases, these rules limit politicians' ability ever to return to their hard-earned state.

The conflict of interest issue should revolve around benefit, not disclosure. Every elected official should be forced to disclose their holdings; this will remain a discouragement to some but is required for the integrity of the system. We must develop sensitive mechanisms to protect the privacy of politicians when the public's need-to-know is not required, if we don't we will only deprive ourselves of the high quality leadership our circumstances require. A regularized process, under judicial scrutiny, scrupulously observed by all parties, of public declaration of conflict and withdrawal from consideration of any "benefit" issue could suffice.

All of these suggestions are intended to improve the effectiveness of government by enhancing the role of the individual members. While many other modifications are desirable, one additional issue which needs to be addressed is the capacity of government to respond quickly and efficiently to public concerns. Failure to do so in a timely manner has been a long-standing public grievance.

Delay is a valuable weapon in the arsenal of any government. Politicians are sensitive to the fact that there are limits to the public's attention span on most issues, no matter how controversial. Public servants sometimes hope to wait out their Ministers. Similarly, time is money; the private sector would frequently prefer a second-best alternative arrived at promptly than waiting for the best choice. As government's role grows, and its legislative intrusion becomes more complex, the potential for delay increases.

Two initiatives could serve to expedite matters and make government more effective. The first is the mandating of specific sunset limits each time new structures or procedures are put in place. Forced reviews of these procedures require measurements of efficiency; extensions with full public review and debate would limit the growth of government without recourse. This principle could be extended to include sharply reduced time limits on how long government processes could hold up pending decisions. The issue is less increasing efficiency than attacking the paralysis which frequently overwhelms political decision-making and undermines public trust in it.

An admittedly more controversial proposal would be to permit the formal gathering of public opinion by the legislature through officially sanctioned referenda. While non-binding in character, they are a reassuring manifestation of public empowerment in its truest sense.

The possibilities for political reform in the 1990s are rising phoenix-like from the ashes of the missed opportunities of the 1980s. The relationship of politicians to their electors remains the focus for much of the current debate about reforming the system. However, public accountability must be linked to achievement in more demonstrable ways if we are to revitalize the credibility of government and its capacity to act in out interests. If the government is not for us—who will be?

CHAPTER THREE

A Lament for Partisanship

DALTON CAMP

Dalton Camp is a political commentator who recently was a senior advisor to Cabinet in the Privy Council Office. A former President of the Progressive Conservative Party of Canada, he also served as Chairman of the Ontario Commission on the Legislature.

FOR SOME time—certainly since the 1960s—I have been worrying about the withering away of the influence and effectiveness of the political parties in the processes of our democracy. At bottom of this concern was the question, would the withering continue to where the role of the parties became nugatory? What would Parliament and the legislatures be like when their seats were held by members who largely represented either themselves or loosely defined abstractions, such as "my constituency"? It seemed increasingly clear this could be possible even though the members might have been elected with party labels of one kind or another attached to them, but on the understanding that the party affiliation was not a binding one, and of little real importance.

Certainly, over the past three decades, this has been the drift. It has become a large part of the political culture to believe not only that we have been ill-served by partisan party politics but that we would be much better served by a political system free of partisanship. As a result, we are presently engulfed in waves of reformers—mainly representing, signifi-cantly enough, special interest groups—all armed with proposals directed at the heart of our parliamentary system. The traditional parties have been mute or, at best, incoherent, on the issue of reform, which helps to explain the rapid growth of a new party almost wholly devoted to the issue—to wit, the Reform Party.

What do the reformers have in mind? In essence, it seems to me, not a Parliament of political parties but one of free spirits. Reformers support the right of government supporters not to support their government; as a deterrent to endemic instability, the defeat of government legislation would not mean the defeat of the government, merely the legislation. Since reformers suspect, with good cause, a prime minister of coercing or intimidating his caucus colleagues, the more controversial issues would be settled by caucus ballot. (Given this salutary precedent, there would be no reason why cabinet should not do the same.) But should members prove to be too independent of mind, in their voting behaviour, constituents would have the right of recall. Essentially, the member of Parliament must be responsive to the opinion of the majority of his or her constituents at any given time, on any given issue.

The centrepiece for the reformers has been the Senate. Unlike other, less understood proposals, almost everyone believes in some sort of Senate reform. An elected Senate, in itself, appeals to the elementary egalitarianism of Canadians and finds resonance in the common popular wisdom that most appointed senators are either senile or slothful. Other than in universities, where ironically many of Senate's most vocal detractors are lodged, the principle of tenure, or job security, such as the appointed senators enjoy, is alien to Canadian life.

Anyway, it is futile to argue at this late date that the Canadian Senate has served as well as any second chamber as both a chamber of second thought, or second look, and as a general, all-purpose restraining body against the excesses of so-called executive federalism. It would be difficult to create an alternative chamber more "independent" than the present one; demonstrably, the reconfigured model will be no match in experience and wisdom for the present conglomerate of former ministers, provincial premiers, "party hacks" and leavening, legitimate free spirits.

But while coming to bury the old Senate and not to praise it, and to return to my theme, it is prudent to note how many of those who have designs for a reformed Senate also have a concommitant dislike of the present political system. Not everyone is comfortable with the argument for "equal" representation in the Senate, and not all reformers have the same ideal of equality in mind. Were there a consensus among them, it would be to de-emphasize the role of political parties in order to guarantee the representation of designated groups and minorities. Half the senators, for example, should be women; aboriginal Canadians should be guaranteed representation. Whatever the method of election, however many will be elected, as little as possible is to be left to chance, with even less left to choice.

There is small comfort in the knowledge that a good deal of this reform agenda simply will not fly. (There is residual concern about what will.) The heart of the reformist literature, the *geist* of it, is the disavowal of politics, partisanship and the adversary system in Parliament as we know it. This may represent a new populism, but also more than that; it seems to be more the casual dismantling of much of what we have known as parliamentary democracy, including the infinite practicality of majority rule. As a further irony, the majority rule has proven to be the most certain guarantee of the protection of minorities, and the requirement of any advanced society for stable, responsible governance.

It has always seemed to me that political parties were indispensable to parliamentary democracy; indeed, until recently, it would have been a truism. Meanwhile, through my long experience in party politics, it also seemed evident that the power and influence of the parties were in steep decline. The gulf between those elected and those they represented continued to widen, and the assumed articles of faith and belief which bound them together in common cause became increasingly difficult to articulate.

In the end—which for me was 1963 during the controversy in the Tory party over the issue of nuclear arms—it became overwhelmingly evident that political parties no longer had any significant responsibility for policy. Moreover, it appeared fitting this be so; modern government and modern society were each too complex to be guided by the lights of inspired amateurs, however gifted.

This is by way of saying that in the contemporary scenario for our own form of parliamentary democracy, the political parties have been written out of the script, become, as it were, stagehands or props. There remains, however, the authority and right of all political parties to determine who should lead them and, better still, who should represent them. Such power is real and conclusive (although most leaders of most parties, including Reform, enjoy the right to overrule the choice of any of constituency), and—after the confrontation with Mr. Diefenbaker in 1966—the Conservative Party established the further right to dispose of its leader, a refinement now widely accepted.

The result, however, has not been a strengthened, more democratic party system but a more bureaucratized one, leading to inevitable over-centralization. The further result for national parties is not unlike what has happened to the nation itself: increased alienation and the isolation of useful dissent and discourse, further contributing to the exacerbations of regionalism, provincialism, and ultimate and irreconcilable differences. This is not what John Meisel had in mind in the 1960s when he cited Canada's political parties as among the national institutions making an essential contribution to the preservation of national unity.

It should not be overlooked that the general, disengaged, non-partisan public, while tacitly acknowledging the right of the political parties to pick and choose their candidates for office, appear to believe they are doing a poor job of it. Contemporary political literature and journalism imply an unspoken rebuke meant both for the selection process and the end product. We are fortunate, thus far, no one has thought of a better way, otherwise political parties having sacrificed the making of policy and willing to jetison their leaders as required, would have nothing left to do.

The most popular remedy for improving the breed of elected politicians is first to liberate them from the party discipline and thus from their parties; and second, to allow for the recall of those who fail to satisfactorily extricate themselves from the pressures of their leaders and peers. This would, of course, inhibit, if not destroy, the way we do business in our legislatures, which is presently by the consensual method through party caucus and the efficacious use of the simple majority.

If there is a single reason for the protracted spasm of public hostility for its political system, which has generated the headlong rush for reform at any cost, it is that many Canadians have little understanding of the system they already have. There is also the unexplored assumption that somehow, in the new order of things, everyone will be represented and ascendant in some way so as to satisfy, if not sanctify, every opinion. The enemy of this ideal is the caucus system, the creator of the fetish of party discipline and the fetishists, the whips. True democracy, on the other hand, would require the political parties to provide candidates for public office who would, on being elected, turn their coats as it suited them.

This has driven me to a contemplate how our Parliament and legislatures might look. It would be necessary, first of all, to reconfigure the physical appearance: the Government, for practical purposes, would be seated together, with other members seated everywhere else. The need for the aisle separating one side from the other would be eliminated since members, obviously, had been elected to be on all sides of an issue; instead of a single aisle dividing the House, several aisles would be provided to allow for easy access, and for swift flight.

Since all votes, inherently, must be free votes, lest offense be given any constituent or constituency, there would be little need for the caucus. Besides, attendance would be irregular and wildly unpredictable. Caucus confidentiality, something like cabinet solidarity, would become an oxymoron. Anyway, no prime minister would attend caucus, nor would any member of his cabinet (save the foolhardy); no one would ever look to find a minister of finance on hand.

The prime minister, stripped of the power of dissolution, would be reduced to a tiresome wheedler, obliged only to be obliging. Stripped of the loyalty of caucus and, for certain, his cabinet colleagues, he could be identified in the House by the sound of his leper bell. Given the compensatory blessing of a fixed term of office, he could nonetheless be sacked on a day's notice by bad polls, unfashionable legislation, an outbreak of parliamentary distemper and other acts of God. In a House of undisciplined minorities, with equal leverage as every member's joy-stick, government would need, as never before, the guiding hand of a prime minister who is a superior wheeler-dealer.

Finally, with these reforms, the decline of the political parties would be irreversible. As difficult as it is to imagine a party system wherein the principle of party loyalty has been moved to the margins, the thought of one functioning in a parliamentary system bullied by opportunistic and eccentric opinion is inconceivable. In the end, parties would become truly irrelevant: two would be too many, and one would be more than enough.

CHAPTER FOUR

1988 Election Expenditures: A Canadian-American Comparison

DONALD C. MACDONALD

Donald C. MacDonald is Chairman of the Ontario Commission on Election Finances and was previously a Member of the Ontario Legislature. He is a former leader of the New Democratic Party of Ontario.

THE 1988 general elections in Canada and the United States were the most expensive in each nation's history. Skyrocketing expenditures have heightened the public concern that money is eroding the integrity of the electoral process. Fewer people are able to run for public office because their personal wealth and/or fund-raising capacity cannot match that of wealthy opponents. The cynical public reaction is reflected in the button for sale in the local gift shop: "A fool and his money are ... soon elected".

How much is spent on elections? It's impossible to say precisely. Some spending is legitimately unreported because it is part and parcel of voluntary participation. Other more formal expenditures are unreported either because they are not required by law or are deliberately withheld from public scrutiny. But it is possible from official reports and informed estimates to get an overall picture. That is the objective of this essay.

It is easier to obtain reliable data on United States' spending because all major expenditures must be reported to the Federal Election Commission (FEC). These include expenditures not only by parties and candidates, but also the nearly 5 000 Political Action Committees (PACs) established by corporations, trade unions or public interest groups.

Candidates for the Presidency	$ 269 008 934
Candidates for Congress	281 771 577
Candidates for the Senate	195 551 083
Parties	412 302 695
Delegates	119 473
Non-Party PACs	241 903 563
Communication Costs, Fliers	4 336 897
Inividuals' Expenditures	358 863
Total	**1 342 353 085**

PACs have become major players in the political game, in some areas out-spending the local party committees. The summary of the FEC disclosure files in the 1988 annual report [1] reveals that the total expenditures for the election that year were $1 342 353 085.

These American data provide a useful benchmark from which to measure the Canadian equivalent. To be in the same league, given the 1:10 ratio in population, Canadian expenditures would have to be in the range of $134 million.

How did Canadian expenditures compare in the same election year? I have checked with knowledgeable persons in the scores of organizations which were engaged in the campaign—how much money they raised and/or spent, and from whence that money came. Some data were readily available for it had to be reported to Elections Canada. In other instances, it was volunteered from an official source in the organization. Sometimes it was gleaned, in the first instance from media accounts, and then checked out with the organization involved. There are, however, certain major expenditures for which there is no official reporting, and no central recording. For these I had to resort to a consensus among informed estimates by persons intimately involved in the direction of their party's campaign. Following is the comparative analysis which emerged. But first, a note on methodology.

Differences in the Electoral Systems

The United States operates on what is termed an "election cycle", the period of two years between the presidential and mid-term elections. However, the FEC requires financial filings annually, and the figures cited above are for the year 1988. In strictly "election" terms, these figures are somewhat inflated by inclusion of the maintenance costs of the parties during the months leading up to the campaign itself. However, studies in this field, as well as FEC data, usually consider regular maintenance costs as an election expense because they are overwhelmingly election-focused. Therefore, I have followed this practice, not only for the American data above, but also in assembling the Canadian equivalent.

Further, American election statistics include expenditures for the primaries—legitimately so, for choosing candidates is very much part of the election process. Nominating conventions are the Canadian equivalent, but for them there is no official reporting of expenses, merely anecdotal evidence.

Even more important, American election data include the expenditure by PACs—again, legitimately so, for they are very much part of the election process. In Canada, however, so-called "third parties" are totally unregulated. They do not have to register; are not obligated to disclose their contributors or expenditures; and the extent to which they voluntarily disclose their financial position varies greatly.

Bearing these differences in mind, we can proceed to analysis of the Canadian experience in 1988.

Parties

In the Report of the Chief Electoral Officer Respecting Election Expenses, 1988, [2] expenditures for the three major parties were:

Progressive Conservative	$ 7 921 738
Liberal	6 839 875
New Democratic	7 060 563
Total	**21 822 176**

The total expenditures for the nine minor parties (Christian Heritage, Social Credit, Communist, Libertarian, Rhinoceros, Green, Reform, Confederation of Regions Western Party and Commonwealth of Canada Party) were only $603 673.

The overall total for the parties was therefore $22 425 844. But this figure does not tell the whole story. Party spending is categorized, first as "election expenses" for which the aggregate must not exceed the statutory limit, and second, "campaign expenses", which are not included in the Report Respecting Election Expenses, but are picked up (though unidentified) in the parties' expenditures reported in their 1988 annual financial returns.

However, there are other transfers of election spending. Charlotte Gray states that party officials concede "at least fifty percent of the PC election spending occurred pre-writ" [3]. These pre-writ expenditures, though clearly for election purposes, are not classified as election spending, and are picked up in the regular party budget.

Furthermore, the lack of clarity between what is categorized as "election" expenditure and other kinds of "campaign" spending has permitted the transfer of at least a portion of the parties' administrative costs into the unlimited expenditures permitted with so-called "campaign" spending. A very calculated game is played regarding the amount of these transfers.

For example, in commenting on the 1984 election, the late Khayyam Zev Paltiel (hitherto acknowledged as Canada's leading academic authority on election spending) has written that the New Democratic Party attributed all its National Office spending to the election in an effort to maximize the expenditure data upon which the government party subsidies are based. In doing so, it was still able to live within the statutory limits. In contrast, the Liberals attributed only two-thirds, and the Progressive Conservatives only one-half, of the national office administrative spending to the election because to have attributed more would have brought them into serious violation of the legal limits [4].

In the 1988 election, the same practice was followed. Charlotte Gray states that the administrative costs for the election were transferred, and thereby buried in the party's annual budget. "These undisclosed expenses," Gray notes, "included the bulk of their rent, salary, travel, telephone and fund-raising costs." Such transfers left more room for election spending without breaching the limits during the campaign.

Documentation for the extent of these transfers is revealed in the 1988 annual returns of the parties. The Conservative Party spending zoomed to over $22 million, as compared with $13 million in the previous non-election year [5]. Undoubtedly, the opposition parties had pre-writ and administrative spending which was picked up in their 1988 regular party budgets, but it was much less. Both the Liberals and NDP reported an increase of only one million or so over the previous non-election year. Being debt-ridden, the opposition parties were not able to accommodate sizeable transfers.

Finally, public opinion surveys have become a major election expenditure [6]. Particularly when taken in an election year, they are clearly an election cost. Keeping on top of electoral trends, and deciding where to concentrate resources to hold or win

key ridings, are basic elements in shaping election strategy. Yet polling expenditures are exempted from election expenses, and are therefore another item picked up in the regular party budgets.

An overall conclusion emerges from the number and size of these transfers of election spending to the party budget, namely, the validity of the practice of considering all party expenditures in an election year as election expenses. Therefore to the $22 425 844 of party spending during the campaign, there should be added the $47.2 million by the three major parties, and the $988 587 by the nine minor parties, reported in their 1988 annual returns [7].

This brings party election spending to approximately $70 million.

Candidates

There were three categories of spending by candidates: first, "election expenses" which are subject to statutory limits; second, "personal expenses" which are broken down into acceptable categories; and third, "campaign expenses" which are not subject to limits, but concerning which there have been repeated calls for clarification from many quarters, including the Chief Electoral Officer. These other campaign expenses are reported to Elections Canada in order to ascertain whether some of them should be included as election expenses, but they are not listed in the official Report Respecting Election Expenses. However, since they are in the Elections Canada computers, I have been able to obtain the aggregate figures for the other campaign expenses [8].

The total for the three categories of publicly-reported spending is:

Election Expenses	$ 31 341 494
Campaign Expenses	7 968 465
Personal Expenses	1 732 578
Total	**41 042 537**

As with parties, this total does not tell the whole story. There is no limit or reporting of pre-writ spending which is picked up by either the candidate or his/her riding association. Virtually all candidates have some pre-writ spending, depending on available funds and how far in advance of the election nomination takes place. On occasion it is very sizeable; for example, Dennis Mills, now the MP for Toronto Broadview-Greenwood, has admitted to $100 000 pre-writ spending.

Nominating conventions are a second area of unreported candidate spending. For this, there is only anecdotal evidence. It has repeatedly been stated that in hotly-contested ridings in the Toronto area, spending is in the range of $30 000 - $40 000 for each serious candidate. According to Robert Mason Lee, in his book *One Hundred Monkeys*, while seeking the nomination for the riding of York-Simcoe, Frank Stronach "had five full-time and 10 part-time staff for two months ... (and) signed up 2 800 members, 1 200 of them employees in his own company."[9] Such nomination and pre-writ spending by a multi-millionaire would add up to many tens, perhaps hundreds, of thousands of dollars.

The total expenditure for the 1 574 candidates in the 1988 election (as well as the thousands of opponents they defeated in the nomination contest), along with other pre-writ spending, is a matter for informed estimates. I have sought the opinions of persons who were intimately involved in the 1988 campaigns of each of the three major parties, but this proved a most difficult area in which to achieve a consensus. The estimates ranged from as low as $10 to $12 million and as high as $15 to $25 million, while the third was $15 to $16 million. The most reliable figure would appear to be $15 million.

Added to the $41 million of reported spending during the campaign period, total candidate spending would therefore be $56 million.

Labour

Labour played an important role in the 1988 election funding, but for the most part it was through financial help to other organizations. Most of the

Progressive Conservative	$ 1 790
Liberal	5 264
New Democratic	2 718 009
Others	0
Total	**2 725 063**

contributions were to parties, centrally, or to candidates, locally, and were included in their official returns to Elections Canada [10].

A breakdown of labour's $2.7 million contributions to the NDP reveals that approximately 37% came from the central organization, the Canadian Labour Congress—money which had originated with its affiliates—while the remainder had come from scores of trade union locals, or more often, their regional and national organizations. The top ten contributors were [11]:

Canadian Labour Congress	$ 1 014 192
United Food and Commercial Workers	78 877
United Steelworkers of America	72 233
Service Employees International Union	35 210
Ontario Federation of Labour	24 660
Telecommunications Workers Union	22 000
Canadian Union of Public Employees	21 158
Energy and Chemical Workers Union	19 760
Retail, Wholesale and Department Store Union	19 500
International Woodworkers of America	19 200

While the major proportion of labour's contribution to the NDP was made to the party to assist in its national campaign, there were also significant contributions to individual candidates, usually made by union locals in, or near, the constituency. Contributions locally to candidates were [12]:

Progressive Conservative	$ 2 600
Liberal	9 772
New Democratic	1 112 668
Others	200
Total	**1 125 240**

The total of trade union contributions to parties and their candidates, centrally and locally was therefore $3 850 303.

In addition, trade unions contributed to the Pro-Canada Network and to cultural, women's, peace, nuclear disarmament, anti-cruise missiles or nuclear submarines and farm groups. It is impossible to assess with any degree of accuracy the totals of this financial outreach to organizations of like mind. In any case, when this money was used during the election it is included in the spending attributed to third parties.

Third Party Spending

The 1988 election witnessed the largest lobbying and public relations effort in Canadian history. It covered a wide spectrum. Prominent among these private interest groups was the women's movement in its many manifestations, such as the National Action Committee and the pro-life and pro-choice protagonists in the abortion issue; and the peace movement in campaigns against nuclear rearmament, missile testing, nuclear submarines and the establishment of nuclear-free zones. Other groups emerged in opposition to free trade: a coalition of cultural interests which perceived free trade as an added threat to a distinctive Canadian identity, and farm organizations which feared that free trade would undermine, and ultimately destroy, their marketing boards. While this proliferation of private interest groups achieved a very high profile, their expenditures were relatively small, but the financial outlay was supplemented with a great deal of voluntary labour and contributions-in-kind.

During a campaign period (but not pre-writ), parties and candidates have to report all contributed goods and services, calculated at the current market value, but being unregulated, the parties do not. It is extremely difficult to quantify the goods and services made available to the women's and peace movements, but being grass-root organizations, their supporters felt very strongly about the issues, and were, therefore, willing to sacrifice beyond the norm through contributions of goods and services in addition to small financial contributions. Bearing this element of these campaigns in mind, informed estimates indicate that the expenditures ranged up to, perhaps beyond, $1 million.

Free Trade Campaign - Con

The main coordinating body in the campaign against free trade was the Pro-Canada Network, a coalition of 35 trade unions along with women's, cultural and church groups. Much of their effort was voluntary, or made up of services-in-kind which are impossible to quantify financially.

The Network achieved full organization status only mid-way through 1988. Its spending is estimated at $750 000, most of which was devoted to a comic book—the product of Montreal artist, Terry Mosher (a.k.a. Aislin) and Toronto writer Rick Salutin—at a cost of $650 000.

The Council of Canadians was part of the Network, but also operated on its own. It contributed approximately $10 000 to the Network, and spent an estimated additional $50 000. As indicated earlier, the trade unions contributed financially to the Network, and assumed responsibility for various aspects of the Network's campaign.

In total, the campaign against free trade is estimated at little more than $1 million in financial outlay, supplemented by extensive voluntary labour.

Free Trade Campaign - Pro

The pro free trade campaign, centered in the business world, was massive, but again, some of the spending is subject only to informed estimates.

The main coordinating body was the Canadian Alliance for Trade and Job Opportunities. At the

Canadian Pacific	$ 250 000
Alcan Aluminum	250 000
Shell Canada	250 000
Noranda	200 000
Royal Bank	200 000
Imperial Oil	200 000
Sun Life	140 000
Manufacturer's Life	110 000
Northern Telecom	107 000
IBM Canada	100 000
Inco	100 000
Olympia & York	100 000
Texaco Canada	100 000

outset it postured as being non-partisan and promised full disclosure of its contributors. Eventually, it revealed the sources for only $3.78 million (72%) of its publicly-reported $5.24 million election spending. The top business donors, as disclosed by the Alliance, can be seen in the preceding table [13].

Most corporations had already contributed to the Conservative and Liberal parties, sometimes equally, even though those parties held opposing views on the dominant issue of free trade. Their contribution to the Canadian Alliance for the promotion of free trade was, in effect, an added contribution to the Conservative party since it was the only major party favouring free trade. Moreover, it is significant that the corporate contributions to the lobbying efforts of the Canadian Alliance were many times greater than to the parties. A selection of four leading Canadian corporations illustrates the pattern [14]:

| | *1988 Contribution from:* | | | |
	Canadian Pacific	Imperial Oil	Noranda	Inco
P.C.	$ 74 300	$ 0	$ 40 000	$ 19 965
Lib.	79 500	0	39 000	19 866
C.A.	250 000	259 000	200 000	100 000

Indeed, some corporations made a third contribution to the Conservative party in support of free trade. They were among the 40 000 undisclosed contributors to the National Citizens' Coalition which supported the Conservative-sponsored free trade proposal. The non-regulation of third parties invited such multiple contributions, perhaps even encouraged them in order to obscure the magnitude of corporate election contributions.

While the Alliance spending was the centrepiece of the pro free trade campaign, it was supplemented by a wide range of supportive efforts. For example, the Alberta Government spent $500 000 in a newspaper ad campaign. In Manitoba, a Committee for Free Trade spent $60 000 on radio, TV and print ads. In Montreal, millionaire businessman George Petty spent $250 000 on full-page free trade ads that appeared in 75 newspapers across the country. In Quebec, Le Regroupement pour le Libre-Echange spent $300 000 to $350 000 on newspaper, TV and radio advertising. In Toronto, Gallop and Gallop Advertising donated $50 000 of billboard

and bus shelter ads in several cities. The National Citizens' Coalition's (NCC) year-long campaign, with pro free trade ads on 800 radio and 90 TV stations, represented a 1988 expenditure of $842 000 [15].

The list of sizeable individual efforts is by no means exhaustive. Since there is no obligation to report, the total is estimated to have ranged up to $10 million, in combination with the $5.24 million of disclosed spending by the Alliance.

To this must be added the expenditure of business interests at the local level. The Alliance was made up of 34 associations, including the four major national organizations—the Business Council on National Issues, the Canadian Federation of Independent Business, the Chamber of Commerce and the Canadian Manufacturer's Association. These four organizations spent a few thousand dollars each in setting up the Alliance and urging their members to become active in the free trade campaign; together that membership represents hundreds of thousands of local organizations and companies. Their participation was, partly, a financial contribution to the Alliance, and partly, organizing and financing local activities. Given the difficulty with which money "trickles up" from the local to the national level in any federation, it may be assumed that a significant proportion of their spending was locally or regionally. Sometimes staff, and whole departments, were freed for campaigning. Estimates of what proportion of business spending was at the local level range from 10% to 33 1/3%, with the consensus being closer to the latter figure. Therefore, in addition to the $10 million spent nationally, there would have to be added at least another $3 million locally, for an overall total of approximately $13 million.

The validity of these estimates for local business spending is confirmed by the fact that not only did it represent an outreach to the local community but there was another important component consisting of internal lobbying of employees and shareholders.

For example, Stelco and Loblaws inserted pro free trade material in their employees' pay envelopes. In the town of Dundas, Ontario, the president of Valley City Manufacturing, a wood-working company, called a special meeting of the employees and warned that many might lose their jobs without free trade. Many companies, like Crown Life, assembled their employees, all on company time, and lectured them on free trade. Enfield Corporation, a Toronto financial and management company, distributed 10 000 copies of a free trade paper to its employees and shareholders. Many of the more than 1 000 business and trade magazines zeroed in on free trade. These expenditures may have been part of the companies' normal internal communication, but in the lead up to, and during, the election campaign, they were heavily focused on free trade [16].

There is another non-monetary factor which should be borne in mind. Effective campaigning often requires financial reserves for a counter-attack when the ebb and flow of a campaign requires it. When the Liberal polls soared into first place following the leaders' TV debate, the pro free trade forces sprang into action with massive expenditures. Because of a ready response from corporate treasuries, in less than three weeks the Alliance was able to raise $2 million [17] bringing its total budget to over $5 million. The Tories abandoned two-thirds of the commercials they had prepared in the pre-writ period (for which the cost was not reported as an election expense because they were not used), and spent at least $2 million in radio and TV advertising in the final week [18]. At this point, the budgets of the anti free trade campaign among third parties, of the opposition parties, and of labour, were virtually expended. Financially, it was a battle of the pygmies and giants. The augmented free trade campaign was "phenomenally successful" in moving votes back to the Tories in the final week [19].

Government Advertising

The appropriateness of government advertising during an election campaign has long been questioned. Apparently it has not become a bone of partisan contention in the United States, but in Canada the controversy erupts in every election, with parties when in opposition, being critical, but when in government, engaging in the practice. In two provinces, however, the practice has been banned: Manitoba and Saskatchewan permit only "public service" advertising during a campaign.

While there is a blackout period during an election campaign which applies to registered parties and candidates, there are no limits on either the amount or timing of third party advertising; it is permitted even in the blackout period. In effect, advertising by government ministries falls into the category of "third parties"; ministries are not perceived to be legally associated with the government party, and are free to promote their programs at any time. In 1988 free trade was acknowledged to be the major commitment of the government, and therefore of every ministry. No one has been able to calculate exactly how much was spent on advertising and other promotional activities, such as salaries, travel and meetings, but one ministry, External Affairs, set up the International Trade Communication Group which spent $24 million [20].

To put it in perspective, that figure alone exceeds the officially reported spending of all the opposition parties opposed to free trade. It serves as an example, but only partial documentation, of government spending on programs that were high-profile election issues.

Summary of Election Spending

In summarizing the overall picture in light of the foregoing analysis, it should be emphasized once again that while most of the expenditure data is drawn from official reports to Elections Canada, a portion of it had to be estimated. This has been done

Election Spending by:	$ million
Parties	70
Candidates	56
Third Parties	
Peace Movement and	
Women's Organizations	1
Free Trade - Con	1
Free Trade - Pro	13
Sub-Total	**141**
Government Advertising	24
Total	**165**

by striking a consensus of the opinions of individuals who were intimately involved. In brief, the totals err, if anything, on the down-side.

Even without government advertising, this total exceeds the $134 million figure which would place Canada in the same bracket of spending as in the 1988 U.S. elections. Moreover, it should be noted again that the American figure is for three elections—presidential, senatorial and house—whereas the Canadian figure is for one election, to the House of Commons.

Election Administrative Costs

While administrative costs are not the focus of this paper, they should be considered for a full picture of the cost of an election. There is an additional reason: in Canada, some items are part of administration of the election while in the United States, they are excluded. For example, enumeration—the compilation of the voters lists—is an administrative cost borne by Elections Canada. Voter registration, the US equivalent, is voluntary, and efforts to promote it are undertaken by parties and interest groups such as trade unions.

For Canada, the official figure for administrative costs was $124 432 629.89 for the 17 639 001 electors—a per-voter cost of $7.05 [21].

If there are difficulties in making a Canadian-American comparison in other components of election spending, nowhere are they greater than with the administrative costs borne by the States.

Let the FEC speak for itself:

In a formal sense, there are no federal elections in the United States. There are only State elections for federal offices. Although each state has its own election code, the burden of administering (and paying for) all elections (federal, state and local) devolves on over 13 000 local officials—typically to county, city or town clerks and registrars. As you might imagine, these do not keep their accounts in any comparable way. For all these reasons (and more) we simply cannot ascertain with any certainty or utility the cost of administering any one election. The best we have been able to do is to survey estimated election costs over a four-year cycle. We did this through the Bureau of Census in the mid-seventies. And despite my doubt about those numbers, we now estimate the cost of administering elections in the United

States to be approximately $1.5 billion over a four-year cycle which includes all elections for all public offices. Assuming that the presidential general election is the most expensive single event in the cycle, and noting that we had some 90 000 000 voters in 1988, it is a reasonable guess (but only a guess) that our administrative cost per voter is very close to your own figure of about $7.40. Certainly, we are in the same ballpark [22].

It would appear that the cost of administering elections in the United States and Canada is not only "in the same ballpark", but also, that these administrative costs are only marginally less than all the money spent in campaigning by registered parties, candidates and others (PACs and third parties).

Conclusions

What conclusion is to be drawn from this escalation of election spending? Various studies in the field provide a balanced perspective.

For example, Dr. Herbert E. Alexander of the Political Science Department of the University of Southern California, and Director of the Citizens' Research Foundation, has authored a regular flow of books and articles on election spending in countries around the world [23]. Canada has been included in his studies since the days when he was a consultant with the Barbeau Committee in its mid-sixties study of Canadian election spending.

Dr. Alexander warns that election spending will continue to rise, partly because of the professionalization of politics in combination with technological developments, and partly because of the limited capacity of statutory restrictions to counter the ingenuity of parties and candidates to find new ways of spending. He then provides an arresting perspective [24]. His calculations for the two years of the U.S. election cycle of 1987-88 is that $2.7 billion was spent on the combined local, state and federal elections. That figure, he notes, is about the same as what was spent by the nation's two leading commercial advertisers—Phillip Morris and Procter & Gamble. Further, that it is significantly less than what is spent on cosmetics and gambling, and represents a mere fraction of one percent of the $1.9 trillion 1988 budgets of the federal, state and local governments.

While that perspective provides a useful balance, it should not eliminate concern over escalating election costs—as another international study solidly documents. Karl-Heinz Nassmacher, of the Institute of Comparative Politics at the University of Oldenburg in West Germany, visits Canada periodically for an update on electoral changes. In 1989 he published a study, *The Costs of Party Democracy in Canada*, covering all the elections, federally and provincially, between 1976 and 1985. His figures are adjusted for the 1980 Consumer Price Index, so as to provide an average for the decade. They reveal that, federally, the cost per voter was $4.82, while provincially it was $8.10 [25].

That the provincial cost per voter was double that of the federal is a matter which invites further study. However, since the 1988 federal cost per voter was in excess of eight dollars, apparently it has almost doubled over that of a decade ago in Nassmacher's study.

The case for subjecting election spending to legitimate limits is solidly established. There's more than a kernel of truth in the quip that half the money spent on elections is wasted, but nobody is sure which half! Statutory limits on spending can check some of that waste and in the process establish a more level playing field for candidates. Not surprisingly, therefore, legislatures in both the United States and Canada are imposing more restrictions.

In the United States, California has the most expensive legislative races in the country, with Senate and Assembly seats averaging over $500 000. Smaller states have experienced a similar escalation: in the State of Washington, for example, between 1976 and 1986, the average Senate race jumped from $10 226 to $54 322 and campaign costs for the House Seats went from $7 490 to $23 074. As a result, many states are restricting campaign contributions and expenditures [26].

In Canada, seven of the 13 jurisdictions (federal, ten provinces and two territories) have imposed limits on expenditures. Ontario's experience in this connection is noteworthy. In the election previous to the 1986 imposition of limits, candidate expenditures ranged as high as $150 000. Under the new legislation, expenditures were limited to an average of $45 000. None of the 487 candidates breached the limit; and the average spending by the Liberals, as government party, was $36 000; by Conservatives,

$27 000; and by New Democrats, $18 000.

Where limits on contributions and campaign spending are not imposed, there should at least be full disclosure so that the public is fully aware of the sources and amounts of election funds. This is generally the case in FEC regulations in the United States, and increasingly so in Canadian jurisdictions. However, there are, as indicated above, serious omissions in the statutory requirements in Canada such as for candidates' nomination and pre-writ spending and for the growing role of third parties.

In the United States, third parties, whether PACs or individuals, have to register and file financial returns with the FEC. In Canada, there is no such requirement. In Canada there should at least be registration and filing so as to provide full disclosure.

Beyond this, there is the unresolved question of whether, during the campaign period, third parties should be excluded so as to leave the field to the regular players: the registered parties and candidates. In its 1966 report, the Barbeau Committee recommended such an exclusion, and belatedly, in 1983, the Canada Election Act was amended to ban third party advertising during a campaign. The National Citizens' Coalition challenged the legislation, and in an Alberta lower court, won a judgment that exclusion of third parties was a violation of free speech as guaranteed by the Charter of Rights and Freedoms. This judgment was not appealed by the Attorney General of Canada and as a result, in the elections of 1984 and 1988, the judgment of the lower court of one province superseded the law of the land as passed by Parliament.

Quebec provides a contrasting experience. Its legislation bans third party expenditures unless authorized by the chief financial officer of a party or candidate, in which case the expenditure becomes part of their budget which is subject to statutory limits. The Quebec legislation has been challenged, but it has been upheld at both the lower and appeal court levels.

Clearly, this is an issue which should be resolved by reference to the Supreme Court of Canada. The current situation is grossly unfair in that registered parties and candidates are restricted on both contributions and spending, and on blackout periods for advertising, while third parties are totally unregulated.

If a registered party or candidate is faced with

one or more hostile third parties, they will have no alternative but to have organized friendly third parties. The result will be, in the short term, an erosion of the integrity of the existing system, and in the long term, its destruction.

An Historical Perspective

The escalating cost of elections has been a matter of growing concern over the past generation. Five federal elections between 1957 and 1965, in combination with the costly emergence of TV as a major component of campaigning, resulted in the appointment of the all-party Barbeau Committee which conducted the first review of election financing. Its report of 1966 was followed by the establishment of a federal election finance system in 1974.

Beginning with the legislative initiative of Quebec during the Quiet Revolution of the early sixties, both provincial and territorial jurisdictions have passed election finance laws. Those of British Columbia and the Yukon are rudimentary; others range in comprehensiveness to those of Quebec and Ontario which are the most extensive in the world. All jurisdictions, except the Yukon, require full disclosure of monies received and spent. Ten have limits on expenditures. Six have limits on contributions, but these six, plus four more, provide tax credits for contributors in an effort to democratize election funding.

Until a generation ago, election funding in Canada was a clandestine, secretive exercise, often of questionable legality. Nobody knew exactly where the money came from nor how it was spent. Contributions were made for the purpose of influencing government policy or securing government contracts, a form of "influence peddling" which was, strictly speaking, a violation of the Criminal Code. Many of our lawmakers became lawbreakers in the very process of getting elected [27].

Periodically, when sources became publicly known, they found their way into our history as scandals—the Pacific Scandal of 1872, the Beauharnois Scandal of 1930, the Ontario Highway Scandal of the mid-fifties.

Today, the process of election funding is being subjected to ever-increasing disclosure. Admittedly, all election finance systems, even the most comprehensive, are incomplete. But with all their deficiencies, they merit support, protection and completion because they are a basic ingredient of an open and democratic society.

Notes

[1] United States Federal Election Commission Annual Report (1988), Appendix 5, 61.

[2] Elections Canada, Report of the Chief Electoral Officer Respecting Election Expenses (1988), Part 2.

[3] *Saturday Night*, March 1989, 3-16.

[4] Zev Paltiel, Khayyam. "Canadian Election Expenses Legislation, 1963-65." in *Comparative Political Finances in the 1980s*. Cambridge University Press, 1989, 68.

[5] Elections Canada, Report of the Chief Electoral Officer Respecting Election Expenses (1988), Part 1-1.

[6] A detailed account of Canadian pollsters and the role of public surveys in Canadian elections appears in Hoy, Clare. *Margin of Error: Pollsters and the Manipulation of Canadian Politics*. Key Porter Books, 1989.

[7] Elections Canada, Report of the Chief Electoral Officer Respecting Election Expenses (1988), Part 1.

[8] Montpetit, Gerry R., Assistant Director of Election Financing, Elections Canada. Letter to author, 1 February 1990.

[9] Lee, Robert Mason. *One Hundred Monkeys: The Triumph of Popular Wisdom in Canadian Politics*. Macfarlane Walter & Ross, 1989, 121.

[10] Elections Canada, Report of the Chief Electoral Officer Respecting Election Expenses (1988), Part 1-11.

[11] Elections Canada produces two, bulky, mimeographed volumes entitled Registered Parties' Fiscal Period Returns, in which there is listed the names and amounts of all the contributors in excess of $100 for each of the registered parties. These figures are extracted from these lengthy lists, and were reproduced from *Equity Magazine*, February 28, 1990.

[12] Elections Canada, Report of the Chief Electoral Officer Respecting Election Expenses (1988), Part 3-339.

[13] Van Alphen, Tony. "Controversial Free Trade Group Reveals its Who's Who Donor List." *Toronto Star*, December 9, 1989.

[14] These figures are contained in Registered Parties' Fiscal Period Returns to Election Canada (1988). In March 1990, Professor W.T. Stanbury of the University of British Colombia compiled all the Data on Contributions to Federal Political Parties in Canada, 1974-88.

[15] Since there is no legal obligation on third parties to report expenditures, this illustrative list is gleaned from many media sources. Some data, such as those of the NCC, are contained in a report to its members; others are individual projects which were reported in news stories.

[16] For a fuller account of the range of "internal lobbying", see Nick Fillmore, "The Big Oink: How Business Won the Free Trade Battle." in *This Magazine*, March-April 1989.

[17] Fillmore, Nick. "The Big Oink: How Business Won the Free Trade Battle." *This Magazine*, March-April 1989, 14.

[18] Gray, Charlotte. "Purchasing Power." *Saturday Night*, March 1989, 16.

[19] The impact of the competing free trade campaigns is detailed in Caplan, Gerald., Michael Kirby, and Hugh Segal. *Elections: The Issues, The Strategies, The Aftermath*. Prentice-Hall Canada Inc., 1989, Chapter 11., and in Fraser, Graham. *Playing for Keeps: The Making of a Prime Minister*. McClelland & Stewart, 1989, Chapter 16.

[20] *Globe & Mail*, June 13, 1958., and Fillmore, Nick. "The Big Oink: How Business Won the Free Trade Battle." *This Magazine*, March-April 1989, 19.

[21] Elections Canada, Administration Costs (including Subsidies) of the 1988 General Election, 2.

[22] Kimberling, William C., Deputy Director, National Clearinghouse on Election Administration, Federal Election Commission, Washington, D.C. Letter to author, 22 February 1990.

[23] Dr. Alexander's latest book is *Comparative Political Finances in the 1980s*, published by the Cambridge University Press, 1989. It includes an essay on the situation in eight different countries (Britain, Canada, Australia, United States, Israel, Italy, Spain and Holland). The Canadian chapter on Election Expenses Legislation, 1963-85, was written by the late Khayyam Zev Paltiel, to whom the volume is dedicated.

[24] Alexander, Herbert E. "Spending in the 1988 Election." Unpublished paper, 1989.

[25] Nassmacher, Karl-Heinz. *The Cost of Party Democracy in Canada, in Corruption and Reform*. The Netherlands: Clawer Academic Publishers, 1989, 232.

[26] Singer, Sandra. "The Arms Race of Campaign Financing," in *State Legislatures*, July 1988, 24.

[27] Fraser, Blair. "Our Illegal Elections," *Maclean's*, April 5, 1953.

CHAPTER FIVE

The Board of Internal Economy: Comptroller of the Public Purse in Canada's Legislatures?

ROBERT J. FLEMING

Robert J. Fleming, President of Robert Fleming International Research, Inc., was Administrator of the Ontario Legislature from 1974-87. He is a former Executive Coordinator of the Canada-U.S.A. Legislative Project, sponsored by the National Conference of State Legislatures, and has counselled overseas governments in legislature reorganization.

TODAY, VIRTUALLY all institutions in our society are coming under the magnifying glass of public scrutiny. Legislatures are no exception. Taxpayers want to know whether their politicians are offering good value for money spent.

In 1992, the total projected expenditure for all legislatures in Canada at the federal, provincial and territorial levels comes to $585 million—$21.65 for every Canadian.

In terms of overall expenditures by governments in Canada, the cost of footing the bill for the Senate, House of Commons and the twelve provincial and territorial legislatures is dwarfed by those of some government departments which now run into billions of dollars annually. Yet, the level of salaries,

allowances and services provided to elected members, and the professionalism by which our legislatures are administered, tend to establish the criteria by which many voters judge government performance in general.

In the past, Canadians have counted on strong parliamentary traditions and despite occasional lapses, that politicians will do the right thing. Now they are unsure about their legislators. They want questions answered such as "Are our MPs and provincial representatives running a clean shop, and if not, what can be done about it?" and, "What about the whole question of government operations across the board, and the responsibility of elected members, both those in cabinet and outside, for ensuring that dollars are well spent?"

Starting in the mid-1970s many members of the House of Commons and the provincial legislators found themselves asking the same type of questions. Frustrated that they (members from all parties) seemed to have little say in, or control over, the level of services provided to them in their official capacity, they strongly supported the establishment in each legislature of a body to be known as the Board of Internal Economy. The purpose of the Board would be to oversee the financial administration of the legislature and to ensure that all members would be treated fairly and equally in terms of allowances and services. As the legislature equivalent to the Treasury Board or Management Board of the government, the Board of Internal Economy would monitor, and where necessary control and curb spending. The Board, as envisioned, (and as recommended by the Ontario Commission on the Legislature in 1972) would consist of the Speaker of each House as Chairman, together with three or four government members, plus representation by the opposition parties.

The concept behind the Board of Internal Economy, that of a democratic body of elected members deciding what is best for all the members and the legislature in general, rather than having a Government Ministry in charge, has gone ahead in the Senate, House of Commons and all the provincial and territorial legislatures. As of 1992, if the legislature is the heart of government, then the Board of Internal Economy (or its equivalent), now functioning in every legislature, is the heart of the legislature.

Nowadays, notwithstanding the high purpose originally conceived for the Board, it is viewed by some critics as a self-serving body since it is composed of politicians administrating taxpayers' money to pay themselves: their salaries, their benefits, allowances, pensions and so on, plus determining budgets for their offices and caucuses. Further, the minutes of the Board's deliberations are not made public in seven jurisdictions including the Senate and the House of Commons. This is not at all what was planned in the beginning, and it runs counter to the aim of creating a more open and professionally-run legislature.

At the start of their work, some Boards of Internal Economy were able to make major strides in "democratizing" the legislature itself. The Ontario Board, which came into being through an amendment to the Legislative Assembly Act in December 1974 is a good example. Dubbed in its early days by members of the Opposition Party as the Board of "Infernal" Economy, this new creature of the Legislature was mistaken as some sort of an extension of the bureaucracy of government.

However, the main objective of the Board was to run the legislature professionally and in so doing, to put aside the distasteful and corrupting influence of internal patronage by providing members' services on a basis of equal provision for all, regardless of party. And they succeeded in winning over members who were dissidents in fairly short order by demonstrating that they were, in fact, doing what they had set out to do.

One of the first acts of the Board had been to have staff coming under the Speaker examine furniture and equipment requirements for members' offices so that there would be uniform and equitable standards for all.

What followed was an unusual exercise in getting the Board to decide on standards, not only for members' physical office needs, but eventually for every other aspect of the operations of the legislature including the various allowances for travel, accommodation, constituency offices, etc. In those days push-button telephones were considered to be an expensive addition to an office and not entirely necessary. The Board decided that the dial telephone should stay because the cost for push-button telephones was deemed excessive. One cabinet minister on the Board couldn't believe that he was having to decide on clear guidelines for his fellow politicians, rather than placing the onus on staff. "Do we have to do all this housekeeping stuff?" he groaned, "I'm a big picture person." But the point of the exercise was that the members themselves through their representatives on the Board had to come to grips with the professional management of their House. This they did.

The Ontario Board of Internal Economy became a very professional body, and always included staff in their meetings, partly to provide advice, but also to make absolutely clear that the decisions they made were to be passed down the line, and enforced. It was not uncommon for those responsible for carrying out the Board's wishes to encounter an irate member who felt that he or she should be treated differently and that the guidelines in some particular instance didn't apply to them. In fact, one person virtually jumped up and down when he tried to hire extra staff for his Queen's Park office, and was told this couldn't be done. "Can't you see that I'm a Cabinet Minister? I don't seem to get any respect around here!" he yelled. He was told politely that staff were following the instructions of the Board of Internal Economy and that he would have to take his case the Board. He did. The Board rejected his request.

The Board, which met about ten times a year, began to be a constructive force in the Legislature as its members—three Cabinet Ministers, one Government backbencher, the Opposition House Leader and the Third Party House Leader came together with the Speaker, as Chairman, to take responsibility for the financial administration of the legislature. For the most part, political partisanship and bickering were put aside at these meetings, in favour of trying to work towards common goals. The minutes of Board meetings were made public within 48 hours, with a copy being placed in the Legislative Library. As a result, the media were up-to-date on Board affairs, and tracked various items as they moved ahead on Board agendas.

The Ontario Board was the first in Canada to include members of the opposition parties. This actually assisted the flow of business in the House because they were the Opposition House Leaders, and it gave them a chance to interact with the Government House Leader who was also on the Board. In the past, they had seldom ever met.

Before long, the Ontario Board of Internal Economy had become a model for all legislatures in Canada as it went about its business of attempting to determine what was right for members of the legislature. As a result of its work, the Ontario Legislature was able to publish a blueprint for legislature operations in 1980; the first Manual of Administration ever to be produced for a legislature in North America. This document was forwarded by the Speaker of the day to the House of Commons and many of the provincial legislatures. It was generally acknowledged that Ontario was at the forefront of professional legislature management and administration in Canada.

Eventually the Board was working so well in terms of being an all-party forum for the resolution of some of the thornier problems around the Ontario Legislature that it seemed to about the only

place where senior members from all three parties could come together without rancor to think for the general welfare of all the members and the institution of the Legislature itself.

After the Board had been in business for ten years and most of the pressing requirements in the administration and operation of the Legislature had been addressed, the Board began to lose sight of its original purpose. This was partly brought about by the series of new members who joined the Board from all three parties but who had no sense of what had gone on before. They tended to view the Board as a political trade-off centre which would enable them to get what they wanted for their caucus. This began to cloud the work of the Board to such a degree that it ceased to be unbiased and business-like in nature. A few months later, at the time of the 1985 Election, members of the Board were suddenly vying with other Board members for increased allowances and services for their caucuses, and for additional funding.

Office of the Assembly staff, who reported to the Speaker and were required to be scrupulously non-partisan, had to do a double-take at some of the Board decisions. For example, in 1984, members in Ontario had one secretary/assistant in their Queen's Park office in Toronto and one assistant in their constituency office. The salaries of these workers totalled $52 000. In 1985, through a decision of the Board of Internal Economy, members were given a global allowance of $90 986 for their legislature and constituency office staff. It then became possible for individual members to have at least three people on the payroll. In times past, the Board most likely would not have agreed to such an increase. There would have been some concern about "trying to keep the lid on."

It was this major increase of almost $40 000 per politician which raised eyebrows. Applied to the 125 elected members at that time, this meant an increase of almost $5 million in the office staff allowance alone. It was unlikely that some members could ever make use of this extra staff allotment, but they would accept it anyway in order to keep up with their colleagues. The result would be not only more staff, but more paper consumed, more equipment, more strain on the reference and research department of the Library who would be responding to requests by new staff in the member's name; and more demands on the human resources and finance branches of the

Legislature. These are the factors which would not have been taken into account in advance. Correspondingly, the budget for the Legislature ballooned.

The budgetary estimates for the expenses of the Ontario Legislative Assembly for 1985/86 (the year that the staff increase took place) was $52.2 million. The following year it had increased to $67.25 million . For 1991/92 it stands at $131 million.

Having traced the development of one Board of Internal Economy, that of Ontario, and outlined some of the problems which appear to have occurred in recent years, it would be totally unfair to suggest that this has been the case with all Boards of Internal Economy. This of course is not so, as many members across Canada who sit on these boards are doing their level-headed best to serve the legislature and their fellow members, keeping in mind the difficulty of providing needed services, while at the same time opting for restraint. There is also no question that in the "hurly burly" of political life, those who are often at the heart of things on a day-to-day basis, simply don't have the time to consider the "overall picture" and the possible ramifications of some decisions that have very often been made in good faith.

As may be seen from the information contained in this book referring to the budgets of the Senate, House of Commons and the provincial and territorial legislatures, there has actually been a reduction of legislative spending in some jurisdictions, however there had been a substantial increase in others. It is the Board of Internal Economy (or its equivalent) which is the determining factor as to how these budgets should be set (although, as explained elsewhere, it is the government which normally decides on indemnity, tax-free allowance and pension levels and can, if they so wish, be the final arbiter on any financial matter in the legislature, through their membership majority on the Board of Internal Economy) and at times, it can even be convenient for the government to let the Board—which has become part of the Canadian parliamentary fabric— take the "heat" on contentious issues.

It should be a matter of great concern to taxpayers that in some jurisdictions, Boards of Internal Economy (which were created, as the name implies, as a means of controlling expenditures from the public purse) have lost sight of their mission and are initiating and approving expenditures which do not reflect an attitude of rectitude and concern for

restraint. This is reflected in some of the excessive financial provisions for elected members which are outlined in the tables and analysis contained in this book. It is not good enough for members on these Boards to declare that the public has no right to know about the decisions they make at the boardroom table. The public has every right. It is the public who employs the legislators, not the other way around.

Do not forget that California voters, in 1990, frustrated by what they saw as "self-serving" incumbents and the skyrocketing costs of that Legislature moved quickly to clip the wings of their legislators. As a result of Proposition 140, approved by 52% of California voters, representatives elected to the California State Legislature are now prohibited from serving beyond three two-year terms. California senators may not remain in office for more than two four-year terms.

One of the results of that radical step was that in addition to restricting term limits for legislators, the $165 million California Legislature budget for 1991 was cut by 40% to $90 million, where it now stands. The pension plan was abolished for all incoming representatives and senators after 1990. More than 750 House and Senate employees out of a work force of 2 500 lost their jobs due to the budget cuts. Those that are left are having to scrounge for books and research materials as there are no longer monies available for things that are normally taken for granted in a legislature. Said one aide to a senior legislative leader commenting on the California predicament, "In retrospect there are hundreds of things that could have been handled differently here in the past eight to ten years, but that's all hindsight now."

The chances are remote that Canadian voters have the political will to find a way to impose term limits on our elected members, or slash legislature budgets. That type of drastic action hardly seems in keeping with our traditional approach to government. Nevertheless public confidence in our politicians, now at an all-time low, needs to be restored. Canadians need to be able to trust that their politicians will do the right thing—and that they are doing the right thing.

One of the ways politicians can do this is by putting their own "house" in order, by being open and non-partisan about the nature of their expenditures while they are in office.

The following recommendations, based on personal experience, knowledge and research, could work to help achieve greater accountability in the political process. But this can only happen if Canadians—the voters who fund our politicians and our political and governmental institutions—demand that action be taken.

- In every jurisdiction, minutes of the Board of Internal Economy meetings should be made public within 72 hours.

- Recommendations by the Board of Internal Economy for annual increases in members' office budget allowances, including constituency offices; caucus funding; and funding for the offices of Opposition Leaders, Opposition House Leaders, Whips, etc., should be tabled in the House by the Speaker as a Sessional Paper, before implementation.

- The Board of Internal Economy should no later than September 1 of each year, through the Speaker, table a Sessional Paper listing members' individual official expenses, by category, for the previous fiscal year.

- The Board should require that all members who utilize scheduled airlines for round trip flights at public expense, which are outside the regular flights between the constituency and the seat of government, complete a form within 21 days of having made the trip, stating its purpose and destination.

- The Board should set unequivocal guidelines for members' official newsletters (Householders) to ensure that these are non-partisan in nature and controlled in terms of cost, and apply similar controls to first class mail. Guidelines to be placed in the public domain.

- The Board should allocate the cost of computer equipment (other than the basic entitlement provided by the legislature) used in members' offices against the name of the member. There should be clear guidelines regarding the purchase and replacement of computers and computer networks.

- The Board should stipulate that in the matter of the purchase of goods and services, party caucuses and members' offices be required to adhere to the same purchasing policies imposed on the public service.

- The Board of Internal Economy should rule that party caucuses and members' offices be subject to the provisions of the Freedom of Information Act, or its equivalent.

- The Board of Internal Economy, through the Speaker, should refer all questions relating to appropriate levels for members' indemnities, salaries, benefits, and allowances, including the tax-free allowance, committee allowance (where applicable) and travel and accommodation allowance to a body outside the House of Commons, or legislature, for review. This body should consist of at least two persons to be appointed by the Speaker, representing the public at large, of which one will be Chair; and one representative of each party officially recognized in the Legislature, but not an elected member or staff person. This body should make its report to the House of Commons, or the Legislature through the Speaker, on behalf of the Legislature.

- The Board of Internal Economy should issue clear guidelines governing the proper use of public funds in all categories of legislature budgets, and require that these standards be adhered to by members and staff alike.

CHAPTER SIX

Resuscitating Parliament: A Breath of New Life is Needed

DOUGLAS FISHER

Douglas Fisher, an Ottawa-based political commentator and analyst, is a former Member of Parliament, and served as a member of the Ontario Commission on the Legislature.

THE MODERN era of Parliament can be dated from the "pipeline debate" in the House of Commons in 1956. It is obvious the era is near its end. Either the constitutional crisis closes with Quebec parting or Canada will go on with a Parliament that is drastically changed.

It is useful to note this period of some 35 years opened with much enthusiasm for a revitalized Parliament. Since 1957 there have been six prime ministers, twelve general elections and several thousand MPs have been created and rejected. The era is closing with the present members conceding that they and their forum are held in disrespect by a frustrated, untrusting public. The antagonism passes no party or leader by.

It happens that I was in the first four of the twelve Parliaments after 1957, and since then been a columnist fixed largely on parliamentary politics. Wisdom, particularly about Parliament, comes hard, even after much close witness. It makes me despondent that the House and the people who have had so much of my attention and respect are scorned and

suffer under withering criticism in books, editorials and commentary. Yet, it is easy to trace how this disfavour, now chronic, developed. It began with the coincidence of a genuinely national television system and the flowering of colourful John Diefenbaker as his party's leader and then our prime minister. More people than ever before began to follow parliamentary politics.

Television's imperatives on personalities and clash meant the context and complexities of issues and actions were simplified. TV breeds familiarity; it makes most people feel they really know their politicians. They can readily judge them, beginning, unfortunately, with their mannerisms rather than their politics. And the medium has this syndrome: overexposure brings exasperation. The ever-greater fixation on leaders brought forward the personal opinions of millions about them, rather than about the long-established party system or the often arcane ways and means of Parliament. Practices inside politics continued, and gradually these have become targets for public venom—of rewards for the faithful, of opposition for the sake of opposition, of ever tighter rather than looser party discipline in contradiction to the clear shift towards the centre over the period by all parties in the House.

During the era the cardinal rules given new MPs by the veterans held firm (and still do). These were to take good care of the riding, be loyal to the leader, play true and fair with the caucuses and smite the rival parties whenever and wherever possible.

After Diefenbaker's big sweep of the House seats in 1958 there came similar sweeps in 1968 and 1984, each also identified with a fresh party leader who subsequently fell, just like the Chief, far from a crest of national acclaim. Since Laurier's heyday Canadians have not been given to cherishing prime ministers for long; however, by 1991 the last of the sweep winners had become the most unpopular prime minister since polling came into vogue after WW II.

And as leaders and politics were being popularized and then cut down before our eyes on television, the federal government and Parliament were going through an extraordinary period of activism and innovation in policies and programs. In 1957, not one national think-tank existed, today there are a dozen, including five funded largely by Ottawa. In 1957, not a single ombudsman figure, protecting and sustaining a particular mission or the abused; today there are many ombudsman-like agencies at watch over matters like languages, penitentiaries, human rights and the rights to information and privacy. Many of these creations were pushed more by organized interest groups than by the political parties which through this period became more and more instruments for raising money, putting candidates in the field and planning for and fighting elections rather than seed beds for policies and programs.

A national optimism emerged in the late 1960s that idealized the Eden we could make in Canada through legislation and spending. Both a general idealism and the advance of lobbying spawned a rapidly growing host of national associations and groups which relentlessly focused on the people and offices of importance in Ottawa. These interests, whether private or public, came to rely increasingly on "consultants" and communication specialists. The latter multiplied like rabbits in the 1980s, promoting, usually discreetly, particular causes and interests. Most of the consultants had been either active in a party or had held senior posts in the federal bureaucracy.

Of course, almost all this ferment and concerted pushing for action and aid focused on the government in its guise of senior ministers and mandarins rather than on Parliament, let alone on MPs. The growing web of fixers and interveners has mostly had mere afterthoughts for the run of MPs. Their pressure points have been ministers, especially those who headed the so-called central agencies, and on the key personnel in the growing offices at the core—the PMO-PCO establishment.

In the mid-1960s federal employees were almost hurrahed by Mr. Pearson and Parliament into unionization and so-called free collective bargaining. There began a remarkable generosity in pay and benefits, not least at the top where reorganization followed reorganization, each with an attendant flowering of associate and assistant deputy ministers, directors, etc. It is hard to believe that in early 1968 only three public servants made over $28 000 a year.

Many who are now nasty about Parliament and politicians forget or ignore this immensely fertile period in experimentation and ideas, and the steady thrust towards more federal agencies, more bureaucrats and more spending. Its legacies include an immensely wider, thicker federal infrastructure and a remorselessly escalating debt load. During all the innovations those who protested and wanted to go slower were damned as reactionaries, not just by those advancing the many proposals and causes but seemingly by the public as a whole. In truth, there were not many protesters in the House. Most MPs went along overwhelmingly with the tide of idealism for making Canada a model for the world. Almost all the radical programs and institutions created were welcomed by the parties in Parliament, at least until the National Energy Program.

Throughout the era since 1962 when the Social Credit MPs from rural Quebec burst onto the Hill there has been an obsession in the government and among the caucuses with what Quebec wants, much of this leading to talk and negotiations about the constitution and Quebec's place in Canada. Probably the most significant of all developments in the era in terms of Parliament's authority was constitutional and came in 1981 with the Charter of Rights and Freedoms. The Charter epitomizes the idealism abroad in Canadian politics. We would as a people through our courts, not through our politicians, ensure that no persons or collectives like women, ethnic groups and native peoples suffered hurt or harm. The Charter has taken responsibilities from Parliament. The courts will decide many contentious issues, at times literally directing what Parliament may do or should not do.

Out of the dilemma over Quebec came the relatively expensive and perennially contentious program of official bilingualism and later of multiculturalism. It's plain that neither program has ever had broad majority support of the people but both programs seemed imperative and very worthy to the political elites, including the parties in Parliament. Each caucus backed the programs with surface idealism masking an openly-expressed antipathy.

The era had opened with the determination, despite partisan differences over timing and form, to complete the national welfare and health programs. By the end of the '70s we had the national "safety net" fairly well in place. Meanwhile the government began to intervene more and more in the economy, in part in the name of correcting regional disparities, in part to sustain or protect Canadian corporations. And similar interventions and funding developed in the fields of culture and recreation, notably so we could be seen as being world class at our centennial celebrations and later in hosting the Olympics of 1976.

In Diefenbaker's first year there was an extraordinary excitement over what was to become all too familiar, the gathering of first ministers. Along with this came an increase of federal and provincial cadres in specific fields like finance, health, culture, training, etc., which has almost firmed into a new institutional level, based on regular conferences and "in camera" meetings.

Such fertility in programs, spending and bureaucratic structures, almost all of which was introduced and passed by Parliament, helps us understand why the last federal surplus, a tiny one, was in the early 1970s and why we close the era with a federal deficit of $400 billion.

Why give so much time to sketching this sheer fecundity of our politics in this era and the diversity and complexity in our programs? Because Parliament, in particular the House and its members, sometimes pushed by the governments, sometimes influenced by opposition aims and criticisms, has responded by adding and altering services and roles.

The complexity of affairs on the Hill today for the MP as constituency and regional figure, as a member of a highly organized caucus and a participant in a much extended system of committees is as a B747 is to the Viscounts of 1957.

In 1957 most MPs had half a secretary's time and a packet of $10 000 a year; today's MP has a staff of four to five; every modern technical device is at hand, so is unlimited phone and fax use and a packet of income running up from $90 000 a year. A shared office of 300 square feet has become a suite of rooms for each MP. Twenty-two ministers then, thirty-nine now; a dozen parliamentary secretaries then, thirty now. In 1991 some thirty-five House committee chairposts each session; in 1957 about a dozen. Now even deputy whips get bonus pay.

The leadership group in each opposition caucus assigns specific responsibilities to each caucus member, from the grandeur of finance to the slightness of sport. This signifies the intense organization on the Hill, much of it stemming from fierce competition by the third party to be seen and heard despite the advantages of the official opposition in priority and numbers. Once upon a time under the tutelage of Stanley Knowles, the NDP was the most constructive and rule-abiding party but this attitude has faded, replaced by a House strategy in favour of any ways or means to delay and obstruct government intentions.

By the early 1970s even the questions in the House, the order of speakers in a debate and the choices of private members' motions and bills for debate were planned and assigned by the House leader groups. Heaven help the straying MP who lurches into a colleague's assigned domain. In 1957 Question Period often petered out in thirty minutes; the Speaker "recognized" whom he saw fit to, both for questions and as debaters. The order paper in 1957-58 had less than a dozen private members' bills, and only a score or so of private members' motions. This session such bills number over a hundred and there are more than six hundred motions on the list. Busy, busy!

The Library of Parliament had three "reference" assistants in 1957, today it has some seventy experts in a dozen or so fields (most with doctorates) to advise MPs and do research for them and for House committees. In 1957 the MPs and senators with their staff support were all in the centre block and near the chamber; now they are housed in five other buildings, three of them off the Hill and served by a parliamentary bus line.

I make this parade, first of many developments in politics and the shift of reportage, then of comparisons with what was once for MPs so as to make understandable the prevalence of busy work on the Hill. MPs operate within a cocoon of personnel and expensive services; there is a rote obedience to their leaders. Even for government backbenchers access to ministers is more difficult than it used to be. Nothing on the Hill is more apparent than the sheer, scheduled rush of almost every minister, even the ministers of state with secondary responsibilities.

There is much less socializing today than there once was, both within party and across party lines. At night now the buildings are dark and empty. On weekends most Hill doors are locked, even at the Press Gallery. Perhaps the plainest way to put it is that the role of the MP, government or opposition, minister or not, has become thoroughly bureaucratized around parliamentary business, serving the riding and dealing with the government as an administration.

What about the purely political, i.e., the partisan? Here also the run of MPs are more removed from discussing and implementing strategy and tactics. Electioneering has become leader-centred. Regional luminaries of a party have far less importance. Large funds are now available to parties through the use of tax exemption receipts and post-campaign provisions for recapture of expenditures. These sustain a large, professional cadre in each party that manages membership and fund drives and campaigns. Such regulars mesh with the large staffs of the party leaders, in concert carrying out the party functions beyond Parliament which MPs once had.

In my opinion most of today's MPs work harder and longer and lead more complicated lives than those of the 1950s; and by and large they are better educated and more fully committed to careers in politics. As a spur to work, not a tenth of their seats are safe today whereas in 1957 at least a third were.

In such zealous preoccupation it is little wonder that the needs and purposes of MPs are scrambled and are taken by an increasingly critical people to be mindless or useless. In fact most MPs are in their chamber only for the daily Question Period, the "charade" as John Turner called it. Very few MPs ever listen to speeches by other MPs. Far more of their time and skill goes to constituency newsletters and making videos for use in the riding than attending the House or preparing speeches. Why speak if few hear and the media ignores what is said about bills and motions?

The MPs of three decades ago were more reflective than today's but the pace of House and caucus and committees was more leisurely. They had many occasions for talk and socializing; fewer had ambitions for high places; above all, most of them were not so critically exposed at home nor so constrained in Ottawa within the frame of leader and caucus discipline as MPs are today.

To reiterate, my wisdom on what has become the parliamentary scenario comes far easier than that on what should be or may be. The crux is that the public will be increasingly critical of their elected politicians—more populist if you will. They will demand more attention, more respect for their views. But these views are often simplistic and often contradictory as befits a nation in danger of splitting, firstly over one province's uniqueness, secondly on whether the federal government should be interventionist and collective in approach or should avow market forces in the economy and play as minimal a role as considerations of security, health and basic welfare allow.

The shake-out coming from the constitutional crisis should put the left vs. right, the anti-American vs. pro-Canadian, somewhat on hold. The transition may also mean a slackening for a time in the public distaste and contempt for MPs and their institution. Until a fractured Canada emerges or the continuing one gets its new, reformed senate and adjusts administratively to realignments of powers between jurisdictions, MPs and their House could be vital, simply by being the forum for being the final debate and the last decisions on the constitution. My hunch and prayer is that through these stages at least, party discipline and its followership does not prevail.

Beyond this we may get back to basics, first that representative government need not mean dictatorship by a leadership cadre sanctified by a legislative majority, second that the role and rule of parties has been overdone. In times when interest groups generate most legislative initiatives (and oppose them) the elected man or woman must have more freedom to criticize and amend and more independence in voting.

CHAPTER SEVEN

Current Political Processes: A Public Perspective

BY MICHAEL ADAMS

Michael Adams is President of Environics Research Group Limited, one of Canada's leading polling firms.

AT THE time of this writing, Canada's Prime Minister, Brian Mulroney, leads the least popular government in Canadian history and a political party that commands the support of only 12% of the decided electorate. Just 12% approve of the way the Prime Minister himself is handling his job. But, Environics' polls also find a disillusionment with politics and politicians that runs much deeper than dissatisfaction with the prime minister of the day, his party or his policies. Increasingly, This dissatisfaction is focused on the basic elements of the country's political institutions, and on the politicians who people them.

In examining nearly two decades of tracking data on public attitudes, senior researchers at Environics have concluded that this growing crisis of confidence in politicians is indicative of a deeper crisis of confidence in the system of representative government and party politics that evolved out of British colonial rule in the nineteenth century. Environics has further concluded that the institutions and practices that have characterized political process for over 125 years are no longer suited to the values and

expectations of Canadians and that in the absence of democratic reforms the Canadian political system is in danger of losing its legitimacy in the public mind.

Sir George-Étienne Cartier, one of Canada's founding fathers, once described his nation as one that has a "political nationality", that is, one in which the citizens are united, not by language, religion or a common ethnicity, but by politicians and a set of constantly evolving political arrangements. Today, however, the economic and cultural forces currently threatening so many other countries around the world are also causing an irreversible unravelling of the ties that once bound Canadians together.

The governing institutions that have served Canada since Confederation required a relatively passive electorate, one that was willing to let the political elites work out the compromises that kept the country together. However, the massive shift in Canadian social values since the 1960s—away from deference to authority and deferred gratification to values that emphasize increased self-confidence and a sense of individualistic empowerment—has meant that many of Canada's political institutions seem, if not anachronistic, then increasingly ill-suited to serve the needs of a better informed and less deferential electorate. We are in the throes not only of a constitutional crisis but of a crisis of confidence in our democratic institutions.

The watershed event, in both crises, was the failure of the Mulroney government to secure ratification of the Meech Lake accord. Quite apart from the fact that the rejection of the accord polarized opinion on the question of Quebec's place within Confederation, the tactics used by Prime Minister Mulroney to force ratification of the accord, during and immediately after his meeting with the provincial premiers in June 1990, were seen as ineffective, cynical, heavy-handed and all too typical of a government that could not be trusted to lead the country out of the constitutional quagmire created by the nation's politicians.

Yet, despite the mid-term slump plaguing Brian Mulroney's second government, and at a time when sovereigntist sentiment in Quebec is strong and the economy is struggling to find its way out of the worst recession to hit this country since the black days of the 1930s, Mr. Mulroney remains secure in his position. Our polls find no evidence of a Boris Yeltsin, waiting in the wings, primed to spark revolt among the masses clambering for change prior to the next general election, nor even a Michael Hesseltine plotting to instigate a palace coup.

None of the leaders of the opposition parties seem poised to fill the leadership vacuum created by the crisis of confidence in Brian Mulroney's Conservative government. An Environics survey conducted in August of 1991 found public enthusiasm for the main federal party leaders ranged from lukewarm to dismally low. The combined approval ratings of Mr. Mulroney and Jean Chrétien, the current leaders of the only two parties that have ever governed nationally, is at an all-time low. Moreover, the relatively large proportions expressing no opinion regarding the leaders suggested that political ennui may be reaching crisis proportions.

Approval of NDP leader Audrey McLaughlin stood at 40% of eligible voters; 28% disapproved and 32% expressed no opinion. Approval of Liberal leader Jean Chrétien remained about the same as that of his predecessor, John Turner; just 29% approved of the way Mr. Chrétien has been handling his job. As was the case in the previous survey in April 1991, half of eligible voters, 49%, disapproved

and 23% expressed no opinion. Preston Manning of the Reform Party remained largely an unknown factor; 28% approved of his performance, 19% disapproved and a majority of 54% expressed no opinion. Among eligible voters in Quebec, 54% approved of Lucien Bouchard's leadership of the Bloc Quebecois, 19 percent disapproved and 27% expressed no opinion.

More disturbing, however, than the flat or low approval ratings of the three major party leaders, was the finding that none emerged as the electorate's first choice for prime minister. When Canadians were asked to indicate who would be the best person for prime minister, a plurality of 31% offered no opinion. Eight percent either said "none of the above" or named a fourth individual. Among the leaders, support ranged from eight percent for Brian Mulroney to 21% for Jean Chrétien.

A perusal of Environics' surveys monitoring support for the nation's political parties reveals that, if an election were held today, no party would come close to forming a majority government. In addition, as the survey conducted in April of 1991 found the simultaneous emergence of the Bloc Quebecois in Quebec and the Reform Party in the rest of Canada is not only eroding the Conservative party's base of support in Quebec and the West, it is adding an element of unpredictability and volatility heretofore unknown in Canadian politics.

The August survey found that 34% of decided voters support the Liberals; a significantly smaller proportion, 24%, would vote for the NDP. And, for the first time in an Environics survey, support for the Reform Party surpassed that of one of the mainstream parties: 17% of decided voters indicated a willingness to vote for the Reform Party. This proportion was five points higher than that reported for the Conservative party. Although the Reform Party remained largely a Western party (it received the support of 35% of Western Canadians, 16% of Ontarians and 10% of Atlantic Canadians) it did outrank the Conservatives in Ontario. Twelve percent of decided voters overall including 45% of decided Quebec voters said they supported the Bloc Quebecois.

The depth of the electorate's disillusionment with the political process was also reflected in an earlier Environics survey, conducted in October of 1990. That survey found that support for abolition of the Senate had doubled since the previous sampling in May of 1990 and was at its highest level since the question was first asked in 1978.

Relations between the Liberal-dominated Senate and the Conservative government of Brian Mulroney had been particularly rancorous throughout 1990. On September 27, approximately one month before this survey went into the field, Prime Minister Brian Mulroney, in an unprecedented use of his constitutional power to appoint senators stacked the upper house with eight additional senators to help his government push through the highly unpopular Goods and Services Tax Bill. These appointments, coupled with earlier and sometimes equally controversial ones, such as that of former premier John Buchanan of Nova Scotia, brought renewed charges that the Senate is "the hog-trough" of political patronage.

Although their grueling eleven-week fight against the GST had popular support, the Liberal senators fared little better in the public mind. Night after night, Canadians winced as senators from both sides of the floor brandished noisemakers and exchanged schoolboy taunts. It was not a dignified or edifying display, however worthy the cause, and to many it seemed to confirm the need to rethink the role of the Senate in Canadian public affairs.

The survey found that a plurality of 41% of Canadians believed the Senate should be reformed; this finding represented a decrease of twelve points since May of 1990. But, a significant minority of 32% said the Senate should be abolished, and this proportion represented a dramatic increase of seventeen points during the same time period.

As in previous surveys, support for Senate reform was higher in the West, particularly Alberta, Manitoba and British Columbia. Support for abolition was especially high in Quebec and somewhat higher in Atlantic Canada. And, interestingly, there was plurality support for abolition of the Senate among Canadians aged 60 or more. Members of the higher education and income groups were more likely than others to favour reform.

The same survey found that public confidence in government and political leaders had declined markedly from the previous wave. The low levels of confidence in political leaders and governments could be attributed, at least in part, to negative fallout from the Meech Lake debacle, to the plummeting popularity of the Prime Minister, to the introduction of the GST, to the economic recession and to an

increasing belief that the free trade agreement negotiated with the United States had been a bad deal for Canada.

Reported confidence in governments, which had been on the rise in 1988, dropped to its lowest point since the question was first asked in 1983. Just 36% of Canadians, a decline of nineteen points since 1988, said they have a lot of or some confidence in their governments; a sizable majority of 63% said they have little or no confidence in their governments. Confidence in private enterprise, which had changed little, stood at 80%.

However, the most dramatic crisis of confidence in Canadian society was focused on the country's politicians. A large majority of 71% said they have little or no confidence in their political leaders. By comparison, confidence in the nation's police forces stood at 82%, and in judges and lawyers at 62%. Only 28% of Canadians expressed a lot of or some confidence in political leaders; this finding represented a drop of sixteen points from 1988 and of twenty-four points from 1976.

Perhaps the most telling evidence of Canadians' loss of confidence is found in data reported by an Environics survey conducted in April 1991. When Canadians were asked to compare their country and the United States on fourteen dimensions, just 32% said they thought Canada had a better system of government. This proportion was seventeen points lower than that found when the question had been asked in 1987 and was the only area in which there had been a precipitous drop in confidence. By comparison, 93% thought the Canadian health care system is superior and 80% said the same of Canada's social security system. Confidence in these and most other areas had held over the six-year period.

Canadians no longer believe that parliament and the political parties represent the interests of the people. Their MPs, once elected, seem to have become vassals to a system in which they represent the party line rather than their constituents. However well intentioned, party policy and the process of its development lacks political legitimacy. Like the infamous Meech Lake accord, most government policy seems to be the product of a few men making deals behind closed doors and acting with little regard for the wishes of the average citizen. Such elitism is increasingly viewed by a less deferential electorate as anachronistic, and intolerable.

Canada's political institutions will need to be reformed in fundamental ways if the politicians are to win back the confidence of the people they wish to govern. The theatrics of Question Period no longer meet the demand for democratic accountability. Citizens today want government policy to reflect their values and interests and they want clear evidence—both in terms of the substantive outcome and process—that this is happening.

We must recognize and confront the deep levels of disillusionment threatening the future of democracy. If democracy is to survive into the next century, we will need a new mix of democratic initiatives, a mix that includes such populist proposals as MP recall, referenda, more free votes in parliament, an elected Senate and fixed-term parliaments. In other words, we must redefine the concepts of "responsible" and "responsive" government, as implemented through the parliamentary system, the party system and the constitution.

Federal Party Support 1988-1991

Party	1988 Election	Apr. 1991	Aug. 1991
Liberal	32%	31%	34%
New Democratic	20%	29%	24%
Reform	n.a.	14%	17%
Progressive Conservative	43%	14%	12%
Bloc Quebecois	n.a.	10%	12%
Other	5%	2%	2%

PART TWO

A Roundtable on Government and its Institutions

CANADIAN LEGISLATURES represents more than facts and figures. It is an attempt to explain in simple terms the inner workings of the Senate, House of Commons and the provincial and territorial legislatures.

In addition, *Canadian Legislatures* seeks to examine the direction in which our political and governmental institutions should be heading in the future.

For this, our Tenth Anniversary, we invited a cross-section of Canadians to help us in our task.

In the following pages academics, business people, writers and broadcasters, doctors and scientists, association and foundation executives and representatives of the arts all share their hopes and suggestions. All have served Canada with distinction, in government and many other capacities. All are anxious to make their experience count for Canada in the future.

The Cultural Imperative

Louis Applebaum

Louis Applebaum O.C., L.L.D. was Chairman of the Federal Culture Policy Review Committee, and co-authored the Applebaum/Hebert Report in 1982 on the state of the arts in Canada. He has an international reputation as a composer of movie scores.

WHILE WE busily search for ways to reform our political systems or procedures, we cannot escape an issue that is perhaps more vital, viz: what do we Canadians believe, what do we stand for and are ready to battle for. The best way to get a grip on that collective self-understanding is to pay attention to what our artists have to say.

Given our geographic positioning, something that cannot be altered through a referendum or amended after a poll or two, Canadians must contend with demands and dangers that face no other nation. The power that the American cultural generating station is able to put out is electrifying the whole world, and that is something the U.S. is ready and happy to develop with impunity. Canada's only recourse is to build up, as effectively and as quickly as possible, our own ability to create and to disseminate our creative output widely.

In 1982 a large committee, which I had the honour to chair, was asked to advise the federal government about its future cultural policies. The most telling recommendation, one that coloured and shaped all the others, was simply this: the cornerstone on which all cultural policies should be built, is the encouragement and support of our creative individuals. We have succeeded in building up an impressive infrastructure of theatre and dance companies, orchestras and galleries; we have justified support to record, film and publishing ventures; and we have developed performing artists of the highest calibre in both the popular and more esoteric art forms. Unfortunately, too many of them still find it necessary to build their reputations and achievements on how well they present the creations of other times and other cultures.

We have come to understand that the good health of our industries demands that we support research. We, therefore, encourage our scientists and designers to reach out, to try the untried, to push at the margins as hard as they dare, in the conviction that basic research will ultimately have a practical pay-off.

In the realm of the arts, however, we still find it easier to pay for new buildings (who was it that first called it the "edifice complex"?) than to provide for novelists, composers, choreographers and painters. The exaltation generated during the Centennial year netted us a goodly number of halls and arenas while giving only passing thought as to how to sustain them, let alone how to instill in them the life-giving breath of creativity.

This is not to diminish the enormous success won by our artists and arts companies in the last few decades. But we have not yet been able to raise the status of our prime creators above the bottom rungs on the ladder of recognition and support. It is they who extract out of the air our songs, symphonies, poems and plays, who shape our dances and sculptures, who imagine our films and TV shows. Too few of them can make a living doing what they were destined to do. Even fewer are recognized by autograph seekers; they are not the heroes and icons they should be.

All governments, their politicians and bureaucrats, must recognize the fundamental need to muster much greater backing behind the creative innovators among us. Our future as a nation is irrevocably tied to the products of their imagination. Through the work of our creative artists we, and the rest of the world, can capture the essence of what it is to be a Canadian. It is about time.

A Problem of the Spirit

John Robert Colombo

John Robert Colombo, an award-winning writer and author of "Colombo's Canadian Quotations" and the "Dictionary of Canadian Quotations" is well-known to Canadians for his pungent observations and prolific books on the Canadian scene.

WHOEVER EXAMINES the constitutional history of this country is overcome with a sense of *déjà-vu*. When the country's past is viewed through a long-range telescope, rather than through a short-range microscope, it becomes apparent that we have been through all this "double trouble" not once, not twice, but innumerable times in the past. It seems that every succeeding generation of Canadians has been anxious to avoid the issues of the day by attempting to rewrite or rework the constitution, as if changes to a piece of parchment, drawn up by Parliament and interpreted by the Supreme Court, will automatically bring about social harmony and put this country back to work economically, politically, socially, culturally and spiritually.

Yes, especially spiritually. Canada's problems are not legislative or constitutional in nature, but spiritual. The legislatures and courts of this country have worked well in the past; they are working now, if on short rations and at cross-purposes; and they could work better in the future. The patriated Constitution with its Bill of Rights is an uninspired but workable document as it stands—given only the will of Canadians to make it work. Too many groups want to rewrite the Constitution *their* way—to bring it closer to *their* heart's desire. The Constitution and federal-provincial relations are beginning to resemble those dilapidated buildings seen in every city in Eastern Europe: no one can tell whether they are being built or being demolished, so much are they in shambles. The Meech Lake Constitutional Accord, the call for a Triple-E Senate, the demand for a Constituent Assembly, the requirement of "distinct society" status are all instances of needless and heedless revisionism. It is possible that one of these measures, or a number of them, could be of assistance; but I doubt it very much.

There is no need to despair of this country, despite its patchwork of federal and provincial governments, its political parties (which so resemble teams in the closed competition of the expanded National Hockey League—fire on ice, ideas on ice). George Woodcock quite rightly referred to our system as "five-year fascism". Despair is not required because compared with systems of government found in other countries, our system is distinctive and still reasonably workable.

Canada is a country that has produced two moral movements and two moral organizations that are respected throughout the world. Although Canadians seem unaware of the importance of these movements and organizations, one has only to travel in the Third World to see the influence in villages of the credit union movement and the co-operative movement. Both movements are of Canadian origin and have saved hundreds of thousands of people

from starvation and given hope to millions more.

The two moral organizations have also earned international respect. The Pugwash conference has done much to contain nuclear adventurism during the Cold War. Greenpeace, with its policy of "direct action," has become, more perhaps than any other single organization, the ecological conscience of mankind.

Any country that assists individuals in the development of credit unions, co-operatives, Pugwash and Greenpeace, is a country with a system of government that has worked.

Here is what I would like to see. Canadians should set themselves the task of drawing up a list of questions to be directed to proponents of specific proposals for constitutional reform. Any proposed legislative change should be measured against answers to questions like these:

- Will the proposed change result in meaningful work for more Canadians?
- Will the proposed change ensure the prosperity of future generations?
- Will the proposed change bring about a more just and equitable society?
- Will the proposed change guarantee individual rights as well as the responsible expression of collective interests?
- Will the proposed change reduce the influence of politicians and political parties and public and private bureaucracies?
- Will the proposed change increase the quality and diversity of cultural expression in the country, as well as the dissemination of civilized values throughout Canada and the world?

Measured against criteria like these, I predict that all the proposed changes will be found wanting because proponents of constitutional reform have their own agendas, often secret or self-seeking, which advance the interests of one group at the expense of another group, specific cultural concerns at the cost of general civilized values. It is better, then, to try to realize the *spirit* of the constitution that is still in place rather than the dead letter of some grand scheme for future betterment. Otherwise (in the words of T.S. Eliot) we will continue to "dream of systems so perfect no one will need to be good."

Reforming the Senate

A. Jean de Grandpré

A. Jean de Grandpré, C.C., is Founding Director and Chairman Emeritus of BCE Inc., a director of various Canadian corporations and a former Chancellor of McGill University, Montreal.

THE WESTERN Provinces have been demanding a reformed Senate which would be Elected, Equal and Effective.

The federal proposals have indicated a willingness to accommodate the request for the "Triple-E" Senate but have been short on the methods of implementation, leaving to Canadians the task of putting some flesh around the base structure of the proposal.

This short paper is an attempt to do just that.

My first assumption is that Canadians are over-governed and subjected to too many elections.

My second assumption is that Ontario and Quebec will find it extremely difficult, if not politically suicidal, to give Prince Edward Island the same weight that they would have. The argument that Rhode Island or Montana have the same number of senators as Texas or California is not convincing when one bears in mind that there are 50 states, thereby diluting the imbalance.

Could Canada attempt to find a compromise by creating five regions with equal representation: British Columbia, the Prairies, Ontario, Quebec and the Atlantic Provinces, in which each region would be entitled to ten senators?

These senators would be appointed by the political parties officially recognized by the Chief Electoral Officer, according to the percentage of the vote received on a regional basis by party at the last federal election. They would hold office until the next federal election.

For instance, if the popular vote at the regional level had given 30% of the ballots to the NDP, 30% to the PCs and 40% to the Liberals, the split would entitle the parties each to appoint three, three, and four Senators.

This approach would have the following advantages:

- It would be far less costly than another election.
- It would not require the drawing of a new electoral map, which would be necessary if the election was based on constituency representation, because there are less senators than MPs. If on the other hand the election is on a provincial-wide basis the ballots would probably list some 50 candidates or more by regions, thus imposing a formidable task on the voter trying to make an intelligent choice. The appointment would eliminate an expensive process.
- The Senate would not likely be a carbon copy of the House of Commons, a danger that could exist if an election is simultaneous with an election for the House of Commons.
- The Senate could no longer be controlled by a majority of a ruling party for a generation, or more.
- The appointment could only be renewed for a second term.
- The Senate would at all times, be an exact image of the opinion of the electorate on a regional basis, thereby giving a strong voice to the regions.
- It would probably attract a different type of candidate to the Senate; individuals who could not or would not run for office but, if appointed, could contribute substantially to the legislative process.

A couple of footnotes:

- The President of the Senate would be selected amongst the senators appointed by the government.
- Any fraction of the percentage applied to the regions for the appointment to the Senate would be rounded up or down if over or below 50 basis points; e.g., 45% of the popular vote justifies five Senate appointments, 44% four appointments. Any unused percentage, like 4% of the regional vote, would have to be assigned to the parties entitled to appoint senators on a proportional basis.

In just such an easy-to-implement and inexpensive process, Canada could not only achieve an elected Senate but also become a stronger country through increasing the voices of its regions. What an exciting and challenging opportunity.

Simplifying the Political Process

William A. Dimma

William A. Dimma, P.Eng, M.B.A. is Vice Chairman of Royal LePage Ltd. and a director of other companies. A former Dean of Administrative Studies, York University, he also served as Chairman of the Niagara Institute.

AS PART of constitutional reform, Canada will probably end up with an elected Senate. Inevitable partisanship means that, from the perspective of the effectiveness of government, a verdict to put in place a second elected, competing chamber will turn out to be one of the great maladroit decisions of our times.

The case for eliminating the Senate is stronger than the case for strengthening it. But this latter is alien to that part of the Canadian psyche which prefers process to results. The idea that we might simplify the political process is viewed blankly like a Baroque architect considering the simplicity of a Doric column.

There is, of course, no doubt that voices beyond those of Ontario and Quebec need to be listened to more carefully in Ottawa. But instead of setting up a competing body, we might consider, inter alia, providing additional seats in the House of Commons to smaller provinces. Deviations from the principle of one person-one vote already exist and could be extended some further distance.

Furthermore, constitutional reform includes a proposal to minimize conflicting jurisdictions by allocating various powers more fully to the provinces while retaining more certain economic powers for Ottawa. If implemented, this will help to reduce in intensity and frequency the squabbles which led to the pressures for an elected Senate in the first place. Several other proposed new consultative mechanisms will also help.

If we sacrifice governability in order to satisfy regional concerns, we are trading one serious problem for another. In an increasingly competitive global world, we will live to regret it. Australia's two-chamber system is an unalloyed disaster and is widely recognized to be such, especially by Australians.

In the U.S., so frequently cited as a model for Canada to adopt, the political process is close to paralysis on domestic issues though, like the story of

the emperor with no clothes, tradition causes perceptions to lag reality.

The four-legged stool of national governance in the U.S. (Administration, Senate, House of Representatives and Supreme Court) was designed with checks and balances foremost in mind. Two hundred years ago, the despotism of divine-righted kings was still real. But in today's fractious world, the result, increasingly, is stalemate and ungovernability. Too many decisions emerging from the political process in the U.S. today are so distorted that the outcome is worse than what came before. If a camel is a horse built by a committee, a law emerging from the U.S. legislative process under full sail is often a two-legged camel with three humps and one eye.

Canada's constitutional proposals attempt carefully to limit the powers of an elected Senate. But I predict that, within a decade, this monstrous hybrid creature, swollen by incremental empowerments over the years, will create far more serious problems than it solves. If the price of holding this country together includes, finally, an elected and empowered Senate, so be it. But it is a very high price which, with political will and a dollop of imagination and good will, need not be paid.

Three Rational Prerogatives for Government

Barbara Eastman

Barbara C. Eastman, D.Phil. (Oxon.), is Secretary-Treasurer and Director of Probyn & Company Limited and Treasurer of Kirkland Lake Power Corp. Dr. Eastman served as Director and Chairman of the Legislative Committee, Canadian Association of Women Executives, and was President of the Couchiching Institute on Public Affairs.

WITH ITS habitual condescension to the former Dominion, *The Economist* magazine once proposed a World's Most Boring Headline contest. The hands-down winner was "Worthy Canadian Initiative".

Even on issues of national importance—and none greater than National Unity—an awkward truth still applies to our domestic political scene: We Canadians have managed to stupefy ourselves with boredom and an overwhelming sense of political impotence. Nothing else explains the public apathy that humiliated the Spicer Commission; the rednecks and radicals outside and inside Quebec demonstrating disrespect for the visible symbols and processes of government; or popular cartoons depicting 'Everlasting Constitutional Debates' as the circle of Hell reserved for Canadians.

Whether or not we accept that a written Constitution and a Charter of Rights have enshrined our national disenfranchisement, or that proposals for a U.S.-style Senate foreshadow the ultimate victory of regional over national interests, the supreme governmental authorities in Canada today are, unquestionably, the extra-Parliamentary institutions of the Supreme Court and the First Ministers' Summit.

Designed to protect the interests of the minority, the result is an oligarchical system consisting of a mere eleven elected representatives and nine appointed justices. In the case of Meech Lake, a single provincial premier—representing less than two percent of Canada's 27 million people—proved capable of thwarting the will of the vast majority.

Our justices act outside our legislatures and the voter's control. On the abortion issue, our highest Court's decision matched the weight of national opinion. A fortunate coincidence. In the name of regional "fairness" and justice, parliamentary democracy is going down in flames.

This spectacle of failure demands immediate and lasting change. To restore representational balance and reactivate a *national* electorate, our federal government has three rational prerogatives to hand:

- **National Referenda** to be used to cast the deciding vote on matters of supreme importance to the country's well-being.
- **Compulsory Voting** required for federal elections and national referenda. (The Australian model, complete with penalties, provides a useful example.)
- **National Telecommunications Net Access** for comprehensive remote polling of the national consensus. The application of Canada's superior telecommunications technology, systems and expertise to the creaking machinery of 19th Century democracy, could easily advance universal suffrage by early in the 21st Century.

A worthy (and not boring) Canadian initiative indeed.

Improving the Public's Perception of Elected Representatives

Paul Fox

Paul Fox, Ph.D, is Professor Emeritus of Political Science at the University of Toronto. A former Principal of Erindale College, he is the author of various books on politics and government in Canada.

IT CANNOT be denied that the public has a poor opinion of elected officials. An Environics poll published in *Canadian Legislatures: The 1986 Comparative Study* revealed that 54% of Canadians sampled believed that most members of Parliament were less than honest and sincere.

Criticisms abound on every side. Whether or not the negative views are deserved, many members of the public think that elected politicians are overpaid, self-serving, under-worked, rude and excessively partisan.

These opinions can be changed by removing the grounds for the complaints. To begin, elected representatives should be paid a reasonable stipend in a straightforward manner without any gimmicks to conceal the actual amount.

What is a "reasonable" salary? It would vary with the office filled and the amount of work involved. A member of Parliament who attended a longer session than a member of a provincial house would receive more, as would a councillor in a large city compared to an alderman in a small municipality.

The basic emoluments now paid to various elected representatives are probably about the right amount. They could be increased each year by the equivalent of a rise in the cost-of-living index. But there would be no supplementary payments. Gone would be the tax-free allowances and such things as extra rewards for sitting on committees. It is these special privileges that are particularly galling to ordinary wage earners who do not enjoy them.

Eliminating these perquisites would do much to change the public's perception that elected politicians are self-serving profiteers lining their own pockets. To prove that they earn their money, elected members should be paid only if they attend a certain percentage of sessions and meetings, which would eliminate absentee members living off public largesse.

To regain the respect of the public, our representatives must also display a higher standard of deportment. Parliament, legislatures and councils are now often the scene of such boorish behavior that school children are shocked and adults mortified.

Name-calling, rudeness, vulgarity and innanity can be stopped by stringently applying the rule of "naming". The speaker or chairperson would simply name the offending member. The first time would involve a warning, the second a suspension from the sitting, and the third an expulsion from the session. If pay were docked for the period of exclusion, there would no doubt be an astonishing transformation in manners.

Deportment could also be improved by taking some of the partisanship out of the proceedings. Excessive party loyalty leads inevitably to vituperation and the accusation that elected members are nothing but trained seals, honking and waving their flippers in unison.

To dispel that impression, parties must allow more free votes. That is an easy reform to accomplish. Governments and opposition parties can merely alter the custom of making every vote a matter of confidence.

If these reforms were adopted, there would be a great improvement in the process of government and in the public's opinion of our elected representatives, which would benefit everyone.

Nurturing Areas for Change

Reva Gerstein

Dr. Gerstein, O.C., O. Ontario is a psychologist and a past member of the Premier's Council on Health Strategy. She is currently Chairman of the Canadian Institute for Advanced Research.

WE MUST genuinely prepare ourselves, i.e., our mind set, for change. This can only be done by increasing the number of occasions for face-to-face dialogue between and among all levels of governments with a broad spectrum of their constituents.

The underlying prerequisite must be "trust" and "credibility" among the participants, which must be perceived far beyond buzz words, but as bench marks which are slowly earned on a daily basis, not by words but by actions.

Key players who "kindle the flames of change" must be civil servants, legislators and the public at large, energized by responsible media and committed leadership.

Among the areas to be nurtured and explored:

- The development of positive attitudes towards management and labour policies at all levels, and closer working relationships with more participation in decision making throughout.

- The encouragement of research and innovative ideas for future growth by new funding approaches and tax incentives.

- The important place in our society of poets, philosophers, artists and musicians. Progress is not made entirely by complex, computer-assisted mathematical modelling. There is a place for vision, metaphors, dreams and creative leaps. From this comes commitment, sacrifice and inspiration.

- The need for literacy and numeracy skills must be recognized. Scientific evidence indicates these skills have important roots in the stimulating experiences of childhood. Greater attention must be given to learning opportunities for children so that words like "daycare" and "babysitting" may become obsolete in our rhetoric, and words like "human development", "learning opportunities", "continuous learning" and "coping skills" will take their place.

- The limits of growth and development in economic theory should be shifted away from classical theory. Young people, particularly, must be made to feel that we count on them. We need new insights, new paradigms, fresher points of view, new solutions and an open mindedness to new ideas.

- The recognition that a country's health status is dependent on more than the treatment of illness. We must begin to appreciate the impact of areas such as early childhood development, socioeconomic factors and stress in the work place on health.

A genuine appreciation for every person in this country of must be nurtured.

Legislatures are not corporate bodies. Their very essence lies in the minds and hearts of the people. They are the ones who must work to reshape Canadian politics realistically from the grass roots upwards.

Getting Politicians to "Do the Right Thing"

Peter Hanson

Peter Hanson, M.D., is an internationally recognized author and lecturer to Fortune 500 companies on stress. He is known as the "Stress Doctor" to many Canadians who listen to his regular radio broadcasts.

IN JUST the same way that businesses have had to go through gut-wrenching changes in their habits, traditions and focus, it is now high time that politicians bow to the inevitable and go through the same process.

To restore credibility and relevance, politicians are going to have to face the same facts that have confronted the rest of us. Politicians have always maintained that their work should not be run like a business. In fact, corporate leaders have maintained that their businesses should not be run like a business either, until the gloves came off in the global economy.

While the public may think politicians and bureaucrats may be of the lowest standing in the zoological kingdom, in fact most of them work long hours, dedicated to doing things right. The problem is that they are not doing the right things. Time spent creating new rules that add to the public's burden of paperwork does not keep our country competitive.

The only companies that have been able to survive in the information age are those who change their focus from the company to the customer. The dinosaurs that resisted have faced extinction. The only countries that will be able to retain their leadership status in the world will be those that shift their focus from the government to the people. Politicians, once in power, quickly forget their roots, and their agenda shifts from helping the voter to helping themselves. The recession and the technological and information revolutions have been hard on companies, both large and small. Both management and labour fear for their very jobs, and are constantly under attack by global competitors. So while it may seem a good idea for politicians to reduce a tax like the Manufacturer's Sales Tax, the businesses lose any competitive gain if the replacement tax requires a mountain of expensive paperwork, which the Goods and Services Tax most assuredly does. While labour can understand wage restraints and lay-offs if they

see management undergoing the same fate, the public cannot tolerate politicians of all parties who lavish taxpayers' money to buy constituents' votes. With corporations trimming fat, the public cannot understand why the government continues to throw away so much money with so little return.

Changing the Political Culture

Frederic L.R. Jackman

Frederic L.R. Jackman, Ph.D., an observer of political and cultural affairs, graduated from the University of Chicago in the Department of Human Development and Psychology. He is President of Invicta Investments Inc. and Chairman of the Jackman Foundation.

THE CULTURE supporting political leadership in Canada has fallen prey to cynicism. In this disaffected climate, our electorate has no heroes, our leaders no followers.

In a three party system, where a party can win with less than half the vote, the majority of voters may not feel represented. Even if they want to stand behind our parliamentary system—our Team Canada—voters are uncertain what is reasonable to expect or how "responsible government" works. Many feel disillusioned.

Unfortunately, there is little to counteract Canadians' disillusionment. Few organizations encourage Canadians to support their leadership and the institution of government, but a multitude criticize and condemn them.

Disillusionment quickly becomes disbelief when the public's most vivid view of the government at work is the televised Question Period—a pseudo-debate from which journalists choose episodes of MPs shouting vulgarities or otherwise trying to discredit and embarrass one another. It is believable that members are staging a ten-second news clip, but it is unimaginable that they are serious about running a country. Opposing parties do, in fact, work co-operatively and constructively in committees, writing and improving legislation, but this is not well-known. That is not what the public sees. It is not entertaining.

The media loves the shenanigans of the House for they justify the media's own efforts to ridicule parliament. Journalists' penchant for highlighting dissent and inappropriate behavior in our politicians seems to pander to the public's view. The resulting news and opinion aids and abets public cynicism.

How can we restore the willingness of the public to follow elected leaders in the face of these powerful, negative influences? How can we attract the best leaders if our culture remains so cynical?

First, parliamentarians should stick to debating. If they persist in acting up, then the televising of Question Period should be modified or cancelled. When television entered the House our MPs, finding they looked like infants banging their fists on their dinner trays (as a form of applause), changed their behavior overnight. It is time they changed again. Question Period should be aired with a description of the other activities within the House of Commons, along with an explanation that Question Period is not where MPs spend all day, only a fraction of it. Other parliamentary activities should be televised.

Second, the media must take more responsibility to understand and manage its impact. Is the influence of the electronic and print media combined greater than the sum of its parts? If there is a collective impact, who is responsible for managing it? Some question whether the traditions of peer group review, Press Councils, Ombudspersons, are sufficient. The media must consider its responsibilities to help our political system work.

Third, citizens should be educated about their responsibilities to "responsible government", encouraged to express their opinions directly to their elected representatives and advised how they can make a positive contribution to our political culture.

The Malaise is in our Heads

J.R. Mallory

J.R. Mallory, M.A., LL.D., F.R.S.C., is Professor Emeritus of Political Science, McGill University. A former Chairman of the Social Science Research Council of Canada, he is the author of various books relating to government and politics.

J.R. Mallory, M.A., LL.D., F.R.S.C., is Professor Emeritus of Political Science, McGill University. A former Chairman of the Social Science Research Council of Canada, he is the author of various books relating to government and politics.

IT SEEMS to me that the most visible disease of our political system does not lie in our institutions but in a change of values which has not yet been assimilated into the vocabulary of politics. The old values, which were not inappropriate in the deprivations of the dirty thirties, or the necessary austerity of the war years, accorded with the assumptions of the political and bureaucratic elites of the time. These seem now to have been submerged by the ostentatious and offensive consumerism which peaked in the eighties.

The old elites retained a sober view of the transience of possessions which derived from the religious standards in which that generation had been brought up. Even in post-war Ottawa these standards prevailed. The offices of senior civil servants, ministers and ordinary members of Parliament were sober and unadorned, and it was not uncommon for such people to walk to work. Arthur Meighen, who, when Prime Minister, was in the habit of walking to his office was contemptuous of Mackenzie King, who often did not. Subservient minions did not surround ministers, and junior members of Parliament shared offices, telephones and possibly a typist. That generally austere style contrasts with the imperial splendor of our modern political and bureaucratic masters.

This change was, in part, an unconscious emulation of the privilege flaunted by the Kremlin and the White House and is illustrated in small things. Ministers and Deputy Ministers used to be distinguished from the rest of the Ottawa world by having rugs on the floor of their offices. Now even the lowest bureaucrat of deputy minister rank has his office embellished by a flag, as well as other highly visible attributes of rank. Of course some of the cocoon around the mighty is designed to meet the need for security in a world of real or apprehended terrorists. Some of it, in other words, is necessary, but for much of it there is no need. Such display of expensive furniture and gadgetry, while it may give an illusion of self-importance to the occupants, serves no useful purpose.

While the signs are not good, they are perhaps not as bad as they look. We cannot, in our much more diverse and multi-cultural society, return to the simplicity of the past. We cannot count on common values to provide the bonds of civility and compassion which, in many ways, made Canada an enviable place. But something else is happening which may provide the necessary social bonds. What is noticeable is the change in political language which is fermenting in the electorate. The things that seem to matter are an emphasis on human rights and the importance of the fairness of the system which the Charter of Rights and Freedoms has done so much to strengthen. All sorts of diverse but hitherto powerless groups, such as women and aboriginals, have now been legitimized by the system and have a sense of being empowered by the Charter.

We should remember that the civility of the old elites had its limits. It did not extend to the plight of either immigrants or aboriginals. In the future our elites, both in the bureaucracy and the political parties, will be coming more and more from this multi-cultural and variegated mix as we become more open to a world of equal opportunity. It is to be hoped that they will carry with them the best values of our changing society.

If we cannot go back to what seems like a golden age of civic virtue we may develop a new sense of community based on humane values more appropriate to our present society. If we do, the chances are that everything from our perverse electoral system to the distortions of the power structure will be meliorated. Our institutions won't be made to work perfectly, but they will work better.

The National Government: Can it be Federalized?

Susan McCorquodale

Susan McCorquodale, PhD., is a Professor of Political Science at Memorial University, St. John's, and specializes in the study of governmental institutions, policy making and bureaucracy.

IT MAY be a weakness of our Canadian system that the current national institutions are not "federalized". But can it be that provincial governments have not thought clearly when they argue that one cure to their problems with Ottawa is an Elected, Effective, Equal Senate? Alternatively, could it be that the lawyers and politicians in Ottawa have created for themselves and all future governments, two sticks with which to beat their own back? Let us start by agreeing that the new Senate will not be without power if it comes into being, which the current proposals suggest. The "double majority" in matters of language and culture will be a formidable barrier to any government, partly for practical reasons of getting a measure through to the Governor General and partly because definitions of language and cul-

ture are open to debate. Likewise, a suspensive veto over matters of "national importance" might raise another set of definitional problems. Add to this approval powers over such a wide variety of appointments and you are left with a new and powerful body. Election will give it the legitimacy to exercise those powers. Governments who find it hard enough to pass legislation in one Chamber might more than double their problems when two Chambers and more political parties are involved. I said "two sticks" because we should consider also the Council of the Federation and what that may portend.

First, however, consider what the new Senate might mean for provincial governments. Is it not possible that an upper house, elected on the basis of intraprovincial regions and proportional representation, will not reflect the political party make-up of the provincial governments? Might we not see a situation where a provincial government sitting with a majority of seats, drawn from 40% of the popular vote, might find itself with a Senate representation drawn largely from the other 60%? Would an Effective Senate really serve the interests of the provincial governments, *qua* governments? I think not.

And for the rest of us, what about the other "stick": the Council of the Federation? Composed of federal and provincial *delegates*, appointed by their governments, it would "test-drive federal proposals in a limited range of very important issues" [1]. Plans for managing the economy, national standards for skills-development programs and the harmonization of fiscal policies would all be subject to Council approval by the federal government and the provinces using the 7:50 formula. We are assured that this would not be another layer of government, but I have doubts. We know that there are over 500 federal-provincial conferences a year and both orders of government have significant and powerful bureaucracies which oversee the whole process. Add a formal, open body, with decision-making powers and you have either a unique new system of checks and balances or a permanent source of federal-provincial confrontation and legislative deadlock [2].

Could we not "federalize" our national institutions and avoid a new layer of government? Could not a new Senate be modelled more on the lines of the German Bundesrat? The 1991 proposals specifically enjoin readers to consider the Bundesrat on the matter of an equitable vs. equal representation. Why not consider this example further? The German upper house is small compared to the much larger number of deputies elected on a representation-by-population basis to the Bundestag. What is significant however is that the members of the Bundesrat are appointed by the state government. The result is more or less a permanent federal-provincial conference. What started as a body concerned with administrative detail has evolved into a national forum for minister presidents. In one writer's opinion the "...Bundesrat wields more political influence than most second chambers in other parliamentary systems such as the French Senate or British House of Lords." [3]

Reform of the current Canadian Senate seems based either on the preference for a federalized national institution more sensitive to regional concerns or on the desire of western provinces to have their governmental concerns heard in Ottawa. I would suggest that the first objective is already effectively met in the functioning of a representative Cabinet. Here indeed "regional ministers" look after their provinces and a powerful cabinet minister, preferably one on the Policy and Procedure Committee, is more than able to look after the province, and trade benefits with colleagues as much as fiscal and party constraints permit. What the western provinces seem to want, however, is the second choice. It seems to me that the German second house presents us with a model for federal-provincial relations that is well worth exploring in the debate about Senate reform.

In an article dealing with the workability of Executive Federalism, Dupre considers that recent Canadian experience of federal-provincial summit relations has for a variety of reasons ended up in a state of "disarray". He cites cases in point in the fields of fiscal arrangements, regional development and social policy [4]. His prescriptions for improvement centre around what he calls "routinized summitry". His argument is that the pressure to "show results" might breed trust and workability at the officials level and perhaps even "constitutional morality" amongst first ministers. I suggest that we examine more closely the next step in the evolution of routinized summitry and put on the table an alternative modelled on the Bundesrat. Surely we already have more experience of Continuing Committees on this or that, specialized expert committees on a

whole range of functional concerns, Ministerial meetings with agendas and rotating chairmanships which taken together must make the Canadian system unique amongst the world's federations. The federal 1991 proposals already see the Council of the Federation as a forum for the harmonization of fiscal policy and legislation concerning the economic union. Why not establish this forum as the new second chamber of the federation?

Notes

[1] Howard, Ross. "Checks and Balances Could Check Ottawa." *Globe & Mail*, October 1, 1991.

[2] Ibid.

[3] Dalton, Russell J. *Politics in West Germany*. Scott, Foresman/Little Brown. Glenview, Illinois, 1989: 57.

[4] Dupre, Stefan J. "The Workability of Executive Federalism in Canada." in *Federalism and the Role of the State*. ed. Herman Bakvis and William M. Chandler. University of Toronto Press. 1987: 243.

Seeking the Common Good

John Meisel

John Meisel, O.C., Ph.D. is Sir Edward Peacock Professor of Political Science, Queen's University, Kingston. A distinguished educator and political scientist, Dr. Meisel is a former Chairman of the Canadian Radio-Television and Telecommunications.

PLURALISM HAS run wild. We have become so blinded by the notion that "there is no national interest, only *interests*" that we are quite incapable of pursuing policies designed to be of general benefit to the whole community. The result has been that the goals of society have come to be seen as merely the sum of individual or specific group goods and not some over-arching purpose transcending the narrow, usually self-seeking concerns of particular interests.

Almost no political and bureaucratic agencies are now able to take the long-term viewpoint; vital national interests are consequently neglected by default. Examples abound but here are a few matters desperately requiring attention: widespread functional illiteracy; colossal expenditures on primary and secondary education with pedagogic results that compare uncomfortably with almost all modern states; serious neglect of science, technology, research and intellectual endeavors generally, crippling our capacity to compete economically and otherwise in the emerging new global order; genuine (as distinct from cosmetic) attacks on the degradation of the environment and so on and on and on.

What can we do to bring about a change?

So fundamental and complex a socio-political flaw is clearly not amenable to correction by a single, simple expedient. It can only be tackled on a broad front and over a long period of time. But unless a beginning is made, solutions will elude us. It is therefore utterly realistic to start tackling the problem at once, even if the results are certain to be delayed. It is particularly imperative to launch remedial action at a time when so much attention and energy is focused on other important matters, notably constitutional change.

Half a dozen steps seem essential.

- The problem needs to be identified and made known. Consequently, scholars, journalists and intellectuals must propagate the nature, existence and urgency of what needs to be confronted.
- Having been sensitized to the issues, significant members of the public must make the effort of will to do something about the situation.
- The excesses of "interest group pluralism" can only be contained when it is realized that the decline of communism and socialism in the world has not solved all the important problems: capitalism, too, is sick, and must be overhauled. Market mechanisms are ethically and aesthetically blind, and often ignore sensitive human concerns.
- The federal and provincial governments must realize that there is life after the Constitution; the latter is meant to facilitate problem solving, not paralyze it.
- It will be well to launch a "Coalition for the Public Interest", which would direct the gaze of interest groups to the broader, shared issues, and would further their pursuit.
- Political parties and the party system will have to be revitalized and changed so as to escape the crippling effects of excessive brokerage politics

at the cost of pursuing long-term, collective goals.

The task is formidable, to be sure; it is also imperative and pressing. A Chinese saying has it that a long voyage must begin with a first step. Other claims on reforms notwithstanding, Canadians must start the journey soon, if they wish to continue the life to which they not only aspire but to which they have to some measure already become accustomed.

Innovation, Prosperity and Government

J. Fraser Mustard

J. Fraser Mustard, M.D., F.R.C.P. (C), F.R.S. (C) is President of the Canadian Institute for Advanced Research, former Vice President, Health Sciences, McMaster University and author of over 300 scientific articles.

OUR FAILURE to develop new ways to produce wealth is increasingly eroding our ability to sustain the social and political institutions that have made Canada a tolerant, fair and decent society. We can reverse the slide of recent years and move Canada into a new era of economic and social progress, but to do so depends on finding new methods of wealth creation. We have to recognize that the basis for economic growth has changed and that this will require the creation of new institutions.

Ideas and technological change have become the sources of constant innovation and economic growth. We have to shift our institutions and policies to reflect the central role of ideas, technology and innovation as the principal source of our future wealth. In the process, we will create new institutions and new relationships.

A characteristic of societies that create wealth from ideas is that they have private institutional structures that can mobilize the talent to innovate, and also to finance, the necessary processes involved in creating wealth. These are paralleled by governing structures that help but do not hinder the innovation process.

It is a challenge for our public sector to evolve innovative flexible policies that enhance the work of these new private sector initiatives that link talented Canadians in universities and business across the country rather than continuing with old policies appropriate for a resources-based economy. For example, the policies of provincial governments tend to balkanize the country and have, for example, hampered the efforts of PRECARN in building a national cluster in artificial intelligence and robotics necessary for an idea-driven economy.

The governing structure suitable for an idea-driven economy will have to get rid of the provincial barriers to a new economy. The federal governing structure will have to be able to create a "partnership" with the private sector so as to create the incentives and infrastructure necessary for the time horizons (long-term) and financing of an idea-based innovative economy. At present Canada has no long-term institutional capacity in its governing structure to do this. If we are to create a modern economy we will have to create new institutions of governance that are capable of establishing policies for the long-term time horizon of an innovation-driven economy, that can adjust to the cyclical changes in the elected government effectively, and link the regions of the country.

Giving the Public More Ice Time

Knowlton Nash

Knowlton Nash is Senior Correspondent of CBC Television News and one of Canada's most distinguished journalists. A veteran of print as well as broadcast journalism, he serves as Co-Chairman of the Canadian Journalism Foundation.

THE GREATEST challenge politicians face today is to recapture their credibility.

Across the country changing values and lack of leadership have made Canadians both rootless and rudderless, intensifying their distrust of politicians to an unprecedented level. As we face the greatest political debate in our history, we are a country in crisis and a nation of cynics. The shareholders are simply in revolt.

Pollster Allan Gregg has said the public is so cynical of politicians today that they wouldn't trust them to run a two-hole outhouse, let alone a country.

After years of executive federalism culminating with the Meech Lake closed-door process, something snapped among Canadians. Meech became a metaphor for failure to understand the public

demand for participation, and Meech itself failed as much, or more, because of its closed-door appearance as its substance. Although in fact the process was more open than ever before, it wasn't good enough for a public demanding ever more political participation and political visibility; demanding a late 20th century TV-age version of Woodrow Wilson's plea for "open covenants ... openly arrived at."

The loss of public confidence in politicians in Canada is unparalleled and so, too, is the challenge in retrieving that confidence. But retrieval is essential if Canada is to survive.

"Openness" is a clear and easy answer in recapturing credibility, but how to achieve such "openness" is the perplexity. As a start, there must be "openness" in process; "openness" in evaluation; "openness" in decision-making; "openness" in sharing with the public. While backroom process was easier, cheaper and quicker, it no longer works in Canada on the eve of the 21st century. "Openness" is painful, tedious, frustrating, time-consuming and expensive, but it's the essence of the democracy of our age. It demands new political skills in listening, formulating, articulating and persuading. Executive federalism and elected automatons are no longer tolerable for most Canadians. The nation's shareholders are no longer satisfied with having a say every four years or so in an election, and then sitting back until the next one.

The challenge, of course, is how to give the public more ice time in the political process.

Although the Spicer Commission on national unity had its detractors and could be justifiably criticized on occasion, the exercise was a vivid and, in the end, highly effective example of participatory democracy. The use of cable television by the Spicer Commission both in linking communities in participation and in simply being on display to the rest of the country, demonstrated an openness in reality and in perception that has considerable potential. People had their ice time. The objective was not just "information out" but "information in" and, for all its peculiarities, it worked. Genuine public forums of this type can provide a valuable vehicle for highly visible sharing of the process. The shareholders are in revolt.

The media, too, is clearly a key vehicle for participation in "openness" and that demands that politicians (and reporters, too, for that matter) recognize that the media are not adversaries, but agents for the public in seeking out information on what's happening, where, when and why, and in offering differing perspectives on issues. And the media themselves can do more in explanation and stimulation of national issues.

"Openness", too, in the legislatures is increasingly being sought by the public in the sense that they want their elected representatives to be less Pavlovian in support for any and every government initiative. That has obvious implications on party discipline and could translate into greater freedom of thought and action for government MPs in the House, in Committees and less impact in the Whip's lash.

"Openness" may not be the total answer to recapturing political credibility, but it is the first building block of that credibility.

Business Can Aid Government

Christopher Ondaatje

Christopher Ondaatje is Chairman and Chief Executive Officer of The Ondaatje Corporation Limited, a former Olympic athlete and author of books including "The Prime Ministers of Canada: 1867-1967."

WE HAVE reached the end of a 25-year wave of prosperity that is marked by very different structures and attitudes from the beginning of the 1960s.

The intervening years have seen the debt burden of business and government soar. The cost of manufacturing has increased highly and disposable income is similarly diminished. At this juncture in the past, government has stepped in and through either increasing taxes or inflating the economy, has kept the country running. This time, unless there is an economic recovery, and there is something to tax, the government is simply going to run out of money.

It is imperative that the private sector come to the aid of the government and take on some of the financial burden of running the country.

How do we do this? Not only do our attitudes have to change, but government attitudes have to change as well. Studied proposals have to be made on joint ventures that will enable responsible members of the private sector to finance, organize, and administer key areas of Canadian life (e.g. Canada Pension and Old Age Security.)

One of the problems in Canada is that the private sector has not had a significant say over the societal commitment of our dollars. For example, in Canada we are allowed to donate up to 20% of our income for charitable purposes and this is written off against our taxable income. In the U.S., the comparable limit is 50%. For potentially significant donors, this difference is important. It gives the American individual a much greater say in where his money should be going, and Americans have responded with much higher contributions to the arts, education, charities to assist the poor, etc. Giving is a responsibility welcomed and accepted by Americans.

In contrast, in Canada the attitude has often been that the government will provide. History supports this evidence and the tax system has been biased to encourage that attitude. You do not have much say on how your taxed dollars will be spent. As a result, Canada has bred a nation of hit-and-run millionaires. People make their money and leave. This was true in England too when giving was discouraged. The wisdom of Margaret Thatcher created significant changes in the system. Now a British person may redirect his income to recognized charities provided the commitment is made for a period exceeding three years. People there are responding.

We can start right now to encourage donations which will help government foot the bill of running the country. For example, "gifts to the crown" are not subject to that 20% limitation. Why not set up agencies to accept directed gifts for educational and charitable purposes? If you want to endow a chair at a university, for example, by channeling your payment through such an agency set up by a provincial government, the entire amount would be deductible. But we need direction. People must be able to commit their money to particular projects and purposes. They must feel the responsibility for their actions.

This is a time for change, and this is a time for action. Changing the tax rules and changing the attitudes of Canadians towards giving may be a first step, but it will not be significant enough soon enough. We are in the midst of a national crisis and a brain-trust of a few clear thinking inventive members of the government and responsible Canadian business people might be able to change the direction of the country and lead us into the 21st century.

Building up a Core of Prospective Leaders

Timothy Reid

Timothy Reid, M.A., is President of the Canadian Chamber of Commerce. Before becoming a Member of the Ontario Legislature and senior federal civil servant, he was a Rhodes scholar and a professional football player.

THERE ARE too many solitudes between those who argue public policy issues in Canada and, in the end, it makes for bad policy. Here I refer not to the public arguments among partisan (party) politicians but to a much deeper division. And that is the isolation from one another of our leaders in the different worlds of business, the public service, labour, academia, social agencies and politics. Theirs is an isolation caused by a terrible ignorance of the perspective, experience and ways of doing things of the others. It is a kind of multiple "disconnect" of understanding.

This mutual "ignorance syndrome", rather than intentional confrontation, is the major cause of the decline of the formation of effective Canadian public policy and of the decline in Canadian political life more generally.

I submit that if over the past decade we had had 500 or 1 000 Canadians (instead of two dozen or so) in leadership positions inside and outside of partisan politics who had lived in three or four of these different worlds, we would now have a much more cohesive and more creative and constructive system of governance and, therefore, much better public policy.

What to do? Herewith a modest proposal.

We need to build up a core of prospective leaders in Canada who have experience in, and understanding of, these different solitudes; Canadians who are "bridge crossers"; who can move freely from one culture to another; who can bring these diverse worlds and their respective leaders together in the interests of seeking the common good.

One means of doing so would be through an endowment fund. Each year twenty Canadians between the ages of twenty-five and thirty-five would

be chosen and given a base salary renewable every two years, for a total of ten years, based on performance. This would involve an active placement program: two-year stints in business, the labour union movement, the public service, a social agency, academia, politics. In order to be eligible, an applicant would: have to be fluently bilingual in French and in English with a working ability in a third language; have two university degrees, one of which must be in the humanities; have lived in at least two of Canada's regions; and have lived outside of North America for at least one year.

Hopefully, a number of these people would continue to play an active leadership role during their lives in bringing a broad understanding and perspective to the debates on public policy issues which, in the end, would make for good policy in the interests of all Canadians.

Polls, Politicians and the Media

David Taras

David Taras, Ph.D., is Dean of the Faculty of General Studies, University of Calgary, and a well-known writer and commentator on contemporary Canadian politics and government. He is a former parliamentary intern.

THE WIDESPREAD cynicism and disenchantment that Canadians have toward their political leaders is rooted in part in the belief that politicians no longer have strong convictions. One of the culprits may be our politicians' obsessive reliance on public opinion polling. Instead of seeing their role as being public persuaders leading public opinion, politicians are using polls as both a compass and a map. When they are ahead in the polls they are afraid to do anything that would upset the applecart. When they are behind they search desperately for a hot issue that will ignite voter response. Polls allow parties to target swing voters, identifiable sub-groups with certain demographic characteristics. Too often principles are packaged, downplayed or ignored in order to shape policies that can succeed in the political marketplace.

Polls have also become part of media election extravaganzas. During the 1988 federal election, twenty-four polls were reported; on each occasion a flurry of publicity, horse race journalism and the reactions of politicians to how they had fared blocked out discussion of important national issues. Far more of the media's time was spent reporting poll results than reporting party positions on the deficit, the constitution, Quebec's role in Canada, health care or the problems of aboriginal Canadians. As a consequence, we elect governments that in some sense are without mandates because the public has not been informed adequately about the positions that the parties have taken.

Moreover, vacuous polls that tell us little about the hardness of public opinion and are leader—rather than issue—oriented inevitably influence voting decisions. A bandwagon effect has been detected in national voting studies that rewards the party that's ahead in the polls, the party that the media has, in effect, already declared the winner.

Defenders of the current system argue that the public should have access to all available information, and that poll results help voters make informed decisions. What they ignore, however, is that the polls and the ways in which polls are reported are often misleading. The significance of sampling, questionnaire design and margins of error are sometimes ignored by media organizations that use polls as a means to sell papers or promote their broadcasts.

My suggestion is not that the music stop but that the tune be changed. Although polls are now an entrenched part of the Canadian political landscape, reasonable limits can be placed on their use. The amount of money that parties can spend on "research" during elections could be specified and sharply curtailed, and the media's reporting of polls could be banned during the last two weeks of an election campaign. These measures would reduce the excessive dependency on polls by the political parties, give the parties equal access to polling and reduce the amount of polling contamination that voters are exposed to. Such changes might ensure a little more conviction and a little less manipulation in our politics.

PART THREE

Legislative Information

IN 1992 CANADIANS are being asked by Government to participate in the restructuring of their nation. Government institutions are under scrutiny. Recommendations for change have become a priority.

In this Part of *Canadian Legislatures* complete information is given on the indemnities, salaries, allowances and services which are provided to members of the Senate, House of Commons and the provincial and territorial legislatures. In addition, the various management processes of the legislature as an administrative unit are outlined, along with trends and forecasts.

Canadian Legislatures began in 1979 as a questionnaire circulated informally between provincial legislatures in an attempt to discover how each jurisdiction handled its internal operations. The first "Comparative Study" tabulating the responses consisted of 32 pages of typewritten tables, without comment.

In the intervening years *Canadian Legislatures* has been in the privileged position of being able to report on, and trace the growth which has taken place in Canada's legislatures, as well as tabulating facts and figures. This has provided the basis for continued analysis as new allowances and services are made available to members, and for an assessment of these emoluments in terms of their impact on the legislature as an institution.

CHAPTER ONE

Financial Management of the Legislature

THE SENATE, House of Commons and the provincial and territorial legislatures each have an internal management body of elected members who oversee the financial management and administration of their institution. While the legislatures use a variety of names to refer to this body, the duties are essentially the same. For the purposes of uniformity, the term "Board of Internal Economy" (BOIE) will be used for identification purposes.

Prior to 1974, when a Board of Internal Economy was established for the Ontario Legislature, the only legislature in Canada to have a similar body was the House of Commons which had a Commission of Internal Economy. It was chaired by the Speaker and included the Government House Leader, the President of the Privy Council and the President of the Treasury Board, but no opposition members.

Starting in 1974, the concept of the Board of Internal Economy gathered momentum largely because of the recommendations of the Ontario Commission on the Legislature which was formed in 1972 to examine the role of the backbencher in Ontario (elected members who are not members of Cabinet). The Chairman, Dalton Camp, and his fellow commissioners, Farquhar Oliver, and Douglas Fisher, representing the three parties in the Ontario Legislature—Progressive Conservative, Liberal and New Democratic—determined that if backbenchers were to have greater power vis-a-vis the Government, then the Legislature itself would have to be given new powers. Essentially, they

recommended that the Speaker assume the responsibility of being the Chief Administrative Officer, in addition to the Chief Procedural Officer of the House, and that rather than having the Ministry of Government Services administer the legislative building (as was the case historically) the Speaker be given sufficient staff for this purpose. The Speaker would also become the paymaster for all elected members, administering salaries, benefits, pensions, allowances, and meting out office services and all common services. In the past, the Management Board of Cabinet (known as the Treasury Board in most jurisdictions) had had the final say on budgets and spending related to members and the legislative building. Under the new plan the Board of Internal Economy, with the Speaker as Chairman, would take charge. The majority of the Camp Commission recommendations were approved.

One of the outcomes of this new approach to managing the legislative building facilities and services for members in Ontario was that civil servants in a government ministry would no longer decide on the operating budgets or expenditures of elected members. Instead, there would be a self-regulating process through the Speaker and the BOIE, with their staff, servants of the Legislative Assembly, implementing their wishes.

By 1979, the Board of Internal Economy concept had spread to Manitoba, Quebec, New Brunswick, Nova Scotia and Newfoundland, in addition to the House of Commons and Ontario.

However, with the exception of Quebec, government Treasury Boards still had a final veto over expenditures in these provinces. In 1992, the Board of Internal Economy, or its equivalent exists in all provinces. Opposition members participate in the deliberations of all Boards, whereas in 1974, only Ontario had opposition members on the Board.

The review procedure for Legislative Assembly Estimates is now similar in all jurisdictions. The Board of Internal Economy receives the annual budgetary estimates for members' salaries, allowances and contingent expenses for the operation of the legislative building which are prepared by the Clerk's Office or by designated administrative offices within the legislature. The BOIE reviews these estimates and revises or approves them accordingly. These estimates are then forwarded to the Treasury Board (or its equivalent) for tabling in the House when the General Estimates of the government are heard. There have been no instances of the Estimates of the Legislature being reduced once they were tabled in the House.

The Board of Internal Economy is always chaired by the Speaker of the House. (A list of the Speakers of Canada's legislatures appears on Page 240.) Membership normally includes at least one cabinet minister, and in all jurisdictions there are more government members on the board than opposition members. The size of the Board ranges from three members in Prince Edward Island to eleven members in Alberta.

The frequency of Board meetings varies in each jurisdiction. They occur almost weekly at the House of Commons when the House is in session, and usually take place on a Wednesday during the dinner hour. Key officers (staff) of the House are present as well as Board members. The Ontario Board meets 13 or 14 times a year, and the staff Management Committee of the Assembly is present. In Prince Edward Island and Saskatchewan the Board averages less than six meetings a year. In all cases, BOIE meetings take place most frequently in the jurisdictions which have the largest budgets.

Often Canadians have no access to the deliberations of their elected members who sit on Boards of Internal Economy. Ontario is the only jurisdiction where the minutes of the Board are made available 48 hours following a meeting and are placed in the Legislative Library. Alberta has a similar arrangement. The minutes of Senate and House of Commons BOIE meetings are not made public, nor are minutes made available in Nova Scotia, Prince Edward Island, British Columbia, Yukon or the Northwest Territories. The legislatures of Newfoundland, New Brunswick, Quebec, Manitoba and Saskatchewan have a variety of approaches to placing the minutes of their Board meetings in the public domain, usually through tabling them in the House on an occasional basis.

When currently evaluating the effectiveness of the Board of Internal Economy as the main instrument of management and financial control in Canada's legislatures, there are clearly some questions which beg answers:

- Can the Board of Internal Economy be responsible for controlling legislature expenditures while at the same time having the powers to provide and expand various allowances and services to members?

- Would the expenditures of the Senate, House of Commons and the provincial and territorial legislatures have risen as rapidly since 1974 if the Cabinet had continued to be the final authority on budget levels?

- Is it fair or reasonable to expect that the Board of Internal Economy—which in all cases includes government and opposition members—should be the final authority when it comes to the administration of funds which directly benefit the members of the Board and all other elected members?

- Can or should the Board of Internal Economy be the watchdog over itself at a time when taxpayers want to see controls placed on government?

These are issues which will be examined in the ensuing pages which review the Board of Internal Economy as the key body in all legislatures responsible for financial administration.

Financial Management

H of C **Body Responsible:** Board of Internal Economy.

Composition of Management Body: Speaker (Chairman), Deputy Speaker, two members of the Queen's Privy Council (appointed from time to time by the

Governor in Council), the Leader of the Opposition (or his or her nominee) and four other members of the House of Commons (of these four, two are appointed by the government party, one is appointed by the opposition party and one is appointed by the third party).

Reporting Relationship: Proceedings for the preceding session are tabled in the House within ten days of the start of each session. Decisions relating to committee budgets are tabled immediately.

Average Number of Meetings per Year: 15-20.

Minutes: Become public when they are tabled in the House.

Powers and Duties of Management Body: Mandate is outlined in the House of Commons Act and the Standing Orders of the House of Commons.

Estimates which are Reviewed by Management Body: Committee budgets and House of Commons Estimates.

Newf. **Body Responsible:** Internal Economy Commission.

Composition of Management Body: Speaker (Chairman), Deputy Speaker (Vice-Chairman), Government and Opposition House Leaders, two members of the Executive Council and one opposition member.

Reporting Relationship: Does not report to the House.

Average Number of Meetings per Year: 15.

Minutes: Tabled annually.

Powers and Duties of Management Body: Mandate is outlined in statute.

Estimates which are Reviewed by Management Body: Legislative Estimates.

P.E.I. **Body Responsible:** Standing Committee on Internal Economy.

Composition of Management Body: Speaker (Chairman), Opposition Leader and Government House Leader.

Reporting Relationship: The Committee has the authority to report to the House.

Average Number of Meetings per Year: 6.

Minutes: Neither published nor available to the public.

Powers and Duties of Management Body: Mandate is not precisely defined.

Estimates which are Reviewed by Management Body: The Committee does not review estimates. Estimates of the Legislative Assembly are devised by the Standing Committee on Internal Economy, reviewed by the Treasury Board, and approved by Cabinet.

N.S. **Body Responsible:** The Legislature.

Composition of Management Body: Speaker (Chairman), Government House Leader (Vice-Chairman), Chairman of Management Board, Minister of Finance, Deputy Speaker, Chairman of Government Caucus, one member from the Opposition Caucus and one member from another recognized party caucus.

Reporting Relationship: Does not report to the House.

Average Number of Meetings per Year: 12-15.

Minutes: Neither published nor available to the public.

Powers and Duties of Management Body: Mandate is outlined in statute.

Estimates which are Reviewed by Management Body: Any estimates will be reviewed.

N.B. **Body Responsible:** Standing Committee on Legislative Administration.

Composition of Management Body: Speaker (Chairman), two Cabinet Ministers and two members from each recognized party.

Reporting Relationship: Reports to the House after each meeting. Does not report when the House is not sitting.

Average Number of Meetings per Year: 10.

Minutes: Neither published nor available to the public. Orders or Decisions are available.

Powers and Duties of Management Body: Mandate is outlined in Standing Rules of the House 104 (2).

Estimates which are Reviewed by Management Body: Legislative Assembly Estimates are reviewed under the Committee of Supply.

Que. **Body Responsible:** Office of the National Assembly.

Composition of Management Body: Speaker (Chairman), five private members from the Government, three Opposition members and one member from another political party.

Reporting Relationship: All decisions are tabled in the House.

Average Number of Meetings per Year: 20.

Minutes: Not published, but available to the public after tabling.

Powers and Duties of Management Body: Mandate is outlined in statute.

Estimates which are Reviewed by Management Body: Legislative Assembly Estimates.

Ont. **Body Responsible:** Board of Internal Economy.

Composition of Management Body: Speaker (Chairman), three Ministers and one private member from each party.

Reporting Relationship: Does not report to the House.

Average Number of Meetings per Year: 13.

Minutes: Published periodically and available in the Legislative Library. Available to the public within 48 hours of each meeting.

Powers and Duties of Management Body: Mandate is outlined in statute.

Estimates which are Reviewed by Management Body: Legislative Assembly, Ombudsman, Provincial Auditor, Election Office, Election Finances Commission, Information and Privacy Commission and Commission on Conflict of Interest.

Man. **Body Responsible:** Legislative Assembly Management Commission.

Composition of Management Body: Speaker (Chairman), five Government Caucus members, three Official Opposition Caucus members and one Second Opposition party caucus member.

Reporting Relationship: Required by legislation to report to the House annually.

Average Number of Meetings per Year: 9.

Minutes: Become public when tabled in the House.

Powers and Duties of Management Body: Mandate is outlined in statute.

Estimates which are Reviewed by Management Body: Legislative Assembly, Election Office, Ombudsman and Provincial Auditor.

Sask. **Body Responsible:** Board of Internal Economy.

Composition of Management Body: Speaker (Chairman), two Ministers, two private members from the Government and two private members from the Official Opposition.

Reporting Relationship: Has the authority to report to the House.

Average Number of Meetings per Year: 5.

Minutes: Not published. Available to the public only upon request.

Powers and Duties of Management Body: Mandate is outlined in statute.

Estimates which are Reviewed by Management Body: Legislative Assembly Estimates, including the Legislative Library, Legislative Counsel, Law Clerk and Provincial Auditor.

Alta. **Body Responsible:** Special Standing Committee on Members' Services.

Composition of Management Body: Speaker (Chairman), one Minister and six members from the Government, two Official Opposition members and one third party member.

Reporting Relationship: Has the authority to report to the House and does so on an *ad hoc* basis.

Average Number of Meetings per Year: 8.

Minutes: Published and available to the public.

Powers and Duties of Management Body: Not outlined.

Estimates which are Reviewed by Management Body: Legislative Assembly Estimates.

B.C. **Body Responsible:** Board of Internal Economy.

Composition of Management Body: Speaker (Chairman), one Minister, two Government members and two opposition members.

Reporting Relationship: May report to the Assembly from time to time.

Average Number of Meetings per Year: 8.

Minutes: Formally recorded and adopted, but neither published nor available to the public.

Powers and Duties of Management Body: Mandate is outlined in statute.

Estimates which are Reviewed by Management Body: Legislative Assembly Estimates.

Yukon **Body Responsible:** Members' Services Board.

Composition of Management Body: Speaker (Chairman), the Premier, Opposition Leader, Third Party Leader and Government House Leader.

Reporting Relationship: Has the authority to report to the House and does so on an *ad hoc* basis.

Average Number of Meetings per Year: 4.

Minutes: Neither published nor available to the public.

Powers and Duties of Management Body: Mandate is outlined in a resolution of the House.

Estimates which are Reviewed by Management Body: Legislative Assembly Estimates.

N.W.T. **Body Responsible:** Management and Services Board.

Composition of Management Body: Speaker (Chairman), at least one Minister and three private members.

Reporting Relationship: Does not report to the House.

Average Number of Meetings per Year: 10.

Minutes: Neither published nor available to the public.

Powers and Duties of Management Body: Terms of reference are set by Sections 35-37 of the Legislative Assembly and Executive Council Act.

Estimates which are Reviewed by Management Body: Legislative Assembly Estimates.

CHAPTER TWO

Legislative Budgets

THE TOTAL cost for the administration of the Senate, House of Commons and the provincial and territorial legislatures has increased dramatically in the past five years. Combined budgets for their operation for Fiscal 1986/87 came to $401 million. For 1991/92 this figure increased to $585 million, a growth of 46% or 9.2% per annum averaged out over five years.

The 295-member House of Commons accounts for $229 million of the total expenditures on legislatures, or approximately 39%. As far back as 1981/82, the House of Commons budget stood at $126 million. By 1986/87 it had advanced to $178 million. The annual increase over the past decade averaged about 8.2%.

One of the major reasons for this growth was that following the 1988 federal election the House of Commons expanded from 282 to 295 seats. This expansion was the result of redistribution—a process whereby the Federal Redistribution Commission evaluates population growth and concentration as they relate to the number of members in the House—and meant an allocation of additional funds to defray all the costs associated with the maintenance of new members of Parliament.

Another factor to consider when examining the House of Commons budget is the decision to broaden the provisions of the members' travel allowance and accommodation allotment which also caused an overall increase. These are issues which will be reviewed in other areas of this section.

Yet, when comparing the expenditures of the House of Commons over the past ten years with the provincial legislatures, there has been a definite upward trend towards proportionately greater spending by the sub-national assemblies. In 1981/82 the total budgets of the provincial and territorial legislatures amounted to $238 million (47% of the total outlay). The House of Commons at $126 million represented 53% of the total outlay, compared to 39% today. When examining these figures it should be kept in mind that from 1975 to 1985 the House of Commons was spending significant amounts on the introduction of electronic Hansard (gavel-to-gavel televising of House proceedings), computers for members' offices and OASIS, an elaborate internal communications network involving computers, video equipment and television monitors. Increased funding for travel and constituency offices was also provided. With the exception of Ontario and Quebec, it was several years before provincial legislatures began to enter the electronic age, although by 1983 Saskatchewan had scored somewhat of a coup by installing a television system and an outlet via cable television, and in the late 1970s British Columbia had rebuilt the ceiling of its Chamber and installed permanent television lights.

There is no question that areas such as non-partisan staffing, the costs of Hansard (verbatim transcripts of House and Committee proceedings produced in all legislatures except Prince Edward Island) and legislative libraries have helped to edge up costs. However, these are marginal when compared to expenditures which can be directly attributed to elected members and their offices at the seat of government, their constituency offices, commu-

Legislative Budgets

	1990/91	1991/92	% increase or decrease (-)
House of Commons	216 500 000	229 350 000	5.6
Senate	38 007 500	43 489 300	12.6
Newfoundland [1]	6 670 400	6 752 700	1.2
Prince Edward Island	2 577 500	2 542 100	-1.4
Nova Scotia	8 217 000	7 648 600	-7.4
New Brunswick	6 981 800	6 602 000	-5.8
Quebec	69 600 000	76 000 000	8.4
Ontario	116 492 700	129 131 700	9.8
Manitoba	10 759 800	9 749 800	-10.4
Saskatchewan	13 488 700	14 435 700	6.6
Alberta	21 199 064	23 346 717	9.2
British Columbia	19 291 000	24 711 000	21.9
Yukon	1 910 000	2 196 000	13.0
Northwest Territories	8 959 000	9 209 000	2.7
Total	**540 654 464**	**585 164 617**	**7.6**

[1] Figure provided for 1991/92 is an estimate.

nications and mass mailings to constituents. For it is at this point that costs take another quantum leap upward. The greatest growth in expenditures, in general, is in the following areas: travel allowances, staffing for members' offices, caucus support at the seat of government and computer and other electronic equipment (although this would not apply to the smaller legislatures of Newfoundland, Prince Edward Island, Nova Scotia, New Brunswick, Manitoba and Saskatchewan). In the Senate, House of Commons, Ontario and Quebec, followed by Alberta and British Columbia, there is no question that the bulk of spending is "member-driven" as opposed to housekeeping costs represented by the Speaker and the various offices reporting to him or her, namely the Clerk, Sergeant-at-Arms, Administrator, Human Resources, Information Services, Hansard, the Legislative Library and Building Services.

While *Canadian Legislatures* tracks various upfront expenses (such as the costs of Hansard) and provides information on the various entitlements and emoluments which are available to members (e.g. $.29 per kilometre automobile allowance for Ontario Members, 64 round-trip points for federal members, etc.) it is difficult to assess the very large total sums of money which are actually spent by some jurisdictions in covering these costs, sometimes running into tens of millions of dollars.

In case the impression has been left that legislature expenditures can only move in one direction—up—it should be noted that in the following instances budgets in 1991/92 have actually decreased from the previous year: Manitoba (-10.4%), Nova Scotia (-7.4%), New Brunswick (-5.8%) and Prince Edward Island (-1.4%). Undoubtedly the governments in those provinces, which also control the Boards of Internal Economy, took the position that in keeping with government policy in general, legislature spending must be cut following the considerable growth during the period of Fiscal 1989/90-1990/91 which had seen increases in Manitoba (23%), Nova Scotia (14%), New Brunswick (5%) and Prince Edward Island (28%).

Seeing legislature budgets rise and then fall, or continue to rise, leads to an obvious question: why are some legislatures curbing spending while others are not? These are some factors to be taken into account when answering this question:

- Strong majority governments (if they have the will and the fortitude to act regardless of opposition from some of their own members) are most likely to put the brakes on legislature spending through exercising control at the Board of Internal Economy, or its equivalent.

- The smaller provinces are more likely to exercise controls than the larger ones because the spending of the legislature is much more visible in the community, particularly in relation to government programs in general.

- The various legislatures tend to look at comparable legislatures to see how they handle certain allowances or services, and this serves as a restraint. (In the mid-1980s Quebec reigned in a proposed members' pension-enrichment plan, and Ontario took notice.)

- Under minority governments, legislature expenditures tend to escalate substantially, with government members wanting more in case they become the opposition, and opposition members bargaining for more money and staff.

- The media may think they have some influence on moderating legislature expenditures, but this is questionable. In the late 1970s Ontario's Board of Internal Economy, acting under pressure from government members on the Board, decided that they would permit a certain cabinet minister whose constituency was some distance from Toronto to use his accommodation allowance to help defray some costs associated with the operating expenses of a home he was about to purchase in Toronto, even though the guidelines said that the allowance could only be applied against the rental of a room or apartment. The proposal reached the media and an editorial soon appeared in one of the Toronto daily newspapers pointing out that the minister, who happened to be the Minister of Housing, could be seen to be using Legislative Assembly funds for his own profit in a rapidly escalating house market. This publicity may have caused the Board of Internal Economy to briefly postpone their amendment, but before long the guidelines were changed to meet the needs of the minister.

- From time to time some members may express concern as to how the public might view legislature expenditures, however it appears almost impossible for members, at least from their vantage point, to relate levels of legislature spending to public attitudes about elected officials. By and large, members can't seem to make the connection between their demands for more allowances and services and the demands of the voters for restraint in government. In short, they have no motivation to push for restraint, particularly when they would be the losers.

In analyzing the 1991/92 budgets, the decrease in spending of most of the smaller provinces stands out in stark contrast against the increases over the preceding year in British Columbia (21.9%), Yukon (13%), Ontario (9.8%), Alberta (9%), Quebec (8.4%), Saskatchewan (6.6%) and the Senate (12.6%).

In 1987 legislation was passed in British Columbia to create a Board of Internal Economy. Prior to that time legislature administration was handled by the Speaker's Office in consultation with the Select Committee on Standing Orders, Private Bills and Members' Services. The budget for 1986/ 87 was $14.2 million and reflected the additional costs incurred on behalf of twelve new members who were elected to the House in October 1986 as a result of redistribution. Since 1987, there has been a $10.5 million increase in the budget of that legislature. An example of the type of pressures exerted on the British Columbia budget is that the 75 members are now provided with a global budget of $43 200 per annum for office staff and constituency office rent and, undoubtedly, caucus funds have been substantially increased, although these figures have not been provided. Travel expenditures have also increased substantially. It is interesting to note that over the years Alberta legislature expenses have tended to parallel those of British Columbia, and 1991/92 is no exception. There are 83 legislators in Alberta compared to British Columbia's 75.

Quebec's budget seems strangely modest when compared to that of the Ontario legislature—$76 million vs. $129 million. In fact, these figures are startling when compared with 1986/87, just five years ago: Quebec was at $56 million and Ontario was at $68 million. Part of the explanation is that in the intervening years the Speaker and the Board of Internal Economy assumed responsibility for all the maintenance and renovation costs of the Ontario legislature, costs that were shouldered in the past by the government, through the Ministry of Government Services. It is likely that in the case of the National Assembly of Quebec similar costs are borne by the equivalent ministry. One has to bear in mind, however, that non-partisan employees are actually classed as civil servants and may be charged against the docket of a government ministry.

The cost of administering the Ontario legislature—$129 million in 1991/92— is very large. It is not only higher than the House of Commons' budget of a decade ago, but it is larger than the budgets of all of the other provinces and territories (except Quebec) combined. One of the reasons for this is that in Ontario the Election Office, the Commission on Election Finances, the Office of the Provincial Auditor, the Freedom of Information and Privacy Commission and the Conflict of Interest Commissioner come under the jurisdiction of the Legislature and the Board of Internal Economy; their costs are allocated against the Legislative Assembly budget. The Information and Privacy Commission which is comparatively new in the Province of Ontario and has only recently been brought to full-staffing strength, employs 84 persons.

It is interesting to note that in 1974 when its Board of Internal Economy was first constituted, the budget of the Ontario legislature was $9 million. Seven years later in 1981, it had increased to $30 million, reflecting the fact that various groupings of employees who had been paid by both the Legislative Assembly and the Ministry of Government Services were brought together and placed under the Speaker. Facilities such as the Legislative Library, which had previously been administered by the Ministry of Government Services, was also brought into the fold, and the Office of the Ombudsman with over 100 employees was added.

As is noted elsewhere in this book, Ontario's legislature budget surged forward during the period 1985-1987 and since that time it has continued to grow significantly. Some of this can be attributed to the costs of the agencies listed above, but much larger amounts of money have been directed to members for increased personal staff ($136 865 each, as compared to $98 883 in 1987), caucus

support services, travel and, in particular, the introduction of large numbers of computers for individual members' offices, caucus offices, Legislative Assembly staff offices and networks of computers linking many different areas of the legislature.

The majority of Canada's legislatures are considered to be full-time operations, the possible exception being Prince Edward Island although those members are paid a basic indemnity of $32 000 per annum plus a non-taxable allowance of $9 700 which could justify full-time status.

There is no question that those who are fortunate enough to to be elected to Canada's legislatures have joined what could be described as a burgeoning business. This is in sharp contrast to those who are elected to the 50 U.S. state legislatures of which only eight are considered to be full-time, and only two (both with Upper and Lower Houses) have substantial budgets: California (population 30 million)— $179 million, now reduced to $90 million by California voters, and New York (population 18 million)—$164 million.

Per Capita Cost

The following Table should illustrate economies-of-scale in per capita legislature costs in which the lowest cost is seen in the largest population centre (Ontario) and the highest cost in the least populated district, the Yukon. In fact, these economies-of-scale must be working in British Columbia which has the lowest cost, and the third-largest population. Northwest Territories, though, with the next-to-smallest population has, by far, the highest cost. This cannot be attributed to the cost of constructing their new legislative assembly building since it is being privately financed by debentures. Beyond these extremes, there seems to be little to account for the per capita cost variation, except that some legislatures are obviously managed with more of an eye to the bottom line.

In comparison with U.S. per capita costs (see Page 195), the most northern state, Alaska, is also the most expensive. However, the average U.S. per capita cost is $6.02 and the Canadian is $30.47.

Per Capita Legislative Costs

Jurisdiction	Legislative Budgets 1991/92	Population	Per Capita Cost of each Legislature	Total Per Capita Cost [1]
Canada: House of Commons	$ 229 350 000	27 023 100	$ 8.49	$ 8.49
Canada: Senate	43 489 300	27 023 100	1.61	1.61
Newfoundland	6 752 700	571 700	11.81	21.91
Prince Edward Island	2 542 100	129 900	19.57	29.67
Nova Scotia	7 648 600	897 500	8.52	18.62
New Brunswick	6 602 000	725 600	9.10	19.20
Quebec	76 000 000	6 811 800	11.16	21.26
Ontario	129 131 700	9 840 300	13.12	23.22
Manitoba	9 749 800	1 092 600	8.92	19.02
Saskatchewan	14 435 700	995 300	14.50	24.60
Alberta	23 346 717	2 501 400	9.33	19.43
British Columbia	24 711 000	3 185 900	7.76	17.86
Northwest Territories	9 209 000	54 000	170.54	180.64
Yukon	2 196 000	26 500	81.33	91.43

[1] Includes the per capita costs of the Senate, House of Commons and the respective individual legislature.

CHAPTER THREE

Legislative Assembly
Estimates Review Procedure

THE SPENDING Estimates for the Senate, House of Commons and the provincial and territorial legislatures come under the purview of the Board of Internal Economy (or its equivalent), and are prepared under the direction of the Clerk of the House or through the Administrator's Office. Following review and approval by the Board of Internal Economy, the Estimates are usually forwarded to the Treasury Board or the Management Board of Cabinet for tabling in the House by the Minister of Finance, the Treasurer or the Chairman of the Management Board.

In seven jurisdictions (Prince Edward Island, Nova Scotia, Quebec, Manitoba, British Columbia, Yukon and the Northwest Territories) Legislative Assembly Estimates are considered in the Committee of the Whole House (actually in the Chamber of the House, by the members of the House, as opposed to a separate Committee). Other legislatures refer the Estimates to standing committees.

In the past, before the emergence of the Board of Internal Economy as the financial review body, it was always the Minister of Finance, the Treasurer, the Chairman of the Management Board or in some cases, the Premier, who defended the budget of the Legislative Assembly (the Premier still performs this duty in Prince Edward Island and New Brunswick). Currently, the Speaker defends the Estimates in the House of Commons, Nova Scotia, Quebec, Ontario, Saskatchewan and the Northwest Territories.

Although the Speaker and the Board of Internal Economy became responsible for the financial administration of the Ontario Legislature in 1974, it was the Clerk of the House and the Administrator who represented the Board when the Estimates were reviewed by the Standing General Government Committee. Several years later, the Honourable Jack Stokes became the second Speaker in Canada to go before his own colleagues for questioning on the Assembly Estimates (the first was in the House of Commons). This represented a major departure from the tradition that only a government minister could speak to the Estimates, as they involved the expenditure of government funds.

There is one difference between the Estimates approval process as it relates to the government and the legislature: government ministries must appear before Estimates Committees for a line-by-line defence of their proposed spending plans. In this forum, opposition members use every opportunity to question and to try to embarrass the government in front of the media. However, when the Speaker or a Minister of the Crown appears before an Estimates Committee on behalf of the Board of Internal Economy, government and opposition members of the Committee alike must change horses and remember that they are reviewing the Spending Estimates for the Legislature prepared and approved by their colleagues on the Board. As a result, questions rarely focus on matters of substance, and often run the gamut from the state of restaurant services, to questions about the need for flags in offices.

CHAPTER FOUR

Remuneration Entitlements

THE TERMINOLOGY in reference to members indemnities, salaries and allowances requires some definition prior to any analysis of current levels in the various areas. "Indemnity" and "Sessional Allowance" are held-over terms dating back to an earlier era when Canada's legislative institutions met for short "sessions" and members were paid an "indemnity" to reimburse them for the time that they were forced to be absent from their place of work. The same terms are still used today in many jurisdictions when referring to the basic annual remuneration of an elected member, which would otherwise be known as a "salary". At present, the term "salary" applies principally to those members who hold additional offices and are compensated accordingly (e.g. the Government Leader of the Senate, Prime Minister, Speaker, Members of Cabinet).

Over the years, a system has come into place (which began with the House of Commons) whereby members receive an annual tax-free allowance in addition to their indemnity. According to Revenue Canada Taxation, this payment may represent up to 50% of the member's basic indemnity and is considered non-taxable in the case of personal income tax. The original purpose of the tax-free allowance was to assist in defraying certain expenses incurred by members in carrying out their official duties, such as a hotel room at the seat of government, a rented room in a home, rental of an apartment, local transportation costs, hospitality for visiting constituents, laundry and dry-cleaning, meals while travelling, etc.

The tax-free allowance has a considerable impact on members' compensation. In some cases remuneration paid to legislators in the smaller provinces is now out-stripping the larger ones, due to the size of the tax-free allowance. In every jurisdiction, however, one must also take into account that in addition to regular indemnities and tax-free allowances, a number of members serve in other capacities—e.g. Committee Chairman, House Leader, Chief Whip, Committee member, etc. and are paid an additional salary.

Members of the House of Commons still receive the highest pay in Canada ($64 400 + $21 300 tax-free allowance). However one jurisdiction—the Northwest Territories—has actually surpassed the Government of Canada in terms of the salary paid to its Government Leader (Northwest Territories' Government Leader—$74 715 vs. the Prime Minister—$73 600). This, in a sense, is like comparing apples with oranges, because the remuneration of the Prime Minister of Canada is $64 400 (basic indemnity) plus $21 300 (tax-free allowance), plus $73 600 (additional salary for the position of Prime Minister), which equals a total package of $159 300. The remuneration for the Northwest Territories Government Leader is $38 701 (basic indemnity) plus $1 000 (tax-free allowance), plus $74 715 (additional salary for the position of Government Leader) for a total of $114 416. However, the Northwest Territories package contains only $1 000 tax-free monies and the Government Leader's remuneration can be seen to represent what might be termed as a "true" salary with which the public can identify.

To continue with some analysis of the Northwest Territories (which covers an area of approximately 3.3 million square kilometres, and has a population of 54 000), members of that Legislature were paid an indemnity of $18 720 in 1987, the second-lowest in Canada at the time (after Prince Edward Island), plus a $1 000 tax-free allowance, totalling $19 720. As of January 1, 1991 the Northwest Territories basic member's indemnity had moved to $38 701, however it was still the lowest in Canada because the tax-free allowance remained at $1 000 while Prince Edward Island politicians, formerly in last place, were receiving $32 000 plus a tax-free allowance of $9 700, totalling $41 700.

The provincial and territorial members who have made the greatest gains in their total basic remuneration in the past five years, *based on rolling together the indemnity and the tax free allowance* are:

	1987	1991	% increase
N.W.T	$19 720	$39 701	101
Alta.	35 649	57 502	61
P.E.I.	27 000	41 700	54
Sask.	31 452	46 168	47
Yukon	36 656	45 730	25
B.C.	40 047	49 218	23

It should be pointed out that even though the Northwest Territories increased its total basic remuneration by slightly more than 100% from 1986/87 to 1991/92 the actual amount of remuneration remained the lowest of all jurisdictions.

The method and timing of setting indemnity, tax-free allowance and salary levels in the various jurisdictions is at best a patchwork approach, badly in need of restructuring and simplification. To better illustrate this one should examine the salaries paid to Premiers and Chief Ministers of provinces or territories. Setting aside the basic members' indemnity and tax-free allowance, the premier of Ontario, Canada's most populous province, receives a salary of $45 240 which ranks very low nation-wide. The Alberta premier, on the other hand, ranks third with a Premier's salary of $59 858 (a total pay package of $117 360 as opposed to Ontario's $103 162. And these figures don't take into account the impact on take-home pay of Alberta's tax-free allowance which is about $4 000 higher than Ontario's).

A glance at the salaries for ministers with portfolios illustrates that next to the Northwest Territories ($67 275), Alberta pays its cabinet members the most ($47 053), followed by Quebec ($45 092), Newfoundland ($39 834) and so on. Ontario, in this case, is again well down the list ($31 749) with only Yukon and Manitoba ranking lower.

The highest-paid Speaker in Canada is that of the Northwest Territories ($67 275) who receives the salary of a Cabinet Minister in the same jurisdiction. The Speaker of the House of Commons follows ($49 100), then the Speaker of the Alberta Legislature ($47 053), and the President of the Quebec National Assembly ($45 092). The Ontario Speaker is paid $24 139 and ranks towards the bottom of the list with Saskatchewan, Prince Edward Island, Manitoba and Yukon. Eight Speakers in Canada receive a salary equivalent to that of a Cabinet Minister in the same province. The exceptions are the Speakers of the Senate, Ontario, Saskatchewan, Manitoba, Prince Edward Island and Yukon.

A degree of fairness must be introduced into indemnities and tax-free allowances. Alberta, Saskatchewan and the Northwest Territories are perfect examples of provinces where legislators, for one reason or another, decided not to adjust these payments four or five years ago, and then made up for it in the past couple of years. Alberta did this partly by raising its tax-free allowance for members from $7 883 in 1988 to its current $19 167. Saskatchewan actually lowered its tax-free allowance from $10 484 to $7 622 in 1991, while at the same time moving the indemnity of its members up from a level of $20 968 in 1984 (where it remained stationary for the following several years) to $38 546 in 1991.

It seems strange that there has been a reluctance on the part of successive Ontario governments to equate the responsibilities of the Speaker with those of a Cabinet Minister, and to set remuneration accordingly. The Speaker oversees not only all staff matters in the House but also heads a very sizeable administrative staff which look after all aspects of members' services and the operation and maintenance of the legislative building itself. In terms of protocol, the Speaker ranks next to the Premier, and above members of the Cabinet. However, the fact that he ranks near the bottom of the scale in terms of remuneration paid to Canadian Speakers, is indefensible. It again suggests that a better way must be found to equitably compensate elected members in Canada.

When it comes to setting levels of compensation only the Parliament of Canada, Ontario, and Nova Scotia have bodies outside the legislature who can make recommendations on this matter to the government or the Speaker.

In Ottawa, the Commission to Review Allowances of Members of Parliament, appointed under the terms of Section 68 (1) of the Parliament of Canada Act has the mandate to make recommendations respecting the allowances paid to senators and members of the House of Commons. This Commission has been constituted on five occasions and has produced the Beaupré Report (1970), the Hales Report (1979), the McIsaac-Balcer Report (1980), the Clarke-Campbell Report (1985) and the St. Germain-Fox Report (1989).

The St. Germain-Fox Commission Report addressed the 60-80 hour work weeks which are routine for some members of Parliament. The Commissioners saw the pressures involved in that type of schedule as more than offsetting the pomp, ceremony, importance and glamour of being a legislator. They felt it made sense to pay a member according to the actual job, rather than paying a reduced salary because of the aura surrounding the job.

Various comparative figures and charts were provided in the Commission Report which indicated that on the "outside", businesspeople would be earning as much as $20 000-$25 000 more than MPs. It was calculated by Hay Management Consultants, who did a study for the Commission establishing certain benchmarks for members, that in the private sector, based on an equivalent weighting, a member of Parliament would actually be paid $78 673 (in 1989 dollars). However, the Commission pointed out that "If the private-sector comparison set out in the Hay Management Consultant's Report were to be adopted, the salaries of MPs would have to be increased by $18 693, or 31%. The Commission is not prepared to make such a recommendation." The Commission instead went on to make the following recommendation: "Considering all of the factors set out in this Report and assuming the indexing formula for MPs salaries and expenses is implemented, then the Commission is prepared to recommend

that the salaries of Members of both houses of Parliament be increased by four percent effective immediately following the next general election."

On January 1, 1990 MPs indemnities were raised by 3.5% (an index) to $62 100, and increased again by 3.7% indexing to $64 400 on January 1, 1991. Considering that their report was tendered in 1989 and that the intervening years have seen no federal election, the additional four percent recommended by St. Germain-Fox would presumably not kick in until the next Parliament comes in following the federal election which must take place by the end of 1993.

For the past ten years or so in Ontario, the question of compensation for members of the legislature is referred to the Ontario Commission on Election Finances, which in turn makes its recommendations to the House through the Speaker. The members of the Commission—which was established to monitor and regulate election and political party financing—are appointed by the three parties in the legislature. This body obviously has the welfare of Ontario members in mind. It forwards specific recommendations to the Speaker regarding indemnities, salaries and tax-free allowances, however no government to date has implemented the "pay package" recommendations of the Commission. The recommendations, if anything, may have been overly generous, which is probably why the government has been hesitant to act, preferring more modest increments, usually introduced during the last week of the session before the House recesses in late June. The Commission recently recommended that the tax-free allowance of Ontario members be removed, the indemnity increased and committee per diems be assessed as income in order to represent a true salary. The government has not indicated that it plans to act on these recommendations in the future.

In Nova Scotia, the Commission of Inquiry on Remuneration of Elected Provincial Officials is constituted by the Speaker under the provisions of Chapter 29 of the Statutes of Nova Scotia (1983) and makes its recommendations directly to the Speaker in a Report "respecting the indemnities, allowances and salaries to be paid under the House of Assembly Act and the Executive Council Act," submitted annually. The Commission, which has three Commissioners who have not held political office but have considerable understanding of the environment surrounding the House of Assembly, as well as operations and administration, is the best possible example in Canada of a remuneration-setting body outside the political system which goes about its work in a diligent, methodical and realistic manner. It has the statutory powers to make recommendation on members' indemnities, salaries and tax-free allowances so that they are consistently implemented. The Commission also makes recommendations regarding compensation for officers of the House (senior staff), and at times, on an informal basis, makes comments on the organization and administration of various offices in the legislature which are maintained at legislature expense, including the caucus offices. The Commission carefully monitors all questions relating to legislators' compensation across Canada and produces a major report each year in November or December. It is also charged with the responsibility of inquiring into, and reporting on, the Members' Retiring Allowance Act of Nova Scotia.

The impact of the members' tax-free allowance in every jurisdiction (except the Northwest Territories) has a major impact on "take-home pay". This is by far the most contentious issue when considering compensation for members of Canadian legislatures at the federal, provincial and territorial levels. Also, the validity of the tax-free allowance cannot be assessed without looking at the level of living accommodation allowances, travel expenses and committee per diems also being provided.

If the total remuneration package is approximately equal in two jurisdictions, this doesn't mean that the respective members have the same take-home pay. Province A may provide a tax-free allowance of 50% of the basic indemnity. Province B may only pay a 25% tax-free allowance. The result is that the actual take-home pay of members in Province A will be higher than Province B. The presence of a tax-free allowance creates a great deal of confusion when attempting to evaluate all the factors which today should determine the actual compensation of an elected member in any jurisdiction.

In order to try to dissect the tax-free allowance conundrum, it is necessary to examine the level of tax-free allowances paid in each jurisdiction starting with Fiscal 1987/88, and then to move on to the present to attempt to assess their validity.

In Fiscal 1987/88 five jurisdictions (Newfound-land, Prince Edward Island, Manitoba, Saskatchewan and British Columbia) paid a tax-free allowance of 50% of the indemnity to their members. Yukon paid 44%, Nova Scotia 38% and the House of Commons 33%.

By Fiscal 1991/92, some interesting changes had taken place. Eight jurisdictions were now paying a tax-free allowance of 50% of the indemnity: Newfoundland, Nova Scotia, Manitoba, Alberta, British Columbia and Yukon. Alberta found its way onto this list by moving from 27% to 50%. At the same time, Prince Edward Island had left the list as a result of lowering its 50% tax-free allowance to 30% and Saskatchewan was also off the list as it had reduced the allowance to 20% of the indemnity. During this fiscal period, New Brunswick paid a 40% tax-free allowance, Ontario 34% and Quebec 18%.

This confusing juxtaposition of provinces and percentages translates into the information contained in the 1991 Actual Earnings Table on page 76. From this it can be clearly seen that the tax-free allowance in relation to the indemnity can create a very lopsided situation in terms of how much individual members in different jurisdictions are remunerated in actual (or street-level) dollars. MPs receive the highest compensation package followed by the Senate, Quebec, Newfoundland, Alberta, Ontario, New Brunswick, British Columbia, Nova Scotia, Yukon, Saskatchewan, Prince Edward Island, Manitoba and finally Northwest Territories.

In order to consider the effect of accommodation allowances on indemnities and tax-free allowances, consult the chapter outlining those allowances. It seems apparent that in every jurisdiction, with the exception of the House of Commons and Prince Edward Island, adequate arrangements are in place to look after the bulk of out-of-pocket expenses incurred by elected members either when they are at the seat of government during a session, or between sessions. This, then, appears to underline the fact that although there are some personal expenses being incurred by members as a result of their public persona, the original purpose for a non-taxable allowance no longer exists, except possibly in one case—the House of Commons.

In Ontario, for some years now, it has been generally acknowledged by the party leadership and the membership of that Legislature that *in fact* the tax-free allowance has come to be considered a part of the indemnity received by a member, rather than a separate amount of money to defray official expenses. Consequently the tax-free allowance has not been increased except for cost-of-living increments. It would appear that Saskatchewan is heading in the right direction by lowering its tax-free allowance, while considerably increasing the indemnity, as is Prince Edward Island, which has pretty well held to its former tax-free allowance, while substantially increasing the indemnity or salary.

It is significant to note that of all the various jurisdictions, the House of Commons does not provide its out-of-town members with an accommodation allowance as such. On the other hand, Ontario provides backbenchers from outside Toronto with an accountable accommodation allowance, which is currently $13 825 for members

and $14 825 for cabinet ministers and party leaders. The same holds true for Quebec where members of the National Assembly may receive up to $10 300 in an accommodation allowance, and senior elected officials of the House up to $13 300.

As a result of a recommendation contained in the St. Germain-Fox Commission Report, all members of the House of Commons were granted up to $6 000 for reimbursement of "travel status expenses" when the member is at least 100 kilometres away from his or her primary residence. This, in a sense, is meant to be equivalent to the accommodation allowance recommended by St. Germain-Fox which was apparently not implemented due to taxation implications. It is, in any case, considerably less than the allowance provided by legislatures in Ontario, Quebec and several other jurisdictions. It would

1991 "Actual" Earnings [1]

	Basic Indemnity	Tax-Free Allowance	Marginal Tax Rate [2]	Gross Earnings Equivalent to Tax-Free Allowance	"Actual" Earnings (Basic plus Gross) [3]
House of Commons	$64 400	$21 300	49.10 [4]	$41 846.76	$106 246.76
Senate	64 400	10 100	49.10 [4]	19 842.83	84 242.83
Newfoundland	38 024	19 014	43.40	33 593.64	71 617.64
Prince Edward Island	32 000	9 700	41.80	16 666.67	48 666.67
Nova Scotia	30 130	15 065	42.77	26 323.61	56 453.61
New Brunswick	35 807	14 323	42.90	25 084.06	60 891.06
Quebec	60 123	10 574	49.70	21 021.87	81 144.87
Ontario	44 665	14 984	41.08	25 431.09	70 096.09
Manitoba	27 963	13 982	28.68	19 604.60	47 567.60
Saskatchewan	38 546	7 622	42.30	13 209.71	51 755.71
Alberta	38 335	19 168	39.89	31 888.20	70 223.20
British Columbia	32 812	16 406	40.69	27 661.44	60 473.44
Yukon	30 487	15 243 [5]	37.80	24 506.43	54 993.43
Northwest Territories	38 701	1 000	38.70	1 631.32	40 332.32

[1] Indicates the "street value" of the Basic Indemnity and Tax-Free Allowance.
[2] The Marginal Tax Rate applies at these rates to every dollar earned above the Basic Indemnity. The Basic Indemnity itself is not taxed at this amount. These tax rates include federal and provincial surtaxes or reductions, provincial flat taxes, where appropriate, and reflect budget proposals to June 15, 1991.
[3] Actually, this would be "minimum earnings" since it assumes there is no other income received and is based on the basic personal exemption.
[4] An average of the Marginal Tax Rate for that income ($64 000) across all ten provinces.
[5] Rural allowance.

seem that there is cause, at least in part, to continue to provide a tax-free allowance to federal members. It appears that the federal tax-free allowance is being used more in keeping with its original purpose—to cover the cost of accommodation and personal out-of-pocket expenses for out-of-town members in connection with their official duties at the seat of government. At the same time it is clear that members whose constituencies are in or near Ottawa should not be receiving the full benefits of the tax-free allowance.

The fact that all members of the House of Commons receive the same tax-free allowance would seem to suggest that, regardless of whether provincial legislatures abolish tax-free allowances, there is cause to lower the House of Commons tax-free allotment by about $10 000 in the case of out-of-town members, and almost totally for Ottawa-based members, while at the same time properly adjusting all members' indemnities upwards.

As part of the process of restructuring legislative institutions in Canada in order to have a solid base from which to face the future, and to provide public confidence in the political system, it seems clear that politicians should seriously consider turning over the responsibility of determining remuneration and allowance levels to bodies outside the legislature. In the end, it would most likely benefit the politician enormously, both financially and from the standpoint of feeling that his or her worth was adequately recognized by those outside the system.

Canadian legislatures have grown like topsy in the past fifteen years in terms of members, staffs, budgets and services. Unfortunately, the handling of members' remuneration and the financial structur-ing of countless other areas of legislature operations have developed in the same way, and now resemble an ill-patched quilt that needs taking apart and redoing. Elected and non-elected people in the Senate, House of Commons and the provincial and territorial legislatures simply do not have the time, nor in many cases, the inclination to tackle such a mammoth and thankless job. This provides another compelling reason why a cadre of professionals should be built up outside the legislatures who can do the research and studies and make recommendations which will go to the heart of straightening out what has become a very confused scene.

The St. Germain-Fox Commission recommended that, in the future, a commission should be established to examine remuneration levels for MPs and senators consisting of a Chair and one Commissioner both of whom would be non-politicians, and one Commissioner who would be a former parliamentarian.

The Canadian public wants to see excellence in their legislators and legislatures. Elected members should be adequately and fairly compensated for their work and they should not in any way suffer any pecuniary losses by going into public service. To enable this, the tax-free allowance must be abolished, a proper assessment made of the allowances and how they affect personal incomes, and then reasonable salaries put in place, even if it means substantially increasing current salaries. This process can no longer be left to political considerations alone. That is why it is important that outside bodies replace the present, hopelessly inadequate method of setting the compensation of elected members in Canada.

House of Commons Remuneration

BASIC	1990	1991
Members' Basic Indemnity	$62 100	$64 400
% Increase over Previous Year	3.5	3.7
Tax Free Allowance	20 600	21 300
Remote Districts	25 200	26 200
Northwest Territories	27 100	28 200
Total Basic Remuneration	82 700	85 700
Remote Districts	87 300	90 400
Northwest Territories	89 200	92 600

ADDITIONAL	1990	1991
Prime Minister	71 000	73 600
Cabinet Minister	47 400	49 100
Speaker	47 400	49 100
Deputy Speaker	24 800	25 700
Leader of the Opposition	47 400	49 100
Third Party Leader	28 500	29 500
Chief Government Whip	12 800	13 200
Chief Opposition Whip	12 800	13 200
Chief Third Party Whip	7 300	7 500
Parliamentary Secretaries	10 200	10 500
Deputy Chair, Cmte of Whole	10 200	10 500
Ass't Deputy Chair, Cmte of Whole	10 200	10 500
Opposition House Leader	23 000	23 800
Third Party House Leader	9 800	10 100
Deputy Government Whip	7 300	7 500
Deputy Opposition Whip	7 300	7 500
No. Receiving Additional Salary	n.a.	n.a.
% Receiving Additional Salary	n.a.	n.a.

Newfoundland Remuneration

BASIC	1990	1991
Members' Basic Indemnity	$38 024	$38 024
% Increase over Previous Year	0.0	0.0
Tax Free Allowance	19 014	19 014
Total Basic Remuneration	57 038	57 038

ADDITIONAL	1990	1991
Premier	54 923	54 923
Minister with Portfolio	39 834	39 834
Parliamentary Assistant	18 673	18 673
Leader of the Opposition	39 834	39 834
Speaker	39 834	39 834
Deputy Speaker	19 917	19 917
Deputy Chair, Cmte of Whole	9 983	9 983
Standing Committee Chair [1]	8 000	8 000
Standing Committee Vice-Chair [2]	6 000	6 000
Opposition House Leader	19 917	19 917
Chief Government Whip	6 000	6 000
Chief Opposition Whip	6 000	6 000
No. Receiving Additional Salary	15	15
% Receiving Additional Salary	29	29

[1] Payable to the Chair of the Public Accounts Committee only.
[2] Payable to the Vice-Chair of the Public Accounts Committee only.

Prince Edward Island Remuneration

BASIC	1990	1991
Members' Basic Indemnity	$32 000	$32 000
% Increase over Previous Year	46.3	0.0
Tax Free Allowance	9 700	9 700
Total Basic Remuneration	41 700	41 700

ADDITIONAL		
Premier	48 200	48 200
Minister with Portfolio	37 000	37 000
Leader of the Opposition	37 000	37 000
Speaker [1]	15 700	15 700
Deputy Speaker [1]	7 900	7 900
Deputy Government House Leader	5 000	5 000
Opposition House Leader	3 500	3 500
Chief Government Whip	3 000	3 000
Chief Opposition Whip	3 000	3 000
No. Reciving Additional Salary	19	23
% Receiving Additional Salary	59	72

[1] Includes expenses.

Nova Scotia Remuneration

BASIC	1990	1991
Members' Basic Indemnity	$30 130	$30 130
% Increase over Previous Year	9.8	0.0
Tax Free Allowance	15 065	15 065
Total Basic Remuneration	45 195	45 195

ADDITIONAL		
Premier	52 012	52 012
Minister with Portfolio	37 055	37 055
Minister without Portfolio	37 055	37 055
Leader of the Opposition	37 055	37 055
Third Party Leader	18 533	18 533
Speaker	37 055	37 055
Deputy Speaker	18 533	18 533
Deputy Government House Leader	3 000	3 000
Opposition House Leader	2 000	2 000
Chief Government Whip	2 380	2 380
Chief Opposition Whip	1 785	1 785
Chief Third Party Whip	170	170
No. Receiving Additional Salary	52	52
% Receiving Additional Salary	100	100

New Brunswick Remuneration

BASIC	1990	1991
Members' Basic Indemnity	$35 807	$35 807
% Increase over Previous Year	5.1	0.0
Tax Free Allowance	14 323	14 323
Total Basic Remuneration	50 130	50 130

ADDITIONAL		
Premier	48 936	48 936
Minister with Portfolio	32 625	32 625
Minister without Portfolio	24 469	24 469
Leader of the Opposition	n.a.	32 625
Third Party Leader	n.a.	12 000
Fourth Party Leader	n.a.	12 000
Speaker	32 625	24 469
Deputy Speaker [1]	16 313	15 000
Chief Government Whip	1 500	1 500
Chief Opposition Whip	n.a.	1 500
Chief Third Party Whip	n.a.	1 500
No. Receiving Additional Salary	25	27
% Receiving Additional Salary	43	47

[1] At the time of publication, the duties and salary of the position of Deputy Speaker were being shared by two persons.

Quebec Remuneration

BASIC	1990	1991
Members' Basic Indemnity	$57 260	$60 123
% Increase over Previous Year	4.0	5.0
Tax Free Allowance	10 070	10 574
Total Basic Remuneration	67 330	70 697

ADDITIONAL		
President	60 123	63 129
Minister with Portfolio	42 945	45 092
Parliamentary Assistant	11 452	12 025
Leader of the Opposition	42 945	45 092
Third Party Leader	20 041	21 043
Speaker	42 945	45 092
Deputy Speaker	20 041	21 043
Standing Committee Chairman	14 315	15 031
Standing Committee Vice-Chairman	11 452	12 025
Deputy Government House Leader	11 452	12 025
Opposition House Leader	20 041	21 043
Deputy Opposition House Leader	8 589	9 018
Chief Government Whip	20 041	21 043
Assistant Government Whip	8 589	9 018
Chief Opposition Whip	17 178	18 037
Assistant Opposition Whip	8 589	9 018
Chief Third Party Whip	8 589	9 018
No. Receiving Additional Salary	99	103
% Receiving Additional Salary	79	82

Ontario Remuneration

BASIC	1990	1991
Members' Basic Indemnity	$43 374	$44 675
% Increase over Previous Year	0.0	3.0
Tax Free Allowance	14 548	14 984
Total Basic Remuneration	57 922	59 659

ADDITIONAL

Premier	45 240	45 240
Minister with Portfolio	31 749	31 749
Minister without Portfolio	15 942	15 942
Parliamentary Assistant	9 808	9 808
Leader of the Opposition	31 749	32 701
Third Party Leader	22 602	23 280
Speaker	23 436	24 139
Deputy Speaker	9 808	10 102
Chair, Cmte of Whole House	n.a.	10 102
Deputy Chair, Cmte of Whole	6 813	7 017
Standing Committee Chairman	8 827	9 092
Standing Committee Vice-Chair	5 313	5 472
Opposition House Leader	12 127	12 491
Deputy Opposition House Leader	5 995	6 175
Third Party House Leader	10 345	10 655
Dep. Third Party House Leader	n.a.	5 613
Chief Government Whip	12 127	12 491
Assistant Government Whip	8 311	8 560
Government Whips	n.a.	6 175
Chief Opposition Whip	9 297	9 576
Opposition Whips	5 995	6 175
Chief Third Party Whip	8 367	8 618
Assistant Third Party Whip	5 450	5 613
No. Receiving Additional Salary	93	93
% Receiving Additional Salary	72	72

Manitoba Remuneration

BASIC	1990	1991
Members' Basic Indemnity	$26 782	$27 963
% Increase over Previous Year	3.4	4.4
Tax Free Allowance	13 391	13 982
Total Basic Remuneration	40 173	41 945

ADDITIONAL

Premier	26 600	26 600
Minister with Portfolio	20 600	20 600
Minister without Portfolio	15 600	15 600
Parliamentary Assistant	2 500	2 500
Leader of the Opposition	20 600	20 600
Third Party Leader	15 600	15 600
Speaker	12 000	12 000
Deputy Speaker	3 500	3 500
Deputy Chair, Cmte of Whole	2 500	2 500
Opposition House Leader	2 500	2 500
Chief Government Whip	2 500	2 500
Chief Opposition Whip	2 500	2 500
No. Receiving Additional Salary	24	54
% Receiving Additional Salary	42	95

Saskatchewan Remuneration

BASIC	1990	1991
Members' Basic Indemnity	$38 546	$38 546
% Increase over Previous Year	4.1	0.0
Tax Free Allowance	7 622	7 622
Total Basic Remuneration	46 168	46 168

ADDITIONAL		
Premier	54 444	52 300
Deputy Premier	43 555	41 840
Minister with Portfolio	38 111	36 610
Minister without Portfolio	n.a.	36 610
Parliamentary Assistant	8 167	8 167
Leader of the Opposition	38 111	36 610
Third Party Leader	19 056	19 056
Speaker	21 778	21 778
Deputy Speaker	8 167	8 167
Deputy Chair, Cmte of Whole	4 084	4 084
Standing Committee Chairman	4 084	4 084
Opposition House Leader	8 167	8 167
Chief Government Whip	8 167	8 167
Assistant Government Whip	4 084	4 084
Chief Opposition Whip	8 167	8 167
Assistant Opposition Whip	4 084	4 084
Chief Third Party Whip	4 084	4 084
No. Receiving Additional Salary	41	21
% Receiving Additional Salary	64	32

Alberta Remuneration

BASIC	1990	1991
Members' Basic Indemnity	$38 335	$38 335
% Increase over Previous Year	0.0	0.0
Tax Free Allowance	19 167	19 167
Total Basic Remuneration	57 502	57 502

ADDITIONAL		
Premier	59 858	59 858
Minister with Portfolio	47 053	47 053
Minister without Portfolio	20 914	20 914
Leader of the Opposition	47 053	47 053
Third Party Leader	20 914	20 914
Speaker	47 053	47 053
Deputy Speaker	23 526	23 526
Deputy Chair, Cmte of Whole	11 763	11 763
Standing Cmte Chairman [1]	4 200	4 200
Opposition House Leader	10 000	10 000
Third Party House Leader	8 000	8 000
Chief Government Whip	8 000	8 000
Assistant Government Whip	6 000	6 000
Chief Opposition Whip	6 000	6 000
Assistant Opposition Whip	5 000	5 000
Chief Third Party Whip	5 000	5 000
No. Receiving Additional Salary	n.a.	n.a.
% Receiving Additional Salary	n.a.	n.a.

[1] Salary applies only to class "A" chairmen. Class "B" chairmen receive an increased hourly rate.

British Columbia Remuneration

BASIC	1990	1991
Members' Basic Indemnity	$31 249	$32 812
% Increase over Previous Year	5.0	5.0
Tax Free Allowance	15 624	16 406
Total Basic Remuneration	46 873	49 218

ADDITIONAL		
Premier	45 000	45 000
Minister with Portfolio	39 000	39 000
Minister without Portfolio	25 000	n.a.
Parliamentary Secretary	6 000	6 000
Leader of the Opposition	39 000	39 000
Speaker	39 000	39 000
Deputy Speaker	19 500	19 500
Deputy Chair, Cmte of Whole	3 000	3 000
Standing Cmte Chairman [1]	225	225
Standing Committee Member [1]	100	100
Opposition House Leader	6 000	6 000
Government Whip	6 000	6 000
Deputy Government Whip	3 000	3 000
Opposition Whip	6 000	6 000
No. Receiving Additional Salary	35	31
% Receiving Additional Salary	53	41

[1] Paid this daily allowance only when the House is not sitting and business has been referred.

Yukon Remuneration

BASIC	1990	1991
Members' Basic Indemnity	$29 035	$30 487
% Increase over Previous Year	4.6	5.0
Tax Free Allowance		
Whitehorse:	12 675	13 309
Rural:	14 517	15 243
Total Basic Remuneration		
Whitehorse:	41 710	43 796
Rural:	43 552	45 730

ADDITIONAL		
Premier	30 496	30 496
Minister with Portfolio	22 260	22 260
Leader of the Opposition	22 260	22 260
Third Party Leader	4 452	4 452
Speaker	7 420	7 420
Deputy Speaker	5 565	5 565
No. Receiving Additional Salary	8	9
% Receiving Additional Salary	50	56

Northwest Territories Remuneration

BASIC	1990	1991
Members Basic Indemnity	$36 858	$38 701
% Increase over Previous Year	n.a.	5.0
Tax Free Allowance	1 000	1 000
Total Basic Remuneration	37 858	39 701

ADDITIONAL		
Government Leader	71 155	74 715
Minister with Portfolio	64 070	67 275
Speaker	15 000	67 275
Deputy Speaker	n.a.	6 000
Deputy Chair, Cmte of Whole	n.a.	3 500
Standing Committee Chairman	n.a.	3 000
No. Receiving Additional Salary	n.a.	24
% Receiving Additional Salary	n.a.	100

ONE MEMBER'S PAY AND PERQUISITES: A FICTIONAL CASE STUDY

In order to explain how the indemnities, salaries, allowances and pensions outlined in this book actually relate to Members of the House of Commons, this article, using documented figures, sketches a scenario of how they apply to a fictional Member of Parliament elected in 1974. Figures provided, although accurate in all respects are given as examples only and do not relate to the specific accounts of any present or former Member. This is a fictitious person.

Personal Background

"Charles Canadore" was born in Windsor in 1949; he is married and lives with his wife and two children in his Windsor riding.

Charles was a member of a small but prestigious law firm where he specialized in corporate law, until he was first elected to the House in 1984. The partners at his law firm held his position for him should he ever return to private life.

Political Career

Charles was sworn in by the Clerk of the House as a Member of the House of Commons in September 1984. To acquaint him with the costs and perks of holding elected office, he received a book dealing with such items as allowances, salaries, office facilities and staff.

He discovered that he would earn less than he used to at the law practice. He would receive a $52 800 Sessional Allowance (salary) plus a Tax-Free Allowance of $17 600.

Charles couldn't figure out why he wasn't given a salary for doing this full-time job; instead he received an "allowance," plus a tax-free allowance that seemed to be part of his salary, but actually isn't treated as such. In terms of "street dollars," the $17 600 would be closer to $25 000 before tax. This meant that if he translated his MP's basic remuneration into salary it would come to about $78 000.

But, if he subtracted all the extra expenses he would incur in Ottawa and Windsor, such as accommodation in Ottawa, meals, taxis on wintry days, furniture, pots and pans and other furnishings, small gifts and meals for visiting constituents and flowers for staff on special occasions, he figured his take-home pay out of the $78 000, after expenses, would be about $60 000 compared to the $100 000 that was his share of the income at the law firm.

Charles took the time to review his allowances, to see if he would be able to recoup some of his lost income.

Travel Allowances (1984)

- Maximum of 52 travel points per year for travel between Ottawa and the constituency—10 of the 52 may be used for travel to any place in Canada—3 of the 10 may be used by the spouse, and/or a designated family member—9 of the 52 may be used by a family member and/or full-time eligible staff for travel to and from the constituency;
- Travel within the constituency by road, water or air is limited to between $1 180 and $5 900 per year depending on the type of riding. This portion of the allowance was restricted to the member.
- Air: First Class for Member (1 point deducted); spouse or designated family member may travel First Class (1 1/2 points) or economy (1 point)—the First Class entitlement was established in 1980; economy class for staff.
- Bus or Boat: within the allowance.
- Train: Unlimited; VIA rail passes are issued to both the member and the family; not included in the 52 point entitlement unless meal and accommodation charges are claimed.
- Car: travel to and from Ottawa under the 52 point system at $.236 per kilometre, to a maximum of the cost of round trip air travel; travel within the constituency was also at $.236 per kilometre to the established maximum.

Pension Benefits (1984)

Someone said that the "life-expectancy" of an MP is actually not much more than four-and-one-half years, and to get a pension Charles would have to be in office for six years.
- Mandatory contribution of 11%.
- No minimum age (to receive pension).
- Full pension after 15 years, based on 75% of the six highest consecutive years' earnings, otherwise 5% per year for those qualifying.
- The pension is indexed to rise according to the Consumer Price Index—retired members are not entitled to indexing until age 60 when they receive the benefit on a cumulative basis of all indexing awarded since the date of their retirement.
- The spousal benefit consists of 60% of the Member's allowance, plus 10% for each dependent child (subject to specified maxima).

Office Allowances (1984)

Charles would have to interview staff for his Ottawa office and look at possible constituency offices in his riding. He was allowed: office supplies and equipment provided by the House of Commons—including a word processor, up to four typewriters (including one electronic memory typewriter), a photocopying machine, a television set and dictation equipment. Then, a total allowance of $94 200 for both Ottawa and constituency office staff (with a maximum of $75 400 for Ottawa). There were no restrictions on the number of staff, but there was a maximum salary of $36 729 for any staff member.

He'd calculated that with his office budget he could hire a senior assistant and an administrative assistant, plus a staff person at the constituency office. Charles thought that the special allowance of $2 000 to enable new members to buy furniture and equipment in addition to what was already in the office on Parliament Hill would be useful.

In Windsor, he headed out to look at possible constituency offices. He knew that he would have to stick within the budget. In the House of Commons' book it said "up to $10 650" for rent, and it had to be taken out of his office operations budget.

As he was driving from place to place, it suddenly

occurred to Charles that his $.236 per kilometre automobile allowance could be used "for travel within the constituency," which he was actually doing at that very moment.

Charles decided he'd better drive to Ottawa to arrange for an apartment in the capital. Checking the book again he saw that under the 52-point system he could make 52 round trips a year by air or car. Having established that the exact distance between his constituency and Ottawa was 760 kilometres, Charles did some quick calculations. For the round trip this worked out to 2 x 760 km x $.236 = $358.72. But, for every round trip he made by car he would have to deduct the equivalent trip he could have taken by air. If he kept the car long enough it would pay for itself and then some.

Once in Ottawa, Charles found a one-bedroom apartment from which he could walk to the Hill in about 15 minutes. The rent was $565 all-inclusive, except for electricity, and would have to be paid out of his own pocket ($6 780 annually).

Charles' wife and two children came to the Visitor's Gallery to witness his first day as an MP. His wife told him: "We read your House of Common guide and discovered that we, too, had some benefits. The only problem was that the regulations under Travel said that the spouse and/or a designated family member could use 9 of your 52 travel points to fly round trip from the constituency to Ottawa, but we couldn't figure out whether the children could qualify as the designated family member". Finally we agreed that I would fly at House of Commons expense, and we'd buy round trip economy tickets for the children using our own money."

Soon, Charles's constituency office was up and running, and a newsletter (Householder) had gone to every home in the community. These would be paid for by the House of Commons up to four times a year, and would keep his constituents up to date with things in Ottawa as well as helping to assure his re-election. This would mean he could hopefully fulfill the required six years of service in order to qualify for a pension.

In 1986, Charles was named to the Finance and Economic Affairs Committee, one of the most important committees in the House. He didn't receive additional remuneration to serve on the committee but, when the committee travelled, the expense allowance covered any additional costs that might be incurred.

Charles survived another election in 1988 and was re-assigned to his old committee.

By February 1992 Charles had been in Ottawa for almost eight years. A lot had happened in that time. Salaries, allowances under all categories, and costs attached to members' services had changed dramatically since he first came to the House in 1984. Although he is extremely hard-working, Charles knows he won't become a committee chairman, nor will he be appointed to cabinet. He is looking towards the future. He knows another election is due in 1993 and the odds are heavily weighed against his winning his riding again. He therefore expects to find himself rejoining his law firm at the end of 1993.

Charles checked his most recent House of Commons book and looked at various salaries, allowances and emoluments as they stand in 1992.

When Charles had come into the House in the fall of 1984, the Sessional Allowance was $52 800, and the Tax-Free Allowance was, $17 600. In 1991 these figures had increased to $64 400 and $21 300. In terms of "actual earnings", taking the tax-free allowance into account, this came to $106 247. He noted that members would be receiving no increase in 1992 due to the across-the-board government restraint program. This would have an effect on his pension and he made some calculations, based on the pension formula, which had not changed in recent years.

Charles pinpointed the first week of September 1993 as the date for the next election. This would mean that when he retired he would have completed nine years of service. Based on the formula of averaging the best consecutive six years' earnings, including a sessional allowance of perhaps $67 900 which he projected for 1993, he came up with a mean amount of $62 900. In these calculations he noted that he could not include any tax-free allowance for pensionable purposes. He then applied the formula of 5% per year of his nine years' service and found that he would be entitled to a pension of 45% of $62 980. This came to $28 300.

Fortunately his retirement allowance would start immediately in 1993. He would be 44 years of age, and the pension would continue for life. Indexing would be withheld until age 60 when he would receive the sum of all indexing awarded since the date of his retirement. Charles felt he was lucky. If he had been a civil servant rather than a politician he would have had to have worked for approximately 18 years to receive the same pension, which, in that case, would be payable at age 55.

Based on a standard life expectancy chart, Charles can expect to live until he's 73. Therefore, before indexing, he will earn $820 700 in pensions for nine years of public service.

In 1992, Charles also realized how much the travel allowance for MPs had changed in nine years. For one thing, he could now be reimbursed for taxi fares up to $45, with receipts only being required for amounts exceeding $20; there was also a per diem of $45.45 for the reimbursement of meals and incidental expenses while members are in travel status. It looked more and more like the famous annual "tax-free allowance" could now be treated as actual pay with the allowance going into Charles's pocket instead of towards expenses. Car mileage had gone up to $.32 from $.236. This meant if he drove the car back and forth from Windsor to Ottawa he would be reimbursed $486.40 instead of the old $358.72. This wasn't bad, because in nine years of driving, particularly when the House wasn't in Session, the mileage allowance had actually paid for more than the cost of a car.

But the greatest increase had taken place in the number of points available for travel, both for the MP and his or her spouse and children. As of 1989, members were allotted 64 points per annum as opposed to the previous 52. All 64 points (a point being the equivalent of one round trip) could be used for travel between the constituency or Ottawa, and any place in Canada. In addition, an MP could allocate six of the 64 points to designated family members for return trips between the member's constituency and Ottawa (15 of these points could be used by a member's office staff). In 1984, travel had been strictly limited to round trips between the constituency and Ottawa.

Charles decided to look at possible travel requirements for himself and his family in 1992, and came up with some calculations. What really surprised him was that he would be reimbursed by the House of Commons for these expenses under the 64-point system of travel.

Charles calculated that during 1992 he would make 40 round trips from Windsor to Ottawa, 30 by air and 10 by car. Air fare, according to the travel agent, was $502.90, and car mileage reimbursement $486.40.

- Total for air travel: 30 x $502.90 = $15 087
- Total for driving: 10 x $486.40 = $4 864
- He then built in 4 round trip air flights to Ottawa for his wife: 4 x $502.90 = $2 011.60
- and one-round trip each for the two children: 2 x $502.90 = $1 005.80

Charles had some official business travel in mind to other parts of Canada (although he realized that under terms of the House guidelines he didn't need to declare the purpose of his trip in order to qualify to have his air fare paid for by the House of Commons). He wanted to fly to Regina to meet with some economists at the University of Saskatchewan. The travel agent quoted $1 208.73.

Charles then had Sidney, Nova Scotia on his list where he wanted to talk to some government officials in charge of economic expansion in Cape Breton. The fare quoted was $849.58.

His wife would have to fly to Halifax, probably twice during the year, in order to see her mother. This would mean two round-trip flights for her. Ordinarily this would be a considerable extra expense for Charles, and he was relieved to find this qualified for payment by the House of Commons. This meant saving himself the flight costs of 2 x $988.68, or $1 977.36.

He was fortunate enough to be able to make reservations for the March school break at a ski lodge in Whistler, B.C. This is where the 64-point system would come in handy. The family of four could fly to Vancouver round-trip for $604.55 each based on an excursion fare. Thus, Charles is saved the expense of 4 x $604.55 = $2 418.20.

In the summer Charles planned to accompany his son to Victoria, again on personal business. He saved himself another $2 192.43. His daughter's flight to summer camp would have been $437.75 out of Charles's pocket if it hadn't fallen under the point travel system.

Charles also had to take one other factor into account. He was a member of three of the eight Parliamentary Associations it is possible for MPs to join. The Commonwealth Parliamentary Association held his main interest, however he did attend occasional meetings of the Canada-U.S. group, and the Canada-Japan group. It was the "CPA" which would be having its regional meeting in Canberra, Australia in mid-August, and though this trip would not come under the 64-point travel provisions, all out-of-pocket expenses would be met by the Directorate of the Commonwealth Parliamentary Association in Ottawa. Charles found that he could purchase round trip economy fares to Canberra from Windsor for his wife and himself at $2 100. Therefore the government, through another funding mechanism, would pay an additional $4 200 (2 x $2 100) in flight costs plus full expenses for the five-day meeting. Having reviewed these various proposals, Charles calculated amount for anticipated 1992 travel:

Windsor to Ottawa (round trips)	
Charles:	
by air	$ 15 087.00
by car	4 864.00
Wife (air):	2011.60
Children (air):	1 005.80
Charles to Regina	1 208.73
Charles to Sidney	849.58
Wife to Halifax	1 977.36
Family to Whistler	2 418.20
Charles and son to Victoria	2 192.43
Daughter to summer camp	437.75
Charles and Wife to Canberra	4 200.00
Total Travel Expenses	**36 252.45**

Charles was inwardly concerned about the efficacy of some of the proposed trips when he reviewed these final figures, even though they would be quite within the House of Commons guidelines. He counted how many of the 64-travel points would be applied. He found that if he went ahead with his plans 57 out of 64 points would have been used. Undoubtedly some of the Windsor constituency staff would have to visit Ottawa and vice-versa. The seven extra points would cover this or any emergencies.

Charles checked the Budgetary Estimates for the House of Commons for Fiscal 1991/92 and found that the average travel costs for members in 1991 came to $33 900. On that basis he decided to go ahead with his plans. He felt somewhat justified in letting the House help him with some of the expen-

ditures which he would otherwise have had to pay for out of his own pocket, because his pay package didn't seem to reflect the demands of the job of an MP.

While he was looking at the House of Commons Guidelines, Charles thought he'd better review the levels of his current Office Operating Budget in relation to 1984. He remembered that in 1984 he had a total office budget of $94 200 for both Ottawa and the constituency, and that he could pay a maximum of $36 729 to his senior staff person. For 1992, the budget for the office had gone up to $164 600 for urban/rural constituencies of less than 25 000 square kilometres. This applied to his riding. And the salary for the top staffer could now be as high as $58 700.

In addition, Charles noted that "Elector and Geographic Supplements" had been added for constituencies that included more than 70 000 electors or are more than 8 000 square kilometres in area. These were on a sliding scale ranging from $5 150 annually to $20 600. These allowances were designed to "supplement" the Members' Operating Budgets, it said. Approximately 142 members of the House of Commons qualified for this extra stipend and Charles felt that his constituency would probably meet the criteria, and he would receive an additional $5 150.

In October 1990 all members became entitled to claim reimbursement of up to $6 000 for accommodation, meals and incidental expenses incurred by them while they are in travel status. This was fortunate, because Charles's apartment rental, which had been $565 in 1984, had gone up to $804. This new allowance would help cover that.

In the cool light of day, and trying to view his own circumstances as dispassionately as he could, Charles realized that in 1992 MPs were now having to take very little out of their own pockets to pay for expenses. The tax-free allowance which was established so many years ago, was no longer fulfilling its original purpose of offsetting the official out-of-pocket expenses of a member. Instead, it should now be considered personal income, and in fact, some members stood to gain additional personal income through the new travel provisions which were so "open-ended".

It seemed to Charles that he was right to wonder in 1984 why MPs weren't getting a salary. "Surely," he said to himself, "the time has come to call a spade a spade. The $64 400 sessional allowance should be rolled in with the $21 300 tax-free allowance. In terms of 'real money' it would exceed $100 000." He then prepared an accounting of his overall support package at the House of Commons.

Total Cost to Legislature (1992)

Sessional Allowance	$ 64 400.00
Tax Free Allowance	21 300.00
Travel Allowance	36 252.45
Constituency Support	169 750.00
Travel Status Support	6 000.00
Total	**297 702.45**

Total Cost to Legislature (Post-Retirement)

Pension (before indexing, to age 73)	820 700.00

Post-Retirement Remuneration (Age 44)

MP Pension	28 300.00
Law Firm Salary	150 000.00

Charles was troubled over the secure type of life and perquisites he had enjoyed in Ottawa. Admittedly he had a workload that was large by any standards, nevertheless as he prepared to go back into "civy street", he could see that there was a big gap between his parliamentary life and that of his law colleagues and friends back home in Windsor.

CHAPTER FIVE

Pension Benefits

ALL MEMBERS of the Senate, House of Commons, and the provincial and territorial legislatures who qualify under the terms and conditions outlined by their institution receive a pension, or a "retirement allowance" as it is better known in legislature circles. The service requirement for eligibility ranges from a minimum of one year in Saskatchewan through five years and/or two elections (twice elected) in Nova Scotia, Ontario and several other provinces, to a maximum of eight years or three legislatures in Manitoba.

In some Canadian legislatures there is no minimum age requirement for the payment of retirement allowances. For instance, those members who meet the service stipulations may collect their pensions immediately upon leaving the House of Commons and the New Brunswick legislature. Pensions for members of the legislatures of Ontario, Manitoba and Alberta are payable when their age and years of service total 55. The British Columbia legislature has a minimum age requirement of 55 or when the age and years of service total 60. Saskatchewan and Yukon have a minimum age requirement of 55 (with an option for a reduced pension at 50). Northwest Territories stipulates a minimum age of 55.

Retirement allowance plans for members were principally established between 1955 and 1970, with Prince Edward Island, Nova Scotia, New Brunswick and Manitoba later implementing plans between 1967 and 1971. The Northwest Territories and the Yukon developed pension legislation in 1983 and 1984 respectively.

As can be seen, the service and age requirements vary considerably between jurisdictions, as do the contribution levels which range from none by members in Yukon to a high of ten percent of the basic annual indemnity for federal MPs, plus one percent for supplementary benefits payable after age 60. The mean average contribution level by members of the House of Commons and all provincial and territorial legislatures, exempting Yukon, is 8.9 %. It is difficult to assess why the arrangements for retirement allowances differ so much between legislatures. In fact, little seems to have changed from the beginning of the last decade, although Nova Scotia improved its provisions and three of four provinces increased the contribution levels by members by an average of 1.5% to 2%.

Traditionally (and to this day) members' retirement allowance plans have been administered by the Ministry of Finance, the Ministry of Government Services, or their equivalents. The terms and conditions of the various plans are, however, largely the prerogative of the government, the prime minister or the premier, who have the final say in any amendments to the Legislative Assembly Retirement Allowances Act, or its equivalent. They also make the final determination with regard to members' indemnities, allowances and salaries. Obviously, those who have this authority take advice from professional and political sources. In some cases, a body outside the government is appointed to make an inquiry and report on members' retirement allowances.

As mentioned in the Remuneration Entitlements chapter, the Nova Scotia Commission on Inquiry on Remuneration of Elected Provincial

Officials reports to the Speaker annually on matters relating to compensation and benefits. In 1989, this Commission was asked by the Speaker to look into the question of allowances being paid under the Members' Retiring Allowances Act. It appears that the majority, if not all recommendations of the Commission, were accepted by the government. This is an example of an exception to the rule in terms of how retirement allowance standards are set for Canadian legislatures.

Pension plans for most employees in municipalities, government or business are funded. Funding means that sufficient interest is generated from investments by equal employee/employer contributions to a plan so that an actuarial amount of retirement income is paid to the recipient for his or her lifetime, usually with an indexing factor build in for inflation. Retirement allowance plans (pensions) for members of the Senate, House of Commons and the provincial and territorial legislatures are not funded. This means that the plans do not pay their own way because the matching payments by the legislators and the government have over the years been insufficient to create an adequate pool of capital.

The only way around this conundrum is for government actuaries to annually determine the shortfall in contribution to the members' retirement allowances fund and for the government to make payments from the Consolidated Revenue Fund (the main income base of the government) directly into members' pension fund. This process is known as "topping up". The amounts drawn for this purpose by various governments are recorded as a bookkeeping entry against the Consolidated Revenue Fund, and the funds are usually added as an additional item to the budgetary Estimates of the Legislative Assembly for transfer to the Minister of Finance or the Treasurer. The actual dollars involved in this type of transaction depend on an actuarial evaluation of the plan in question to determine the shortfall. In the instance of the Ontario Legislature, amounts of $1 million to $2 million have been transferred to that Plan from time to time. It is possible that the Plan could be deficient in excess of $10 million. The deficit of the fund intended to provide pensions for members of the House of Commons would be considerably larger than that of Ontario.

The problem of the funding of members pensions is compounded by the indexing of retirement allowances in all jurisdictions in Canada (mostly according to the Consumer Price Index), with the exception of Newfoundland where there is no post-retirement adjustment. In Ontario, the Speaker has statutory authority to adjust existing pensions, subject to the approval of the Board of Internal Economy, and in Yukon increases are by regulation, on the recommendation of the Members' Services Board.

In six jurisdictions what constitutes payment of a "full" pension to members is usually predicated on a formula that establishes 15-20 years as the period of service required in order to draw a pension that represents 75% of the average annual remuneration over the final one-to-six years of being a member. In one case the level is 70% (the standard normally set by government and other pension plans), and elsewhere, 80% and even unlimited.

There is another factor that has a considerable bearing on the level of retirement allowances paid to former members of Canada's legislatures: legislation is in place in some jurisdictions which permits serving members to make contributions to the retirement allowance plan by including the annual non-taxable allowance as part of the total remuneration package. This means that members of some medium- and smaller-sized legislatures who receive indemnities (salaries) considerably less than those of some larger legislatures can, in fact, receive pensions which can be as large or larger than those paid by some large legislatures. The legislatures which permit the indemnity and non-taxable allowance to be added together for pension purposes are Newfoundland, Prince Edward Island, Nova Scotia, Manitoba, Saskatchewan, Alberta and British Columbia. It is interesting to note that Newfoundland excluded the non-taxable allowance for contribution purposes until 1987, while Nova Scotia included the non-taxable allowance in 1983. The other jurisdictions all allowed this practice prior to 1982, with the exception of British Columbia, which introduced the provision that year.

The following examples are provided in order to illustrate the effect that rolling the indemnity and non-taxable allowance together has on pension income for retired members of Manitoba and British Columbia as compared to those of Ontario which permits contributions to be made on the indemnity alone. The figures provided are based on the indemnities and non-taxable allowances and the application of the formulas outlined for the respective provincial legislatures in the Pension Benefits Table accompanying this analysis, and utilizing researched indemnity and non-taxable allowance figures of immediate past years. In all cases, the retirement allowance figures listed are based on a member having completed 15 years of pensionable service and meeting the age requirements. It is difficult to provide figures in absolute terms due to the complicated structuring of some of the annual increments that have taken place in several jurisdictions in the past couple of years, however the amounts listed are as accurate an approximation as can be provided under the circumstances.

Sample 1992 Retirement Allowance for members who are only permitted to make pension contributions based on their indemnity (salary):

- Ontario
  1992 indemnity $44 665
  full pension $32 837

Sample 1992 Retirement Allowances for members who are permitted to make pension contributions based on their indemnity and non-taxable allowance combined:

- Manitoba
  1992 indemnity $27 986
  tax-free allowance $13 982
  total pensionable earnings $41 945
  full pension $27 300
- British Columbia
  1992 indemnity $32 812
  tax-free allowance $16 406
  total pensionable earnings $46 218
  full pension $33 765

Because Manitoba and British Columbia allow the tax-free allowance to be rolled in with the indemnity, the actual pension almost equals the final, 1992 salary in those provinces. It also means that the British Columbia pension actually exceeds that for members of the Ontario Legislature, although the annual indemnity of British Columbia is almost $12 000 less.

It is a strange anomaly that pension legislation in seven jurisdictions permits the non-taxable allowance to be added to the indemnity as pensionable income, while the Senate, House of Commons and the legislatures of New Brunswick, Quebec and Ontario do not make provisions for this practice. The situation is further complicated because it is the former group which, for the most part, provide their members with the highest non-taxable allowance in

Canada. Newfoundland, Nova Scotia, Manitoba, Alberta and British Columbia have a non-taxable allowance which is 50% of the indemnity (the maximum level permitted by Revenue Canada Taxation).

The fact that an allowance which is non-taxable (provided originally to meet the official out-of-pocket expenses of members) is automatically added to the indemnity (salary) to produce pension income is a further dichotomy, as the allowance is actually treated as income rather than a non-taxable, official business expense. The fact that seven provinces are treating the tax-free allowance as members' personal income, and that the other jurisdictions by and large do the same thing but do not permit it to be rolled into pensionable income, is sufficient reason for the tax-free allowance to be done away with in every jurisdiction. As proven elsewhere, the allowance no longer serves its original purpose, and what is more, is distorting the pension levels for members of Canadian legislatures so that those who belong to some of the medium-sized and smaller legislatures, in provinces where there are smaller populations, now receive proportionately higher pensions than members of larger legislatures.

In reviewing and comparing some "basic" pension arrangements for members in several jurisdictions and providing sample calculations, it should be remembered that this is the "stripped down" pension (one that includes only the indemnity, or the indemnity plus the tax-free allowance). This covers the entitlement of a "backbench" member—not a member of Cabinet, Leader of the Opposition, Whip, or other holder of official office in a caucus for which remuneration is paid (see Remuneration Entitlements)—nor does it include the per diem payments for committee membership in some provinces. Thus, some members by reason of their office may add additional income to their basic indemnity or indemnity/non-taxable allowance structure for pension purposes.

Premiers, cabinet ministers (and most Speakers who receive salaries equivalent to cabinet ministers, and add those salaries to their members' basic indemnity, or indemnity/tax-free allowance for pension purposes) receive pensions which are considerably higher than those of backbenchers. In the House of Commons and Ontario where the retirement allowance may become immediately payable based on the formula "years of service plus age equals

55" relatively young cabinet ministers can retire and qualify for hefty pensions. It would be possible, for example, for an Ontario member who was elected in 1975 at the age of 25, and who had served as a member of Cabinet from 1987 to 1992, to retire at the end of 1992, aged 42 (years of service plus age = 55), with an annual pension of approximately $56 000. Cost of living "catch-up" increments would not be payable until age 60.

Turning to the House of Commons, and perhaps a more typical example, a member could have been elected in 1979 at the age of 42 and served as an opposition member before moving up in seniority when the government came to power in 1984. In 1986 he or she joined Cabinet and now plans to retire at the age 56 in 1993. His or her pension, which may be collected immediately, will be not less that $78 000, and is indexed to rise according to the Consumer Price Index. He or she will not be restricted from taking a position as chairman of a Crown Corporation or any equivalent salaried position in a quasi-government agency or, of course, in private business. The House of Commons pension will remain in effect.

The question of the level and fairness of elected members' pensions in Canada in comparison to most other pension plans is a debate that has gone on for some time. One of the key arguments that is put forward in support of pensions which are considerably more generous than any other in Canada, is that if good people are to be encouraged to go into politics and serve their country, then they should not be at a personal disadvantage in terms of salary, benefits, pensions and the type of perquisites which they might have had in their previous career. There is no question that political life disrupts so-called "normal" life, and the fact that an elected member very often has to fight a number of elections in a comparatively short period of time adds to this disruption. A member elected to the House of Commons in 1972 would have had to seek re-election in 1974, 1979, 1980, 1984 and 1988. This could be seen as an obstacle course of considerable proportion in comparison to the careers of most business executives. In order for elected members to get some type of "job security" they have had to make a point of winning elections to try and stay in office for as long as possible. With this uncertain livelihood, and having stepped out of their previous careers, a case was made for the provision of some

type of "buffer" so that a defeated or retiring member would be eased back into private life and not have to face undue hardship in the long run for having sought elected office.

The idea of compensating legislators in Canada for the inherent risks faced in running for elected office probably made sense during the 1960s and 1970s, a time when those in the working world expected to enter a job and stay with the same organization for many years. However, in the 1980s and 1990s, due to massive changes developing in the economic structuring of the country, career patterns in all areas of society began to be altered, and in 1992 the concept of job security has all but vanished. This means that the original idea of providing politicians with some type of special financial cushioning to compensate them for a period of uncertain employment is at odds with what is happening to the constituents they represent. The idea, in particular, of providing "beefed up" indexed pensions which offer constant protection and security to the retired member as he or she advances through life runs counter to what ordinary citizens can expect now or in the future.

How do the pensions of MPs and members of provincial legislatures equate with those employed in the private sector, or as civil servants in government departments? First of all, there are a large number of Canadians who, although employed full-time, will receive no pension at all. There are also those who will receive pensions not indexed against inflation. Finally, there are those who are civil or public servants, employees of large public institutions and those who work for medium- to large-sized organizations relating to the private sector, who will receive pensions which are indexed. It is only the latter group whose pension entitlements can be compared to those of Canadian politicians, and they do not fare very well.

First of all, private pension plans are usually predicated on the employee working for 35 years in order to receive what is described as a "full" pension, normally 70% of an averaging of several final years of salary (the "best" years). If the employee elects to receive his or her pension at an age less than 60 (and in some cases 55), then pension payments are reduced on a percentage basis until the retiree reaches the qualifying age for a full pension. For the purposes of comparison with MPs and the private sector, should a 40 year-old employee who is a member of a private pension plan, say, after 17 years with an organization move away to another job, he or she may either leave their pension contributions in the "company pension plan", or under the provisions of "portability" which exist under certain conditions, have them moved, together with the employer's share of the contributions, to the new job. The employee may not draw an immediate pension or, in fact, any type of reduced pension until at least age 55.

The actual pension level at any given point during employment is usually determined by multiplying the years of service by two percent a year, and then applying this against the final average salary formula to obtain a dollar amount. Thus, 2% x 17 years of service = 34% of the final average salary, or 2% x 35 years of service = 70% of the final average salary ("full" pension).

Using this formula we can take a typical civil servant in Ontario who joined a government department in 1975 (paralleling the elected member mentioned earlier), and decides to leave the public service in 1992 after 17 years of service. The final salary of the civil servant in 1992 is the same as that of the politician $77 375. The politician's pension accrued at the rate of five percent per year so that after fifteen years he or she qualifies for a "full" pension. The civil servant has had an accrual rate of two percent per year, or 34% of the final salary. In order to receive a "full" pension of 70% of the final average, the civil servant would have had to work for 35 years (age plus years of service = 90). Applying these formulas, the Ontario politician would retire in 1992 at age 42 with a full pension of $56 000 per year, payable immediately, with indexing (determined every year by the Speaker and Board of Internal Economy) accruing to his or her pension account and to be paid in a lump sum at age 60, when the member would receive an actuarial adjusted pension which would be considerably in excess of $56 000. On the other hand, the civil servant with the equivalent time served would, on retirement, have accrued a pension of about $25 000 which could only be received at a reduced rate when he reached the age of 55, and not in full until 65.

What this means in reality is that the retired politician would receive eighteen payments of $56 000 by the time he or she reached 60, a total slightly in excess of $1 million, while the civil servant with the same length of service and salary structure would receive no pension monies during the same period.

If this example is transferred to the House of Commons and a cabinet cinister retiring in 1993 with a pension of $78 000 payable immediately, the federal civil servant with the equivalent length of service and salary structure would receive approximately $35 000 payable in full not before age 65.

Pensions for employees outside government do not exceed those in government, except in unusual cases, therefore the pension arrangements for the person on the street are also considerably restrained and modest in comparison to that of the politician.

In order to attempt to assess pension levels of Canadian politicians and to arrive at a conclusion as to whether they are fair and reasonable, or whether, in fact, notwithstanding the "uniqueness" of the job, the formulas for their retirement allowances are excessive, some comparisons with pension levels of U.S. state legislatures can be made.

Sample Legislators' Pensions [1]

Canada	Pop. (million)	Salary	Approx. Pension
Ontario	10	$ 45 000	$ 33 000 [2]
British Columbia	3.2	49 000	34 000 [3]
Manitoba	1.1	42 000	27 000 [2]
Prince Edward Island	0.13	42 000	23 500 [4]
United States			
California	30	50 000	21 500 [5]
New York	18	57 000	16 000 [6]
Illinois	12	36 000	23 000 [7]
Michigan	9	46 000	29 000 [7]

[1] Canadian pensions are based on contributions ranging from 7% to 10%. U.S. pensions are based on contributions ranging from 8% to 11.5%, hence the reduced pension.
[2] When the age and years of service total 55.
[3] Age 55, or when the age and years of service total 60.
[4] A minimum age requirement of 50 years.
[5] Age 60, or following twenty years of service.
[6] Age 62, following ten years of service.
[7] Age 55.

The Sample Legislators' Pensions Table is based on 1991 salary figures and provides approximate pensions in Canadian dollars for retiring members with 15 years service in some Canadian and U.S. state legislatures. The U.S. legislatures are designated "full-time" legislatures, as are the Canadian. The figures listed are based on contributions made from basic pensionable remuneration. (A detailed listing of American legislators' pension arrangements appears on Page 207.)

The U.S. individual pension levels are considerably less than the Canadian for the same period of legislative service with the exception of Michigan, however members' pensions cannot be paid out in that state until age 55. Illinois also withholds pensions until age 55, and California and New York set the age at 60 and 62 respectively.

Legislators in the assemblies of the four largest states receive smaller pensions than the sample of Canadian legislatures with the exception of Michigan, which pays more than Prince Edward Island. California, New York, and Illinois, however, now provide smaller pensions to their members than does the Prince Edward Island legislature for the same length of service, and the U.S. legislators may not collect their pensions until they are five to twelve years older than Prince Edward Island members.

It is worth noting that out of the 52 U.S. states, the legislatures in 26 of those states gear the pensions of their lawmakers to state employees' standards. In the sample provided, this includes New York and Illinois, however the California and Michigan legislatures do not relate the pensions for their members to those of state employees. In any event, the size and terms of the pensions provided by the four largest states, considering the population of those states and the length of legislative sessions, are far more modest than almost any jurisdiction in Canada.

The reason U.S. state legislature pensions are much smaller than those in Canada probably relates to the fact that, in terms of historical tradition, serving as a state legislator was not a full-time occupation in most legislatures and incumbents were able to carry on with their outside profession between sessions. For most states this tradition still carries on, however that is not so in California, New York, Illinois, Pennsylvania, Michigan, Ohio, Massachusetts and several other states, where the job of lawmaker is full-time.

There are also a large number of "watch-dog" groups in the U.S., including such well-known organizations as Common Cause, a Washington, D.C.-based organization which has the capacity to monitor legislature operations nationwide, and has a reputation for thoroughness and fairness. Citizen groups of all sorts monitor the salaries and pensions of legislators, their attendance records, the conferences they attend and travel. The local media in every state capital (and in the legislators' home town) are quick to report any actual or perceived transgressions on the part of the members. In Canada, an equivalent agency does not exist.

The foregoing, together with the fact that U.S. voters have traditionally been inclined to be a little less trusting of their elected members than have Canadians, have probably combined to put a damper on legislature salaries and pensions, to say nothing of a range of other members' perquisites.

It could be said that the more generous pensions that exist in Canada (as compared to the U.S.) have reflected the Canadian sense of fairness in providing "safety nets" to various segments of society. In this situation, however, it is the elected members (through the premier and the cabinet, in consultation with the opposition leaders) who have determined what they believe to be right. In the past, there has been little opportunity for ordinary citizens to participate in this process, although there have been exceptions, such as the Nova Scotia Committee of Inquiry. Consequently, taxpayers have not been able to decide what is fair and right in terms of pension provisions for those they voted into office, because they simply aren't aware of the facts.

As this review has pointed out, there are a large number of confusing and complex issues at the heart of attempting to determine what is fair, and what is right about retiring allowance plans for Canadian legislators as presently constituted. In order to clarify the situation for Canadians in every province several steps should be initiated.

- In every jurisdiction the shortfall in the members' retirement allowance fund should be clearly spelled out and tabled as a Sessional Paper in the legislature, and any monies drawn on the Consolidated Revenue Fund to add to the retirement allowances fund in the future, should also be made public.

- The formulas governing the members' retirement allowance plan in each jurisdiction, together with current levels of annual remuneration for pension purposes should be tabled in the House each year together with sample calculations, so that the public may be aware of members' pension entitlements. It is clear in 1992 that the whole question of the current level of members' pensions needs to be examined in the light of changing economic and social conditions, and against the broader pension picture throughout Canada. For instance, it has been suggested that no elected member should qualify to receive any pension before age 50. If this were to be the case, then a reasonable severance allowance would have to be put in place to enable the legislator to be integrated back into "mainline" society.

It appears certain that given the overall conditions confronting Canadians in 1992 when politicians are often labelled as lacking in integrity and credibility, they would be wise to no longer place themselves in the position of having to justify their own pension arrangements. A wide range of issues surrounding retirement allowances for elected members should be examined outside the House of Commons or the legislatures, therefore: Members' Pension Commissions should be struck in each jurisdiction consisting of qualified persons from outside the legislature, including persons with actuarial skills, a knowledge of the legislature environment and representatives of the broader community, with the purpose of examining existing legislation governing members' retirement allowances and recommending whatever changes may be required to provide a plan that is fair and equitable for members and the community at large.

Pension Benefits

H of C   **Contribution Level:** 10% of the basic indemnity (contributions based on the tax-free allowance are not permitted). An additional 1% is contributed for supplementary benefits payable after age 60.

Those members receiving salaries in addition to the basic indemnity (e.g. Minister, Whip, Parliamentary Secretary, etc.) may contribute up to 10% of these salaries as well. These addtional contributions are used to purchase further pensionable service credits and increase the retiring allowance payable. An additional year of pensionable service is creditied for each contribution equal to 10% of the sessional indemnity payable for that year.

Minimum Age Requirement: None.

Minimum Service Requirement: 6 years.

Basis of Pension Calculation: Based on the average of the best consecutive 6 years of earnings.

Maximum Pension Level: 75% after 15 years (5% per year of service).

Post-Retirement Adjustment: Indexed to rise according to the Consumer Price Index. Retired members are not entitled to indexing until they reach the age of 60, at which time benefits are received on a cumulative basis of all indexing awarded since the date of retirement.

Spousal Benefit: An annual allowance equal to three-fifths of the basic allowance. To each dependent child, an annual allowance equal to one-tenth of the basic allowance, or, if the member died without leaving a surviving spouse or if the surviving spouse is dead, two-tenths of the basic allowance. The total amount of allowances for dependent children shall not exceed three-tenths of the basic allowance, or, if the member died without leaving a surviving spouse or if the surviving spouse is dead, eight-tenths of the basic allowance.

Newf.   **Contribution Level:** 7% of all indemnities and salaries (including tax-free allowance).

Minimum Age Requirement: When age plus years of service equal 60 (55 in the case of the Premier).

Minimum Service Requirement: Two elections and five years.

Basis of Pension Calculation: Based on the average earnings of the member's best three years. Five percent for each of the first ten years, 4% for each of the five years thereafter and 2.5% for each of the next two years.

Maximum Pension Level: 75%

Post-Retirement Adjustment: None.

Spousal Benefit: 60%

P.E.I. **Contribution Level:** 8.5% of all indemnities and salaries (including tax-free allowance). Legislative Assembly contributes 6.5 times the member's contribution.

Minimum Age Requirement: 50

Minimum Service Requirement: Two elections (twice elected).

Basis of Pension Calculation: Average of last five years as a member. A minister's pension may not exceed 50% of the highest salary year.

Maximum Pension Level: 75% of contributions.

Post-Retirement Adjustment: Indexed to rise according to the Consumer Price Index (8% per year max.).

Spousal Benefit: 60% of the member's allowance. No allowance for dependent children.

N.S. **Contribution Level:** 10% of indemnity, expense allowance and salary payments.

Minimum Age Requirement: 50

Minimum Service Requirement: At least 5 years during two or more General Assemblies.

Basis of Pension Calculation: The average indemnity for the last three years as a member is multiplied by 5% and then multiplied by the total years and months of service (max. 15 years). This formula would also apply to the expense allowance and salary, if applicable.

Maximum Pension Level: 75%

Post-Retirement Adjustment: Indexed to rise according to the Consumer Price Index (6% per year max.).

Spousal Benefit: 60% of the member's allowance. Dependent children receive 10% of member's allowance up to a maximum of four children.

N.B. **Contribution Level:** 9% of all indemnities (excluding the tax-free allowance), 6% of ministerial salary (if applicable). All contributions are matched by the Legislative Assembly.

Minimum Age Requirement: None.

Minimum Service Requirement: Ten sessions. Military service may be counted as pensionable service if certain conditions are met (each year of military service is equivalent to one legislative session).

Basis of Pension Calculation: Highest three year-average.

Maximum Pension Level: Must not exceed sessional indemnity in effect at date of retirement. There is no maximum on the ministerial portion, if applicable.

Post-Retirement Adjustment: Indexed to rise according to the Consumer Price Index (6% per year max.).

Spousal Benefit: 50% of member's allowance. No allowance for dependent children.

Que. **Contribution Level:** 10% of all indemnities (excluding tax-free allowance) up to the amount of the personal exemption under the Quebec Pension Plan, plus 8.2% of excess up to the level of maximum pensionable earnings under the Quebec Pension Plan, plus 10% of the remainder.

Minimum Age Requirement: a) Without reduction: when age and years of service total 65 or more and the member is not less than 50 years of age, or, when the Member reaches the age of 71.

b) With reduction: when the member reaches the age of 50.

Minimum Service Requirement: See Minimum Age Requirement.

Basis of Pension Calculation: 3.5% of the total indemnity received, including any additional indemnity (excluding tax-free allowance), reduced by 0.7% of the maximum pensionable earnings as defined by the Quebec Pension Plan. (70% of the highest three-year average.)

Maximum Pension Level: n.a.

Post-Retirement Adjustment: Indexed on Jan. 1 of each year by the amount by which the rate of increase in the Pension Index exceeds 3%.

Spousal Benefit: A member may elect to replace his or her pension with a life annuity, the benefits of which pass on to the surviving spouse. Such election must be made before the pension begins, and can be either 100% or 50% of the member's entitlement, adjusted accordingly by actuarial analysis.

Ont. **Contribution Level:** 10% of all indemnities and salaries (excluding the tax-free allowance). All contributions are matched by the Legislative Assembly.

Minimum Age Requirement: When age and years of service total 55.

Minimum Service Requirement: 5 years.

Basis of Pension Calculation: Highest 36 month average.

Maximum Pension Level: 75% of highest 36 month average.

Post-Retirement Adjustment: The Speaker has statutory authority to adjust existing pensions, subject to the approval of the Board of Internal Economy.

Spousal Benefit: The greater of 25% of the annual indemnity or 60% of the member's allowance, plus 10% for each dependent child to a maximum of three children.

Man. **Contribution Level:** 7% of all indemnities and salaries (including tax-free allowance).

Minimum Age Requirement: When age and years of service total 55.

Minimum Service Requirement: 8 years or 3 Legislatures.

Basis of Pension Calculation: Average annual indemnity for the last 5 years or, if less than five years of service, for the years served as a member.

Maximum Pension Level: 70% of the above.

Post-Retirement Adjustment: Indexed to rise according to the Consumer Price Index (no maximum).

Spousal Benefit: 60% of the member's monthly allowance. No allowance for dependent children.

Sask. **Contribution Level:** 9% of all indemnities and salaries (including tax-free allowance). Contributions are matched by the government, which increases its contribution as the sign-up age of the member increases (adds 2% if member is between 41 and 50 years of age, and adds 4% if member is 51 or older).

Minimum Age Requirement: 55 (option for reduced pension at 50).

Minimum Service Requirement: One year.

Basis of Pension Calculation: Plan One: (formula style for Members elected prior to April 1, 1979) monthly allowance based on earnings and years of service. Plan Two: (money purchase plan for Members elected on or after April 1, 1979) purchased annuity based on contributions plus earnings of the pension plan.

Maximum Pension Level: None.

Post-Retirement Adjustment: Automatically increased by an amount equal to any increase awarded to retired civil servants.

Spousal Benefit: Plan One: (for members elected prior to April 1, 1979) 60% of the member's pension. Plan Two: (for members elected on or after April 1, 1979) guaranteed life annuity and/or postponed guaranteed life annuity based on amount of contributions plus earnings of the pension plan.

Alta. **Contribution Level:** 7.5% of indemnities, pensionable allowance and salaries received (including service on committees, service as an officer of the House or as a leader of a recognized party in the House).

Minimum Age Requirement: When age and years of service total 55.

Minimum Service Requirement: 5 years (max. 20 years). Eligible periods of prior service in the public sector may be established as pensionable service if the required contributions and interest with respect to that service were paid.

Basis of Pension Calculation: 4% of the member's average pensionable allowance during the three highest consecutive years, multiplied by the total years of pensionable service.

Maximum Pension Level: The 4% base may only be multiplied by years of service up to 20.

Post-Retirement Adjustment: A cost-of-living adjustment may be applied. There is no formula for an automatic annual increase.

Spousal Benefit: 75% of member's normal pension.

B.C. **Contribution Level:** 9% of all indemnities and salaries (including tax-free allowance). Contributions are matched by the Legislative Assembly.

Minimum Age Requirement: 55, or when age and years of service total 60.

Minimum Service Requirement: 7 years, or more than two parliaments.

Basis of Pension Calculation: 5% of the highest four-year average legislative allowances multiplied by the number of years of pensionable service (maximum 16 years).

Maximum Pension Level: None.

Post-Retirement Adjustment: Indexed to rise according to the Consumer Price Index.

Spousal Benefit: Amount is dependent on plan chosen (all plans include a continuing pension for the surviving spouse).

Yukon **Contribution Level:** No contribution by member.

Minimum Age Requirement: 55 years, but Member may elect to receive a reduced amount anytime after 50 years.

Minimum Service Requirement: 6 years.

Basis of Pension Calculation: The average of the highest three consecutive years (basic indemnity, tax-free allowance plus salary) is multiplied by 2.5% of the number of years of service.

Maximum Pension Level: None.

Post-Retirement Adjustment: By regulation upon the recommendation of the Members' Services Board.

Spousal Benefit: A lump-sum payment. (15% of the basic indemnity plus tax-free allowance in force at the time of death, multiplied by the number of years of service.)

N.W.T. **Contribution Level:** 9% of yearly pensionable remuneration and earnings (does not apply to members with 15 years of service).

Minimum Age Requirement: 55

Minimum Service Requirement: 6 years.

Basis of Pension Calculation: The number of years of service since March 10, 1975 (max. 15 years) multiplied by 2% of the average annual pensionable remuneration (excluding earnings) of the four consecutive years of service of the member's choice. The Speaker, Deputy Speaker, chaipersons of the Committee of the Whole, chairpersons of Standing Committees and ministers receive an additional allowance equal to the number of years of service (in that capacity) since March 10, 1975 (max. 15 years) multiplied by 2% of the average annual earnings received by the member during the four consecutive years of service (in that capacity) of the member's choice. If service in that capacity is less than four years, 2% of the average annual earnings in that capacity is multiplied by the years of service in that capacity.

Maximum Pension Level: None.

Post-Retirement Adjustment: A supplementary retirement benefit is paid based on the Benefit Index. The pension allowance is multiplied by the ratio that the Benefit Index for the year in which a given monthly payment falls, bears to the Benefit Index for the year in which the member retired. The pension allowance is subtracted form the resulting figure, and this amount is the supplementary benefit.

Spousal Benefit: An annual allowance equal to 60% of the basic allowance of the member is payable for the life of the surviving spouse. Each dependent child receives an annual allowance equal to 10% of the basic allowance of the member. If the member dies without leaving a surviving spouse, each dependent child receives an annual allowance equal to 25% of the basic allowance of the member until the child reaches the age of majority, marries or ceases to be in full-time attendance at a school or university.

CHAPTER SIX

Accommodation Allowances

IF A business person is required to work in a city other than their home-base, accommodation, meals and other such out-of-pocket expenses are met by the employer, either with a per diem or a reimbursement of costs. In the same way, members of provincial and territorial legislatures who represent constituencies some distance from the capital are provided with an accommodation allowance, designed to wholly, or at least in large measure, offset the extra costs incurred by being away from home. However, in some cases, members who represent ridings either in, or bordering on, the city where the legislature is located, also receive an allowance to defray the cost of meals, etc. This was not the original intent of such an allowance.

In this section, Ontario and Quebec are outlined as examples of jurisdictions where a lump sum of money for each out-of-town member—$13 825 in the case of Ontario and $10 300 in Quebec—may be drawn down to cover the cost of rental accommodation in Toronto and Quebec City. Meal expenses are not provided for. It is appropriate that Ontario has the largest allowance since Toronto has the highest cost of living in Canada. The House of Commons has an maximum annual allowance of $6 000.

All other jurisdictions (except Prince Edward Island which has no accommodation allowance), rely on per diem arrangements to look after their members.

The actual cumulative total of the various financial arrangements for members depends on the number of sitting days of the legislature in question, and in some instances there is a ceiling on the number of days for which a member can claim his or her allowance.

In Newfoundland, based on an average of 80-90 sitting days (the House actually sat longer in 1991) and a per diem for out-of-town members of $40 for meals (without receipts), and up to $75 for accommodation (with receipts), it would be possible for an individual member to receive $9 200-$10 350 annually. A member of the Assembly representing a constituency within the district of St. John's could claim $25 per weekday for meals, with a possible cumulative total of $2 125.

In Nova Scotia, the allowance of up to $85 per day (on submission of receipts) available to members from outside Halifax could mean that they would receive as much as $7 225 per annum, based on an average of 85 sitting days. And in the case of Saskatchewan, based on a maximum of 70 sitting days, members of that Assembly who represent constituencies outside Regina can be reimbursed as much as $10 850 annually, based on a per diem of $155. Similar hospitality is extended to Regina-based members who can claim a per diem of $94, also up to a maximum of 70 sitting days. This could amount to approximately $6 580 annually—well above the provisions of the out-of-town members' accommodation/expense allowance of any other jurisdiction.

The Saskatchewan Accommodation Allowance has risen considerably during the past few years and could be part of the reasoning behind the voluntary decision of Saskatchewan politicians to lower their individual tax-free allowances to $7 622 (see Remuneration Entitlements). In this way the costs incurred for out-of-pocket official expenditures could be allocated as a legitimate charge against the Assembly rather than paying an outright tax-free amount to the member.

Alberta's Capital Residence Allowance is based on an allocation of up to $1 000 a month for members who represent ridings outside Edmonton and must acquire temporary accommodation. British Columbia has an arrangement which provides members who live outside Victoria with an allowance of $100 per day, with ceilings of 60 days when the House is sitting and 20 days when it is not. This would mean a maximum draw of $8 000 for those members. British Columbia also provides a $45 per diem to those members who live in Victoria, or within reasonable commuting distance, which could total $3 600 annually.

The Northwest Territories Legislature sits for an average of 60 days a year and provides its members with a per diem accommodation allowance of $185 (non-accountable) for "members residing outside the locality where the session is being held." This could work out to be as much as $11 100 cumulatively. Members living in the locality where the session is being held receive a per diem of $53 and, using the same formula, could receive as much as $3 180 per annum. However, it should be noted that in the Northwest Territories living costs are considerably higher than most other jurisdictions. The Yukon Legislature meets on an average of 50 days annually, and the Legislature provides actual accommodation expenses for its members plus a per diem of $52.85 for meals and incidental expenses.

By and large, the accommodation allowances seem fair and reasonable in most of the situations outlined, although it would appear that granting an allowance of this type to members residing in, or very near, the capital is stretching the purpose of the allowance considerably. If it is being done either as a way of assuaging the feelings of some members who don't really qualify for an accommodation allowance, or as a means to place more money in the pockets of some members, it is not a good thing. Ordinary Canadians in the regular work force do not receive an allowance from their employer for meals and incidentals if they live in the same city in which they work.

The accommodation allowance for members should be treated as what it is: an allowance to defray the out-of-pocket expenses of members who represent constituencies away from the seat of government and who should be reimbursed for the additional expenses they are forced to incur by reason of being away from home.

Accommodation Allowances

H of C   An annual maximum of $6 000 for reimbursement of travel status expenses when the member is at least 100 km away from his or her primary residence. Receipts are required for accommodation, which must not be in a residence owned by the member.

Newf.   Members who reside more than 60 km from St. John's are reimbursed up to $40 per day for meals (without receipts) and $75 per day for accommodation (with receipts). Members living in, or representing a St. John's district, may claim only $25 per weekday for meals. The Speaker, ministers and the Leader of the Opposition are not entitled to a meal allowance.

P.E.I.   None.

N.B. $60 per day for accommodation and $40 per day for meals when the House is sitting. Ministers are not eligible. Established and reviewed by the Standing Committee on Legislative Administration 1990.

N.S.   Up to $85 per day on submission of receipts. Established and reviewed by the Legislature. Last revised Jan. 1, 1991.

Que. $10 300 per year. Members may rent or buy their accommodation, although the allowance is based on rental values. The President, Leader of the Official Opposition, Government House Leader, Opposition House Leader, Chief Government Whip, Chief Opposition Whip and the Caucus Chairman of the Government Party receive an allowance of $13 300. Established and reviewed by the Office of the National Assembly.

Ont.   Up to $13 825 for members and $14 825 for ministers and party leaders. The Speaker is provided with an apartment in the Legislative Building. Members may rent or buy, but claims on owned accommodation are restricted to specified operating expenses. Established and reviewed by the Board of Internal Economy in 1974. Last revised April 1, 1991.

Man. Members representing a constituency that is wholly outside the city of Winnipeg receive an allowance of $50 per day when the House is sitting. However, if the member maintains residences in both the constituency and Winnipeg, he or she receives $82 per day (unless the House is adjourned for 10 days or more) up to a maximum of 90 days per session. Those members who maintain two residences receive an allowance of $41 per day for five days a week while the Legislature is not in session. Established by statute. Revised in 1988 and annually indexed to the cost of living.

Sask. $94 per day for Regina members, $155 per day for other members (including the Speaker) while the House is sitting, up to a maximum of 70 sitting days. Intersessional caucus per diem: the same rates are applied up to a maximum of 24 days per year. Established by the Board of Internal Economy in a 1989 directive. The annual increase is tied to the Consumer Price Index for Saskatchewan.

Alta. Temporary Residence Allowance: Allowances under this category may be claimed only by members representing constituencies outside the city of Edmonton. When a member must live in a temporary residence in, or near, the city of Edmonton in order to carry out the duties of his or her office, the member may claim an allowance of $100 per day for accommodation, meals and living expenses in accordance with the following guidelines.

Sessional Allowance: A member may claim one of the following allowances:

a) Non-sessional allowance of $100 per day for each day (max. 30 days within a three-month period) that the member is in, or near, Edmonton on public or offi-

cial business and has maintained that Edmonton residence; or,

b) Capital Residence Allowance of $1 000 per month if the member owns or leases a temporary residence in the member's name or, in the case of a part month, $100 per day to a maximum of $1 000. This allowance applies only when the House is not sitting.

B.C. $45 per day for members representing ridings within the capital district or within commuting distance of the capital. $100 per day for other members. The allowance is paid for the first 60 sitting days of each sitting of the Legislature, plus up to a maximum of 20 days out-of-session when conducting business in the capital.

Yukon When the House is sitting, members are reimbursed for their actual expenses for accommodation, plus $52.85 per day for meals and incidental expenses (no maximum; ministers are excluded). When the House is not sitting, there is a maximum of $8 800 per year, or members may rent accommodation in Whitehorse up to a maximum of $594 per month (effective April 1, 1989), plus up to a maximum of $4 400 per year for meals.

Ministers whose constituencies are outside Whitehorse may claim actual expenses for accommodation plus $52.85 per day when visiting their constituencies, and may rent accommodation in Whitehorse up to a maximum of $594 per month if they maintain a residence in both Whitehorse and their own electoral district (effective April 1, 1989).

N.W.T. "Living Allowances" established by statute in 1988: members residing outside the locality where the session is being held may claim a $185 per day, non-accountable allowance when the House is sitting. Members may rent or buy. Members living in the locality where the session is being held are entitled to a sessional "living allowance" of $53 per day.

CHAPTER SEVEN

Travel Allowances

SINCE 1867, when MPs were authorized travel expenses of six cents per kilometre for a return trip, once per session, between Ottawa and the constituency, travel allowances have been steadily increasing.

The various legislatures take different approaches to providing travel allowances to their members. These tend to be based on the size and population of the jurisdictions involved. Over the years and, it appears, based on original travel concepts established for members of the House of Commons, the provinces and territories have developed their own regulations to meet a number of circumstances.

As far back as 1903, MPs were provided with free and unlimited rail transportation, which also included their spouses and dependent children. This concept advanced over the years to the point where not only the House of Commons provides for the families of members, but similar arrangements are in force in Newfoundland, Quebec, Ontario, Alberta and British Columbia. The original concept of members' spouses being able to travel to the seat of government has, on occasion, been considerably expanded in some jurisdictions so that now spouses and designated children can, if needed, use some of the travel points or round trip allotments to make trips of their own without the member, to places other than Ottawa or the respective provincial capital.

Travel provisions for MPs and senators in Ottawa have now reached the point that in 1992, a 64-point system prevails which translates into 64 round trips annually between the constituency and Ottawa, or the constituency and any other place in Canada. A member, therefore, representing a riding in or near the National Capital Region who would not need the travel points for constituency-to-Ottawa purposes, may use all 64 points for flights to other parts of Canada.

Following the Senate and the House of Commons are Nova Scotia, Quebec, Ontario, Manitoba, Saskatchewan, Alberta and British Columbia which annually make 52 round trips available to the members of their legislatures. In Alberta, air travel between the constituency and Edmonton is unlimited; the 52 round trips only apply to automobile travel.

Of these provinces, Ontario members are permitted to use up to twelve of their 52 round trip allotment for official travel within the province using whatever means of transportation is required, although air travel is limited to regularly scheduled airline flights. Alberta has a similar arrangement in place, although province-wide air travel is limited to five round trips for members. British Columbia is the third jurisdiction to make this provision, however members of that legislature are provided with ten round trips to anywhere in the province in addition to their 52 constituency-capital round trip flights.

Alberta actually goes one step further than any other jurisdiction. There, the member may claim "the reasonable travelling and living expenses of a spouse, family member or guest who accompanies the member to, or joins him or her in Edmonton or, providing the trip is related to the member's public or official business, any other part of the province, subject to the following conditions: *a)* the expenses are related to travelling and living within Alberta, and *b)* no Member may claim for more than six round trips under this category." Alberta also permits a member to claim reasonable travel and living expenses for a spouse, family member or guest who accompanies the member to a function or meeting sponsored by the Commonwealth Parliamentary Association, or any of its regions or branches, or any other parliamentary association, meeting or function attended by the member as a representative of the Legislative Assembly or the Speaker.

In 1975, the Ontario Board of Internal Economy authorized spouses to use up to four of the 52 round trips allocated to the member for travel by air between the constituency and Queen's Park, and up to six such trips by bus or train. In 1981, this allotment was increased so that both spouses and other family members could travel six times a year to Toronto, as in the case of bus or train travel. In 1984, the allotment for spouses and family members was raised to twelve of the 52 round trip flights, as were the bus and train provisions. These allotments have remained constant since that time. Current Ontario regulations do not include any provisions for members' spouses or family members to travel within the province, other than to the seat of government, or to accompany the member to functions outside the province or overseas at public expense.

It has been customary both in the private sector and in the public service, that if a business person or civil servant wished to have a family member or other person accompany them while they were travelling to meetings, conferences etc., then they would have to pay any extra expenses out of their own pocket. During the early 1980s this became an issue at the Ontario Legislature. Several members who were required to travel outside the province (and in one case overseas) with committees of the House, chose to take a family member or friend with them, then submitted some of the personal costs incurred for reimbursement by the legislature. These expenses were not allowed by the legislature accountant because they were outside the members' travel regulations. Similarly, some members felt that if they were nominated to attend an overseas conference as an official representative of the Ontario Legislature, then the expenses of their spouse, or the person accompanying them, should also be covered in full. This was debated by the Board of Internal Economy on several occasions, and it was determined that if the member chose to attend such a meeting, then it was up to him or her to personally look after any additional costs.

During those discussions the point was made on a number of occasions by various members of the Board of Internal Economy that the whole question of extending travel benefits beyond the member could open a real "Pandora's Box". The two most worrisome issues were efficacy and cost. Eventually, several other jurisdictions decided to extend the members' travel allowance provisions. This not only gave some members travel arrangements which are unique only to politicians, but it also provided them with the option of including spouses, family members and friends in these special provisions.

1981 marked the first time that spouses and designated family members could travel by air at public expense to anywhere in Canada. Members, then, were permitted to use three of their travel points for that purpose. In 1989, an MP (or his or her spouse), was permitted to use all of what had then become 64 points for air travel anywhere in Canada and, in addition, a member could allocate as many as six of these to designated family members.

This year the House of Commons budget presentation estimated that because of the "flexibility" introduced in the application of the 64 travel points (referring to spouse and designated family member travel, and the fact that MPs and spouses can now use all 64 points for travel anywhere in Canada) overall travel costs for Fiscal 1991/92 would rise by $3 million. An examination of the House of Commons Estimates for the same period indicates an increase in the number of "special trips" taken by MPs, spouses and designated family members over 1989/90, and an average per-member cost for 1990/91 air travel of $31 600 compared to $25 400 for the previous year. Total travel costs (air, car, etc.) for each member for the same year averaged $37 500.

In comparison to an average cost of $37 500 for federal members' annual travel costs, the travel for members of the Ontario Legislature for 1990/91 averaged $10 500. Thirteen members, however, spent between $20 000 and $31 000, and one member ran up a grand total of $59 600, far above the rest. The average per-member expenditure in Ontario is lower than that of the House of Commons for a number of reasons: *a)* Ontario members are unable to travel outside the province, *b)* members may only make twelve air trips to locations within the province (as a part of their overall 52 round trip allocation), *c)* spouses and family members are limited to twelve constituency-Toronto trips and *d)* there is an annual, public disclosure of all travel expenses.

Rather than giving members an outright 52 round trips to the constituency, Newfoundland provides one round trip per week by any means, when the House is sitting, and reimburses all out-of-pocket expenses. When the House is not sitting, a member may be reimbursed for up to 25 trips between the constituency and St. John's. Based on House sittings which can range from 80 to 110 days, this would mean that 37-42 trips can be made by members at public expense.

New Brunswick provides members with a $200 non-accountable allowance per round trip for expenses, plus an automobile allowance for up to 25 round trips between the constituency and Fredericton when the House is not sitting, and a similar per diem for weekly trips when the House is sitting (there is no air travel for members).

Manitoba provides 52 round trips to its members for travel from the constituency to Winnipeg each year. However all members of the assembly receive an additional car allowance of $344 per month, and members whose constituencies are outside Winnipeg may be reimbursed up to $3 000-$4 000 annually for car mileage.

As can be seen from the information contained in the accompanying list, Alberta has outlined a formula for automobile travel which permits rural members to be reimbursed for up to 60 000 kilometres per year on submission of receipts, based on $0.25 per kilometre; urban members may claim up to 25 000 kilometres at the same rate. That is, of course, in addition to reimbursement for out-of-pocket expenses for regular car maintenance (i.e. fuels, fluids, oil and washes). It should be remembered that travel for members by scheduled airline is unlimited in Alberta.

British Columbia has arrangements in place for members' travel which are similar to those of Alberta. There are special annual allowances provided to all members for travel within their constituencies in addition to their regular reimbursement for car mileage based on 52 round trips annually to the capital. These allowances are: Urban ridings $2 640, Semi-Urban $3 600, Rural $4 800 and $6 000 for coastal or remote ridings, which also qualify for an

additional $6 000 on presentation of receipts.

As can be seen, travel allowances are handled in a variety of ways in different jurisdictions; what is presently in place reflects the unique situation confronting each legislature. In several legislatures there appears to be a desire to provide members whose constituencies are in or near the city where the legislature is located with some type of stipend (either relating to travel or accommodation) to offset the fact that they do not receive a travel allowance equivalent to that of a rural or non-urban member. The wisdom of this, in some cases, is questionable, and certainly not cost-effective. The best example of an attempt to provide members with a benefit for which they would not normally qualify, was the 1989 decision of the House of Commons to authorize a member or his or her spouse to use all of the 64 travel points for travel anywhere in Canada, and that six of these points could be assigned to designated family members. Members whose ridings are in Ottawa or just outside, also qualify for these flights and trips. One would be hard-pressed to explain why those members (and more particularly, their spouses and family members) should be included. The member and his or her spouse and family can fly to any part of Canada at will, 64 times a year, without any questions being asked as to the purpose of the trips. Surely this was not the original intent of the allowance.

Part of the problem in trying to establish standards for members' allowances and services is that things tend to go ahead on an *ad hoc* basic. A policy is no sooner established by the Board of Internal Economy than a special situation arises which runs counter to the policy, usually in the form of a problem raised by an elected member who feels that his or her circumstances are unique and must be taken into account. This is, in fact, how the term "designated family member" arose. In the mid-1980s, a single MP requested that the guidelines be changed so that a child would qualify for round trip travel from the constituency to Ottawa. The fact that a family member other than a spouse was unable to travel to Ottawa at public expense obviously caused a major problem for the member, and the regulation was amended. The decision was a right one, of course, but it brought other factors into play, which, in turn, undoubtedly had a bearing on the current travel provisions for MPs. It is possible that the reason the House of Commons travel allowances are now so "open-ended" has to do with a combination of special cases which have arisen, together with some desire to provide MPs whose constituencies are in or near the National Capital Region, with benefits similar to those representing other constituencies.

Whatever the reasons for the extraordinarily generous provisions accorded MPs in their travel allowances, they don't appear to be sufficient to justify an annual allotment of 64 round trip flights for members and their spouses anywhere in Canada, and for up to six of these trips to be made available to designated family members. The number of trips in this category could be substantially reduced.

Canada's national legislators have travel perquisites which far exceed any of those in the legislatures of the provinces or territories, or, for that matter, those accorded to business executives or professional people in the private sector. At present, the travel provision for federal members of Parliament is open to abuse at the taxpayers' expense.

Travel Allowances

H of C   **General:** Travel entitlements are administered by a Travel Point System through which members are entitled to reimbursement of transportation expenses, exclusive of meals. Each member is allotted a total of 64 return trips in Canada per 12-month period, converted into 64 travel points. The member and/or the member's spouse may use all of the 64 points for travel from Ottawa or the constituency to any destination in Canada; the member may allocate 6 of the 64 points to designated family members for return trips from Ottawa or the constituency to any destination in Canada ("special trips"); the member may allocate 15 of the 64 points to designated family members and/or office staff for trips between the member's constituency and Ottawa ("regular trips"); the member may allocate 9 of the 64 to designated family members for trips between the member's constituency and Ottawa ("regular trips"). Independent of the 64-point travel system, members are entitled to reimbursement of transportation expenses which are charged to their Operating Budget, when travelling within the province or territory in which the constituency is located.

Effective October 1, 1990: members are reimbursed for meals, incidental and accommodation expenses while they are in travel status in Canada, up to a maximum of $6 000 per fiscal year. For meals and incidentals, reimbursement is at the rate of $45.45 per day. Rented or leased accommodation (other than a primary residence) qualifies for reimbursement upon presentation of receipts.

Air: Air travel for the member is by first class. An extra one-half point is deducted for first class travel by family members, although only one-half point is charged for each return trip by a member's preschool aged child. Staff are not entitled to reimbursement for travel by first class.

Train: Under the Railway Act and the Canadian Transport Commission, rail transportation privileges are provided free of charge in Canada to members, their spouses and their dependent children.

Car: $.32 per km (independent of the point system). This rate also applies to travel by privately owned, leased or rented automobile, aircraft or boat.

Newf.   **General:** When the House is sitting, members who reside more than 60 km from St. John's are reimbursed for actual travelling expenses (documentation required) for one return home journey each week. This expense may take the form of car mileage, air fare or car rental (not to exceed two days). When the House is not sitting, members are reimbursed for up to 25 return trips between the central point in their district and St. John's. This expense may take the form of car mileage, air fare or car rental (not to exceed two days).

At any time, members may claim up to four spousal trips per annum (with the Speaker's approval) to be deducted from their 25-trip allowance. Members are entitled to claim two trips to Ottawa per annum (with the Speaker's approval) to be deducted from their 25-trip allowance.

Members are reimbursed for documented travel costs within their constituencies up to an annual maximum of $3 000. Members representing specified constituencies may claim up to $6 000; there are eight such constituencies.

Specific Regulations: Commuter's Allowance: members who reside between 10 and 40 km from the House of Assembly may (with the approval of the Internal Economy Commission) be reimbursed for actual return distance travelled between their place of residence and the House of Assembly. This allowance is only payable on weekdays when the House is sitting.

P.E.I. **General:** Restricted to car travel between the capital and a member's constituency. Members are permitted one round trip and a $25 meal allowance per sitting day, plus three round trips per month when the House is not sitting. No allowance exists for travel within the constituency. Rates are tied to civil service rates: $.30 per km. Established by statute.

Specific Regulations: n.a.

N.S. **General:** Maximum of 52 trips per year by any mode of transportation. Reimbursed upon submission of receipts. Established and reviewed by the Legislature.

Air: By economy class.

Bus and Train: In accordance with the general allowance.

Car: In accordance with the general allowance: $.291 per km. For inside members there is an additional allowance of up to $2 300 for travel within the constituency. For outside members, there is an additional allowance of up to $3 400 for travel within the constituency.

N.B. **General:** A maximum of 25 trips per year by any mode of transportation while the House is not sitting. When the House is sitting, one return journey for each week or part thereof. Includes a non-accountable expense allowance of $200 for each trip, plus mileage. Established in 1972 by statute.

Air: No air travel except to conferences, etc. (Economy class).

Bus and Train: In accordance with the general allowance. Includes a $200 non-accountable allowance and expense allowance.

Car: In accordance with the general allowance. Tied to the civil service rates: up to 7 000 km at $.25, 7 000-14 000 km at $.23, 14 000-30 000 km at $.20, over 30 000 at $.16. No travel allowance within the constituency.

Que. **General:** From the constituency to Quebec City. Maximum 52 trips per year and five trips for family members by any mode of transportation, based on the distance from the capital to the constituency. Also includes accommodation expenses based on the rates for civil servants. Ten additional trips may be claimed by the Deputy Speaker, Opposition House Leader, Deputy House Leaders, Chief Government Whip, Chief Opposition Whip, Assistant Whips, Standing Committee Chairmen and Vice-Chairmen and members of the Office of the National Assembly (BOIE). Established in 1969 and reviewed by the Office of the National Assembly (BOIE).

Air: When by economy class, in accordance with the general allowance.

Bus and Train: In accordance with the general allowance. Reimbursed upon submission of receipts.

Car: Unlimited when to and from constituency ($.34 per km). An additional annual allowance of between $5 000 and $15 030 exists for travel within Quebec (inside or outside the constituency) depending on the classification of the riding (urban members excluded).

Ont. **General:** Maximum of 52 trips per year for members in accordance with the specific regulations. A maximum of 12 round trips for spouse or family member by air, bus or train. Established and reviewed by the Board of Internal Economy. Unlimited travel for opposition leaders within the province when on legislative business.

Air: Economy class. Up to 12 round trips for business within the province, special $7 000 travel allowance for northern members.

Bus and Train: Unlimited travel for member.

Car: Unlimited both to and from the capital and within the constituency. $.295 per km for northern members and $.29 per km for southern members.

Man. **General:** By any mode of transportation, the overall travel entitlement including travel within the constituency, is based on the value of 52 round trips per session between the capital and the constituency (calculated by applying the mileage rates payable to civil servants). Established by statute; revised in 1986.

Air: In accordance with the general allowance.

Bus and Train: In accordance with the general allowance.

Car: Each member of the assembly (except cabinet ministers and the Leader of the Official Opposition) is entitled to a car allowance of $344 per month, and any member whose constituency is outside Winnipeg may claim up to $3 000 per year in mileage. A Member whose constituency is more than 350 km from Winnipeg may claim up to $4 000 per year in mileage, paid on the basis of actual kilometres travelled ($.11 per km).

Sask. **General:** The travel allowance is based on a formula that applies to transportation by any mode: the civil service kilometric rate is applied to the total of the distance from the largest centre in the constituency (or the home of the member, whichever is greater) to the capital, plus 20 000 km (or 45 000 km if the constituency is greater than 2 000 square km). This figure is then multiplied by 52. This formula does not apply to cabinet ministers, the Speaker or the Opposition Leader.

Air: The Legislative Assembly will pay the full cost of a member's air travel between the constituency and the capital, reducing the member's allowance by the amount attributable to one return trip. Members living more than 350 km from Regina may travel by Executive Air during session; the full cost will be paid by the Legislative Assembly and the member's allowance will be reduced by the amount attributable to one return trip.

Bus and Train: In accordance with the general allowance formula. Bus passes are issued.

Car: In accordance with the general allowance formula.

Alta. **General:** In accordance with the air, bus, train and car regulations. In addition, a member may claim the reasonable travelling and living expenses of a spouse, family member or guest who accompanies the member to, or joins him or her in Edmonton or, providing the trip is related to the member's public or official business, any other part of the province, subject to the following conditions: *a)* the expenses are related to travelling and living within Alberta, and *b)* no member may claim more than six round trips per year under this category.

A member may claim the reasonable related travel and living expenses of a spouse, family member or guest accompanying him or her to: *a)* a conference, meeting, seminar, or other function of, or sponsored by, the Commonwealth Parliamentary Association or any of its regions or branches, *b)* a meeting of any other parliamentary association or any of its divisions, and *c)* any meeting or function attended by the member as a representative of the Legislative Assembly or the Speaker.

Air: Members are entitled to unlimited regularly scheduled air travel in Alberta between their constituencies or temporary residences and Edmonton. In addition, members on official MLA business may use regularly scheduled air service to points anywhere in Alberta. The assembly pays for a maximum of five such return trips per member in a fiscal year (April 1 to March 31). A member who is the leader of an opposition party is entitled to unlimited regularly scheduled air travel within Alberta. Members representing the constituencies of Fort McMurray, Dunvegan, Lesser Slave Lake, Peace River and Athabasca-Lac La Biche are entitled to chartered air service within the constituency provided that the trip cannot be made with reasonable convenience using regularly scheduled air service. If a member chooses not to travel by air on any or all of the five allotted return trips in the fiscal year, he or she may claim in lieu $.25 per km up to a maximum of 1 500 km per trip of surface travel.

Bus and Train: Members are entitled to free regularly scheduled long-distance bus transportation within the province. A Greyhound Bus Lines pass is available upon written request to the Director of Administration.

Car: Members may claim expenses related to the operation of a private automobile including fuel, oil, lubrication fuel, antifreeze, gas line antifreeze, transmission fluid, brake fluid, steering fluid, windshield washer fluid and car wash and waxing, including labour.

In addition to the expenses listed above, a member may claim an allowance of $.25 per km travelled in his or her private automobile. In each fiscal year a rural member may claim up to 18 000 km if no receipts or claims for automobile fuel are submitted, and up to 42 000 additional km with receipts (making the total maximum for rural members 60 000 km). An urban Member may claim up to 10 000 km in a fiscal year without fuel receipts, and 15 000 additional km with receipts (making the total maximum for urban members 25 000 km).

An allowance of $.25 per km covers up to 52 round trips per year between a member's residence, place of employment, business or constituency and Edmonton. (This is in addition to those listed in the previous paragraph.)

B.C.   **General:** By any mode of transportation, an annual maximum of 52 return trips between the constituency and the capital may be claimed, plus ten return trips anywhere in the province. A spouse or dependent may use any number of the 52 constituency/capital trips, and the constituency secretary or assistant may use three of the 52 constituency/capital trips. For travel within the constituency by any means of transportation, members receive an annual allowance of $2 640 for urban ridings, $3 600 for semi-urban ridings, $4 800 for rural ridings and $6 000 for coastal or remote ridings, without the presentation of claims or receipts. Coastal or remote ridings are also eligible for an additional $6 000 upon presentation of receipts.

Air: When by economy class, included in the 52 return trips mentioned above.

Bus and Train: Passes are issued for travel by bus and ferry. There are no specific allowances for travel by train.

Car: If a private vehicle is used for any of the 52 constituency/capital trips or ten business trips, $.28 per km may be claimed.

Yukon **General:** Unlimited travel while the House is sitting and up to 48 return trips when the House is not sitting (allows the payment of travel expenses within the constituency). Restricted to private members. Ministers whose constituencies are outside the capital may claim 24 return trips to their constituencies for travel on business as an MLA. Recognized leaders who travel within the Yukon in the performance of their duties may claim twelve return trips per year.

Air: When by economy class, in accordance with the general allowance.

Bus and Train: No specific allowances.

Car: In accordance with the general allowance. $.385 per km (tied to civil service rate).

N.W.T. **General:** Established by statute.

Air: Three trips per year within the constituency by chartered aircraft or economy class, and five trips to the capital or nearest regional headquarters when the House is not sitting. When the House is sitting, the member or a designated person may make one economy round trip after five sitting days, another after 20 sitting days and another after 35 sitting days.

Bus and Train: No specific allowances.

Car: Up to 4 800 km per year at $.385 per km (includes to-and-from capital and within constituency). Tied to civil service rates.

CHAPTER EIGHT

Committee Allowances

IN ADDITION to their regular salary (sometimes still referred to as an "Indemnity") and non-taxable allowance, members of the Senate, House of Commons and the provincial and territorial legislatures are all eligible to have their expenses covered for serving on a Standing, Special or Select Committee of the House. As well, members of all legislative bodies with the exception of the Senate, House of Commons, New Brunswick, and Yukon may also receive a per diem for their committee work. Alberta grants the equivalent of a per diem in the form of a "Committee Members' Allowance."

Remuneration for committee service was comparatively unknown until the mid 1970s when Ontario and Quebec introduced a per diem for committee members. In Ontario, as early as 1972, the Ontario Commission on the Legislature recommended to the government of the day that committee members should not be provided with a special emolument, since in its view, committee work was a normal part of the job of an Ontario member for which he or she was already being paid.

In all cases, the entitlement to a per diem and expense allowance is predicated on committee meetings which take place when the House is recessed (thereby requiring that members of the committee make a special trip to the seat of government to be in attendance), when a committee is travelling to various parts of the country (in the case of the Senate and House of Commons, and some provincial committees) or when the committee meets away from the seat of government regardless of whether or not the House is sitting.

In order to examine the impact of the committee per diem on a member's take-home pay, one must also take into account the salary level and expense allowance in effect in his or her province.

The highest committee per diems and expenses currently being paid are in the Northwest Territories, Alberta and Saskatchewan. The Northwest Territories pays a per diem of $218 and a non-accountable expense allowance of $185 for members who are required to attend committee meetings when the House is not sitting. However, when evaluating this total payment of $403 one has to bear in mind that Northwest Territories members receive a salary of $38 701, plus a tax-free allowance of only $1 000 (by far the lowest tax-free allowance paid in Canada).

Alberta's Committee Members' Allowance is based on a sliding scale: $100 per day for attendance at a committee meeting lasting four hours or less, $165 for between four and eight hours and $260 for meetings lasting longer than eight hours. In addition, members may claim an allowance of $100 per day for living expenses for "each day on which they attend a meeting ... or are otherwise engaged in its business and affairs, and for each additional day required for travel in connection with these responsibilities, provided they are required to obtain accommodation by reason of being absent form their normal place of residence." Alberta members receive a salary of $38 335. However , they receive a non-taxable allowance of $19 167, considerably greater than the $1 000 paid in the Northwest Territories, although the Northwest Territories salary is almost identical.

In Saskatchewan, members of committees receive a per diem of $155 which is adjusted annually according to the Consumer Price Index, and are reimbursed for out-of-pocket meal, travel and accommodation expenses, provided receipts are submitted. If receipts are not available, a flat, non-accountable per diem of $24 for meals and $26 for accommodation is provided. Saskatchewan members receive a salary of $38 546 and a non-taxable allowance of $7 622.

Remuneration for actual committee work has advanced slowly in those jurisdictions where it has been in force for the past ten years. In Fiscal 1981/82, Northwest Territories members received a per diem of $138, and an expense allowance of $113.13. Alberta members received a straight per diem of $75. Saskatchewan paid its members an $84 per diem plus actual out-of-pocket expenses.

Members of the House of Commons have never been paid a per diem for serving on committees. In Fiscal 1981/82 they were receiving an allowance for out-of-pocket expenses of $40 per day for those living south of the 60th parallel, and $45 per day for those living north. For 1992, these figures are much the same: $45.45 and $52.85, however both may also be applied against days when the member is travelling either to attend or return from a committee meeting. In addition, actual travel costs are met by the House of Commons, and it is assumed that in the case of travelling committees, accommodation and local transportation are met by the Clerk of the Committee, who would also pick up the tab for joint meals.

Ontario's foray into paying members for committee service has also been restrained in terms of increments during the past decade. In Fiscal 1981/82, Ontario members received a $60 per diem and a $27 non-accountable allowance for personal expenses. The per diem has now increased to $78, however the expense allowance has remained the same. Ontario members are allowed to apply both the per diem and the non-accountable allowance to travel days to and from the location where the committee meeting takes place.

Chairmen of committees, and in some cases Vice-Chairmen, receive special salaries instead of the per diem of regular members. They also receive the same expense allowance provided to members. The following is a breakdown of salaries paid to committee Chairmen and Vice-Chairmen in those jurisdictions where these apply: Quebec: $15 031 (Chairman), $12 025 (Vice-Chairman); Ontario: $8 827 (Chairman), $5 313 (Vice-Chairman); Alberta: $4 200 for what is termed a "Class A" Chairman, and for "Class B," an increased hourly rate over the regular members; Saskatchewan: $4 084; Northwest Territories: $3 000; and in Newfoundland a salary of $8 000 payable only to the Chairman of the Public Accounts Committee, and $6 000 to the Vice-Chairman.

It should be noted that in the case of Chairmen, Vice-Chairmen and all members of committees, salary or per diem payments are considered pensionable income along with their regular annual salary or indemnity. The annual non-taxable allowance, however, in most cases, may not be taken into pensionable income.

Of course, most committee meetings take place during the regular session of the legislature and members may not receive extra remuneration at that time. Special committee meetings to which the per diems and allowances apply are normally scheduled during January and February, occasionally during the summer (in the case of committees with a special mandate, like a Constitutional Committee), and sometimes in the fall weeks before the legislature resumes sitting. The Senate and House of Commons have tighter schedules and expense monies really only apply to travelling committees.

There is an anomaly in some larger provinces that out-of-town members usually maintain year-round residences at the seat of government, in the form of apartments or houses paid by an accommodation allowance. An Ontario committee member for instance, who represents a riding some distance from Toronto, may draw the $78 per diem and $27 a day for committee meetings and travel. A mileage of $.29 for southern members and $.295 for northern members may also be claimed. There is no restriction, for that matter, on a member representing a Toronto riding claiming the $27 daily expense allowance if attending a committee meeting at Queen's Park when the House is not sitting. A similar ambiguity holds true for the Northwest Territories Legislature where a committee member who actually maintains his principal residence in the community where the committee meeting is being held may also receive a non-accountable daily allowance which in this case is set at $50.

Members of cabinet in some of the medium- and smaller-sized provinces still take part in legislature committees as chairmen or members, however this is a thing of the past in Ontario and Quebec. Although they are paid an annual salary as members of the Executive Council in addition to their salary as a member, plus their non-taxable allowance, they may also claim the same per diems and allowances as other members of committees.

It is difficult to assess the impact committee remuneration has on the pay package of individual members in Canada. It appears that in most jurisdictions the committee per diem is being treated as a non-taxable allowance rather than taxable income. If this is so, then the income which some members may receive from this activity—possibly ranging from a low of $1 000 per annum to as high as $3 000-$5 000—could, in real dollar terms and when combined with the regular annual non-taxable allowance, represent anywhere from $2 000-$10 000 in "wage-earner" terms.

It should also be remembered that it is possible for members to be appointed to several committees, and to claim the appropriate emoluments from each, and that the non-accountable meal expense per diems which are provided for committee members, whether they are actually spent or not, are tax-free.

Some members are not appointed to committees, although they are few in number, and a few elect not to sit on committees. However, the majority of members are appointed by their caucuses to one or more. It appears that members are, by and large, happy to settle for the frustration, boredom (and the occasional feeling of satisfaction and excitement) of committee work. The fact that there's occasionally a per diem and a meal allowance attached, as well as some camaraderie, at least makes the work palatable. Still, there is no question that some committees have made a major contribution to provincial and national life. Some examples are those relating to the Constitution, the environment, electric power planning, etc. However, the fact that many members are paid for committee work does have a detrimental effect: it provides a strong temptation to extend committee work, thereby adding to the overall costs of committees; it is difficult for the member to be his or her own person, as committee appointments are made by the caucuses; it tends to help blur the true pay-package of the member; and it increases the level of public distrust of politicians and the political system.

The question of the fairness and justification of committee per diems and allowances has to be looked at in the context of what should be done to provide elected members in Canada with salaries, benefits, pensions and allowances befitting their job, and which can be understood and supported by the public at large. Of course, the main question is that if the role of elected members is considered to be full-time, and their pay is set accordingly, then what is the justification for paying members a per diem if sitting on committees is part of the job? The answer is that in many jurisdictions a system has developed over the years whereby the member's principal salary is treated as a sort of token payment which is bolstered by all sorts of other emoluments, including committee per diems.

Committee Allowances

H of C **Per Diem:** None.

Expense Allowance: South of the 60th parallel, $45.45; north of the 60th parallel, $52.85 (applies within the United States, as well). Outside Canada and the United States, the per diem is set according to the prevailing cost of meals and incidentals in the centre to be visited, and must be approved by the Speaker. For anticipated travel days, the per diem can be paid in advance. Non-accountable. Charged to the committee budget.

Newf. **Per Diem:** The Chairman and Vice Chairman of standing or select committees (other than the Public Accounts Committee) are paid a sitting-day per diem of $100 and $75 respectively, up to an annual maximum of $3 000 and $2 250 respectively, payable only when the House is in adjournment. The following allowances are paid to members of the Public Accounts Committee: Chairman, $8 000; Vice Chairman, $6 000; members, $4 000. No office holder of the Legislature or member of any other committee receives an additional allowance by reason of committee membership.

Expense Allowance: Committee members who must travel in order to attend meetings may claim travel costs plus up to $75 per day for accommodation (receipts required) and $40 per day for meals (or, this allowance can be waived in favour of actual expenses, when accompanied by documentation). A member living in St. John's on a full-time basis may claim $25 per day for meals.

P.E.I.   **Per Diem:** $75 per day when the House is not sitting.

Expense Allowance: $25 per meeting-day for meals, plus mileage at $.30 per km (varies with prevailing civil service rates).

N.B.   **Per Diem:** None.

Expense Allowance: $200 non-accountable allowance for each day the committee meets, plus travel expenses. Established by the Standing Committee on Legislative Administration. Last revised Feb. 23, 1989.

N.S.   **Per Diem:** $100 per day for attendance at all committee meetings. Established by the Legislature. Last revised in 1991.

Expense Allowance: Members are reimbursed for their actual expenses for meals, and up to $85 per day for accommodation on submission of receipts.

Que.   **Per Diem:** $137 per day when the House is not sitting.

Expense Allowance: Members are reimbursed for their actual travel costs when the committee is sitting outside Quebec City, or mileage at $.34 per km; $137 per day for meals and accommodation. Established by Order-in-Council.

Ont.   **Per Diem:** $78 per day ($90 for chairmen) for meeting and travelling days when the House is not sitting or when the committee is travelling (whether or not House is sitting). Last revised April 1, 1989.

Expense Allowance: $27 per day non-accountable allowance ($38.30 outside Canada), plus travel and accommodation

expenses on submission of receipts. Established by the Board of Internal Economy.

Man.   **Per Diem:** $92 per day when the House is not sitting or has been adjourned for four days or more (cabinet ministers and Opposition Leader excluded). Established by statute and annually indexed by the cost of living.

Expense Allowance: Members are reimbursed for expenses for meals, accommodation and travel as required. This allowance is not necessarily increased on an annual basis.

Sask.   **Per Diem:** $155 per day. Last revised Jan. 1992, with an annual increase tied to the Consumer Price Index for Saskatchewan.

Expense Allowance: Members are reimbursed for their actual expenses for accommodation, meals and travel (if other than by private automobile) on submission of receipts. A per diem of $24 (plus GST and PST) per day for meals and $26 per night for accommodation is applied if no receipts are available. Automobile travel: reimbursement of mileage based on the per km rate paid to public employees ($.2566 per km as of April 1, 1991).

Alta.   **Per Diem:** None.

Committee Members' Allowance: $100 per meeting lasting four hours or less; $165 per meeting lasting more than four hours but less than eight hours; $260 per meeting lasting longer than eight hours.

Committee Chairman's Allowance: The chairmen of the following committees receive an additional allowance of $350 per month: Standing Committee on the Alberta Heritage Savings Trust Fund Act, Standing Committee on Private Bills, Standing Committee on Public Accounts, Standing Committee on Legislative Office, and Special Standing Committee on Members' Services. The chairmen of the Standing Committees on Law and Regulation; Privileges and Elections; Standing Orders and Printing; and Public Affairs may claim the following additional allowances: $35 per meeting lasting four hours or less; $65 per meeting lasting more than four hours but less than eight hours; $105 per meeting lasting longer than eight hours.

Expense Allowance: Members who serve on committees appointed by a resolution of the assembly may claim an allowance of $100 per day for living expenses for each day on which they attend a meeting of one of these committees or are otherwise engaged in its business and affairs, and for each additional day required for travel in connection with these responsibilities, provided they are required to obtain accommodation by reason of being absent from their normal place of residence.

B.C.   **Per Diem:** $100 per day payable to all members when on committee work (committee chairmen receive an additional $125 per day). This per diem can only be claimed when the House is not sitting and business has been referred.

Expense Allowance: Members are reimbursed for their reasonable out-of-pocket, travel and other expenses. This allowance can only be claimed when the House is not sitting and business has been referred.

Yukon   **Per Diem:** None.

Expense Allowance: $52.85 per day for meals and incidental expenses, plus actual expenses for accommodation. Travel allowances are equivalent to the rates paid to civil servants ($.385 per km for car, or actual expenses for other modes of travel). These allowances are available only if the committee meets on a day when the House is not sitting.

N.W.T.   **Per Diem:** $218 per day when the House is not sitting. Outlined in statute and approved by the Management and Services Board, usually once a year. Last revised April 1, 1991.

Expense Allowance: $185 per day non-accountable allowance for members residing outside the locality where the committee meeting is being held; $50 per day if the meeting is held in the member's own riding. Established by statute.

CHAPTER NINE

Support Services at the Legislature

THERE IS a wide variation between the office facilities and staff support services provided to members of the Senate, House of Commons, and the provincial and territorial legislatures. Members of the Senate, House of Commons, the Ontario Legislature and the Quebec National Assembly each have private offices or a suite of several rooms, executive-type furniture, personal staff and sophisticated computer and video equipment. Members of the House of Commons, with a 1992 global office budget of $164 600 can employ as many as five or six people to staff their Ottawa and constituency offices.

The first year that members of the House of Commons were provided with a private secretary was 1968. However it was not until 1978 that a member's staff budget of $58 000 was established, enabling MPs to hire two people for the Ottawa office and one for the constituency. In 1981 MPs were provided with $3 900 in addition to their $74 100 office budget to allow them to rent word processing equipment, electronic typewriters or photocopiers for their parliamentary offices.

Newfoundland, Saskatchewan, Alberta, British Columbia and the Yukon provide private offices for their members, and Northwest Territories members representing the Yellowknife area each have their own office, however none of these legislatures provide even one personal staff person for their members. In other jurisdictions, members often share offices and secretaries, or work out of a block of offices supplied to a caucus with administrative

staff being provided on an "as-required" basis.

All legislatures in Canada provide substantial sums of money to enable their members to communicate with constituents. The Senate, House of Commons, the Ontario Legislature and the National Assembly of Quebec have print shops to facilitate the preparation of newsletters (Householders), or this is handled by government printing plants or outside, commercial printers. At the Ontario Legislature each caucus has its own print shop, and any suggestion that there should only be one common print shop has been resisted.

Householder newsletters are perhaps the most visible communication by politicians to their constituents. They are distributed by Canada Post to every residence and are usually limited to four mailings a year. They range from fairly straightforward four-to-eight page productions with three or four black-and-white photographs outlining the various activities of the member, up to productions with as many as 15-20 photographs. (Recently one member sent out a 50-page newsletter to constituents.)

The original concept behind Householders was that they were meant to provide an opportunity for elected members to keep their constituents—regardless of party affiliation—abreast of developments at the legislature, in the constituency and in the government in general. In the same way that constituency offices were established so that the member could serve the whole community on a non-partisan basis, Householder newsletters were developed to provide a strictly non-partisan report of the member's activities.

Householders in Canada had their origins in the larger jurisdictions in the early 1970s. At that time there was a similar development in some of the larger U.S. state legislatures, and it was there that standards of ethics were set for these folders produced, printed and distributed at government expense. In 1978, both the Republican and Democratic caucuses in the New York State Assembly strictly adhered to a policy that Householders could not be more than eight pages in length, could only carry a head-and-shoulders portrait of the member in black-and-white, and any colour reproductions were not permitted. The rationale for this was that if public rather than party funds were provided for the newsletters, they could not be partisan instruments.

Even in the bigger legislatures in the early 1970s, when most office and staffing facilities were provided for members by the Government through the equivalent of the Department of Public Works or the Ministry of Government Services, tight controls existed for what were then termed "Constituency Newsletters," first class mail, and telephone usage. In fact, all jurisdictions imposed definite limits in these areas. The content and make-up of newsletters was carefully monitored. First class mail in some legislatures was limited to official correspondence and no bulk mailings were permitted. In many cases telephone calls could only be made within the province using government trunk lines or credit cards. These controls were relaxed, however, with the passage of time and because the policy issues regarding the operation and administration of legislatures were increasingly determined by the members themselves through their duly appointed Board of Internal Economy, rather than the government. A self-regulating process by elected members regarding the level and standards of service was seen to be preferable to having civil servants arbitrarily set standards.

One result of all this is the veritable explosion of costs in some of the larger jurisdictions in terms of the dollars spent by members to communicate with their constituents.

In 1992 the original concept of the Householder is probably being breached in various ways. When the program of Householders was originally introduced, any mention of party affiliation in a newsletter was strictly forbidden. Yet, last year one elected member referred to, or gave credit to her party (which happened to be the governing party), at least five times in a newsletter. Colours denoting specific parties are also used in some newsletters.

Little information has been tabulated concerning Householders, however the House of Commons and the Ontario Legislature both make their figures public. They serve to illustrate that the production and distribution of Householders has become a major operation.

Prior to the 1988 Federal Election, MPs sent out 815 Householders reaching virtually every household in Canada, and following the September 4 election, 285 Householders were distributed. The total 1988-1989 cost was approximately $4.5 million. The following year, 1989-1990, the total number of newsletters was slightly reduced, however the cost increased to $5.6 million, an average of $19 600 per elected member. The Main Estimates for the House of Commons for 1991-1992 quote a reduced cost, this time of $4.6 million. It is interesting to note in this connection that for 1989-1990 the average annual telephone cost for an individual MP was $32 100, although the amount forecast for 1991-1992 was $28 800.

At the House of Commons, effective April 1, 1989 the Principal Office budget, Constituency Operating Allowance, and the Constituency Travel Allowance (which originally made up the member's office budget) were renamed the "Members' Operating Budget". This budget principally takes care of staff salaries, constituency office rent, staff travel in the constituency and out-of-pocket expenses incurred in the operation of the constituency office. All costs of furniture, hardware, etc. in the House of Commons and constituency offices are borne separately by the House of Commons.

The way in which individual members choose to use their operating budget has been left by those in authority as a matter for the member to decide, although certification of their expenditures is required by the Comptroller of the House of Commons, and members may not pay any one assistant in their office more than $58 700 annually. (Ontario members are limited to $41 000). The question of confidentiality of accounts relating to Member's Operating Budgets was examined at great length by an all-party committee of senior members of the House who sought to amend the Parliament of

Canada Act so that from their standpoint there would be no unwarranted intrusion into the private affairs of MPs by the R.C.M.P. The Act, which was finally amended in 1991, gave them almost every protection they sought, and we can no longer learn just how much Canadian taxpayers are paying for each member to operate the constituency office.

Support Services at the Legislature

H of C **Office:** Each member is provided with an office on Parliament Hill furnished and equipped with a personal computer, laser printer, word processor, typewriters, television set and converter, photocopier, telephones, stationery, office supplies and other equipment as needed, e.g. calculators, dictating equipment, etc. Translation services, electronic mail, internal mail and messenger services, printing (including four Householder mailings per year), dining room, cafeterias, security, galleries, tours, health, language training, gymnasium and steamroom, parking, picture framing ($400 annual ceiling), souvenir boutique and liquor store, daycare, barber and hairdresser, tailor, shoeshine and masseur are also provided.

Global Operating Budget: (urban constituencies: $164 600; urban/rural constituencies with less than 25 000 square km: $167 500; rural/urban, rural and urban/rural constituencies with more than 25 000 square km: $170 400) is used for staff, supplies, travel, etc., for both the Parliament Hill and constituency offices.

Staff: Global Operating Budget is used to pay the salaries of secretarial, research, administrative or support staff working for a member at the Parliament Hill office or the constituency office.

Members recruit, hire, promote and release employees, as well as determine their duties, hours of work, job classifications and salaries. Employee relations are the member's responsibility. No limit on number of employees. Salary limit set by Board of Internal Economy (current limit $58 700).

Office Mail: Mail sent to and addressed by the member is unlimited.

Telephone: Unlimited regular- and long-distance telephone service is paid by the House. Answering machines are purchased using the Global Operating Budget.

Newf. **Office:** One office per member. Supplies and furniture are provided by the legislature. Each caucus receives an operating grant based on the formula of $1 000 per member per annum.

Staff: Each member has a secretary. The government caucus has 3 researchers and the opposition caucuses have one researcher, one chief of staff and one policy advisor. The Leader of the Opposition has one executive assistant.

Office Mail: Unlimited.

Telephone: Unlimited. Each member is provided with a credit card.

P.E.I. **Office:** A block of offices is supplied to each caucus. Space is allocated by the Standing Committee on Internal Economy. Office supplies are provided by the caucus; office equipment is provided by the Legislative Assembly.

Staff: The government caucus has 3 secretaries and 2 researchers (entitlement established by the Standing Committee on Internal Economy). Salaries are established by the Standing Committee on Internal Economy. Staff are employees of the Legislative Assembly. No union.

Office Mail: Only when the House is sitting.

Telephone: Unlimited regular- and long-distance telephone services are paid by the Legislative Assembly. No credit cards.

N.S.

Office: Each caucus is supplied with a block of offices (allocated by the Internal Economy Board). Supplies and equipment are provided by the Legislative Assembly.

Staff: Each caucus is given funds for support services. Salary is based on the classification of the employee position, and tied to the civil service ranges. Employees are hired for a term by the Legislative Assembly. No union.

Office Mail: Charged to member's caucus.

Telephone: Unlimited regular telephone services are paid by the Legislative Assembly. The only long-distance calls that can be placed from legislature telephones are those within the 902 (N.S. and P.E.I.) and 613 (Ottawa) area codes. Paid for by the Legislative Assembly. No credit cards.

N.B.

Office: Progressive Conservative, New Democratic and Confederation of Regions parties each have office space allocated by Standing Committee on Legislative Administration. Government caucus office has an office in the Legislative Assembly. Staff and office expenses for each registered political party member: $11 366.

Staff: No staff provided. Legislative Research Service, a temporary service attached to the Legislative Library during the Fifty-first Legislature (which elected no official opposition), was at the disposal of registered political parties, but has now been phased out.

Office Mail: Charged to caucus allowance by the Standing Committee on Legislative Administration. Based on budget figures determined by the Clerk of the House.

Telephone: Unlimited regular- and long-distance within the province. Credit cards are issued. Unlimited facsimile.

Que.

Office: One office per member. Space is allocated by the Speaker. Furniture is provided by the government department; supplies and equipment are provided by the Legislative Assembly.

Staff: Member has an annual sum of between $98 300 and $115 500 for hiring personnel (funding level established by the Office of the National Assembly). At least 25% of this sum must be used for the Legislature office. The remainder may be used for the constituency office. Staff are employees of the member, and are not civil servants. No union.

Office Mail: Unlimited. Paid by the government.

Telephone: Unlimited regular- and long-distance costs paid by the government. Credit cards are issued and members are provided with cellular telephones.

Ont.

Office: One office per member. Space allocated by the Speaker in consultation with the House Leaders. Supplies and equipment are provided by the Legislative Assembly.

Staff: Member has an annual global sum of $136 865 (includes 4% vacation pay and sick leave allowance) for hiring personnel to work in either the Legislature office or the constituency office. No restriction on staff numbers. Salary range is established by the Board of Internal Economy. Staff are employees of the caucus. One caucus is unionized.

Office Mail: Unlimited. Paid by the Legislative Assembly.

Telephone: Unlimited regular- and long-distance service paid by the Legislative Assembly. Credit cards are issued.

Man.

Office: Each caucus is supplied with a block of offices. Space is allocated by the Department of Government Services.

Staff: 12 staff-years for the Government; 9 staff-years for the Official Opposition; 6 staff-years for the second opposition caucus office. The classifications are established by the Legislative Assembly Management Commission and the salary range is based on that provided to civil servants. No union.

Office Mail: Unlimited. Paid by the government. Two constituency Householder mailings will be paid for by the Legislative Assembly.

Telephone: Unlimited regular- and long-distance service paid by the Legislative Assembly. Credit cards are issued.

Sask. **Office:** One office per member. Equipment and supplies are provided by the Legislative Assembly.

Staff: Secretarial services, according to the following formula: a) Sessional: the government and opposition caucuses receive one secretary for every 2.8 private members; the third party receives one secretary for three hours per day. b) Inter-sessional: the government and opposition caucuses receive one third of their sessional allotment.

The salary range for a secretary is $24 432 to $28 752. Caucuses are also given research and secretarial grants to hire staff and may set salary levels. If the secretaries are paid by the Legislative Assembly, their benefits are the same as those received by civil servants. If the secretaries are paid by the caucuses, their benefits are established by the caucuses.

Office Mail: Included in the communications allowance (equal to four first-class letters multiplied by the number of registered voters in a member's constituency).

Telephone: Unlimited regular- and long-distance service paid by the Legislative Assembly. No credit cards.

Alta. **Office:** One office per member. Space is allocated by the Executive Council. Standard equipment is supplied by Public Works Supplies and Services. Stationery is supplied by the Clerk's Office. Data processing entitlement established by the

Special Standing Committee on Members' Services.

Staff: One legislative assistant for every two members (entitlement established by the Special Standing Committee on Members' Services). Pay rates are established by the caucus. Staff are employees of the Legislative Assembly but are hired only for the life of the parliament. Benefits, including pension, are the same as for other Legislative Assembly staff. No union.

Office Mail: Unlimited. Paid by the Legislative Assembly.

Telephone: Unlimited regular- and long-distance service paid by the Legislative Assembly.

B.C. **Office:** One office per member. Space is allocated by the Board of Internal Economy. Furniture, equipment, stationery and supplies are provided by the Legislative Assembly.

Staff: Each caucus receives a global allowance for hiring personnel. The number of employees and salary range is established by the caucuses. Staff are employees of the Legislative Assembly.

Office Mail: Unlimited. Paid by the Legislative Assembly.

Telephone: Unlimited regular- and long-distance service paid by the Legislative Assembly. Credit cards are issued for use within the province.

Yukon **Office:** One office per member. Space is allocated by the Speaker; equipment and supplies are provided by the Legislative Assembly.

Staff: Supplied by the Clerk's Office on a request basis.

Office Mail: Unlimited. Paid for by the Legislative Assembly.

Telephone: Unlimited long-distance per member per year. A long-distance calling card is issued upon request.

N.W.T. **Office:** One office for each local member. Seven offices are shared by out-of-town members when in the capital on business. Space is allocated by the Speaker; equipment and supplies are provided by the Legislative Assembly.

Staff: Sessional staff is supplied by the Legislative Assembly as required. Inter-session requirements are supplied by the Clerk's Office. Staff are casual employees in the civil service; some are unionized, depending on their status in the civil service.

Office Mail: Unlimited. Paid for by the Legislative Assembly.

Telephone: During session, unlimited regular- and long-distance service is paid for by the Legislative Assembly. No credit cards. When not in session, the member has the use of telephone credit cards, but pays for all calls.

CHAPTER TEN

Support Services in the Constituency

ONCE AGAIN, it is the House of Commons, the Ontario Legislature and the National Assembly of Quebec leading the way in expenditures by providing their Members with the most extensive constituency office arrangements in Canada.

British Columbia has the next most generous constituency office assistance for its members, followed by Alberta. British Columbia provides a specific "Global Constituency Budget" of $43 200 for salaries, office rental, and general overhead. It is significant that both British Columbia and Alberta, according to available information, provide a higher level of funding for members' constituency offices than for the offices at the seat of government. Alberta also has a dedicated budget for constituency offices: $38 036 is available to its members, and staff may travel to the constituency or to the legislature up to three times a year.

The only legislatures which do not make provisions for some type of constituency office support are Prince Edward Island, New Brunswick, and the Yukon. All others have varying levels of assistance.

To illustrate just how much the constituency office has become an accepted extension of the member's office at the seat of government during the past decade, one may look back thirteen years to 1979. At that time there were no entitlements in Newfoundland, Prince Edward Island, Nova Scotia, New Brunswick, Alberta or the Northwest Territories. Ontario and Quebec both provided approximately $7 000 annually for constituency offices, Manitoba members received a yearly allowance of $900, Saskatchewan made $6 000 available to each member, and British Columbia offered up to $12 000. The Yukon actually provided its members with a constituency allowance of $2 835, but withdrew it the following year.

The purpose of constituency offices is to make it possible for the member to act as the constituency representative by providing a facility where citizens, regardless of political stripe, can come to discuss their problems or concerns with government, and seek redress. The constituency office has to be seen to be totally non-partisan so that it can serve all citizens equally. For identification purposes, it must display a sign which simply indicates that it is the office of the elected representative for the constituency—Joe R. Smith, MP—and there can be no party symbols attached. The question of maintaining impartiality is helped in part by the vigilance of individual citizens who may contact the legislature (or the media) concerning the sign on the constituency office, and for that matter, the general usage of the office, particularly when they suspect that political meetings may be taking place in that venue.

It is obvious that liaison is necessary at times between the member's constituency office and his or her office at the seat of government. The House of Commons, Ontario Legislature, the Quebec National Assembly and Alberta make it possible for staff to travel between these two offices, and as noted in the Travel Allowances Chapter, a portion of the members' travel funding may be allocated for that purpose. A similar arrangement is made for staff travel within the constituency, although to a lesser degree. In the case of the House of Commons, the Ontario Legislature and the Quebec National Assembly, the Global Office Budget may be used to pay staff in the constituency office or in the office at the seat of government, and the question of the deployment of staff is left to the member.

For a detailed outline of how constituency office funding is handled, review the Support Services at the Legislature Chapter as well as the information that follows.

Supprt Services in the Constituency

H of C **General:** The House of Commons provides each member with an Operating Allowance to be used under directives prescribed by the Board of Internal Economy.

Categories of Allowance: Global Operating Budget (urban constituencies: $164 600; urban/rural constituencies with less than 25 000 square km: $167 500; rural/urban, rural and urban/rural constituencies with more than 25 000 square km: $170 400) is used for staff, supplies, travel, etc, for both the Parliament Hill and constituency offices. In the constituency, the Operating Budget is also used for rent, telephone, utilities, furniture and equipment.

Members who represent constituencies that include more than 70 000 electors and/or are more than 8 000 square km in area are entitled to Budget Supplements ranging from $5 150 to $20 600 per year. These supplements may be used for expenses incurred in the constituency only.

Members are entitled to a Constituency Furniture and Equipment Allowance under which re-elected members receive $3 000 over the life of a Parliament for furniture and equipment for their constituency offices, and newly-elected members are entitled to $5 000 for the same purpose. This allowance extends over the life of a Parliament and is not renewed annually.

Staff: Global Operating Budget is used to pay the salaries of secretarial, research, administrative or support staff working for a member in the Parliament Hill or constituency offices.

Members recruit, hire, promote and release employees, as well as determine their duties, hours of work, job classifications and salaries. Employee relations are the member's responsibility. No limit on number of employees. Salary limit set by Board of Internal Economy (current limit $58 700).

Mail: Charged to the Global Operating Budget (excluding four annual Householder mailings). Electronic mail (Office Automation Services and Information Systems) provided by the House.

Telephone: Long-distance calls to all points in Canada and most of the U.S.A. on the government network are paid by the House. Charged to the Global Operating Budget.

Administration: The Comptroller's Office of the House verifies that all expenses charged to the member's budget were incurred in accordance with the rules prescribed by the Board of Internal Economy.

Newf. **General:** Each member is entitled to an accountable constituency allowance of $7 500 per annum. This allowance is for the payment of expenditures incurred in the performance of constituency business as approved by the Internal Economy Commission. Receipts are required for all expenditures.

Only equipment and furniture purchases valued at $500 or more shall be deemed the property of the House of Assembly. All equipment or furniture is depreciated in value by one-third per year and at the end of three years becomes the personal property of the member.

Categories of Allowance: Up to $5 000 may be used for the use of office rental, secretarial assistance, furniture, equipment, office supplies, etc.. Up to $1 000 may be used for non-partisan newspaper and radio advertising, the purchase of flags or pins, Christmas cards, etc. Up to $1 500 may be used for discretionary spending by the member. An amount of up to $1 000 may be transferred from any of the above allotments, with the prior approval of the Speaker.

P.E.I. **General:** No constituency program. Members may use office space free of charge on a weekly basis in any of five regional offices operated by the Department of Industry.

Telephone: The Legislative Assembly pays for the installation of a private telephone line for all rural members, plus monthly charges equalized to the lowest rate in the province. Established by the Standing Committee on Internal Economy.

N.S. **General:** Monthly allowance established by the Legislature.

Categories of Allowance: $300 per month for services in the constituency, up to $1 900 per month for actual expenses for office space, equipment and secretarial services on submission of receipts. Furniture and equipment may be leased by the member and charged to the office allowance.

Staff: No specific allowance. Staff are employees of the member and are paid on a fee-for-service basis upon submission of account. No restriction on the number of employees.

Mail: $3 500 per calendar year.

Telephone: Charged to the office allowance.

Administration: Administration is the responsibility of the Speaker's Office. There are no formal restrictions on the use of the office.

N.B. No constituency program.

Que. **General:** Annual allowance established by the Office of the National Assembly.

Categories of Allowance: Between $19 000 and $22 100 for the office, depending on the classification of the riding. Actual operating expenses are reimbursed upon submission of receipts. Furniture and equipment may be rented by the member and charged to the office allowance. An additional $2 000 per length of Legislature may be used for the purchase of furniture or equipment.

Staff: Members have an annual sum of between $98 300 and $115 500 for hiring personnel. At least $23 400 of this must be used for the Legislature office and the remainder may be used for the constituency office (an additional $17 200 is available for selected large ridings). Funding level established by the Office of the National Assembly. Staff are employees of the member, and are not civil servants. Salary range is established by the member. No union.

Mail: Unlimited. Paid by the Legislative Assembly upon submission of receipts.

Telephone: Unlimited. Regular- and long-distance costs are paid by the Legislative Assembly upon submission of receipts.

Administration: Administration is the responsibility of the Office of the National Assembly. Formal guidelines prohibit partisan political activity, the use of the Member's home and the use of the office for campaign purposes.

Ont. **General:** Annual allowance first established by the Board of Internal Economy in 1977.

Categories of Allowance: Up to $15 600 for office accommodation expense and $15 766 for office operations and maintenance expense. Furniture, equipment and office automation equipment are provided by the Legislative Assembly.

Staff: The member has an annual global sum of \$136 865 for hiring personnel to work either in the Legislature office or the constituency office. Staff are employees of the member, but are on the payroll of the Legislative Assembly. Salary range is established by the Board of Internal Economy. No restriction on the number of employees.

Mail: Paid by the Legislative Assembly.

Telephone: Unlimited. Regular- and long-distance costs are paid by the Legislative Assembly. The Legislative Assembly pays for toll-free calling within the constituency.

Administration: Administration is the responsibility of the Legislative Assembly (Office of the Controller). Formal guidelines prohibit partisan political activity, employment of the member's spouse or children and the use of the office for campaign purposes.

Man. **General:** Allowance established by statute.

Categories of Allowance: A constituency allowance of \$25 823 per year is provided for expenses identified in the rules made by the Legislative Assembly Management Commission and incurred by the member in serving residents of his or her constituency (including rent, utilities, salaries, stationery, supplies and equipment, meetings with constituents, and the preparation and distribution of material of a non-partisan nature to constituents). Submission of receipts is required.

Staff: No specific allowance. Included in the \$25 823 constituency allowance.

Mail: Charged to the \$25 823 constituency allowance.

Telephone: Credit cards are issued. Paid by the Legislative Assembly.

Administration: Administrated by the Legislative Assembly Allowances Officer of the Administration Branch.

Sask. **General:** Established by statute in 1979. Board of Internal Economy directives establish annual and monthly allowance amounts.

Categories of Allowance: \$25 872 per year for constituency secretary, \$1 198 per month for constituency office. \$1 565 per year for telephone (without receipts), unlimited payment of telephone bills or reimbursement (with receipts). Furniture and equipment may be rented or bought by the member and charged to the office allowance, the telephone allowance or the communications allowance.

Staff: \$25 872 per year. Staff are employees of the member. Pay rate established by Board of Internal Economy directive (top of the range of a Clerk Steno 3 in the public service). Member may also use the office allowance to hire staff. No restriction on number of employees. Members may choose to have staff on time sheets in order for them to receive benefits equivalent to those of civil servants (benefits are paid by the Legislative Assembly).

Mail: Charged to the communications allowance. Equal to four times the cost of a first-class letter multiplied by the number of registered voters in a member's constituency.

Telephone: Up to \$1 565 per year without receipts. Unlimited with receipts or credit card. Monthly rental may be charged to either the telephone allowance or the office allowance. Members may lease cellular telephones and fax machines using the telephone allowance (all usage and rental charges of these items are paid/reimbursed to an unlimited account).

Administration: Administered by the Clerk's Office. There are no formal guidelines concerning the use of the office.

Alta. **General:** Members' Service Allowance established by the Special Standing Committee on Members' Services.

Categories of Allowance: $38 036 per fiscal year for securing office space and furnishings, retaining office and secretarial assistance and providing related services. May also be used for the reasonable living and travel expenses of staff working for the member and travelling to the legislature or to the member's constituency for a maximum of three occasions per fiscal year. Each member is provided with a standard constituency office package. Typewriter, dictaphone, transcriber, answering machine, photocopier and electronic data processing equipment are provided by the Legislative Assembly. Standard furniture is provided by government department. A standard stationery package is supplied for each constituency. Standard business and compliment cards are provided.

Staff: Included in fiscal allowance. Staff are recruited by the member and hired through the Personnel Services Branch.

Mail: General Administration pays postage for single mailings, but not for bulk mailings of letters, pamphlets, brochures or greetings to constituents. Postage for large mail-outs to constituents is charged to the Members' Services Allowance. General Administration pays the postage for Christmas cards to constituents.

Telephone: General Administration arranges and pays for the installation, rental and tolls for two telephones and three incoming lines in the constituency office. Members may rent or purchase telephones for their private automobiles and pay for them from their Members' Services Allowance. Tolls are paid by General Administration.

Administration: Administration is the responsibility of General Administration. The constituency office may not be used for promoting partisan political activities, nor may constituency office staff engage in such activities during their hours of work as constituency office staff.

B.C. **General:** Annual allowance is established by the Board of Internal Economy.

Categories of Allowance: Each member receives a maximum global budget of $43 200 for salaries, office rental and overhead.

Staff: Salaries are included in the $43 200 global constituency budget. Staff are employees of the member, and pay scales are established by the member. No restriction on the number of employees.

Mail: Charged to the $43 200 global constituency budget.

Telephone: Members are provided with direct-access lines to the provincial government network for outgoing calls and for fax machines. Other telephone services are charged to the $43 200 global constituency budget.

Administration: Responsibility of the Board of Internal Economy. Furniture and equipment may be rented or purchased by the member and charged to the $43 200 global constituency budget.

Yukon No constituency program.

N.W.T. **General:** Annual allowance first established by statute in 1975.

Categories of Allowance: Telephones, office supplies, advertising and furniture are supplied by the Legislative Assembly Office. Rental arrangements must be approved by the Management and Services Board.

Staff: Stenographic/interpreters as needed. A full-time constituency assistant may be hired (maximum salary $20 000).

Mail: Unlimited.

Telephone: $3 000 per year for long-distance. Credit cards are issued.

Administration: Administration is the responsibility of the Speaker's Office.

CHAPTER ELEVEN

Caucus Services

THE CAUCUSES in each legislature represent the common partisan thrust of elected members as they act as a group to pursue the various policies and platforms of their political party. In order to sustain this action the caucus has its own administrative organization headed by a manager which takes care of such matters as political research, speech preparation, the production and distribution of members' constituency newsletters, televised messages for cable distribution, liaison with the party machine throughout the province and in Ottawa, media relations, the staffing of caucus meetings, arrangements for travelling, investigative committees of caucus members, and so on.

Substantial sums of money are now being spent to maintain the operations of the party caucuses in all the legislatures, with the exception of the Northwest Territories which has no parties and is based on consensus government. For the purpose of this analysis, the budgets of the Opposition Leaders and House Leaders are included where applicable.

In every jurisdiction in Canada, the legislature provides public money in varying amounts to the party caucuses to defray their considerable administrative expenses. Twenty years ago, at a time when the public service basically ran the administration and services of most legislatures, party caucuses were provided with modest funding for their operations. The concept behind this funding was that opposition parties must have the necessary financial resources to best act in their capacity as critics of the government and its various ministries and departments. On the other hand, the premier and the members of his party who had been appointed to cabinet, could count on the considerable resources of government to maintain their political thrust in the legislature. Therefore it was generally felt that the level of government caucus funding should be based on the number of backbenchers only and should not include cabinet members. Funding provisions, in general, began to increase as Boards of Internal Economy came into being, and the members of those boards, elected politicians, started to think of various types of services which would enable them to compete more effectively with each other in the legislature.

The result of more funds being made available to the caucuses, particularly in Ontario and Quebec, was the building of a cadre of professional staff capable of handling a wide range of administrative, communications, research and policy assignments. Word processors, mass letter writing and mailing systems, and computer networks were also introduced.

Invariably, security became a key issue for the caucuses. The members of one party wanted to be sure that another party could not have access to their private print shop or their computer system. In Ontario this meant a triplication of equipment.

In the past it was always assumed that the federal or provincial organizations of the individual parties would cover the costs of maintaining and running party operations outside the legislature. That would include office headquarters, rental, staff, travel, advertising and promotion, meetings, retreats, etc. These expenses were traditionally met by the parties themselves through fund-raising endeavors, and were not taken out of public funds allocated to the caucuses in the legislature intended to defray internal operating and support costs.

In all legislatures, funding levels for caucuses are determined using a formula calculated either on a per-member basis, or on party standing in the House. It appears that in almost every case there is no limitation on the actual use of the funds, although in several instances phraseology such as "intended to cover the cost of staff salaries and contracts for temporary services" or "subject to audit by the Provincial Auditor" are cited in connection with caucus funding in several jurisdictions. In Ontario, caucus funding is considered to be an outright or non-accountable grant, and the Provincial Auditor therefore views the overseeing of the use of caucus funds as being outside his mandate.

Considering the large amounts of money now being spent in some provinces, the question is increasingly bound to be asked whether caucus funds are being spent in keeping with their designated purposes, or whether they are being used to defray expenses which historically have been the responsibility of the party organizations themselves. The fact that auditors who are appointed to ensure that public funds are being wisely used are unable to comment on whether caucus funds are being properly spent, may place a new responsibility on legislators to publicly state how those funds have actually been used.

In order to give some idea of the size and scope of caucus funding and its increases in recent years, it is worthwhile looking back at the 1982 expenditures of the House of Commons. That year, the Government, Official Opposition and Third Party received a total of $1.4 million for the operation of caucus research departments. (Traditionally in Ottawa the caucus funding allotment has gone entirely to a research component, as the House of Commons has provided the necessary staff to help individual members with the preparation of Householders, mass mailings, etc., and printing is handled through the House of Commons and government print shops, rather than through caucus print shops.) For the operation of the offices of the Official Leader of the Opposition and the Third Opposition Party, a further $1.65 million was provided in 1992. This meant a total expenditure at the House of Commons in 1982 of approximately $3 million for the three

caucuses and opposition parties' support.

Turning to 1982 figures for the Ontario Legislature, the Board of Internal Economy in that year allocated funds to the caucuses under two categories: Administration and Research. The combined amounts came to $2.6 million plus $640 000 for the combined offices of the Opposition Leader, Third Party Leader and Opposition House Leaders, totalling approximately $3.2 million.

It is interesting to note that in 1982, the House of Commons had 282 members and the Ontario Legislature had 125, yet both legislatures spent virtually the same amount for caucus services and Opposition Leaders' offices.

The printing of caucus materials in Ottawa (including Householders) is carried out in printing facilities which are open to public inspection, whereas at the Ontario Legislature caucus-owned printing presses produce substantial numbers of letters, flyers, brochures and reports. How much, if any, of this printing is being used to further the political thrust of the parties outside the legislature is known only to the caucuses themselves.

Since 1982 there has been a steady increase in the caucus and Opposition Leaders' budgets in the House of Commons; they now total $5.7 million. In the meantime, however, the Ontario Legislature has moved ahead to almost double the expenditures of the House of Commons with fewer than half as many members. The 1992 figure for the Ontario Legislature (revealed not by the legislature itself, but by independent research considered to be accurate) comes to approximately $11.5 million for caucus, Opposition Leaders' and House Leaders' budgets. Of this, approximately $9 million is earmarked for the caucuses alone.

It is certain that these budgets far exceed the provisions for any legislature caucuses in North America, at the provincial or state level, and that they most likely dwarf those of many national parliaments around the world where there is a party system in place.

In the Quebec National Assembly it could be suggested that the total caucus budget of $738 000 is not fully accurate. The reason it might appear low is that many of the services traditionally performed by a caucus are, very likely, being done elsewhere, and being charged elsewhere. In this case, the bulk of caucus support funds could be going through the office of the Opposition Leaders, and these figures have not been provided.

Looking at the rest of the country, Alberta and British Columbia appear to fund their caucuses at about the same level: Alberta has indicated a total figure of $2.8 million. There are no up-to-date figures for British Columbia, however research would indicate that the budget for the caucuses in that legislature for 1991-1992 is in the range of $2.5 to $2.7 million.

Nova Scotia comes in this year with caucus budgets totalling almost $2 million, followed by New Brunswick at slightly under $1 million, Manitoba spends $735 000, Saskatchewan approximately $600 000, Yukon follows with a budget of about $500 000 and finally Newfoundland and Prince Edward Island, both of which have budgets below $150 000, although Newfoundland's figure is difficult to pinpoint.

It appears from an examination of the figures in the following List and the implications for growth in the future, that the Board of Internal Economy in some provinces may soon wish to examine the original purpose of caucus funding in an attempt to simplify what has become a very confused area of legislature administration.

Caucus Services

H of C **Funding Mechanism:** Funding levels set by the Board of Internal Economy. Annual staff budgets for the Leaders of Opposition are approved at twice the amount provided for research to each party. Resources for translators may be assigned to research units or opposition leaders' offices.

Restrictions on use of Funds: Funds are intended to cover the costs of staff salaries and contracts for temporary services.

Employees: n.a.

Funding Levels: Research (all figures include Translation Resources): Government, $1 115 100; Opposition, $951 700; Third Party, $664 700.

Leaders' Offices: Opposition, $1 663 200; Third Party, $1 329 400.

Newf. **Funding Mechanism:** Each caucus receives an operating grant based on the formula of $1 000 per member per annum.

Restrictions on use of Funds: None.

Employees: The government caucus has three researchers. The opposition caucuses have 1 researcher, 1 chief of staff and 1 policy advisor. The Leader of the Opposition has 1 executive assistant.

Funding Levels: n.a.

P.E.I. **Funding Mechanism:** Funding levels are established by the government based on the recommendation of the Standing Committee on Internal Economy. First established in 1979 (Government caucus) and 1971 (Opposition caucus).

Restrictions on use of Funds: None.

Employees: Government, 5; Opposition, 5 (plus 1 during session and 1 summer student per caucus). Staff are employees of the Legislative Assembly and are hired on a casual basis. Pay rates are established by the Standing Committee on Internal Economy. Benefits include vacation, pension and sickness. No union.

Funding Levels: Government caucus $56 700 (total grant), Opposition caucus $77 500 (total grant).

N.S. **Funding Mechanism:** Funding levels established by the Legislature.

Restrictions on use of Funds: Funds cannot be transferred between categories.

Employees: Government, 9; Opposition, 13; Third Party, 1; Fourth Party, 1. Staff are employees of the Legislative Assembly. Pay rates are tied to civil service standards (benefits are the same as other Legislative Assembly staff, including pension). No union.

Funding Levels: Government caucus $476 800, Opposition caucus $634 500, Third Party caucus $55 100, Fourth Party caucus $36 400. Opposition Leader $518 800, Third Party Leader $224 700.

N.B. **Funding Mechanism:** Funding levels established by the Standing Committee on Legislative Administration based on budget figures determined by the Clerk of the House. First established in 1981.

Restrictions on use of Funds: None.

Employees: Government Members Office, 7 (2 researchers); Official Opposition, not finalized as of Dec. 3, 1991; Third Party, 4 (1 researcher).

Funding Levels: Government, $306 900; Opposition, $90 928; Third Party, $34 098; Fourth Party, $11 366. Leader of the Opposition, $320 625; Third Party Leader, $126 000; Fourth Party Leader, $93 400. (Leaders' figures include salary.)

Que. **Funding Mechanism:** Funding levels established by the Office of the National Assembly, which also establishes total allocation. Party leaders negotiate the breakdown among caucuses. First established in 1974.

Restrictions on use of Funds: None.

Employees: Number of employees fluctuates widely. Staff are employees of the caucus and pay rates are established by the caucus. Benefits, including pension, are established by the Office of the National Assembly. No union.

Funding Levels: Government caucus, $382 200; Opposition caucus, $312 700; Other, $43 100.

Ont. **Funding Mechanism:** Funding levels established by the Board of Internal Economy using a formula based on party standings. First established in 1975.

Restrictions on use of Funds: Expenditures are monitored by Legislative Assembly Administrative staff and are subject to audit by the Provincial Auditor.

Employees: Number of employees in each caucus varies from year to year. Pay rates are established by the caucus. Group insurance, hospital, dental and pension are provided by the Legislative Assembly; all other benefits are provided by the caucus. The NDP caucus is unionized.

Funding Levels:

Administration:

a) $8 000 per member. This is a formula allowance based on the assumption of 30 members per caucus. Therefore, each caucus receives $240 000.

b) $16 000 per backbencher. This is a formula allowance based on the assumption of a minimum 30 backbenchers per caucus.

NDP: 46 x $16 000 = $736 000

Lib.: 36 x $16 000 = $576 000

PC: 30 x $16 000 = $480 000

(The PC Party, although represented by 19 backbenchers, receives the minimum grant based on the assumed minimum of 30 backbenchers.)

Research:

$26 000 per member. This is a formula allowance based on the assumption of a minimum 30 members per caucus.

NDP: 73 x $26 000 = $1 898 000

Lib.: 36 x $26 000 = $936 000

PC: 30 x $26 000 = $780 000

French Language Operations: A formula allowance of approximately $250 000 per caucus.

Non-formula allowances:

a) For employee benefits and miscellaneous:

NDP: $448 000

Lib.: $422 000

PC: $376 000

b) Approximately $200 000 per caucus for office automation.

c) Approximately $200 000 per caucus for capital projects (maintenance of printing shops, equipment, etc.)

d) Approximately $200 000 per caucus for maintenance and leasing of equipment.

Man. Funding Mechanism: Operating budget for each caucus set by Legislative Assembly Management Commission.

Restrictions on use of Funds: All operating expenditures are processed by the Administration Branch of the Legislative Assembly and are subject to audit by the Provincial Auditor.

Employees: 12 staff-years for the Government caucus, 9 staff-years for the Official Opposition caucus and 6-staff years for the second opposition caucus. Staff are employees of the Legislative Assembly and pay rates are established by the Legislative Assembly Management Commission. Benefits, including pension, are similar to those of civil servants. No union.

Funding Levels: A base of $50 000 for the first four members and $3 000 per member thereafter.

Sask. Funding Mechanism: Funding levels for research, secretarial and operating expenses are established by the Board of Internal Economy, and by statute, using a formula based on party standings. The Legislative Assembly supplies dictating equipment, copiers, telephones, fax machines, stationery and office supplies. First established in 1976.

Restrictions on use of Funds: Funds for caucus research are separate from operational grants.

Employees: Total number of employees unknown. Research staff are employees of the caucus (some are on the Legislative Assembly payroll). Pay rates are established by caucus and benefits are provided by the caucus. A certain number of secretaries are supplied by the Legisla-

tive Assembly and their pay rates are established by the Legislative Assembly. Benefits, including pension, are the same as for civil servants.

Funding Levels: Secretarial: a per caucus grant of $35 945.96. For research, each caucus receives two separate grants, each calculated using a formula based on the number of private members in each caucus.

Grant One:

$6 365.87 per member (excluding the Speaker, the Cabinet and the Leader of the Opposition). Government members are increased by two for the purposes of this calculation.

Grant Two:

Calculation based on a formula involving the salary for a Research Officer in public service.

Opposition Leaders: Official Opposition Leader receives an additional allowance of $38 623.55. The Opposition Leader's Office also receives a grant of $119 817.41. The Third Party Leader receives an additional grant of $20 104.08 and an office grant equal to one-half of that received by the Leader of the Official Opposition.

Alta. Funding Mechanism: Established by the Special Standing Committee on Members' Services. First established pre-1970.

Restrictions on use of Funds: Funds may not be transferred amongst caucuses or to constituency offices (however 25% of a constituency budget may be transferred to the respective caucus).

Employees: Government, 34; Official Opposition, 24; Third Party, 14.

Funding Levels: Government, $1 347 570; Official Opposition, $979 894; Third Party, $551 941; Funding for research (caucus and opposition leaders) is included in caucus budgets.

B.C. **Funding Mechanism:** Funding levels established by the Board of Internal Economy and based on party standings.

Restrictions on use of Funds: Funds are basically for salaries, staff, travel, etc., but further allocation is at the discretion of the caucus chairman.

Employees: Staff are employees of the Legislative Assembly. Pay rates and certain benefits are established by the caucus. Most fringe benefits are the same as for public service employees.

Funding Levels: No specific funding is provided (part of global caucus budget and distributed at the discretion of each caucus).

Yukon **Funding Mechanism:** Established by Members' Services Board and based on party standings. First established in 1978.

Restrictions on use of Funds: Funds are generally to be used for research and secretarial services.

Employees: 2 full-time researchers and 1 full-time secretary (Government), 2 full-time researchers, 1 full-time secretary and 1 part-time secretary (Opposition), 1 full-time secretary/researcher and one part-time secretary/researcher (Third Party). Staff are employees of the caucus. Pay rates are established by the leader of each party and are subject to the policies established by the Members' Services Board.

Funding Levels: $24 400 per member for research funds, $30 500 per caucus for secretarial funds.

N.W.T. Members do not belong to party caucuses. The Northwest Territories operates on a basis of consensus government.

CHAPTER TWELVE

Employees of the Legislature

THERE ARE the equivalent of 3 788 full-time persons (sometimes referred to as "person-years") and 447 sessional employees currently working in our legislative institutions at the federal and provincial level. In Fiscal 1986/87 there were 2 856 full-time and 541 sessional. These figures, however, apply strictly to those employees who work for specific departments of the legislature (e.g. the Clerk's Office, Hansard, Food and Beverage Services, etc.) and, in most instances, do not include the large numbers of political staff—those employees who work directly for members as secretaries or assistants at the seat of government, in the constituencies or for the party caucuses. Based on an examination of legislature budgets, numbers of members in the Senate and elected members in the House of Commons, provincial and territorial legislatures as well as figures provided in the list that follows, it is estimated that approximately 3 000 more people are employed full-time in positions directly relating to members or caucuses. Taking into account that there are also a number of part-time employees working in the constituencies for members, and that maintenance and janitorial duties are carried out in some legislatures by employees of a Ministry of Public Works, or its equivalent, it could be concluded that the total number of Canadians providing support and/or services to 1 168 legislators in fourteen legislatures could range in the neighbourhood of 7 000 full-time and 1 000-2 000 part-time or sessional.

Ontario led the increase with 495 full-time employees in 1991/92, compared to 320 five years ago, however some of the increase can be attributed to agencies which come under the umbrella of the Legislative Assembly but are not part of the legislature operations (e.g. The Information and Privacy Commission).

House of Commons staffing since 1986/87 as represented by full-time employees has grown from 1 666 person-years to 1 731—an increase of 65 person-years. (It should be noted, however, that in Fiscal 1981/82 the House of Commons registered 1 898 person-years.)

Considerable gains in full-time staff also took place in Nova Scotia —28 as opposed to eighteen five years ago; Prince Edward Island—13 compared to one in 1986/87; Manitoba—52 up from 35; Saskatchewan—up ten to 47; and British Columbia where there are now 147 full-time staff in place compared to 136 in 1986/87.

The Prince Edward Island increases signal that the legislature in that province is beginning to function as an institution which now requires a full-time commitment from most of its members, and an examination of members' remuneration for that province, found elsewhere in this book, supports this suggestion.

It was not until 1974 that those working in legislatures began to be directly employed by the individual legislatures, with the exception of the Senate and the House of Commons. Up until that time, all were employees of various government departments which were responsible for the upkeep and maintenance of the legislative buildings, and for providing the staffing to look after the legislature as a legislative and administrative body. In other words, they were civil servants serving the legislature and all its elected members, reporting to other civil servants, and through them to the Ministers of the Crown. Nevertheless, they were employees of the government and this caused a conflict of interest for some. A former Director of Government Services explained "It was simple: we always put the needs of our *Government* members first."

In 1974 the House of Commons, the Ontario Legislature, the Quebec National Assembly and the legislatures of Alberta and British Columbia were considered full-time. The remainder were considered to be part-time. In most instances, there weren't any full-time legislature employees. Any necessary duties were looked after by the appropriate civil servants, with the exceptions of the Clerk of the House, who was either on the payroll of the appropriate government ministry or on retainer from a local law firm, and his staff. To augment the Clerk's staff and the civil servants, part-time or "sessional" employees were retained for the duration of a session so that peak workloads could be met. Sessional employees then, and still today, in some cases, might include court reporters, pages, messengers, food service staff, etc., who were able to organize their private working lives so that they could be available to "serve the House" when it was in session.

When the Ontario Commission on the Legislature was holding its hearings during the period 1972-1974, a great deal of discussion took place concerning the impartiality of those employed in the legislature. The Commission envisioned a legislature wherein, regardless of party, staff reporting to the Speaker would meet the needs of all members equally. The Commission felt that those employees should be hired under terms and conditions equivalent to those employed by government ministries and departments.

The Commission recommended that civil servants who were already working in the legislature be transferred over to become employees of the legislature itself and retain their full government benefits. It was anticipated that the result of all this would be a cadre of employees of the Office of the Legislative Assembly who would be loyal to the Speaker and all members of the Legislature.

Since 1974 the concept of legislatures staffed by their own employees, rather than those of the government, has gained considerable headway across Canada. Only the National Assembly of Quebec and

the legislatures of Nova Scotia, the Northwest Territories and Yukon continue their tradition of having government employees look after the affairs of the legislature. By administering the National Assembly through civil servants, rather than employees of the legislature, the Quebec Government could be seen to be in a position to exercise control over the operations of the National Assembly and to be able to give its own members an advantage as they go about their day-to-day work, although there is no evidence that this is the case. In the Northwest Territories and Yukon, it is unlikely that those governments would consider creating a special category of employee due to the very small numbers of full-time staff, and because the Northwest Territories government is by consensus rather than party.

During deliberations in 1972, the members of the Ontario Commission on the Legislature met with the three party leaders to discuss their views on a great many issues. There was some concern on the part of the Commission as to how to handle the transfer of non-management employees—who were members of the Ontario Public Service Employees Union (OPSEU)—to the Office of the Assembly. It was finally agreed that in the absence of a union the Commission would recommend that the Board of Internal Economy do everything possible to ensure that the pay and perquisites for employees of the Assembly were at least equal to those in the civil service, where there was a union. This met with general agreement, however the leader of the NDP of the day was quite insistent that those persons who were already employed by the NDP caucus remain in OPSEU. As a result, all employees working for the NDP caucus in Ontario today continue to be OPSEU members. There are equivalent arrangements for some of the employees in the House of Commons, Quebec National Assembly and, as suggested earlier, in Nova Scotia, the Northwest Territories and Yukon.

It is interesting that in the case of Ontario the NDP through its representatives on the Board of Internal Economy has, over the years, reminded the other members of the Board that OPSEU represents its employees. There have, however, been no instances of the OPSEU Local not negotiating suitable contracts with management, in this instance the NDP caucus in the legislature. There have been rumours of possible skirmishes between the members of the public service union and the administrators of the House of Commons but that is as far as it has gone. These examples perhaps best serve to illustrate that working conditions in Canada's legislatures are such that it is unlikely there is any cause for grievances to be carried to the point of strike action or any other serious disruption of the operation of the legislature.

It is clear that during the past ten years the job of an employee of a Canadian legislature at the federal or provincial level has become recognized and institutionalized. There is now a sizeable workforce across the country maintaining and operating legislatures and offering a wide range of support services to elected members.

It is unlikely that the future will bring staffing increases like those experienced in the recent past. In 1992 most of the needs for staffing in Canada's legislatures have been met; in fact, one legislature, the Quebec National Assembly, has reduced its full-time staff from 410 to 397 and its sessional staff from 163 to 150.

Nevertheless, legislatures, like other institutions, tend to have a life of their own. The question must be asked whether these bodies must, by needs, continue to grow: are current staffing levels an example of the expansionist '80s? The 1990s, as Quebec is proving, may show a marked trend beyond curbing growth, to actual reductions.

Employees

H of C   **Total Full-time:** 1 731 person-years.

Total Sessional: Included in person-years calculation.

Clerk's Office: 368 person-years (includes Deputy Clerk, 59; Law Clerk and Parliamentary Counsel, 13; Director General of Parliamentary Operations, 290).

Administrator's Office: 5 person-years.

Legislative Library: 252 person-years.

Hansard Reporting Service: 35 person-years (included in the figures for the Clerk's Office under Parliamentary Operations).

Parliamentary Relations Office: n.a.

Comptroller's Office: 89 person-years.

Status of Employees: Employees of the House of Commons. Some are unionized.

Newf.   **Total Full-time:** 68 (45 with caucuses).

Total Sessional: 3

Clerk's Office: 4

Administrator's Office: 2

Legislative Library: 3

Hansard Reporting Service: 14

Parliamentary Relations Office: None.

Status of Employees: No union.

P.E.I.   **Total Full-time:** 13

Total Sessional: 21 (including pages).

Clerk's Office: 15 (3 are full-time).

Administrator's Office: Included in figure for Clerk's Office.

Legislative Library: Legislative collection is maintained by the Provincial Library Service (a part of the Department of Community and Cultural Affairs).

Hansard Reporting Service: None.

Parliamentary Relations Office: None.

Status of Employees: Casual employees of the Legislative Assembly. No union.

N.S.   **Total Full-time:** 28

Total Sessional: 40

Clerk's Office: 2 (full-time).

Administrator's Office: 6 (including Personnel and Finance).

Legislative Library: 6 (full-time).

Hansard Reporting Service: 8 full-time and 9 sessional.

Parliamentary Relations Office: None.

Status of Employees: Civil servants. Some are unionized.

N.B. Total Full-time: 52

Total Sessional: 22

Clerk's Office: 32 (including 7 caucus staff and 11 translation staff).

Administrator's Office: Included in figures for Clerk's Office.

Legislative Library: 7

Hansard Reporting Service: 13

Parliamentary Relations Office: None.

Status of Employees: Employees of the Legislative Assembly; not civil servants. No union.

Que. Total Full-time: 397

Total Sessional: 150

Clerk's Office: 4 full-time and 1 sessional.

Administrator's Office: 3 (full-time).

Legislative Library: 59 full-time and 24 sessional.

Hansard Reporting Service: 40 full-time and 32 sessional.

Parliamentary Relations Office: 10 full-time and 3 sessional.

Status of Employees: Civil servants. Some are unionized.

Ont. Total Full-time: 495 (includes Office of the Chief Elections Officer, 17; Commission on Election Finances, 12; Information and Privacy Commissioner, 84; Conflict of Interest Commissioner, 2; Office of the Speaker, 10).

Total Sessional: 2

Clerk's Office: 107 (including Hansard Reporting Service, 45).

Administrator's Office: n.a.

Legislative Library: 93

Hansard Reporting Service: 45 (included in the figures for the Clerk's Office).

Parliamentary Relations Office: n.a.

Office of the Controller: 102

Assembly Services: 70

Status of Employees: Employees of the Legislative Assembly; not civil servants. No union.

Man. Total Full-time: 52

Total Sessional: 48

Clerk's Office: 8

Administrator's Office: Personnel and some financial functions of the Legislative Assembly are performed by the Director of Administration of the Department Cooperative, Consumer and Corporate Affairs. The Director has a staff of 11.26 staff-years, but not all are associated with the Legislative Assembly.

Legislative Library: Not a part of the Legislative Assembly.

Hansard Reporting Service: 3 full-time and 31 sessional.

Parliamentary Relations Office: These functions are performed by the Speaker's Office and the Clerk's Office.

Status of Employees: Employees of the Legislative Assembly. Not civil servants. No union.

Sask. Total Full-time: 47 (includes 4 contract employees and 8 permanent caucus employees currently on the Legislative Assembly payroll).

Total Sessional: 66 (includes 15 members' secretaries paid by the Legislative Assembly).

Non-permanent: 73 (includes 56 constituency secretaries on the Legislative Assembly payroll).

Clerk's Office: 5

Financial Services and Administration: 5

Legislative Library: 14 (full-time).

Hansard Reporting Service: 1 full-time and 35 sessional.

Parliamentary Relations Office: These functions are performed by the Speaker's Office and the Clerk's Office.

Status of Employees: Employees of the Legislative Assembly. Not civil servants.

Alta.

Total Full-time: 50 (plus 223.6 full-time equivalent).

Total Sessional: 45

Clerk's Office: 10 (includes Clerk's Assistant, 4; Parliamentary Counsel, 3; House Services, 1).

Administrator's Office: 13 (includes General Administration, 9.5; Personnel, 3.5).

Legislative Library: 16 full-time (plus 18 full-time equivalent).

Hansard Reporting Service: 6.75 full-time (plus 13.6 full-time equivalent).

Parliamentary Relations Office: None.

Status of Employees: Employees of the Legislative Assembly. No union.

B.C.

Total Full-time: 147

Total Sessional: 45

Clerk's Office: 4 table officers and 3 full-time secretaries.

Administrator's Office: Support services for the Legislative Assembly are performed by the Speaker's Office (3 employees), the Clerk's Office (see above) and the Comptroller's Office (6 employees).

Legislative Library: 34 full-time and 2 sessional.

Hansard Reporting Service: 8 full-time and 18 sessional.

Parliamentary Relations Office: None.

Status of Employees: Employees of the Legislative Assembly, except Library staff who are civil servants.

Yukon

Total Full-time: 5

Total Sessional: 1

Clerk's Office: 5 full-time and 1 sessional.

Administrator's Office: Included in the figures for the Clerk's Office.

Legislative Library: No Legislative Library.

Hansard Reporting Service: Handled under contract by a commercial firm.

Parliamentary Relations Office: None.

Status of Employees: Civil servants. One unionized employee.

N.W.T.

Total Full-time: 21

Total Sessional: 4

Clerk's Office: 21

Administrator's Office: 5 permanent, full-time employees (included in the Clerk's Office).

Legislative Library: Included in the figures for the Clerk's Office under Research Services: staffed by a Director, two Research Services employees and one Research Assistant/Library Technician.

Hansard Reporting Service: Handled under contract by a commercial firm.

Parliamentary Relations Office: This function is performed by the Clerk's Office through the Coordinator of Commications Services.

Status of Employees: Civil servants. Some are unionized.

CHAPTER THIRTEEN

Hansard Reporting Service

HANSARD, THE verbatim transcript of House debates, covers all proceedings which take place in the legislature, including those of the committees. A Hansard Reporting Service exists in the Senate, House of Commons and each of the provincial and territorial legislatures, with the exception of Prince Edward Island. In all cases, the transcripts of debates which take place in the actual Chamber of the House are printed and made available to the general public (in Prince Edward Island only Question Period is printed for distribution). Hansard may normally be purchased either in single copies or in subscription form through those agencies responsible for the sale of government documents: government bookstores or special bookstores which specialize in stocking government publications. The price is extremely modest given the volume of material and the production costs involved, and sales contribute little to the overall expense for Hansard. All elected members receive Hansard free of charge.

Hansard originated in the British House of Commons in the early 19th century, where a Mr. T.C. Hansard was responsible for printing the Debates of the House, and spread from there to other countries of what was then the British Empire. Hansard came to Canada in 1880 when it was adopted by the Canadian House of Commons, and then the various provinces.

In 1992, members of the Senate, House of Commons and provincial and territorial legislatures have come to attach more importance to the actual words spoken in their debates and proceedings than any other country on earth. No less than 200 people across the country are employed full-time, and 125 part-time (or sessional) in reporting, transcribing and printing Hansard at a cost for 1991/92 in the neighbourhood of $18 million.

It is significant to note that in the United States, where there are different traditions, none of the 50 state legislatures produce a verbatim transcript of their proceedings, and even the U.S. Congress does not print a gavel-to-gavel account of its debates equivalent to Hansard.

Hansard, in Canada, began with trained court reporters taking down the debates of the House of Commons in shorthand, with reporters spelling each other off on a regular basis, enabling each to dictate his or her notes to a typist or transcriber. As Hansard spread to the provincial legislatures, other techniques such as the stenograph and stenomask were developed by court reporters .

Right up to the 1960s most provincial legislatures contracted out their Hansard reporting requirements either to commercial firms or individual contractors. This is still the case in Northwest Territories and Yukon. When legislative sessions were much shorter, it was quite possible for a local firm to take on the job of producing Hansard, and in most cases to move into offices in the legislature itself for the duration of the session.

There were other arrangements as well. For instance, in Ontario, a number of the Hansard staff were part-time editors with commercial publishing houses. They were available to be recruited by a full-time Hansard manager and his small full-time staff, when the session was about to start.

An examination of the current costs of Hansard across Canada shows that what began as a comparatively simple process has, by 1992, become a very substantial operation. Hansard budgets for the past year, particularly in jurisdictions like Newfoundland, Nova Scotia, New Brunswick and particularly Manitoba, have been reduced. However, in the past few years, Hansard budgets in other jurisdictions have advanced by leaps and bounds. In 1986/87, for instance, the Ontario Hansard cost stood at $2.5 million. In 1992 it is $4 million, an increase of approximately 60% over five years. Similarly, the cost of producing Hansard in British Columbia rose from approximately $1.3 million last year to $2 million in 1992. Yet, a sampling of the average number of sitting days for these two legislatures over the past ten years shows that they have remained relatively constant (Ontario:1981/82— 106 days, 1986/87—92 days and 1991/92—100 days; British Columbia: 1981/82—89 days, 1986/ 87—79 days and 1991/92—85 days).

Any attempt to assess the reasons in general for an increase in the overall costs for Hansard would seem to point to the increased cost of labour, printing and distribution, electronic equipment which has replaced the "quill pen" approach, the more widespread practice of recording, printing the proceedings of Committees of the House and the additional costs which may be included in some Hansard budgets, such as Ontario, which relate to the technical support services for electronic Hansard (televised gavel-to-gavel coverage of debates and proceedings in the Chamber of the House).

But, in order to examine the steadily growing cost of Hansard in Canada it is necessary to look at some of the precedents establishing how the service actually operates. It is customary, for instance, in the House of Commons, the Ontario Legislature and the Quebec National Assembly and in lesser degrees for other provincial legislatures, for a draft copy of Hansard to be produced for circulation to, and review by, House Officers, legislative counsel, the media, caucus offices, etc. Sometimes members who have taken part in House debates may be asked by Hansard staff to clarify statements, or provide corrections to name spellings. The intent is not to permit changes to what was actually said during the debate, but merely to "clean up" the text before committing it to print. The draft copy is usually produced as soon as possible following the debate, and any alterations must be made within several hours so that it can go to press within 24 hours. There is, of course, additional expense involved in printing and circulating this "rough draft" edition before it is forwarded to the printers.

The House of Commons, Ontario Legislature, Quebec National Assembly and the Saskatchewan Legislature have electronic Hansard (television) which in all cases provide distribution of House debates to the public through cable television channels. In addition, the Hansard offices in almost all legislatures are equipped with sophisticated computer systems. Yet, in some legislatures there continues to be a reliance on manual reporting as a "back-up" to this system. For example, in the province of Ontario, a Hansard reporter is still seated at a desk on the Floor of the House where this person takes shorthand, then after a certain number of minutes he or she is replaced by another Hansard reporter who has been observing the proceedings from the Speaker's Gallery. In Ontario, the actual debate in the House is also being taken off the audio tape by a transcriber. The reporter isn't really necessary, and is there only as a sort of "double-checker", particularly in relation to "interjections" from the Floor (off-hand comments uttered by members who do not have the Floor and who have not been recognized by the Speaker). Essentially, this way of doing things means a complete duplication of effort.

Members obviously have a very direct interest, not only in how their statement or speech is reported, but how the general debate is handled by Hansard and particularly the fairness by which interjections are included in order to give as true a picture of the debate as possible. This is a very sensitive business in all legislatures as it is from the accuracy of this process that constituents, members of the public and the media will form their impressions, good or bad, of individual members and the contribution they make as legislators.

It is up to the manager of Hansard to ensure that a proper weighting or balance exists in the preparation of the printed debates. The process by which Hansard staff make the final determination as to whether a certain interjection is "relevant to the debate," or how much to "clean up" the comments of a member speaking extemporaneously is indeed tricky, to say the least. And yet, through a process which is almost impossible to define, the written word, when it comes out as the authorized verbatim debate of the House in the form of Hansard, seems to be accepted by all concerned as "the gospel". This past year saw several remarkable comments issued in the House of Commons, one ascribed to the Prime Minister, of particularly unparliamentary language. These remarks, however, were allegedly excised from Hansard and, officially, were never made.

To illustrate the sensitivities involved in one province, again Ontario, the Chief of Hansard in the mid-1980s proposed that in order to reduce expenses the traditional reporter on the Floor of the House be removed because the audio recording system tied into the Hansard computers could do the job. When the Government and the two Opposition Parties heard of this proposal, they objected strenuously and insisted that the status quo be maintained. The reason they gave was that they wanted to have a person present who could be aware of the circumstances of the debate, and what was being said by whom. They were unwilling to leave this to an electronic recording device.

In recent years, those responsible for Hansard have been looking at various technologies which might improve the way in which verbatim reporting is handled, while helping to save on costs. However, this is not a matter of urgency to elected members; their main concern is that their constituents, and the media, receive a full accounting of their participation in the House, regardless of the cost. In Canada, verbatim transcripts have, for all elected members, become as dependable and solid as the seats which they occupy in the legislatures.

There is no question that a great deal of effort is extended by many legislators in Canada to get "on the record", or at least to be seen on the fringes of the record.

To produce Hansard in Canada costs around 3.1% of the $585 million total budget of all legislatures in Canada. The cost could actually be more, since it is almost impossible to determine whether the costs of outside printing plants or work performed by personnel who may be employed in government departments outside the legislature, are recorded in the figures.

Projections for Hansard costs in Canada, based on past performance, and taking into account unusual situations and longer legislative sessions in the future, as well as increased staffing costs, etc., might indicate that the total annual Hansard costs could rise to $40 million by the very early part of the 21st century.

An "unusual situation" could be identified as the Legislature of the Northwest Territories where some verbatim translation and transcription is handled in six native languages, plus English and French.

It is likely that legislatures in Canada will, in general, become places of increasing legislative activity, as populations increase and governments wrestle with wider-ranging agendas. Television, or electronic Hansard, is also bound to become more widespread.

All of this raises the question of whether full Hansard in its present form (rooted in a 150 year-old tradition and demanding an increased expense) is really necessary. Is there a simpler way of going about things? Does the cost attached represent a wise expenditure of public funds?

Prince Edward Island is the one jurisdiction where debates are recorded in full, but only Question Period is transcribed and printed. Other proceedings are recorded on tape and transcribed only on request. Could there be merit in having this applied nation-wide, including the House of Commons? In the Senate, House of Commons and provincial and territorial legislatures all committees are recorded, but only the committees of the Senate, House of Commons and the larger legislatures are transcribed and printed in Hansard, usually within ten days. The transcription and printing of committee deliberations is an area which has increased substantially in recent years, and a considerable number of staff are involved in this work. Would the simple minutes of committee meetings suffice in all jurisdictions, rather than having verbatim Hansard?

The late professor Norman Ward, a distinguished political scientist at the University of Saskatchewan who wrote the entry for Hansard in *The Canadian Encyclopedia*, described the use of Hansard as "partly for the immediate convenience of legislators but also as an indispensable historical archive." Many will agree with this statement, however once again the cost factor must be taken into account.

It would, of course, be ridiculous to propose that Hansard be done away with altogether, nevertheless those responsible for charting the future course of legislature operations in the various jurisdictions should be examining what can be done to provide proper coverage of legislature debates and proceedings at a reasonable expense, given the historical rate of growth in many Hansard budgets. In any event, it is likely that electronic Hansard will sooner or later become the principle provider of archival material.

Hansard Reporting Service

H of C   **1989/90 Budget:** $4 009 400

1990/91 Budget: $4 304 800

1991/92 Budget: $4 799 500

Service: Bilingual. Available within 24 hours. Published and available to the public.

Note: Figures include the Hansard budget and the Committee Reporting budget.

Newf.   **1989/90 Budget:** $272 600

1990/91 Budget: $473 400

1991/92 Budget: $369 777

P.E.I.   There is no Hansard service in P.E.I. Proceedings are recorded on tape and transcribed only upon request. Question Period is transcribed and printed in-house for delivery the next day. Committee proceedings are recorded on tape and transcribed at the request of the committee.

N.S.   **1989/90 Budget:** $447 300

1990/91 Budget: $538 000

1991/92 Budget: $433 800

Service: English only. Printed by government department; final House copy is produced by the morning following the debate (two days for committees).

N.B.   **1989/90 Budget:** $558 100

1990/91 Budget: $584 800

1991/92 Budget: $513 100

Service: English and French. The first edition (without translation) is photocopied by the Government Copy Centre. Several months are required to produce the translated version, which is printed by the Queen's Printer. Committee transcripts are produced within two weeks.

Que.   **1989/90 Budget:** $1 960 000

1990/91 Budget: $2 008 800

1991/92 Budget: $2 045 100

Service: French only. Final House copy is produced in 48 hours and is printed by a commercial firm. Committee copy is produced in three to four weeks and is printed by the National Assembly.

Ont.   **1989/90 Budget:** $2 783 600

1990/91 Budget: $3 872 300

1991/92 Budget: $4 061 300

Service: English only. Final House reports are produced within 24 hours (up to 10 days for committees). Printed by a commercial firm.

Man.   **1989/90 Budget:** $440 900 (represents actual expenditures. The budget for 1989/90 was $592 300.)

1990/91 Budget: $818 600

1991/92 Budget: $654 400

Service: English only. Final House copy is produced in 24 hours. Typeset by a commercial firm and printed by the Queen's Printer.

Sask.   **1989/90 Budget:** $442 730

1990/91 Budget: $459 110

1991/92 Budget: $461 790

Service: English only. Both final House and final committee copy are produced in 24 hours. Typeset in-house and printed by a commercial firm.

Alta.   **1989/90 Budget:** $715 729

1990/91 Budget: $697 266

1991/92 Budget: $814 542

Service: English only. Printed by a commercial firm. Final House copy is produced in 24 hours; final committee copy is produced in 48 hours. Electronic blues and hard copy blues are produced within 1 1/2 hours. Hansard text is stored on a mainframe computer for on-line searches using key words. Limited copy of current session index is produced and published at the end of each session.

B.C. **1989/90 Budget:** $1 259 277 (includes cost of printing by Queen's Printer)

1990/91 Budget: $1 292 500 (includes cost of printing by Queen's Printer)

1991/92 Budget: $1 992 000 (includes cost of printing by Queen's Printer and provisions for televising debates).

Service: English only. Printed by the Queen's Printer. Final House copy is produced in 36 hours. Committee copy is printed but not published.

Yukon **1989/90 Budget:** $228 000

1990/91 Budget: $317 430

1991/92 Budget: $330 301

Service: English only. Transcribed and printed by a commercial firm under a five-year contract that commenced Jan. 1, 1989. Final House copy is produced in 48 hours; time to produce committee copy varies.

N.W.T. **1989/90 Budget:** $325 000

1990/91 Budget: $330 000

1991/92 Budget: $346 500

Service: English only. Printed by a commercial firm. Final House copy is produced in 5 days.

CHAPTER FOURTEEN

The Legislative Press Gallery

CANADIANS FROM coast to coast have received an increased diet of political reporting in the past decade. This is reflected in the overall numbers of those who are a part of press gallery operations, and they will continue to grow.

It is estimated that approximately 750 reporters, technicians and support staff are engaged in providing media coverage of the Senate, House of Commons and the provincial and territorial legislatures. About half are based in Ottawa. This group alone has grown from about 270 ten years ago to 365 in 1992. Over the same period, there were modest increases in the ranks of the media covering some of the provincial legislatures. In 1981/82, 79 media personnel were attached to the Quebec National Assembly. Today that figure stands at 105. Nova Scotia registered an increase from 10 to 23. Saskatchewan went from a press gallery of 34 members to one of 47. In many other provinces, however, figures have remained constant.

Members of the media reporting on politics and government do so under a wide range of working conditions. The hub of operations for media attached to the Senate and the House of Commons is the National Press Building, which is located directly across from Parliament on Wellington Street. Here, representatives of the print, radio and television media (including the wire services and national magazines), are in a position to observe federal politics up close. It is in the media studio of the National Press Building that major press confer-

ences are held before the television cameras of the networks, with reporters and correspondents filling the seats and standing in the aisles.

The House of Commons, in the Centre Block, maintains a large office area for working journalists equipped with television monitors linked with OASIS, the House communications network which carries the proceedings live. OASIS also pipes the television feed into the National Press Building as well as the other buildings within the precincts of Parliament.

At Queen's Park in Toronto, media representatives covering that legislature are ensconced in a variety of offices, ranging from cramped, round tower offices accessible only by a circular metal staircase, to large offices with lofty ceilings looking out over University Avenue. Gallery members have a large sitting room, and an adjacent area which includes a full bar and board room table. Several attendants are provided to the media to handle bar service which includes light refreshments, and there is an attendant who provides gallery members with legislative papers and notices. The Press Gallery in the Chamber proper, which is directly above the Speaker's Chair, can be accessed directly from the press gallery quarters, and media people normally crowd their gallery during Question Period, although there is a direct television feed to their offices.

At Province House, in Halifax, Canada's oldest and smallest seat of government, built in 1819, surroundings for the media are definitely spartan compared to Parliament or the Ontario Legislature. Press Gallery members occupy a large room just inside the entrance to the building, and maintain private offices in a variety of downtown buildings. They do not have the luxury of being able to watch the proceedings of the House on television.

Although working conditions for the media vary in legislatures across Canada, there does appear to be a common culture surrounding their operations. Invariably members of press galleries are organized into a formal Press Gallery Association with its own officers. The president of the Press Gallery, or his or her designate, is usually the person who sits with the prime minister or a premier at a press conference and formally opens and closes the proceedings. The president also negotiates with the Speaker for office space for gallery members, and any other services which may be required. If a gallery member has to be spoken to, or disciplined for some reason, it is up to the president to take action. There is a "pecking order" in press galleries, and the officers are usually drawn from a small pool of the most

experienced media representatives assigned to the legislature.

To be appointed "Bureau Chief" of a news organization covering the Ontario Legislature or the Quebec National Assembly is considered to be a significant plum for a reporter or correspondent, and a major step on the ladder which may lead to a senior position such as Bureau Chief in Ottawa, the ultimate in Canadian political reporting. There seems to be an "ebb and flow" of media personnel in all legislatures as they arrive to take up a post, and then move on after several years. Some continue in political reporting; others return to a fresh assignment with whatever news organization they represent (or in some cases change careers and join a government department).

It is significant that the landlords of the press galleries across the country—the Speakers of the individual legislatures, or the government—do not charge gallery members or the organizations they represent for the space they occupy (with the exception of the National Press Building). They also provide telephone lines and equipment to offices in

Press Gallery Membership

	Radio	T.V.	Print	Freelance	News Agency	Honorary	Total Members
House of Commons [1]	64	118	81	16	86	5	365
Newfoundland	6	5	2	0	0	0	13
Prince Edward Island	3	2	2	0	0	0	7
Nova Scotia	7	6	4	4	2	0	23
New Brunswick	11	6	0	0	0	2	21 [2]
Quebec	19	46	21	1	16	2	105
Ontario	7	14	24	2	0	0	47
Manitoba	5	5	9	3	2	0	21
Saskatchewan	14	13	20	0	0	0	47
Alberta	6	7	17	0	2	0	32
British Columbia	4	6	16	1	3	5	35
Yukon	3	1	2	1	0	0	7
Northwest Territories [3]	n.a.	n.a.	n.a.	n.a.	n.a.	n.a.	n.a.

[1] Members of the House of Commons Press Gallery also report on the proceedings of the Senate.
[2] Total includes one mixed-media member.
[3] The Northwest Territories have no official Press Gallery. Members of the press are accredited on request.

the legislative buildings, although long distance charges are the responsibility of the news media. Office furniture and the provision of appropriate staff to meet the various information needs of gallery members are also supplied at legislature or government expense.

During the 1972-1974 deliberations of the Ontario Commission on the Legislature, the suggestion was made by one commissioner (who happened to be a journalist) that perhaps it would be better if the Press Gallery of the Ontario Legislature could be moved out of the main building and dispatched to the Whitney Block, which is across the street and connected by tunnel. The Press Gallery offices, then, were described by Ministry of Government Services personnel as "rabbit warrens" badly in need of total renovation. There was also the question of the efficacy of media representatives attempting to operate at arm's length from politicians and the government when, in fact, they were beholden in many ways to those very bodies for their office space, bar, and other facilities. Gallery members, when they got wind of the suggestion went up in arms. The government of the day had the same reaction.

There is no question that media representatives who are assigned to cover Parliament and the provincial and territorial legislatures have considerable influence on elected politicians (although the media may claim this isn't so). Politicians, by and large, will do everything possible to curry favour with press gallery members, either individually or collectively; their political livelihood and that of their government or party depends on it. They are not about to do anything which will upset the media.

In this case both groups are determined to get something from the other—a news story in the case of the journalist, and exposure, either personally, or for an initiative (or preferably both) on the part of the politician.

The media can "go for the jugular", within reason. They are, after all, in the business of looking for news. At the same time, they can't afford to close down their sources by being too hard on the politicians they cover everyday. They also know that in

terms of career paths, one direction in which to move is towards a government ministry and a possible job as Director of Communications. These jobs don't just fall out of thin air, they come from "catching the eye" of cabinet ministers and developing the right contacts, friendships and confidences.

Those associated with press galleries across the country represent a force of slightly more than half the number of elected members at the federal and provincial level in Canada. Politics would not be politics without the media. For that matter, the media would be quite different without politics.

Because of the "intertwining" relationship between politicians and members of the media in general, it is difficult to assess whether in fact the media is really doing its job, or whether they have been "sandbagged" by the politicians, in spite of their protestations, and what appears to be just the opposite. There is evidence that some of those who are a part of the media cadre could be accused of "taking" news, rather than digging, probing and analyzing, that the perquisites provided by some legislatures and governments have dulled their senses as newshounds.

Media scrums (a horde of reporters and photographers crowding in on a "hot" politician) seem to best represent the curious mating rite which brings opposites instantly together. It wouldn't be worth the political life of a prime minister or a premier to refuse to stop at a certain place in a stairwell or a corridor and engage in this ritual. The question might be asked why the media don't demand that prime ministers and premiers give formal press conferences; the media scrum, as it exists in Canada today, is probably doing as much as any other single element in parliamentary and legislative life to make a mockery of the political process.

In 1992, all politicians in Canada are automatically involved in a complicated and massive building project—that of architecting the future of a people and their basic institutions. It may be that members of press galleries have to seriously debate their own position, if any, individually and collectively, in relation to this process.

CHAPTER FIFTEEN

Research Services

ALL LEGISLATIVE bodies in Canada at the federal and provincial levels provide some form of research services to their members, always through the party caucuses (except Northwest Territories), sometimes through the library, and to a lesser degree by the provision of funding to enable individual members to retain the services of a personal research assistant. As is the case with members' services in general throughout Canada, the research function has come to the fore mainly during the past ten years.

Prior to 1970, only members of the Senate and the House of Commons were provided with research services through a legislative library, in this case the Library of Parliament, which had developed its own research department. In 1971 the Quebec National Assembly offered its members research services, and in 1979 the Ontario Legislature initiated the Legislative Library, Research and Information Services division of the Office of the Assembly. The hallmark of these research services (as compared to those offered by the party caucuses and members' personal research assistants) is that they are provided by the library on a strictly non-partisan basis. A member, for instance, may commission a research paper from the library, but that paper may not be slanted in any way. It is up to the member, then, to either use the material as it is, or to convert the substance of the paper to meet whatever other requirements may exist, including those of a political nature. The Research Branches of the Library of Parliament and those of Ontario and Quebec (there are no others in Canada) jealously guard their neutrality and do everything possible to ensure

integrity. As a result, they have gained an excellent reputation for their work.

It is the caucus researchers who are involved in major research projects of a political nature, designed in the instance of opposition caucuses to produce new evidence or information which can strengthen their position in Question Period, before the media, or in buttressing the probes of an investigative committee constituted by the party to examine an issue of public concern. As a result, in some cases, and as can be seen from the accompanying list, substantial budgets are devoted to supporting caucus research operations. The Ontario Legislature, with 155 fewer members, actually manages to out-spend the House of Commons and has a 1992 total research budget for all three caucuses of $3 632 000, plus additional funds for French language applications. The House of Commons budget for the same period was $2 731 500 for the research services provided by the three federal caucuses to their members.

Only the House of Commons, the Ontario Legislature, and Quebec National Assembly provide funds for a personal research assistant, should the member wish to use part of his or her global office budget for that purpose. Newfoundland members may also have access to personal research assistance, but approval must first be sought from the Board of Internal Economy. Saskatchewan members may also use their secretarial or constituency office allowance for the purpose of hiring a research assistant.

It should be noted that until the late 1980s,

there was a Research Department of five persons in the Legislative Library of the Alberta Legislature, however that service was discontinued. It was the only source of non-partisan research at that legislature.

The Research Branches of the Library of Parliament, the Ontario Legislature and the National Assembly of Quebec have bred a number of highly skilled people who have undertaken ground-breaking research projects and, as well, have gone on to author various books relating to their field of specialization. Some caucus research alumni have moved on to elected office, to the top echelons of party organizations, to the media, or have made a significant contribution in endeavors relating to business or the labour movement.

Research Services

H of C   **Personal Research Assistant:** Within the limits of the overall staff budgets.

Caucus Research: Within the limits of the authorized budget.

Library Research: The research department of the Library of Parliament has a staff consisting of 88 person-years.

Newf.   **Personal Research Assistant:** As per Internal Economy Commission approval.

Caucus Research: Government caucus: 2 researchers and 1 public relations officer. Opposition caucuses: 1 researcher and 1 public relations officer.

Library Research: Total staff of 3 who assist with research.

P.E.I.   **Personal Research Assistant:** None.

Caucus Research: Government, 2; Opposition, 2. Pay rates are established by the Standing Committee on Internal Economy. Staff are employees of the Legislative Assembly and are hired on a casual basis. No union.

Library Research: There is no Legislative Library *per se*. Library service is provided on demand by the Provincial Library Service.

N.B.   **Personal Research Assistant:** None.

Caucus Research: Staff are employees of the Legislative Assembly. Pay rates are established by the Standing Committee on Legislative Administration. Benefits, including pension, are the same as other Legislative Assembly staff. No union. Two Government Members' Office employees are researchers, one Third Party employee is a researcher.

Library Research: Legislative Library research is available.

N.S.   **Personal Research Assistant:** None.

Caucus Research: 6 staff.

Library Research: No separate research department in the Legislative Library.

Que.   **Personal Research Assistant:** Members may hire a personal research assistant using the annual global staff allowance of between $98 300 and $115 500.

Caucus Research: Number of employees fluctuates widely. Pay rates are established by the party leader. Staff are employees of the caucus. No union.

Library Research: 8 employees. Department was established in 1971. Employees are civil servants. Research is restricted to legislative business. Non-partisan research is provided to members, the Speaker, ministers, party leaders and committees.

Ont.   **Personal Research Assistant:** Members may hire a personal research assistant using the annual global staff allowance of $136 865.

Caucus Research: $26 000 per member. This is a formula allowance based on the assumption of a minimum 30 members per caucus.

NDP: 73 x $26 000 = $1 898 000

Lib.: 36 x $26 000 = $936 000

PC: 30 x $26 000 = $780 000

Library Research: 21 employees (16 research officers). Department was established in 1979. Staff are employees of the Legislative Assembly. Non-partisan research is provided to members, ministers, party leaders and committees.

Man. **Personal Research Assistant:** There are no personal research assistants *per se*. However, there are research staff attached to each caucus office. Also, members may use funds from their $25 823 global constituency allowance to fund research assistants or other personal assistants.

Caucus Research: Government, 3 staff years; Official Opposition, 3 staff years; Third Party, 2 staff years.

Library Research: Legislative Library is not a part of the Legislative Assembly.

Sask. **Personal Research Assistant:** Member may hire research assistant using the secretarial allowance or constituency office allowance. No restriction on number of employees.

Caucus Research: Total number of employees unknown. Staff are employees of the caucus, and pay rates and benefits are established by the caucus. Some employees are on the Legislative Assembly payroll.

Library Research: No separate research department in Legislative Library.

Alta. **Personal Research Assistant:** None.

Caucus Research: Government, 7; Official Opposition, 5; Third Party 5. Pay rates are established by caucus and range from $2 083 to $3 510 per month. Staff are employees of the Legislative Assembly and are hired on a contract basis. No union.

Library Research: None.

B.C. **Personal Research Assistant:** None.

Caucus Research: Pay rates and some benefits are established by caucus. Funding is included in Caucus Services. Staff are employees of the Legislative Assembly.

Library Research: No separate research department in Legislative Library.

Yukon **Personal Research Assistant:** None.

Caucus Research: Government, 2 full-time; Opposition, 2 full-time; Third Party, 1 part-time. Staff are employees of the caucus and pay rates and benefits are established by the caucus. No union.

Library Research: Legislative Library is not a part of the Legislative Assembly.

N.W.T. **Personal Research Assistant:** None.

Caucus Research: There are no caucuses in the Northwest Territories.

Member's Research: 3 researchers and 1 research assistant/library technician. Staff are employees of the Clerk's Office and provide research assistance to all members and assigned Standing Committees.

Library Research: No Legislative Library. A small resource centre maintains a selection of reference materials (i.e. statutes, Hansard, etc.), sessional documents, and other current topical material.

CHAPTER SIXTEEN

The Legislative Library

THERE IS a legislative library in all jurisdictions except Prince Edward Island and the Northwest Territories. Manitoba and the Yukon have legislative libraries, however they do not come under the authority of the Speaker and the Legislative Assembly.

The mandate of most legislative libraries is to serve the elected members and their staffs, the caucuses, the officers and staff of the Legislative Assembly itself, and those people in government departments who are required to interact with the Legislative Assembly, such as the office of Legislative Counsel, the Election Finances Commission (or its equivalent), the Office of the Ombudsman, etc. In some instances, members of the public may also have access to the library if their work involves a specific research project with no resource base other than the legislative library. However, on the whole, the library and its resources exist principally to serve the members of the legislature and any other uses are secondary.

In the Research Services Chapter of this analysis, it is noted that some legislative libraries offer considerable resources in this field, especially the Library of Parliament (which comes under the joint authority of the Speakers of the House of Commons and Senate, and serves members of both equally), and the libraries of the Ontario Legislature and the Quebec National Assembly. Together with reference and research services (and in the case of Ontario, a press clipping service) these libraries provide a service which is not only thoroughly professional but also unique because of their clientele and, as the principal provider of research assistance, the library interacts closely with Committees of the House.

The budget of the Library of Parliament has gone from $8.6 million in 1982 to a little over $16 million this year. Staff levels, as can be seen in the List, range above 250 person-years, however this gives a good indication of the demands which are increasingly being placed on this important unit of Parliament. Similarly, Ontario's library budget has gone from $2.5 million in 1982 when there was a staff of 73 employees, to $6.6 million in 1992, and 93 employees. The library of the Quebec National Assembly, on the other hand, showed a budget increase in the past 10 years to $3.5 million, but a reduction in staff from 87 to the present 83.

During the early 1970s when the Ontario Commission on the Legislature was examining the various facilities and services available to members, considerable attention was paid to the Legislative Library, at that time administered by the Ministry of Government Services. With the exception of a few members, the library was, by and large, being used by persons other than legislators. This was a matter of concern to the Commission, and considerable attention was given as to how to "beef up" the image and role of the library so that members would be more prepared to respond to the ever-increasing challenges of being a lawmaker in a modern legislative institution. Based on the recommendations of the Commission and with the advice of the Librarian of Parliament, the government transferred the Legislative Library to the Speaker's domain, who recruited a person with the professional qualifications and background to enable the Legislative Library to become of significant service to members of the legislature.

At the beginning of the 1980s, the British Columbia Legislative Library was split between the jurisdiction of the Speaker (when the House was in Session) and the Provincial Secretary (during the House recess). It is therefore difficult to assess costs at that time, however by 1987 it appeared to have fully come under the authority of the Speaker and there were 32 full-time staff in place and an overall budget of $1.4 million. In 1992, staff levels have increased to 34, with a projected budget for library services of $2.3 million.

The Alberta Legislative Library has actually seen a reduction in its budget for the same period, due to the closing of the Research Department. In 1992 the library accounts for a budget of $947 237 and a staff equivalent to eighteen full-time employees, whereas in 1987 the budget was approximately $1.1 million and employees numbered 24.

Manitoba and Saskatchewan spend about the same amounts on their legislative libraries. It seems strange that in 1992, Manitoba is really the only legislature of its size where the library does not come under the authority of the Speaker, although this may be explained by the fact that some other services in the legislative building are still handled by government departments. It would appear likely that in the not-too-distant future the library will be handed over to the Speaker in order to give credence to the philosophy which is very much in place throughout Canada: the legislative building and its various facilities, services and appendages should be under the independent authority of the Speaker who acts on behalf of all members, regardless of party affiliation.

Legislative Library

H of C **Number of Employees:** 252 person-years.

1990-91 Budget: $14 997 000

1991-92 Budget: $16 238 000

Number of Employees in Research Department: 88 person-years.

Newf. **Number of Employees:** 3

1989-90 Budget: $104 300

1990-91 Budget: $111 500

1991-92 Budget: $119 800

Number of Employees in Research Department: No separate research department in the Legislative Library.

P.E.I. There is no Legislative Library *per se*. Library service is provided on demand by the Provincial Library Service.

N.S. **Number of Employees:** 6

1989-90 Budget: $356 300

1990-91 Budget: $407 000

1991-92 Budget: $428 200

Number of Employees in Research Department: No separate research department in the Legislative Library.

N.B. **Number of Employees:** 10

1989-90 Budget: $510 290

1990-91 Budget: $531 971

1991-92 Budget: $452 125

Number of Employees in Research Department: 3

Que. **Number of Employees:** 83

1989-90 Budget: $2 799 800

1990-91 Budget: $3 100 000

1991-92 Budget: $3 500 000

Number of Employees in Research Department: 10

Ont. **Number of Employees:** 93

1989-90 Budget: $5 239 100

1990-91 Budget: $5 961 800

1991-92 Budget: $6 642 700

Number of Employees in Research Department: 21

Man. **No. of Employees:** 17.19 staff-years.

1989-90 Budget: $734 000

1990-91 Budget: $795 400

1991-92 Budget: $773 000

Number of Employees in Research Department: No research department (Legislative Library is not a part of the Legislative Assembly).

Sask.   **Number of Employees:** 15

1989-90 Budget: $662 400

1990-91 Budget: $721 100

1991-92 Budget: $811 900

Number of Employees in Research Department: No separate research department in the Legislative Library.

Alta.   **Number of Employees:** 16 full-time and 2 wage employees (totalling 18 full-time equivalents).

1989-90 Budget: $910 388

1990-91 Budget: $883 363

1991-92 Budget: $947 237

Number of Employees in Research Department: None.

B.C.   **Number of Employees:** 34 (plus 1 sessional).

1989-90 Budget: $1 737 228

1990-91 Budget: $1 824 043

1991-92 Budget: $2 303 052

Number of Employees in Research Department: No separate research department in the Legislative Library.

Yukon   Legislative Library not a part of the Legislative Assembly.

N.W.T.   No Legislative Library. A resource centre maintains a selection of reference materials (i.e. statutes, Hansard, etc.), sessional documents, and other current topical material.

CHAPTER SEVENTEEN

The Senate

THE MEMBERSHIP of the 104-seat Senate of Canada is composed of the Prime Minister's appointees from each of the provinces, based historically on a set number of seats for each. Because the Senate is unelected, many of its administrative arrangements differ from those of the provinces and the House of Commons. Senators do not represent constituencies, and therefore there is no need for constituency offices, allowances for travel within the constituency, Householder newsletters, etc. For this reason, it is impractical to try to make operational comparisons between the Senate and the elected Houses across the country.

The Senate was created in 1867, and until such time as the Constitution Act is amended by the provinces, the qualifications for appointment to the Senate will remain as they have existed for the past 125 years: Canadian citizen, domiciled in the province of appointment, at least 30 years of age, with a net estate worth of at least $4 000 including unencumbered land in the province with a minimum value of $4 000.

Senators are currently appointed with no fixed term, however they are required to retire at age 75. Their seats are distributed as follows: Ontario and Quebec each have 24; six seats go to each of the four Western Provinces; New Brunswick and Nova Scotia each have ten; Newfoundland has six; four go to Prince Edward Island, and one each to Yukon and the Northwest Territories.

An annual sessional indemnity of $64 400 is paid to senators in 1992, along with a tax-free allowance of $10 100. Any senator who fails to appear at least once in two consecutive sessions will lose his or her seat. During a session of Parliament, a deduction of $60 from the indemnity and $60 from the expense allowance is made for each missed day in excess of 21.

Senators may carry on with their outside work or profession, however the Constitution Act provides that senators cannot sit on committees which may be examining matters in which he or she has a pecuniary interest.

As the late Senator Eugene Forsey pointed out, the Senate was originally established as a means to protect the less populated regions—Quebec and the Maritime Provinces—against the preponderance of Ontario, to protect minorities, and to provide a "sober second thought" to legislation. It was also intended to protect provincial and regional interests in matters under federal jurisdiction. As matters stand, Quebec and Ontario, with nearly two-thirds of the Canadian population, have less than half of the Senate seats. According to Dr. Forsey, "As long as the Senate has the legal power to throw out—and keep throwing out—any bill passed by the House of Commons, the other provinces can theoretically protect themselves against central Canadian domination." Forsey went on to say in 1988, before the wrangling over the Goods and Services Tax Bill, "As the Senate is appointed, not elected, it has very little political clout: it has not thrown out a bill from the Commons for almost 50 years. So the protection, in fact, does not amount to much. But, such as it is, the smaller provinces are not likely to give it up. They want more protection, not less."

Senator Forsey saw a great many problems on the horizon in connection with trying to abolish or reform the Senate. When asked what internal changes could take place in the Senate, regardless of constitutional considerations, he provided the following check list.

- The abolition of property qualifications for senators.
- A fixed term of office: ten years, renewable for a further term of five years upon the recommendation of a secret-ballot vote by a bi-partisan Senate Committee.
- The removal of any senator who fails to attend at least one-third of the sittings in each of two consecutive years.
- A full pension at 65 after fifteen years' service (or at 70, with ten years' service).
- The establishment of standing committees on regional affairs, official languages (the membership of which would consist of half French- and half English-speaking senators) and on human rights.
- The establishment of regional, all-party caucuses.

An examination of the Table "Structure of Upper Houses Worldwide" on Pages 156-7, shows that Canada is the only country out of 43 nations to have an Upper House which offers what amounts to "lifetime" appointments for all its senators, and Canada has the 11th largest senate in the world. (The U.S. is 12th with 100 members.)

The 1992 Senate budget is $43 million. It is very likely that Canada spends more on its Senate on a per capita basis than almost any other country in the world, and Canadian senators enjoy a security of tenure and income that far exceeds the provisions for senators in any other nation.

It is also clear from the information contained in the Table that, internationally, there are no set patterns for senate development, and that each senate has been constituted in a particular way that reflects the needs of the country in question. In terms of future reform, the question of the cost of the Senate should obviously be kept in mind, and cost translates into size. It is difficult to see how a Canadian Senate of more than 50 or 60 seats could be justified. Any Senate "wish lists" must be tempered by the hard reality of cost. In reality, the whole issue of Senate "reform" is so complex and interlocking—even for the experts (of which there are few)—

that substantial changes are unlikely to take place without very extensive consultations between the provinces and Ottawa.

Some aspects of the Senate, including the legislative library (the cost for which is shared with the House of Commons), the Press Gallery and the budget, have been listed in the appropriate Chapter for comparison purposes.

Senate Remuneration

BASIC	1990	1991
Members' Basic Indemnity	$60 000	$64 400
% Increase over Previous Year	0.0	7.33
Tax Free Allowance	9 500	10 100
Total Basic Remuneration	69 500	74 500

ADDITIONAL		
Speaker [1]	28 900	31 000
Leader of the Government [2]	45 800	49 100
Leader of the Opposition	22 300	23 800
Dep. Leader of the Government	14 000	14 900
Deputy Leader of the Opposition	8 800	9 400
Government Whip	7 100	7 500
Opposition Whip	4 600	4 800

[1] Also receives a $3 000 residence allowance and a $1 000 car allowance.
[2] Also receives a $2 000 car allowance.

Senate Information

Employees

Total Full-time: 458

Total Sessional: n.a.

Clerk's Office: 13

Administrator's Office: n.a.

Legislative Library: n.a.

Hansard Reporting Service: 19

Parliamentary Relations Office: 10

Status of Employees: n.a.

Hansard

1991/92 Budget: $1 221 649

Service: Daily editions of Debates of the Senate for publication; preparation of bound volumes of debates; reporting, dictation and transcription of debates; editing and revision of senator's transcripts (blues); provision of texts to senators and Parliamentary Press Gallery on demand; coordination and submission of texts to the printing bureau and translation bureaus.

Financial Management

Body Responsible: Standing Committee on Internal Economy, Budgets and Administration.

Composition of Management Body: Hon. Senator Lavoie-Roux (Chairman), Hon. Senator R. Leblanc (Vice Chairman) and fifteen senators.

Reporting Relationship: Reports to the Senate.

Average Number of Meetings per Year: 25

Minutes: All meetings are documented.

Powers and Duties of Management Body: The Committee reviews and approves financial, personnel and administrative policies and budgets.

Estimates which are Reviewed by Management Body: Main and Supplementary Estimates.

Committee Allowances

Per Diem: None.

Expense Allowance: $45.45 meal allowance. When travelling by air, senators travel first class, staff travels economy.

Travel Allowances

General: Senators: actual living expenses are reimbursed up to a maximum of $166 per day when supported by receipts. Taxis are reimbursed up to $23 per day without receipts. Unlimited with receipts.

Staff: Per diem of $45.45. Hotel accommodation at Treasury Board-approved rates. Receipts required. Taxis are reimbursed up to $5 without receipts. Unlimited with receipts. Other authorized staff expenses are reimbursed when supported by receipts.

Air: Senators travel first class, staff travel economy class.

Bus and Train: Senators travel first class with a free rail pass, staff travel economy class.

Car: Senators: $.325 per km. Staff: Treasury Board rates.

Pension

Contribution Level: 6% of sessional indemnity (basic pension). An optional contribution of up to 10% of additional salaries may be made.

Minimum Age Requirement: n.a.

Minimum Service Requirement: 6 years.

Basis of Pension Calculation: 3% accrual rate per year, multiplied by the number of years of service, multiplied by the average of the best six consecutive annual earnings. The optional, additional salary pension is calculated in the same manner except with an accrual rate of 5% if the contribution level is at 10% (prorated).

Maximum Pension Level: Basic: 75% (25 years x 3%). Optional, additional salary pension: no maximum.

Post-Retirement Adjustment: Pension escalation is based on cost of living increases.

Spousal Benefit: 60% of senator's pension (also increased by cost of iving).

Library

Budget for the library is shared with the House of Commons.

Structure of Upper Houses Worldwide

Country and Body	No. of Seats	Term (years)	Appointment Arrangements
Afghanistan (Senate)	192	n.a.	One-third are directly elected for a term of five years; one-third are elected by provincial councils for a term of three years; one-third are appointed by the government for a term of four years
Antigua and Barbuda (Senate)	17	5	Appointed immediately following the House elections
Argentina (Senate)	46	9	Indirectly elected; one-third are renewed every three years
Austria (Bundesrat)	63	5 - 6	Indirectly elected
Bahamas (Senate)	16	5	Appointed by the Governor General
Barbados (Senate)	21	5	Appointed by the Governor General
Belgium (Senate)	184	4	106 are elected; 51 are selected by provincial councils; 26 are co-opted, one is a member of the Royal Family
Belize (Senate)	9	5	Appointed by the Governor General
Bolivia (Chamber of Senators)	27	4	Elected
Brazil (Senate)	81	8	Elected; one-third and two-thirds are renewed alternatively every four years
Canada (Senate)	104	n.a.	Appointed by the Governor General upon the recommendation of the Prime Minister, who in turn receives recommendations from the provinces; continuous service until the age of 75, except for those Senators appointed before June 1, 1965 who hold office for life.
Chile (Senate)	48	8	38 are elected; 9 are appointed; one former President is a Senator for life
Colombia (Senate of the Republic)	114	4	Elected
Czechoslovakia (Chamber of Nations)	150	2	Elected
Dominican Republic (Senate)	30	4	Elected
France (Senate)	321	9	Indirectly elected; one-third are renewed every three years
Germany (Bundesrat)	69	n.a.	Appointed by the Lander (states); as elected members of the Lander, their term in the Bundesrat depends on the term of the Lander they represent; 16 Lander are represented by a minimum of three members each
Grenada (Senate)	13	5	Appointed by the Governor General
Haiti (Senate)	27	6	Elected; one-third stand for re-election every three years
India (Council of States)	245	6	233 are elected; 12 are nominated by the Head of State

Country and Body	No. of Seats	Term (years)	Appointment Arrangements
Ireland (Senate)	60	5	43 are elected from five panels of candidates; 6 are appointed from universities; 11 are appointed by the Prime Minister
Italy (Senate)	322	5	Appointed; six appointments are for life
Jamaica (Senate)	21	5	Appointed by the Governor General
Japan (House of Councillors)	252	6	Elected; one-half are renewed every three years
Jordan (Senate)	40	4	Appointed by the King
Malaysia (Senate)	69	3	26 are elected by the 13 state legislative assemblies; 43 are appointed by the King
Mexico (Senate)	64	6	Elected; one-half are renewed alternatively every three years
Nepal (Rastriya Sabha)	60	6	35 (including at least three women) are elected from the House of Representatives; 15 are indirectly elected; 10 are appointed by the King; one-third are renewed alternatively every two years
Netherlands (First Chamber of the States General)	75	4	Indirectly elected
Pakistan (Senate)	87	6	Elected; one-half are renewed alternatively every three years
Peru (Senate)	60	5	Elected; in addition to the 60 regular members, former Presidents serve for life
Philippines (Senate)	24	6	Elected
Poland (Senate)	100	4	Elected
Saint Lucia (Senate)	11	5	Six are appointed by the Government, three by the Opposition and two by the Governor General
Spain (Senate)	251	4	Elected
Switzerland (Council of the States)	46	4	Two are appointed from each of the 20 cantonal governments and one is appointed from each of the six half-cantons
Trinidad and Tobago (Senate)	31	5	Appointed by the Head of State
United Kingdom (House of Lords)	1 188	n.a.	One-third are hereditary peers, 380 are life peers and 25 are archbishops and bishops
United States (Senate)	100	6	Elected; one-third stand for re-election every two years
Uruguay (Senate)	31	5	Elected; Vice-President of the Republic serves as Ex-Officio
Venezuela (Senate)	49	5	Elected; three are life members
Yugoslavia (Chamber of Republics and Provinces)	88	4	Indirectly elected

Source: 1991 report by The International Centre for Parliamentary Documentation, Inter-Parliamentary Union, Geneva, Switzerland.

CHAPTER EIGHTEEN

The Impact of Recent Elections on the Composition of Canada's Legislatures

DAVID DOCHERTY AND PAUL HOLMES

David Docherty was a legislative intern at Queen's Park, Toronto in 1984-1985. A former researcher for the Royal Commission on Electoral Reform and Party Financing, he is presently working on his Ph.D. in Political Science at the University of Toronto where his dissertation will be an examination of career patterns in the House of Commons. Paul Holmes was a legislative intern at Queen's Park, Toronto in 1990-1991. He recently completed his Master's Degree in Political Science at MacMaster University, Hamilton.

THE PROFILE of the legislatures has changed dramatically since the last publication of *Canadian Legislatures* in 1988. At that time, the Progressive Conservative and Liberal parties dominated legislatures across the country. The Conservative Party held majorities in four provinces, while the Liberal Party also held legislative majorities in four provinces. The Social Credit party governed in British Columbia while the New Democratic Party held office in Manitoba. Contemporary commentators on politics have suggested that public disaffection with politics is at an all-time high. Certainly the wholesale change in governing parties as reflected in the following Table lends some credibility to the thesis that this dissatisfaction has been felt at the polling stations across the nation.

As the Table indicates, the governing party

Changes in Government

	1987 Governing Party	1991 Governing Party
H of C	P.C.	P.C.
Newf.	P.C.	Lib.
P.E.I.	Lib.	Lib.
N.S. [1]	P.C.	P.C.
N.B.	Lib.	Lib.
Qué.	Lib.	Lib.
Ont.	Lib.	N.D.P.
Man.	N.D.P.	P.C.

	1987	1991
	Governing Party	*Governing Party*
Sask.	P.C.	N.D.P.
Alta.	P.C.	P.C.
B.C.	Social Credit	N.D.P.
Yukon	N.D.P.	N.D.P.
N.W.T.	Non-Partisan	Non-Partisan

[1] No election held between 1987 and 1991

changed in five of the nine provinces that have held elections since 1988. In each of the four provinces where the governing party retained power after an election, the majority was reduced. The same is true for the federal Conservative party, which though returned in 1988 with a second consecutive majority—the first time that has happened since 1953—saw their majority reduced.

A second indication of voter discontent present in these most recent elections is the success of minor parties and parties that have traditionally not fared well in certain provinces. The Confederation of Regions Party, without even a single seat in the preceding legislature, is now the Official Opposition in New Brunswick. Minor parties collected seven percent of the vote in the 1990 Ontario election even though all seats were still won by the three major parties. The Liberal Party, while it no longer forms the Official Opposition in Manitoba, has re-emerged provincially in both Alberta and British Columbia, two provinces where they have traditionally not been a major electoral factor.

A second trend that runs throughout almost every legislative assembly update, is the increasing numbers of women who are being elected to public office. While gender equality in our representative assemblies has yet to be achieved, the number of females elected to sit has increased dramatically in the past few years. Far more parties are now led by women, a woman has held a brief tenure as a premier, and a woman now heads the Government of the Northwest Territories.

Finally, recent literature on legislative assemblies in Canada has begun to pay more attention to elected life as a career. One indication of this trend is the age at which members first enter legislative life. The earlier a member enters, the more likely they are to see the potential of treating elected office as a career. In order to see if some legislative assemblies are being treated by its members as a possible career choice, this update will look at the age of members when they first entered the legislature. Therefore the data presented on age in this edition is not comparable to the data presented in earlier editions of *Canadian Legislatures*, which calculated the average age of members at time of the most recent election.

THE HOUSE OF COMMONS

Date of Election: November 21, 1988
Date of Previous Election: September 4, 1984
Voter Turnout: 75.9% (1988)

The 1988 federal election led to a second consecutive majority government for Prime Minister Brian Mulroney's Progressive Conservative Party. Many observers considered the election to be a virtual plebiscite on the issue of free trade. However, others argued that because of the distortions inherent in the single member plurality system that transform less than 50% of the popular vote into a majority government, one can never say, with certainty, that a government has been given a "mandate" by the public to carry out a particular policy. Nevertheless, free trade did become the primary focus of the election campaign after the Liberal Party, led by John Turner, followed the NDP lead and presented an anti-free trade campaign.

Since the 1988 election a number of changes in party personnel and leaders have occurred in the House of Commons. Soon after the election, a by-election was held in Alberta to fill a seat vacated by the death of a newly-elected Conservative member. That by-election resulted in the election of the first Reform Party MP, Ms Deborah Gray. While the Reform Party did not officially run a slate of candidates in the 1988 election, they appear ready to do so in the upcoming election, with Ms Gray running as their first incumbent member, and Preston Manning as leader.

Both the Liberal and New Democratic parties saw the retirement of the leaders who had guided them through the 1988 contest. John Turner, the Liberal leader, stepped down from the party mantle, but still holds and represents his Vancouver Quadra seat. Former Liberal cabinet minister Jean Chrétien came out of a brief political retirement and now heads the Liberal Party after defeating, among others, Paul Martin Jr. (son of former Liberal cabinet minister Paul Martin) and Sheila Copps, former Ontario MPP and leadership hopeful. The NDP meanwhile, saw the departure of leader Ed Broadbent, who had guided the party since 1975. Mr. Broadbent, who gave up his Oshawa seat, lead the NDP in 1988 to its best federal showing, winning 43 seats. Mr. Broadbent was replaced by the Yukon's Audrey McLaughlin, who is the first woman to head a national Canadian political party.

The failure of the Meech Lake Accord was felt in the party standings in the House. Some members of both the Liberal and Conservative parties broke to form a new party, the Bloc Québecois, soon after the failure of the constitutional accord's passage in the summer of 1990. In a by-election in Quebec soon thereafter, a Bloc Québecois member was elected to the House.

House of Commons: Party Standings

Party	1984	1988
Progressive Conservative	211	170
Liberal	40	82
New Democratic	30	43
Independent	1	0
Total	**282**	**295**

There is a fairly equitable distribution of members, from the inexperienced to long-serving veterans. Although newly elected members comprise 40% of the House, those having served at least one term total almost 60%.

House of Commons: Years of Service

Years of Service	1988 No.	%
Newly Elected	119	40.3
1 - 5 Years	88	29.8
6 + Years	88	29.8

Once again, the statistics reveal that the 35 to 44 age bracket is the largest single category. Other notable statistics include the four members elected

who were less than 25, and the two members elected for the first time when they were older than 65.

House of Commons: Age Entered Legislature

Age Entered	1988 No.	%
Under 25 Years	4	1.4
25 - 34 Years	51	17.3
35 - 44 Years	115	39.0
45 - 54 Years	88	29.8
55 - 64 Years	22	7.5
65 + Years	2	0.7
No Information	13	4.4

Most federal MPs have attained at least a post-secondary education. Most striking amongst this group is the high proportion of members with professional degrees.

House of Commons: Educational Background

Level Achieved	1988 No.	%
Elementary	2	0.7
Secondary	32	10.9
Post-Secondary	131	44.4
Graduate	50	17.0
Professional	80	27.1

The House of Commons has a comparatively large number of lawyers amongst its members. Lawyers comprise the largest single occupation from those listed below.

House of Commons: Previous Occupation

Previous Occupation	1988 No.	%
Business	55	18.6
Law	60	20.3
Education	50	17.0
Farming	15	5.1

	1988	
Previous Occupation	*No.*	*%*
Government	14	4.8
Other	101	34.2

Over one-third of federal MPs have had previous electoral experience, either at the municipal or provincial levels.

House of Commons: Prior Political Experience

	1988	
Prior Experience	*No.*	*%*
None	199	67.5
Municipal	72	24.4
Provincial	24	8.1

The federal Parliament has a surprisingly poor record with regard to gender parity. Only Newfoundland and Nova Scotia have a lower percentage of elected female members in the legislature.

House of Commons: Gender

	1988	
Gender	*No.*	*%*
Male	258	87.5
Female	37	12.5

THE SENATE

The period following the last federal election has been a historic time for the Senate of Canada. While the Progressive Conservative majority in the House of Commons passed the Goods and Services Tax Bill into law, the Liberal-dominated Senate withheld its support and threatened to defeat the Bill. In August and September of 1990 the Prime Minister both filled all existing vacancies in the Senate and made use of a Constitutional provision which give the him the authority to appoint more than the usual 104 senators in cases of a legislative standoff. The result was the largest Senate in Canadian history. The political fallout, however, has not been favourable for either the senators or the federal government, and calls for Senate reform are increasing. The latest constitutional proposals from the federal government include provisions for an elected Senate.

The second unique development in the Senate was the appointment in June 1990 of Senator Stan Waters from Alberta. The provincial government of Alberta, following through on an election promise, ran a province-wide election for the Senate seat vacancy. Mr. Waters, a member of the Reform Party and a former Lieutenant-General in the Canadian Armed Forces, won the election and was eventually appointed to the Senate by Prime Minister Mulroney. Senator Waters passed away in September 1991.

The combination of new appointments and recent vacancies have put the current total of Senate seats at 103, with three vacant seats. Although this is two more than the Senate normally has, because the west is entitled to twenty-four senators and currently has only twenty-one, the total will remain at 106 until all regional quotas have been filled. There are only two sitting senators who enjoy life appointments, Hartland Molson and John M. MacDonald. Other senators who were appointed before the installation of the seventy-five year age limit have taken their leave instead of serving out their entitlement.

Senate: Party Standings

Party	Feb. 1988	Dec. 1991
Progressive Conservative	32	53
Liberal	61	45
Independent	5	5
Vacancies	6	3

Brian Mulroney's government has been in power since 1984. Thus, in these seven years, he has been responsible for appointing all those who fall within the "less than 5 years" of service category and some of those who currently have between six and ten years' service. In the next year another five senators will reach the obligatory age of retirement, leaving a total of seven vacancies. At this rate, Mulroney's appointees will soon constitute over half the Senate.

Although many Canadians envisage the Senate as being comprised of doddering old political hacks,

Senate: Years of Service

Years of Service	1988 No.	1991 No.
1 - 5 Years	36	52
6 - 10 Years	25	32
11 - 15 Years	13	10
16 - 20 Years	11	5
21 - 25 Years	12	2
26 - 30 Years	0	2
31 - 35 Years	4	0

one look at the following Table will show that most senators assume their seats in the same age group as other elected members, and almost 80 percent are less than the usual retirement age of 65 when they become senators.

Senate: Age

Age	1988 No.	1991 No.
35 - 44 Years	3	5
45 - 54 Years	20	35
55 - 64 Years	37	42
65 - 70 Years	20	14
71 - 75 Years	14	5
76 - 95 Years	6	2

Canada's non-elected chamber differs significantly from its elected counterparts both in terms of educational background and occupation. The Senate is a more educated and professional body. The vast majority of senators have some post-secondary education and most also have graduate or professional degrees. As well, while all legislatures have a significant proportion of business persons and lawyers, none has as high a percentage as the Senate . While the Senate personnel has changed significantly since 1988, the educational and occupational background profile of members has been little altered.

Senate: Educational Background

Level Achieved	1988 No.	1991 No.
Elementary	0	0
Secondary	9	4
Post-Secondary	104	99
Graduate and Professional	most	most

Senate: Previous Occupation

Previous Occupation	1988 No.	1991 No.
Business	39	43
Law	28	24
Education	19	16
Farming	7	4
Other	7	16

Senate: Gender

Gender	1991 No.	%
Male	87	84.5
Female	16	15.5

NEWFOUNDLAND AND LABRADOR

Election Date: April 20, 1989
Previous Election: April 2, 1985
Voter Turnout: 80.6% (1989)

The provincial election in the spring of 1989 returned the first Liberal government in Newfoundland since Joseph Smallwood's government was defeated in 1972. Prior to that, the Liberals under Smallwood had governed Newfoundland continuously since the province entered Confederation in 1949.

Following Brian Peckford's retirement as the leader of the Progressive Conservative Party, and from politics in general, Thomas Rideout was chosen as his successor early in 1989. An election was immediately called. The result was that the Liberals doubled the number of seats they held previously, while the Conservatives lost almost half of their former seats. Clyde Wells, leader of the Liberal Party, failed to win his seat in the general election. A by-election prompted by the resignation of one of the new Liberal ministers, resulted in Wells's victory by acclamation. The NDP lost their only seat in the Legislature, however they later recovered a seat in St. John's in a December 1990 by-election. Rideout resigned as Leader of the Official Opposition in January of 1991.

Newfoundland: Party Standings

Party	1985	1989
Liberal	15	30
Progressive Conservative	36	22
New Democratic	1	0
Total	**52**	**52**

Predictably, the number of newly elected members is quite high, at almost half of all members. This is normally the case when a majority government is replaced by a majority government of another party. More surprising is the close to one-third of the members who have more than six years (at least two terms) experience behind them.

Newfoundland: Years of Service

	1989	
Years of Service	No.	%
Newly Elected	25	48.1
1 - 5 Years	11	21.2
6 + Years	16	30.7

The largest single group of members began legislative life between the ages of 35 and 44. Almost half of the current members had been elected for the first time by the age of 44. As is the case in other provinces, the number of new members steadily drops off past the age of 45.

The vast majority of the members in the Legis-

lative Assembly have attained a post-secondary education. Only two members never attended high school, while eight received graduate degrees and eight others received a professional degree.

Newfoundland: Age Entered Legislature

	1989	
Age Entered	No.	%
25 - 34 Years	12	23.1
35 - 44 Years	16	30.8
45 - 54 Years	7	13.5
55 - 64 Years	2	3.8
65 + Years	0	0
No Information	15	28.8

Newfoundland: Educational Background

	1989	
Level Achieved	No.	%
Elementary	1	2.0
Secondary	6	11.5
Post-Secondary	19	36.5
Graduate	8	15.4
Professional	8	15.4
No Information	10	19.2

Twenty-five percent of the current Legislature is comprised of members who were either elementary, secondary or post-secondary teachers, or were employed in the education field in some other capacity, such as an administrator. Lawyers comprised only 13.5% of the Legislature while business persons held 17.3% of the seats.

Newfoundland: Previous Occupation

	1989	
Previous Occupation	No.	%
Business	9	17.3
Law	7	13.5
Education	13	25.0

Previous Occupation	1989 No.	%
Farming	1	2.0
Government	6	11.5
Union	0	0
Other	16	30.8

Exhibiting patterns found in most of the other provinces, approximately twenty percent of the members had previous elected experience at the municipal level.

Newfoundland: Prior Political Experience

Prior Experience	1989 No.	%
None	40	76.9
Municipal	11	21.2
Federal	0	0
Municipal and Federal	1	1.9

Except for Nova Scotia, Newfoundland has the worst record in the country with respect to gender parity in the Legislature. Only 7.7% of the members are women, while most other legislatures have approximately 20% of their seats filled by women.

Newfoundland: Gender

Gender	1989 No.	%
Male	48	92.3
Female	4	7.7

PRINCE EDWARD ISLAND

Election Date: May 30, 1989
Date of Previous Election: April 25, 1986
Voter Turnout: 82.7% (1989)

Premier Joe Ghiz was returned with a second consecutive majority government in the 1989 general election. The election increased the Liberal majority substantially and, as the Official Opposition, the Progressive Conservative Party now holds only two of the total 32 seats in the Legislative Assembly.

There are sixteen constituencies in Prince Edward Island. Each riding elects both a Councillor and an Assemblyman, who share equal status in the Assembly.

Prince Edward Island: Party Standings

Party	1986	1989
Liberal	22	30
Progressive Conservative	10	2
Total	**32**	**32**

The return of a second Liberal majority had only a minor effect on the level of experience among Councillors and Assemblymen. There is one less member who has served over five years, while the number of members with between one and five years has increased by three to twelve.

Prince Edward Island: Years of Service

Years of Service	1986 No.	%	1989 No.	%
Newly Elected	9	28.3	8	25.0
1 - 5 Years	10	31.2	12	37.4
6 + Years	13	41.9	12	37.4

Based on the age when most members are first elected, few MLAs in Prince Edward Island seem to see service in the provincial assembly as a full-time career. Members seldom enter the provincial House before age 34 and the vast majority first enter between the ages of 35 and 54. None of the current members entered the House after age 55, suggesting that provincial office does not appear to be a reward for years of local community service.

Most members of the Prince Edward Island Assembly have at least a post-secondary education. While there is an increase in the number of MLAs without a secondary school education, the number of individuals with a post-secondary, graduate or a professional degree has also increased.

Prince Edward Island: Age Entered Legislature

Age Entered	1989 No.	%
25 - 34 Years	4	12.5
35 - 44 Years	14	43.8
45 - 54 Years	12	37.5
55 - 64 Years	0	0
65 + Years	0	0
No Information	2	6.2

Prince Edward Island: Educational Background

Level Achieved	1986 No.	%	1989 No.	%
Elementary	0	0	3	9.4
Secondary	14	43.8	6	18.6
Post-Secondary	12	37.6	14	43.8
Graduate	5	15.6	7	21.8
Professional	0	0	2	6.3
No Information	1	3.1	0	0

Although farming remains the most popular outside occupation, there has been a substantial decrease in the number of MLAs whose outside profession is farming, from 15 to ten. Education remains the second-most popular profession for legislators, increasing from seven former educators to nine.

Prince Edward Island: Previous Occupation

Previous Occupation	1986 No.	%	1989 No.	%
Business	5	15.6	2	6.3
Law	3	9.4	3	9.4
Education	7	21.8	9	28.1
Farming	15	46.9	10	31.3
Union	0	0	2	6.3
Other	2	6.3	6	18.6

There has been a slight increase in the number of provincial legislators with previous electoral experience at the municipal level. Even so, only 20% of MLAs from Prince Edward Island have previous electoral experience. Given the smaller size of provincial ridings however, a municipal base may not be the prerequisite to provincial office that it is in the larger, more populous provinces.

Prince Edward Island: Prior Political Experience

Prior Experience	1986 No.	%	1989 No.	%
None	27	84.4	25	78.1
Municipal	4	12.5	7	21.1
Federal	1	3.1	0	0

While far from parity, the number of women in the Prince Edward Island Legislative Assembly has almost tripled since 1986. Now, fully one-quarter of Prince Edward Island MLAs are women. In 1982 there were only two women MLAs, representing only 6.3% of the total Assembly.

Prince Edward Island: Gender

Gender	1986 No.	%	1989 No.	%
Male	29	91.6	24	75.0
Female	3	9.4	8	25.0

NOVA SCOTIA

Election Date: September 6, 1988
Date of Previous Election: November 6, 1984
Voter Turnout: n.a.

Nova Scotia's last general election, on September 6, 1988, once again saw the Progressive Conservative Party returned to power, but with far fewer seats. The PCs, under John Buchanan, managed to retain a majority government by only two seats, holding 28 seats in the 52-seat legislature, down from their previous 42.

The election saw the Liberals increase their seats to 21 from six: a staggering 350% increase in representation. The NDP, under leader Alexa McDonough, lost one seat in 1988 to hold only two. A 1991 by-election saw the Liberals lose a seat to the NDP.

In 1990 John Buchanan resigned as premier and eventually, in a 1991 leadership convention, was replaced by Donald Cameron.

Nova Scotia: Party Standings

Party	1988
Progressive Conservative	28
Liberal	21
New Democratic	2
Independent	1
Total	**52**

Not surprisingly, with the large change in number of seats from PC to Liberal, many veterans of the House were ousted by newcomers. Still, overall, the Nova Scotia Legislature has many members with significant legislative experience.

Nova Scotia: Years of Service

	1988	
Years of Service	No.	%
Newly Elected	17	32.6
1 - 5 Years	8	15.4
6 + Years	26	50.0

Nova Scotia's politicians overwhelmingly began their political career at an early age: almost 60% were first elected by the age of 45. This is not completely attributable to the change in distribution of seats, because most returning members fall into the younger age groups.

Nova Scotia: Age Entered Legislature

	1988	
Age Entered	No.	%
25 - 34 Years	15	28.8
35 - 44 Years	16	30.8

	1988	
Age Entered	No.	%
45 - 54 Years	6	11.5
55 - 64 Years	3	5.8
65 + Years	0	0
No Information	12	23.1

Nova Scotia's legislators are well-educated, with almost 80% attaining some post-secondary education. There were no members who did not attend secondary school.

Nova Scotia: Educational Background

	1988	
Level Achieved	No.	%
Elementary	0	0
Secondary	7	13.4
Post-Secondary	24	46.2
Graduate	8	15.4
Professional	8	15.4
No Information	5	9.6

In members' previous careers, there is a fairly even distribution across the surveyed categories of business and education. Interestingly, in comparison to other legislatures, the number of lawyers is quite low.

No members of the legislature have previous experience as an MP, and most have no municipal experience.

Nova Scotia: Previous Occupation

	1988	
Previous Occupation	No.	%
Business	15	28.8
Law	6	11.5
Education	12	23.2
Farming	6	11.5
Government	0	0
Other	13	25.0

Nova Scotia: Prior Political Experience

	1988	
Prior Experience	No.	%
None	38	73.1
Municipal	14	26.9
Federal	0	0

When Alexa McDonough was elected leader of the Nova Scotia NDP, she became the first woman in Canada to lead a major political party. She continues to hold her seat and is accompanied in the House by two other women. This is the lowest representation by women in all of Canada's legislatures.

Nova Scotia: Gender

	1988	
Gender	No.	%
Male	49	94.2
Female	3	5.8

NEW BRUNSWICK

Date of Election: September 23, 1991
Previous Election: October 13, 1987
Voter Turnout: 80.1% (1991)

Although Premier Frank McKenna was unable to repeat the 1987 "sweep" of the province in the fall 1991 election, his Liberal Party once again formed a majority government. Mr. McKenna won 46 of the 58 seats in this most recent election. This election also saw the dramatic breakthrough of a "minor party" on the political stage, as the Confederation of Regions Party won eight seats to become the Official Opposition. C.o.R., as it is known, won most of its seats in the Fredericton area. The Progressive Conservative Party won three seats and the New Democratic Party won one seat: leader Elizabeth Weir's seat in Saint John.

On a sad note, 1991 also saw the passing of former New Brunswick Premier and Senator Richard Hatfield. A key player in the 1982 Constitutional talks, Mr. Hatfield served as Premier of New Brunswick for seventeen years.

New Brunswick: Party Standings

Party	1987	1991
Liberal	58	46
Progressive Conservative	0	3
Confederation of Regions	0	8
New Democratic	0	1
Total	**58**	**58**

Given the number of returning Liberals from the previous electoral sweep, it is perhaps not surprising that the majority of MLAs have served between one and five years in the New Brunswick Legislature. A few members retired since the last session, so the number of newcomers is not restricted to the opposition benches. As well, two members of the opposition PC party have previous experience in the provincial chamber, but did not sit during the 1987-1991 session. They are, therefore, not rookies. One C.o.R. member also has some legislative experience as a Conservative member who left the party before running for C.o.R.

New Brunswick: Years of Service

	1987		1991	
Years of Service	No.	%	No.	%
Newly Elected	37	63.8	14	24.1
1 - 5 Years	6	10.3	27	46.5
6 + Years	15	25.9	17	29.3

New Brunswick fits the age-of-entry pattern of most Canadian legislatures. The majority of members enter before the age of 45, with the largest single group entering between the ages of 35 and 44. Only two members entered the House after reaching the standard retirement age of sixty-five.

The educational background of the 1991 House is more varied than its immediate predecessor. Graduates and professionals now make up over 35% of the chamber, but there are also more individuals whose formal education ended with secondary school and one MLA with no secondary education.

The occupational profile of New Brunswick

New Brunswick: Age Entered Legislature

Age Entered	1991 No.	%
25 - 34 Years	15	25.9
35 - 44 Years	20	34.5
45 - 54 Years	10	17.2
55 - 64 Years	4	6.9
65 + Years	2	3.4
No Information	7	12.1

New Brunswick: Educational Background

Level Achieved	1987 No.	%	1991 No.	%
Elementary	0	0.0	1	1.7
Secondary	6	10.3	10	17.2
Post-Secondary	36	62.1	25	43.1
Graduate	16	27.6	9	15.5
Professional	0	0.0	13	22.4

MLAs has not changed significantly since 1987. The largest single group remains educators, who still represent over one-quarter of the Assembly. Over ten percent of MLAs are lawyers, just slightly down from the previous Legislature.

New Brunswick: Previous Occupation

Previous Occupation	1987 No.	%	1991 No.	%
Business	15	25.9	12	20.7
Law	7	12.1	6	10.3
Education	18	31.0	17	29.3
Farming	1	1.7	0	0.0
Government	5	8.6	4	6.8
Other	12	20.7	16	27.7

The number of members entering the New Brunswick Legislature with previous elected experience rose as a result of the 1991 election. However, almost two-thirds (63.8%) of New Brunswick MLAs enter the assembly with no prior service in an elected, civic position. As with other provincial jurisdictions, municipal elected service (either municipal, city office or local school board) was by far the most popular form of previous elected service. The one individual with federal experience is Dennis Cochrane, leader of the Progressive Conservative Party.

New Brunswick: Prior Political Experience

Prior Experience	1987 No.	%	1991 No.	%
None	45	77.6	39	67.2
Municipal	13	22.4	18	31.0
Federal	0	0.0	1	1.7

During the 1987-1991 period, when only the Liberals had elected representatives in the New Brunswick Legislature, the two major opposition parties were making major strides in gender representation. Both the Progressive Conservative and New Democratic parties were led by women, Barbara Baird-Filliter and Elizabeth Weir respectively. In the spring of 1991, Baird-Filliter, a political neophyte, resigned in frustration and Dennis Cochrane, a former mayor of Moncton and MP, was chosen at a leadership convention. Both Weir and Cochrane now hold seats in the provincial House.

New Brunswick: Gender

Gender	1987 No.	%	1991 No.	%
Male	50	86.2	49	84.5
Female	8	13.8	9	15.5

QUEBEC

Election Date: September 25, 1989
Date of Previous Election: December 2, 1985
Voter Turnout: 75.0% (1989)

The most recent election in Quebec did not significantly change party standings. The Liberals were returned with their second consecutive majority, losing seven seats to be reduced to 92 of the 125 (redistribution saw a three-seat increase in the House size). The Parti Québecois was returned as Official Opposition. The new leader of the P.Q., Jacques Parizeau, only marginally increased their standing in the House, from 23 seats to 29. The P.Q.'s former leader, Pierre Marc Johnson, (whose father, Daniel Johnson, was also Premier of Quebec) did not run in the 1989 election. The most stunning result of the 1989 Quebec election was the emergence of the Equality Party, whose strength was based in anglophone sections of Montreal. While winning only four seats, and therefore not gaining official party status in the Quebec National Assembly, members of both the governing Liberals and Opposition P.Q. have extended every effort to provide the Equality members with the financial and support services accorded official party caucuses.

Quebec: Party Standings

Party	1985	1989
Liberal	99	92
Parti Québecois	23	29
Equality	0	4
Total	122	125

The 1989 general election did not result in a major turnover in members similar to that which occurred in 1985. As the Table below indicates, fewer than half of the members in 1989 were newly elected, as opposed to the 1985 election when the Liberals replaced the P.Q. government, and slightly more than half of the members were serving their first term.

Quebec: Years of Service

Years of Service	1985 No.	1985 %	1989 No.	1989 %
Newly Elected	64	53.3	31	25.0
1 - 5 Years	36	29.5	53	42.7
6 + Years	22	18.2	40	32.3

Members in Quebec tend to enter the Legislature at a young age. Roughly 65% of the current members were elected before the age of 45. Like their colleagues in other jurisdictions, Quebec legislators appear to be pursuing careers in elected politics.

Quebec: Age Entered Legislature

Age Entered	1989 No.	%
Under 25 Years	5	4.0
25 - 34 Years	26	21.0
35 - 44 Years	49	39.5
45 - 54 Years	37	29.8
55 - 64 Years	5	4.0
65 + Years	1	0.8
No Information	1	0.8

The majority of Quebec MNAs have some form of post-secondary education. One-third of the members have a professional degree (law, medical, engineering, etc.), making Quebec's MNAs perhaps the most highly educated group of elected officials in the country.

Quebec: Educational Background

Level Achieved	1985 No.	1985 %	1989 No.	1989 %
Elementary	0	0	1	0.8
Secondary	6	4.9	13	10.5
Post-Secondary	46	37.7	52	41.9
Graduate	70	57.4	17	13.7
Professional	0	0	41	33.0

The most significant change in 1989 is the fourteen percent drop in the number of members reporting business as a previous occupation. The difference has been redistributed across all the other occupations with education showing the most dramatic increase.

Almost one-quarter of the National Assembly's members have had prior elected experience at the municipal level. This represents an increase from the previous legislature and may be representative of a career trend in politics.

The number of elected women in the National

Assembly has increased since 1985, so that almost twenty percent of all members are women. However, the major political parties in Quebec have, to date, never selected a woman as leader.

Quebec: Previous Occupation

Previous Occupation	1985		1989	
	No.	%	No.	%
Business	48	39.3	32	25.8
Law	16	13.1	17	13.7
Education	24	19.7	32	25.8
Farming	1	0.8	3	2.4
Government	7	5.7	8	6.5
Union	0	0	1	0.8
Other	26	21.3	31	25.0

Quebec: Prior Political Experience

Prior Experience	1985		1989	
	No.	%	No.	%
None	99	81.1	94	75.8
Municipal	23	18.9	30	24.2
Federal	0	0	0	0

Quebec: Gender

Gender	1985		1989	
	No.	%	No.	%
Male	104	85.2	100	80.7
Female	18	14.8	24	19.4

ONTARIO

Election Date: September 6, 1990
Date of Previous Election: September 10, 1987
Voter Turnout: 64.4% (1990)

After 42 years of consecutive Progressive Conservative Party rule in Ontario, the five-year period between 1985 and 1990 saw all three of Ontario's major political parties in power. The Liberal-NDP accord in 1985 saw the Liberals govern for two years under David Peterson with fewer seats than the Conservatives. In 1987 David Peterson led his government to a precedent-setting majority, winning 95 of the 130 seats with just over 47% of the popular vote. Only three years later, Mr. Peterson's accord co-signer, Bob Rae, led the NDP to the first democratic socialist government in Ontario since the 1919 United Farmer of Ontario (UFO)/Labour Party Coalition. The NDP won 76 seats in the election with 38% of the popular vote.

Ontario: Party Standings

Party	1987	1990
New Democratic	19	74
Liberal	95	36
Progressive Conservative	16	20
Total	**130**	**130**

The 1990 election saw a massive turnover in the House, as disgruntled voters halved the Liberal benches and selected many unfamiliar faces from the NDP ranks. Of the 74 NDP members in the Legislature, only sixteen were veterans of the House. The Progressive Conservatives are split with ten new members, and ten veteran members.

Ontario: Years of Service

Years of Service	1987		1990	
	No.	%	No.	%
Newly Elected	49	37.6	68	52.3
1 - 5 Years	37	28.5	36	27.7
6 + Years	44	33.9	26	20.0

Ontario: Age Entered Legislature

Age Entered	1990	
	No.	%
Under 25 Years	4	3.1
25 - 34 Years	27	20.8
35 - 44 Years	47	36.2
45 - 54 Years	28	21.5

	1990	
Age Entered	*No.*	*%*
55 - 64 Years	4	3.1
65 + Years	0	0
No Information	20	15.4

Once again, the largest single group of members was elected between the ages of 35 and 45, repeating a pattern found elsewhere. Perhaps more interesting, are the four members of the Legislature who were first elected before they reached age 25.

All members of the Legislature report that they have attained at least a high school education. Well over half went beyond high school and obtained a post-secondary education. Of those, thirteen percent have a graduate degree (Masters or Doctoral) and 17.7% are professionals.

The number of members with a business background has dropped dramatically since 1987. There are also fewer lawyers present in the House. Signifi-

Ontario: Educational Background

	1987		*1990*	
Level Achieved	*No.*	*%*	*No.*	*%*
Elementary	0	0	0	0
Secondary	20	15.4	29	22.3
Post-Secondary	58	44.6	61	46.9
Graduate	52	40.0	17	13.1
Professional	0	0	23	17.7

Ontario: Previous Occupation

	1987		*1990*	
Previous Occupation	*No.*	*%*	*No.*	*%*
Business	40	30.8	11	8.5
Law	26	20.0	20	15.4
Education	27	20.8	25	19.2
Farming	14	10.8	5	3.9
Government	8	6.2	8	6.2
Union	0	0	7	5.4
Other	15	11.4	54	41.4

cantly, the number of farmers has decreased from fourteen to five, comprising only 3.9% of all members in 1990. Since agricultural issues (such as land-use planning) have become critical, it is surprising to note the decline in agricultural representation. The other significant increases since 1987 are in areas not enumerated in this list. Typically these occupations include such backgrounds as volunteer service, social work and labour or manufacturing positions.

Although the number has dropped since 1987, Ontario still has a comparatively high proportion of members who have had prior elected experience. Close to one-third have served at the municipal level. Only one member, Premier Rae, has served as an MP.

Ontario: Prior Political Experience

	1987		*1990*	
Prior Experience	*No.*	*%*	*No.*	*%*
None	74	47.0	89	68.5
Municipal	54	41.5	40	30.8
Federal	2	1.5	1	0.8

Gender equality took two major steps as a result of the 1990 election; not only were more women elected (increasing from 20 to 28), but the number of women in cabinet also increased. When Premier Rae announced his cabinet in late September, 40% of the new cabinet were female, the largest percentage of any jurisdiction in the country.

Ontario: Gender

	1987		*1990*	
Gender	*No.*	*%*	*No.*	*%*
Male	110	84.6	102	78.5
Female	20	15.4	28	21.5

MANITOBA

Election Date: September 11, 1990
Date of Previous Election: April 26, 1988
Voter Turnout: 69.1% (1990)

The 1990 Manitoba general election saw the return of Premier Gary Filmon. Unlike 1988 however, Premier Filmon's Conservative party managed to secure a majority government in 1990. The Manitoba Liberal Party lost its Official Opposition status to the New Democratic Party, which increased its ranks from eight to twenty seats. NDP leader Gary Doer, a minister under former Premier Howard Pawley, became the leader of the Official Opposition. Sharon Carstairs remains as the leader of the Liberal Party in Manitoba.

Manitoba: Party Standings

Party	1988	1990
Progressive Conservative	25	30
New Democratic	12	20
Liberal	20	7
Total	57	57

Following the 1990 general election, the Manitoba Legislature had fewer newly-elected and senior members in the House. The number of members with up to five years of experience increased significantly. These members are serving in at least their second term, and possibly their third.

Manitoba: Years of Service

	1988		1990	
Years of Service	No.	%	No.	%
Newly Elected	25	43.9	21	36.8
1 - 5 Years	15	26.3	24	42.1
6 + Years	17	29.8	12	21.1

The entry pattern into provincial politics in Manitoba indicates that, like the other jurisdictions, the majority of members tend to enter before the age of 45. In addition, the data available from the 1988 election demonstrates that this is a fairly stable pattern. One interesting difference between 1988 and 1990 is the decline in the number of members age 55 and over entering provincial politics.

Manitoba: Age Entered Legislature

	1988		1990	
Age Entered	No.	%	No.	%
25 - 34 Years	14	24.6	11	19.3
35 - 44 Years	19	33.3	20	35.1
45 - 54 Years	13	22.8	12	21.1
55 - 64 Years	3	5.3	1	1.8
65 + Years	2	3.5	0	0
No Information	6	10.5	13	22.8

The number of members with only a high school education has declined significantly from almost one-third of the Legislature in 1988 to one-quarter in 1990. While the number of members with graduate degrees has held at eleven, there is now one additional member from the professions.

Manitoba: Educational Background

	1988		1990	
Level Achieved	No.	%	No.	%
Secondary	19	33.9	14	24.6
Post-Secondary	20	35.1	18	31.6
Graduate	11	19.3	11	19.3
Professional	5	8.8	6	10.5
No Information	2	3.5	8	14.0

Manitoba: Previous Occupation

	1988		1990	
Previous Occupation	No.	%	No.	%
Business	4	7.0	4	7.0
Law	3	5.3	3	5.3
Education	6	10.5	8	14.0
Farming	13	22.8	10	17.5
Government	1	1.8	2	3.5
Union	2	3.5	1	1.8
Other	26	45.6	21	36.9
No Information	2	3.5	8	14.0

Like several other provinces, Manitoba has also experienced a decline in the number of farmers in the legislature. Nevertheless, farmers continue to be the single largest identifiable group. The number of business persons and lawyers remains unchanged.

The number of members with previous elected experience has declined.

Manitoba: Prior Political Experience

Prior Experience	1988		1990	
	No.	%	No.	%
None	42	73.7	44	77.2
Municipal	15	26.3	13	22.8
Federal	0	0	0	0

Indicating an upward trend, the number of women in the legislature has risen from nine elected in 1988 to eleven elected in 1990. Prominent among them is Liberal leader Sharon Carstairs.

Manitoba: Gender

Gender	1988		1990	
	No.	%	No.	%
Male	48	84.2	46	80.7
Female	9	15.8	11	19.3

SASKATCHEWAN

Election Date: October 22, 1991
Date of Previous Election: October 20, 1986
Voter Turnout: 83.2% (1991)

Saskatchewan saw a dramatic change of government in the 1991 fall election. The New Democratic Party was returned to power after two terms of Progressive Conservative government headed by Premier Grant Devine. The new Premier, Roy Romanow, has extensive legislative and cabinet experience and was the Attorney General under former NDP Premier Alan Blakeney. The Liberal Party was unable to rekindle its historic success in Saskatchewan, and once again was only able to win one seat in the 66-seat Legislative Assembly. In her first election as leader of the Saskatchewan Liberals, Linda Haverstock was successful in winning the riding of Saskatoon-Greystone.

Saskatchewan: Party Standings

Party	1986	1991
New Democratic	25	55
Progressive Conservative	38	10
Liberal	1	1
Total	**64**	**66**

Not surprisingly, the huge turnaround in seats from 1986 to 1991 has resulted in the election of a large number of inexperienced members. Over half of the 66 Saskatchewan MLAs are newcomers to the Legislative Assembly. Only thirteen MLAs can be considered as parliamentary veterans with at least six years service, as compared to nineteen such members in the previous Assembly.

Saskatchewan: Years of Service

Years of Service	1986		1991	
	No.	%	No.	%
Newly Elected	21	32.8	35	53.0
1 - 5 Years	24	37.5	18	27.0
6 + Years	19	29.7	13	20.0

Though it would appear that quite a few members of the newly elected Saskatchewan Assembly entered at a relatively young age, the absence of information on over half the members makes accurate analysis impossible.

Saskatchewan: Age Entered Legislature

Age Entered	1991	
	No.	%
25 - 34 Years	8	12.1
35 - 44 Years	15	22.7
45 - 54 Years	5	7.5
55 - 64 Years	1	1.5
65 + Years	0	0
No Information	37	56.1

The new Assembly has seen a large increase in the number of professionals elected: from none in 1986 to nine in 1991. Almost 75% of the 66 members have at least some post-secondary education. Exactly one-third of the members have either a graduate or professional degree. Only one member has less than a high school education.

Saskatchewan: Educational Background

		1986		1991
Level Achieved	No.	%	No.	%
Elementary	0	0	1	1.5
Secondary	22	34.4	18	27.3
Post-Secondary	24	37.5	25	37.8
Graduate	18	28.1	13	19.7
Professional	0	0	9	13.6

There are three fewer lawyers and five fewer business people in this new Assembly, down to six and seven respectively. There are two more farmers however, and now just under one-third (21) are farmers. While a number of MLAs have been active in the union movement, only one individual left a full-time position in a union to sit as a member of the Assembly.

Saskatchewan: Previous Occupation

		1986		1991
Previous Occupation	No.	%	No.	%
Business	11	17.2	6	9.0
Law	10	15.6	7	10.6
Education	15	23.4	15	22.7
Farming	19	29.7	21	31.8
Government	0	0	2	3.3
Union	0	0	1	1.5
Other	9	14.1	12	18.2
No Information	6	9.4	0	0

While the new NDP government has far less legislative experience than its PC predecessor, the amount of prior elected experience is up considerably. Twenty-three MLAs have some prior elected experience, one at the federal level and the rest either on local councils or school boards. This is a substantial increase from the eight MLAs with previous experience in the 1986 House.

Saskatchewan: Prior Political Experience

	1986		1991	
Prior Experience	No.	%	No.	%
None	56	87.5	43	65.2
Municipal	7	10.9	22	33.3
Federal	1	1.6	1	1.5

The number of women in the Saskatchewan Legislature more than doubled as a result of the most recent election. While still less than twenty percent of the total, the nineteen female MLAs is eight more than there were in both the 1986 and 1982 Assemblies.

Saskatchewan: Gender

	1986		1991	
Gender	No.	%	No.	%
Male	59	92.2	53	80.3
Female	5	7.8	13	19.7

ALBERTA

Election Date: March 20, 1989
Previous Election: May 8, 1986
Voter Turnout: 53.6% (1989)

There was little change in the Alberta House following the 1989 election. The Conservative Party won a majority government for the sixth consecutive time; they have been the ruling party in the province since 1971. Don Getty continues as Premier. Although still few in number, the doubling of Liberal representation is somewhat astonishing given the general anti-Liberal sentiment throughout the province. In fact, the Liberal advance may be due solely to their new leader, Laurence Decore, who assumed this position in 1988; 1989 was his first election leading the party.

Alberta: Party Standings

Party	1986	1989
Progressive Conservative	61	59
New Democratic	16	16
Liberal	4	8
Representative	2	0
Total	**83**	**83**

Although the ruling Conservative party lost only two seats, the overall level of experience in the House did not decrease as a result of the election. As the Table below shows, over twenty percent of the 1989 Legislature consisted of newly-elected members, and well over half of the MLAs have served for five years or less.

Alberta: Years of Service

	1986		1989	
Years of Service	No.	%	No.	%
Newly Elected	41	49.4	19	22.9
1 - 5 Years	11	13.3	35	42.2
6 + Years	31	37.3	29	34.9

Members tend to enter the Alberta Legislature at a fairly young age, suggesting that many view life in the Alberta chamber as a possible political career, or at least as a stepping stone to federal office. As the Table below indicates, over 45% of Alberta MLAs first enter the House before reaching the age of 45, and less than ten percent enter after they have turned 55 years of age.

Alberta: Age Entered Legislature

	1989	
Age Entered	No.	%
25 - 34 Years	14	16.9
35 - 44 Years	24	28.9
45 - 54 Years	22	26.5
55 - 64 Years	8	9.6
65 + Years	0	0
No Information	15	18.0

The majority of members of the Alberta Assembly have at least some post-secondary education. Professionals represent just over thirteen percent of members.

Alberta: Educational Background

	1986		1989	
Level Achieved	No.	%	No.	%
Elementary	0	0	6	7.2
Secondary	19	22.9	19	22.9
Post-Secondary	36	43.4	30	36.1
Graduate	28	33.7	12	14.6
Professional	0	0	11	13.3
No Information	0	0	5	6.1

While the personnel of the Assembly changed substantially from 1986 to 1989, the occupational profile of the Legislature remains largely the same.

Alberta: Previous Occupation

	1986		1989	
Previous Occupation	No.	%	No.	%
Business	22	26.5	16	19.3
Law	9	10.8	9	10.8
Education	16	19.3	13	15.7
Farming	17	20.5	16	19.3
Government	0	0	2	2.4
Union	0	0	1	1.2
Other	19	22.9	26	31.3

The election of 1989 brought with it a more electorally experienced membership. An additional five members hold municipal experience, either gained on a municipal or township council or a local school board.

There was only a slight increase in the number of women holding office as a result of the latest election. Just over fourteen percent of MLAs in Alberta are female, up from ten percent after the 1986 election.

Alberta: Prior Political Experience

Prior Experience	1986		1989	
	No.	%	No.	%
None	64	77.1	59	71.1
Municipal	17	20.5	22	26.5
Federal	2	2.4	2	2.4

Alberta: Gender

Gender	1986		1989	
	No.	%	No.	%
Male	73	88.0	71	85.8
Female	10	12.0	12	14.5

BRITISH COLUMBIA

Date of Election: October 17, 1991
Date of Previous Election: October 22, 1986
Voter Turnout: 75.0% (1991)

1991 was an historic year in British Columbia. Not only was there a change of government, but three individuals served as premier, one of whom was non-elected. The resignation of Social Credit leader William Vander Zalm in the spring signalled the beginning of an eventful political season. Rita Johnston was selected as interim leader and Premier of the province immediately upon Mr. Vander Zalm's departure. Ms Johnston, a trailer park operator and cabinet minister under Vander Zalm became Canada's first woman premier. Her entry into the leadership contest that followed hurt fellow Social Crediter and elder party statesperson Grace McCarthy's chances of becoming British Columbia's (and Canada's) first elected female premier. In the fall election that followed, former Vancouver mayor and present NDP leader Michael Harcourt led his party to victory. This is only the second time the New Democratic Party has held power in British Columbia. The first time was when Dave Barrett was Premier from 1972 to 1975.

While the NDP victory is news in itself, the resurgence of the Liberal Party in provincial politics after an absence that can be traced back to the Liberal-Conservative coalition of 1941-1952, is equally noteworthy. After the coalition failed in 1952, the Liberal Party began a slow decline in provincial politics. However, the collapse of the Social Credit Party in 1991, and a strong showing in the leaders' debate by Liberal head Gordon Wilson, helped the Liberal Party to achieve Official Opposition status with seventeen seats. The Social Credit Party now has third party status with only seven seats. Ms Johnston lost her own riding.

British Columbia: Party Standings

Party	1986	1991
New Democratic	20	51
Liberal	0	17
Social Credit	49	7
Total	**69**	**75**

Not surprisingly, the large turnover in the 1991 election had a high cost in terms of legislative experience. Two-thirds of the 1991 House are newly-elected members, and only three of the 75 members bring more than six years experience with them. After the 1986 election, nineteen members had at least six years experience, and there were 36 rookies, fourteen less than this most recent Assembly.

British Columbia: Years of Service

Years of Service	1986		1991	
	No.	%	No.	%
Newly Elected	36	52.2	50	66.6
1 - 5 Years	14	20.3	22	29.3
6 + Years	19	27.5	3	4.0

The entrance age of members is fairly equitably dispersed amongst all age groups. Twenty-two members first came to the Assembly between the ages of 35 and 44. A similar number were between the ages of 45 and 54 when they first entered the British Columbia Legislative Assembly. There were as many people entering before turning 34, as there were entering after turning 55.

Over three-quarters of the Assembly have at least some post-secondary education. There are eight MLAs with professional degrees, twenty MLAs with, at least, one graduate degree and twenty-seven MLAs with some post-secondary education.

British Columbia: Age Entered Legislature

	1991	
Age Entered	No.	%
25 - 34 Years	8	10.6
35 - 44 Years	22	29.3
45 - 54 Years	22	29.3
55 - 64 Years	8	10.6
65 + Years	0	0
No Information	15	20.0

British Columbia: Educational Background

	1986		1991	
Level Achieved	No.	%	No.	%
Secondary	18	26.1	16	21.3
Post-Secondary	31	44.9	27	36.0
Graduate	20	29.1	20	26.6
Professional	0	0	8	10.6
No Information	0	0	4	5.3

The Assembly under an NDP majority has a quite different occupational composition than it did in 1986. There are far less business people and many more educators. While almost half the Assembly in 1986 listed business as their pre-elected occupation, only nineteen of the 75 MLAs in 1991 considered themselves business people. Educators increased their representation in the House, from six to fourteen. The number of lawyers has remained constant at six.

British Columbia: Previous Occupation

	1986		1991	
Previous Occupation	No.	%	No.	%
Business	34	49.3	19	25.3
Law	6	8.7	6	8.0
Education	6	8.7	14	18.6
Farming	2	2.9	3	4.0

	1986		1991	
Previous Occupation	No.	%	No.	%
Government	0	0	12	16.0
Union	0	0	1	1.3
Other	21	30.4	20	26.6

There has been a ten percent increase in the number of MLAs with previous elected experience since the 1991 election. Now 32 of the 75 members have local elected experience. Gone from the British Columbia House are the two members with House of Commons experience.

British Columbia: Prior Political Experience

	1986		1991	
Prior Experience	No.	%	No.	%
None	44	63.8	42	56.0
Municipal	23	33.3	32	42.6
Federal	2	2.9	0	0

The 1991 election produced somewhat ironic results in terms of an increased role for women in the legislature. While the election brought an almost threefold increase in the number of women elected (from seven to nineteen) it also produced a major setback in the fight for gender equality with the defeat of Canada's first woman premier.

British Columbia: Gender

	1986		1991	
Gender	No.	%	No.	%
Male	62	89.8	56	74.6
Female	7	10.2	19	25.3

YUKON

Date of Election: February 20, 1989
Date of Previous Election: May 13, 1985
Voter Turnout: 78.0% (1989)

Of the four New Democratic Party governments in Canada, Yukon's has held office the longest. Under Premier Tony Penikett's leadership, the NDP has governed the Yukon since the 1985 general election. Like the Northwest Territories, the Yukon constituencies have small populations which are widely dispersed. Elections are close contests with some ridings containing fewer than 300 voters. Unlike the Northwest Territories, however, the Yukon Assembly does use political parties for its organizational basis and elections are fought on partisan lines.

Yukon: Party Standings

Party	1985	1989
New Democratic	8	9
Progressive Conservative	6	6
Liberal	2	0
Independent Conservative	0	1
Total	16	16

The composition of the Legislature did not change appreciably following the 1989 election. Only two new members were elected, although the governing NDP did increase their majority by one seat.

Yukon: Years of Service

	1985		1989	
Years of Service	No.	%	No.	%
Newly Elected	7	43.8	2	12.5
1 - 5 Years	6	37.5	6	37.5
6 + Years	3	18.8	8	50.0

Yukon MLAs tend to enter political life at a comparatively early age. Close to half of the members had begun a political career by the age of 34, and almost 75% had done so by the age of 44.

Most members of the Territorial Assembly have had at least a high school education. More than half have had a post-secondary education.

Yukon: Age Entered Legislature

	1985		1989	
Age Entered	No.	%	No.	%
25 - 34 Years	8	50.0	7	43.8
35 - 44 Years	4	25.0	4	25.0
45 - 54 Years	2	12.5	1	6.3
55 - 64 Years	1	6.3	3	18.8
65 + Years	0	0	0	0
No Information	1	6.3	1	6.3

Yukon: Educational Background

	1985		1989	
Level Achieved	No.	%	No.	%
Elementary	0	0	2	12.5
Secondary	8	50.0	5	31.3
Post-Secondary	3	18.8	5	31.3
Graduate	1	6.3	1	6.3
Professional	4	25.0	3	18.8

Most of the members of the Territorial Assembly were previously employed in occupations other than those listed below. Some aboriginal members have built careers in Band administration, while other members were previously miners or volunteers. A large proportion of members were formerly government employees.

Yukon: Previous Occupation

	1985		1989	
Previous Occupation	No.	%	No.	%
Business	4	25.0	2	12.5
Law	3	18.8	1	6.3
Education	0	0	0	0
Farming	0	0	0	0
Government	0	0	2	12.5
Union	0	0	1	6.3
Other	9	56.3	10	62.5

Unlike politicians in the Northwest Territories, Yukon members were overwhelming inexperienced before entering Yukon politics. Only three members, including Premier Penikett, had prior elected experience.

Yukon: Prior Political Experience

	1985		1989	
Prior Experience	No.	%	No.	%
None	13	81.2	13	81.2
Municipal	3	18.8	3	18.8
Federal	0	0	0	0

The Yukon does not have a female political leader. Since 1985, the number of women in the Assembly has increased from three to four.

Yukon: Gender

	1985		1989	
Gender	No.	%	No.	%
Male	13	81.3	12	75.0
Female	3	18.8	4	25.0

Unlike the Northwest Territories, people of non-aboriginal descent outnumber people of aboriginal descent in the Yukon. This is reflected in the composition of the House.

Yukon: Heritage

	1985		1989	
Heritage	No.	%	No.	%
Aboriginal	5	31.2	4	25.0
Non-Aboriginal	11	68.8	12	75.0

NORTHWEST TERRITORIES

Election Date: October 15, 1991
Date of Previous Election: October 15, 1987
Voter Turnout: 76.4% (1991)

While the first non-elected female premier in Canadian history suffered defeat in the 1991 British Columbia general election, the Northwest Territories made history by selecting as their government leader 51-year old Nellie Cournoyea, the acclaimed member from the district of Nunakput.

Northwest Territorial politics is also unique in Canada for other reasons. The Northwest Territories legislature, while premised on the Westminster system, operates without a party system. After the election, the 24 elected MLAs select the cabinet and government leader by secret ballot. Ms Cournoyea had served for twelve years as an MLA, eight of them as a cabinet minister. She defeated a male candidate for the position of government leader, and succeeds Dennis Patterson. This is the twelfth elected Legislative Assembly in the Northwest Territories.

The 1991 general election did not result in a high turnover in the Legislature. Over 60% of the incumbents returned to office. One-quarter of the current Legislature has had more than six years of elected service.

Northwest Territories: Years of Service

	1987		1991	
Years of Service	No.	%	No.	%
Newly Elected	8	33.3	9	37.5
1 - 5 Years	8	33.3	9	37.5
6 + Years	8	33.3	6	25.0

Members of the Northwest Territories Assembly overwhelmingly enter politics at an early age. Almost 30% were elected by the age of 34, and close to 60% were elected by the age of 44. Although complete information is not provided, it appears clear that relatively few members are elected in later life.

Although most members of the Assembly have received a post-secondary education, few have graduate or professional degrees.

The Northwest Territories' Assembly has lost two lawyers and a businessperson since 1987, while the number of individuals entering elected office

Northwest Territories: Age Entered Legislature

	1991	
Age Entered	No.	%
25 - 34 Years	7	29.2
35 - 44 Years	7	29.2
45 - 54 Years	3	12.5
55 - 64 Years	0	0
65 + Years	0	0
No information	7	29.2

Northwest Territories: Educational Background

	1987		1991	
Level Achieved	No.	%	No.	%
Elementary	0	0	0	0
Secondary	7	29	6	25.0
Post-Secondary	5	21	9	37.5
Graduate	4	17	2	8.3
Professional	0	0	2	8.3
No information	8	33	5	20.8

Northwest Territories: Previous Occupation

	1987		1991	
Previous Occupation	No.	%	No.	%
Business	8	33.3	7	29.2
Law	3	12.5	1	4.1
Education	1	4.1	0	0
Government	5	20.8	7	29.2
Other	7	29.5	9	37.5

Northwest Territories: Prior Political Experience

	1987		1991	
Prior Experience	No.	%	No.	%
None	12	50	11	45.8
Municipal	12	50	10	41.2
First People's Councils	0	0	3	12.5

Northwest Territories: Gender

	1987		1991	
Gender	No.	%	No.	%
Male	22	91.7	21	87.5
Female	2	8.3	3	12.5

represents an improvement from 1987 when only two women held seats.

The proportion of aboriginal peoples in the Territorial Legislature is representative of the demographic profile of the Northwest Territories. Persons of aboriginal descent outnumber all others. Since the Northwest Territories is comprised of aboriginal peoples from several different cultures, proceedings in the House are translated into eight different languages (English, French, North Slavey, South Slavey, Dogrib, Chipewyan, Loucheux and Inuktitut). Furthermore, the previous, non-aboriginal government leader, Dennis Patterson, has been replaced by an aboriginal government leader.

Northwest Territories: Heritage

	1991	
Heritage	No.	%
Aboriginal	18	75
Non-Aboriginal	6	25

from government work has increased from five to seven.

Before entering Territorial politics, over half of the sitting members had previously held elected positions, either at the municipal or Band level.

Although the Northwest Territories now has a female government leader, only three women in total hold seats in the Legislature. This, however,

SUMMARY

While each legislative assembly has its own unique profile, patterns of membership do emerge. Occupational backgrounds differ by region, yet an indication of the increased urbanization of Canada is seen in the reduction of the number of farmers sitting in legislative assemblies. At the same time, redistribution in all jurisdictions has resulted in fewer rural-based seats. While clear patterns do not emerge from the educational profiles of members, elected officials are increasingly drawn from the ranks of those with post-secondary educations.

Although it is clear that none of the legislatures are even close to achieving gender parity, improvements have occurred since the previous general elections. It is interesting to note that the House of Commons has one of the lowest proportions of elected female members in all of Canada.

While conventional wisdom has often suggested that provincial office provides a good reward for past community service for prominent local citizens, the examination of "ages entered" suggests differently. The majority of members in all legislatures began their legislative careers before the age of 45. Although the number of elected provincial officials seeking federal election is declining, it appears that the number of people seeing elected office as a potential career has not simultaneously declined. It may be that there aren't stages to a political career in Canada; political careerists may choose to spend all of their elected life in a single legislature. However, career lengths when seen coupled with the number of large-scale changes in party fortunes as a result of recent elections, suggests that few assemblies run the risk of being dominated by professional politicians. Most elections bring to their respective assembly a new crop of legislators. They may well be seeking a political career, but disgruntled voters have other ideas.

In some cases this has resulted in the election of new, or formally minor, parties. While the most striking example may be the newly attained official opposition status of the Confederation of Regions Party in New Brunswick, the Bloc Québecois and the Reform Party have also translated uncertain political and economic expectations into legislative seats. In other jurisdictions traditional parties have overcome historic obstacles to holding office, most notably the New Democratic Party in Ontario. Future federal and provincial elections will prove interesting as the ebbs and tides of political fortunes continue their effects.

CHAPTER NINETEEN

Composition Of The House, 1991

THERE ARE a total of 1,065 seats in the House of Commons and the ten provincial and two territorial legislatures compared to 1,018 seats in 1982. Redistribution (a process examining census figures, and based on population concentration), has, during the past decade, provided additional seats to the House of Commons (13), Quebec (3), Ontario (5), Saskatchewan (2), Alberta (4), British Columbia (18) and the Northwest Territories (2).

The Composition of the House, 1991 Table shows that with the exception of Nova Scotia, Manitoba and Yukon, relatively strong majority governments are in place in every jurisdiction. However, the substantial majority governments that some provinces enjoyed a decade ago have either been considerably reduced or wiped out all together, with an opposition party forming the government. Such was the case in Alberta in 1982 when the Progressive Conservative Party had 73 seats while the Official Opposition, Third Party and Independent seats totalled only six. By 1992 the Progressive Conservatives in that province have been reduced to 59 seats, with the Opposition and Third Party accounting for 24 in what has become an 83-seat House. In 1982 the Ontario Progressive Conservatives had a majority consisting of 70 seats in a 125-member House, compared to the combined 54 Opposition and Third Party seats. Today, the New Democratic Party government holds 73 seats out of a new total of 130, the Liberal opposition has 35 and the Progressive Conservatives are relegated to third party status with just 20 seats.

One of the hallmarks of the last decade's provincial politics has been the fluctuation of power levels for majority and minority governments alike, and the swings in public attitudes which have ousted a number of governments that had hardly strayed from their original, election-winning agendas. In 1982 the Progressive Conservatives formed the government in eight legislatures. The Liberals did not form the government in any province, and the New Democratic Party were only in power in Manitoba.

Today, this picture has changed dramatically: The Progressive Conservatives form the government in three provinces (Nova Scotia, Manitoba and Alberta), the Liberals in four (Newfoundland, Prince Edward Island, New Brunswick and Quebec), and the New Democratic Party are the government party in the largest provincial jurisdiction (Ontario), and in Saskatchewan, British Columbia and Yukon.

One of the results of these fluctuations is that fairly large numbers of new members with little previous political experience have taken their places in Canada's legislatures. Many of those that lost their seats had only served for short periods, and would not qualify for retirement allowances (pensions).

Composition of the House, 1991 [1]

	Total Elected Members	Distribution of Members					Last Redistribution	Avg. Number sitting days/year
		Govt.	Oppos.	Third Party	Other	Vacant		
H of C	295	158	81	44	12 [2]	0	1988	134
Newf.	52	34	17	1	0	0	1983	110
P.E.I.	32	30	2	0	0	0	1963	29
N.S.	52	27	22	3	0	0	1981	85
N.B.	58	46	8	3	1	0	1974	39
Que.	125	90	30	4	0	1	1991	90
Ont.	130	73	35	20	1 [3]	1	1987	100
Man. [4]	57	29	20	7	0	0	1989	90
Sask.	66	55	10	1	0	0	1991	76
Alta.	83	59	16	8	0	0	1986	90
B.C.	75	51	17	7	0	0	1991	85
Yukon	16	9	5	2	0	0	1989	50
N.W.T.	24	..... consensus government				0	1983 [5]	60

[1] Including information from the most recent elections in New Brunswick, Saskatchewan and British Columbia.
[2] Represents 11 independents, nine of which are members of the Bloc Québecois and one Reform Party member.
[3] Independent Member.
[4] Speaker is included in Total Elected Members, but not in the party breakdown.
[5] The 1989/90 Electoral Boundaries Commission Report was tabled in April 1990 and considered in the fall elections. The recommendations were passed with a few amendments and resulted in some boundary changes.

PART FOUR

The American Counterpart

SINCE ITS inception, *Canadian Legislatures* has included a section on U.S. state legislatures, tabling information concerning legislative salaries, allowances and pensions as well as the budgetary estimates of state legislatures, and other facts that are pertinent to the legislative process in that country.

Although the Canadian federal system of government differs from that in the United States in terms of powers, mandates and the operating style and role of elected members, there is a relevance and similarity in the way that administrative functions are handled. This is particularly true of the large U.S. states where legislators are provided with a range of allowances and services which are somewhat akin to those in Canada.

CHAPTER ONE

Limiting Terms: What's in Store?

KARL T. KURTZ

Mr. Kurtz is the Director of State Services of the National Conference of State Legislatures. This article is reprinted with permission from State Legislatures, *January 1992. Copyright © 1992 by National Conference of State Legislatures.*

WHEN WASHINGTON voters in November dealt the first defeat to term limits, they slowed a movement that only last year seemed indomitable. And in doing so they cast some doubt on the conventional wisdom that frustration with politics coupled with well-heeled organizations promoting limited terms would force lawmakers out of work in state after state. Yet voters in as many as 20 states may decide the question in 1992. For the short term, at least, the issue is here to stay.

Already in California, 120 seasoned lawmakers can see the end of their tenure just ahead, the result of a voter initiative passed by a narrow margin in 1990. That year Oklahoma and Colorado passed term limits, too.

While Washington was the only state to vote on term limits in 1991, 45 states considered legislation that would impose limits on legislative terms. In Oregon, term limit bills passed in both houses, later to die in conference committee at the end of the session. Supporters of term limits filed initiatives for 1992 in at least 10 states, and there's talk of collecting signatures in 10 others. Recognizing that legislators are not likely to impose term limits on themselves and that there are only 23 states that allow voter initiatives, proponents of term limits are mounting major grass roots campaigns to pressure legislatures in states without the initiative, notably Texas and Wisconsin.

Political scientists have begun to focus not only on the intended consequences of this institutional reform but also the likely unintended outcomes. All around the country, political scientists and constitutional scholars are beginning to think about how legislatures may change under term limits. Since the impact of these limitations will not be felt for a number of years, much of this examination is, at best, informed speculation.

Will term limits reduce the advantage of incumbents in elections?

The advantage of the incumbent does not disappear with term limits, but limiting the number of elections in which incumbents are eligible to run will reduce their domination of legislative elections. Shorter limits like the six-year limit for the California Assembly will have greater impacts than longer ones like the 12 years for members of Congress from Colorado. However, Gary Moncrief of Boise State University, Gary Copeland of the University of Oklahoma, David Everson of Sangamon State University and NCSL's own analysts all conclude that term limits will have relatively little effect on part-time, low-salary, small-staff legislatures like Idaho, Oklahoma and West Virginia, which already have turnover rates well over 80 percent without any limit on the length of terms. The greatest change will occur in highly professionalized legislatures like Congress, California and New York where membership turnover is very low because the jobs are basically full time with relatively high pay and generous support staff. A strong staff, along with resources like postage allowances and district offices, allows members in these states to provide effective constituent services that help them get re-elected.

Will term limits lead to greater party competition?

Most observers believe that term limits will have little or no effect on party competition in legislative districts. Moncrief points out that an open seat is not necessarily a competitive seat and that term limitations in many instances will exchange a veteran legislator from one party for a new legislator of the same party. Even if term limits do allow a minority party in a district a better chance, this will happen only when seats come open. If incumbents choose to seek re-election, whenever eligible, these open seats will occur only every six or eight years, depending on the cycle of the term limits.

Will women and minorities gain representation?

Proponents argue that by reducing the number of incumbents eligible to run, term limits will open up more opportunities for women and minorities. Scholars generally agree, provided the group is currently underrepresented in the legislature. Fernando Guerra of Loyola Marymount University says that in

California this means greater opportunity for Latinos and Asian-Americans but not necessarily for African-Americans, who are currently slightly overrepresented in the California Assembly. Others argue that while minorities may gain in numbers in the long term, they may lose influence in the legislature in the short term because powerful senior legislators, like Speaker Willie Brown, from very safe districts will have to leave the legislature.

Will term limits change the types of people who run for the legislature?

When California lawmakers were asked if they would have run the first time had term limits been in effect, more than half said that they would have, one-third said that they would not have and the remainder did not know. Some California legislators told Charles Price of California State University at Chico they thought term limits would change the types of people who serve in the legislature. Several said that if a legislative seat is guaranteed to be a temporary position, only the wealthy and retired will be able to afford to serve.

Linda Fowler of Syracuse University, co-author of *Political Ambition*, a book on motivations for running for office and political careers, doubts that term limits will significantly affect who runs and serves in the legislature. While there is little evidence on state legislatures, she points out that historical research into nearly two centuries of congressional biographical information shows that there has been very little change over time in the occupations and backgrounds of members of Congress under greatly differing levels of pay, length of session and expectations about length of service.

How will term limits affect races for other offices?

By forcing career-oriented politicians to leave the legislature after a short time, the pool of experienced candidates available to run for other state, national or local offices will increase. Whether this is good ("we'll have more competition for other offices") or bad ("legislators will be spending all their time planning their next race for another office") is a subject of debate.

Senators with four-year terms will have even more incentive than they do today to run for other offices when they have a "free ride" in the election two years before their last term ends. While offices such as mayor, county commissioner and state official are likely to be affected by the larger pool of experienced legislators seeking other jobs, Congress is the office to which state legislators are most likely to attempt to move. In California especially, where state senate districts are larger than congressional districts, members of Congress will have to glance frequently over their shoulders at ambitious state senators. The proportion of former state legislators serving in Congress—already large—is likely to increase, especially if term limits on Congress spread and are upheld in the courts.

Term limits will also affect the mobility of members from one chamber to another. In states with specific limits for each chamber (California and Colorado), more members from the lower house are likely to move to the upper house at the enforced end of their term. On the other hand, in states like Oklahoma, where the limit is on total service in either body, most members are likely to devote their entire legislative career to one of the two chambers in order to make the most of their influence.

How will term limits affect the internal distribution of power in legislatures?

Many observers think that term limits will have their most profound impact on the leadership of legislatures. One might assume that leaders in term-limited legislatures will come from the most senior members toward the end of their terms. But, based on historical patterns of legislative turnover, it is possible to project the experience levels of legislators into the future in limited legislatures. For example, term limits will first affect California Assembly members in the 1996 elections when no current members will be eligible to seek re-election. If we assume that recent patterns of 15 percent turnover in each election continue (ignoring the possibility that term limits will increase the amount of voluntary turnover), then we can forecast the numbers of members of each class of the Assembly based on historic

turnover and eligibility for re-election under the six-year term limits.

The Table projects that 61 of 80 members of the California Assembly will be serving their first term after the 1996 elections. Similar analyses for other legislative bodies estimate that 34 of 40 California senators will be in their first term in 1998, and in Colorado 75 percent of House members in 1998 and 82 percent of the Senate in 2000 will be freshmen. These freshman classes are so large that it is possible that the newcomers will be tempted to elect some of their own to leadership positions. In any case, in these years there will not be enough experienced members to dominate committee chairmanships.

Projection of the California Assembly Under Term Limits (80 members)			
	Number of Members Starting		
Election Year	*Term 1*	*Term 2*	*Term 3*
1996	61	10	9
1998	19	52	9
2000	19	16	44
2002	50	16	14
2004	24	42	14
2006	24	20	36
2008	42	20	17
2010	27	36	17

Alan Rosenthal of the Eagleton Institute of Politics at Rutgers University takes this argument one step further and suggests that legislatures with term limits will rotate leaders and committee chairs every year because there will be so many short-term legislators wanting a turn at leadership positions. He argues that limits will accelerate an already existing trend toward weakening leadership in legislatures.

Another likely spin-off is that in states where legislative campaign fund raising has become a major activity and source of power for leaders, the incentive (holding on to leadership positions) for this activity will be greatly reduced. This may mean that state party staff and leadership will have to perform this role or, more likely, that centralized campaign fund raising will die out and individual candidates will have to raise their own campaign money.

Michael Malbin of the Rockefeller Institute at the State University of New York at Albany suggests that term limits may lead to an increase in the number of coalition elections of leaders and more cross-party factional alignments in general. Why? Because short terms of office weaken the ties of political parties and increase the importance of loyalties to the class with which lawmakers enter the legislature.

But there is no consensus on the impact of term limits on party strength within the legislature. David Brady and Douglas Rivers of Stanford argue that parties will be strengthened by term limitations because research shows that historically party-line voting in Congress increases whenever there are large numbers of new members who, presumably, lack experience and knowledge to base their decisions on cues other than party.

How will term limits affect constituency service?

Under Costa Rica's extreme limitation of only one four-year term, legislators pay little or no attention to constituency service, reports Charles Dawson of the State University of New York at Albany. While this may be due at least as much to cultural differences as to term limits and none of the U.S. measures is so stringent as to deny any re-election, this Latin American example suggests the possibility that legislators in their last term who are not planning to run for other office may do less casework.

Will term limits result in better legislation?

Some say this reform will bring much needed "fresh blood" and new ideas into the system and reduce "gridlock" brought about by entrenched powerful veteran legislators. Opponents, on the other hand, say that the business of government is extremely complicated and that legislating should not be left to the inexperienced. In large part because there is no easy way to define what constitutes "better" legislation, objective social science research has very little to contribute to this argument.

To the claim that effective legislating requires experience, Mark Petracca of the University of California at Irvine responds that the principle of rotation in office, long a part of American political theory and history, means that there should always be a mix of new and experienced members in office. An unfortunate aspect of most term limitation proposals is that the limitation clock starts ticking on the same date for all members. The projections in the table for the California Assembly shows that it is likely to take at least two decades before the curve of different levels of experience smooths out. Even in 2008, it is likely that more than half the members of that body will be first-termers.

How will term limits affect the balance of power between the legislature and the executive, lobbyists and legislative staff?

Proponents of term limits argue that the business of legislatures is not so complex that years of experience are required for the legislature to stand up to the executive branch, resist the entreaties of lobbyists and maintain appropriate control of staff. In fact, their argument is that many years of interacting with these groups lead legislators to be too cozy with the "inside the beltway" interests and to ignore the demands of voters. Opponents say that experience and continuity are two of the key advantages that legislators have over governors, that time is required to learn to say no to lobbyists and that staff will tend to dominate term-limited legislatures.

Potential shifts in the balance of power is another issue that is difficult to evaluate through empirical analysis. Most students of Congress and state legislatures fear that legislatures will lose power in relation to the executive as a result of term limits, but reputable scholars can be found on either side of the issue.

In the end, the debate over term limits is highly emotional. Most people will make up their minds on this issue based on their feelings about the need for fresh blood and new ideas versus the importance of experience and knowledge in a legislature. Academic research can shed little light on these two most important issues. Nonetheless, advocates on both sides should take heed of all the possible effects, intended and unintended, that term limitations may have on America's legislatures.

CHAPTER TWO

American State Legislatures

RICH JONES

Rich Jones is Director, Legislative Programs of the National Conference of State Legislatures, Denver, Colorado. The National Conference of State Legislatures is the principal co-ordinating body for state legislatures in the United States.

STATE LEGISLATURES in the United States have undergone a dramatic transformation during the past two decades. Starting in the mid-1960s, legislatures embarked on a major campaign to improve and modernize their operations. They added staff, extended the time spent in session, raised salaries for legislators, built new office buildings, restored state capitols and added district offices for the members. Once considered a purely part-time office, lawmaking has become a full-time career for one out of every five legislators. In some states, the number of full-time legislators exceeds 50%. As a result of these changes, legislatures have become co-equal partners in state government and are a leading source of policy innovation in the United States.

Legislative Sessions

In 1991, state legislatures are meeting in longer sessions and have fewer restrictions on their ability to call themselves into special session than they did 25 years ago. Today, twelve states place no limit on session length, 32 states have constitutional limits and six states have statutory or indirect limitations based on cut-off dates for legislators' salaries or per diem expense payments. All but seven states (Arkansas, Kentucky, Montana, Nevada, North Dakota, Oregon and Texas) currently meet in annual sessions. Following World War II, only four states held annual sessions. In 1966, this number increased to twenty states, and by 1974, 42 states met annually.

More recently, however, there has been increased interest, particularly on the part of the public, in limiting legislative sessions. In 1988, voters in Colorado approved a constitutional amendment limiting legislative sessions to 120 days in both years of the biennium. This is a change from previous years when the General Assembly had no limit on the first year and a 140-day limit on the second. Oklahoma voters passed a constitutional amendment in 1989 that specified that the Legislature could only meet from February through May. This has had the effect of reducing the session length from the previous limit of 90 legislative days. Alaska adopted a 120-day session limit in 1984 and there have been several attempts to limit sessions in Michigan.

Legislative Compensation

Compensation for state legislators has increased as the time spent in session and the complexities of the issues have grown. Proponents of the legislative reform movement argued that increased salaries, additional staff resources and extended time in session would help attract and retain higher quality members. In the mid-1960s, lawmakers' salaries were set in the constitution of 26 states. Those states with constitutionally set salaries paid legislators less than those that set salaries by statute. Over the past 25 years, all but six states have removed legislators' salaries from their constitutions.

Deciding appropriate salaries for state legislators is a difficult task that involves balancing the philosophical idea of a citizen legislature with the practical considerations of the time and cost of serving in the legislature. Legislatures in 28 states are responsible for setting their own salaries. Compensation commissions are used in 21 states. In most of these states, the legislature must approve the commission's recommendations before they can take effect. However, in five states (Delaware, Hawaii, Idaho, Michigan and Washington), the commission's recommendations go into effect automatically unless rejected by the legislature. In Oklahoma, the Compensation Review Board sets legislators' salaries without approval or rejection by the Legislature. Seven states (Florida, Georgia, Kansas, Missouri, Montana, North Carolina and Oregon) tie legislators' salaries to those paid to state employees.

In 1991, salaries range from a low of $100 per year in New Hampshire to a high of $57 500 per year in New York. Ten states will pay legislators $30 000 a year or more in 1991. Annual salaries in some of the largest states include: California, $52 500; Texas, $7 200; Pennsylvania, $47 000; Florida, $22 560; Illinois, $35 661 and Ohio, $40 406.

All but five states pay legislators a per diem to cover living expenses. In 43 states, presiding officers and majority or minority leaders receive additional compensation. In sixteen states, additional pay is given to other leaders such as deputy majority leaders, whips, caucus chairs and policy chairs. Committee chairs get extra pay in fifteen states.

In addition to salaries, legislators are eligible for retirement benefits in 42 states, and in 46 states they receive various insurance benefits such as health and hospitalization, dental, life, disability and opti-

cal. In most of these states, legislators receive the same insurance benefits as state employees. All but three states (Hawaii, Massachusetts and New Jersey) reimburse legislators for the use of their cars. California and Pennsylvania provide monthly allowances to lease automobile, and certain legislative leaders are provided with a state car in Arkansas, Missouri, New Jersey and Washington.

A relatively new and growing aspect of legislative compensation is the allowances paid to members in 33 states for district or capitol office expenses. These range from relatively small postage budgets in Minnesota and Nevada to staffing allowances in excess of $100 000 paid to members in California, Michigan, New York and Texas.

Costs of Operating Legislatures

During Fiscal Year 1990 (the most recent year for which we have data), legislatures across the United States spent almost $1.5 billion on their operations. This works out to an average of $6.02 per citizen, and almost three cents out of every $10 in state general fund expenditures. The large states spend the most on legislative operations. Legislative expenditures totalled $197 million in California, $172 million in New York, $121 million in Pennsylvania and $86 million in Michigan during Fiscal Year 1990. Conversely, the small states spend the least on their legislatures, with Wyoming ($4.2 million), South Dakota ($2.9 million) and Idaho ($4.6 million), spending less than $5 million each. (For expenditure totals for all U.S. state legislatures, see Page 195.) Even with all the changes occurring in state legislatures, the percentage of total state general fund expenditures spent on the legislatures has remained fairly constant through the 1980s.

Legislative Staffing

The cornerstone of the modern state legislature is the legislative staff. The growth and development of legislative staff has significantly affected the operations of state legislatures. Through its ability to gather, evaluate, process and synthesize information, staff provide legislatures with greater independence. No longer must legislators rely exclusively on the information provided by lobbyists and executive agencies.

Legislative staffing underwent several significant changes in the 1980s. First, the number of staff working in state legislatures grew by approximately 24%, from almost 27 000 total staff in 1979 to over 33 000 total staff in 1988. Most of the increase came in the area of full-time professional staff which grew by 5 400 or almost 65%. This growth represents nearly 85% of the total staff change since 1979. The number of session-only staff declined by twelve percent from 1979 to 1988.

The growth rate in legislative staff has not been uniform across all states. The states with the largest number of staff in 1979 accounted for over 65% of the total growth during the 1980s. States with the largest legislative staffs in 1988 are, in rank order: New York, California, Pennsylvania, Texas, Florida, Illinois and Michigan.

The decentralization of legislative staff that has occurred since the mid-1960s is continuing, but in a different way. There have been almost no recent examples of decentralization occurring through the break-up and reassignment of central legislative staff agencies. Rather, decentralization is occurring through growth in staff outside of these legislative staff agencies. Staff added during the 1980s tended to be personal staff to individual members, staff assigned to the party caucuses and policy staff assigned to work directly with legislative committees. Since 1979, at least seventeen states report they have increased the number of personal staff available to members. The growth in this type of staff has decentralized staff resources and consequently, power within state legislatures.

Legislative Facilities

Legislatures have come a long way from the time when the only space the members had was a desk on the chamber floor. Modern telecommunications and computer technology, longer sessions, increased public desire for access to the legislature and the expanding number of staff are some of the factors driving the legislatures' need for additional and more sophisticated space. The Connecticut Legislature recently completed a new legislative office building, Pennsylvania added a new wing to its main Capitol, Alabama renovated a highway department building and converted it for the Legislature's use, and Wisconsin moved legislative staff into leased spaced outside of the capital. Plans are underway for constructing new legislative office buildings in Arizona, Michigan and Texas.

Concurrent with this drive for additional space, legislatures have embarked on an effort to restore and preserve the historic quality of their capitols. During the 1980s major renovation projects were undertaken in California, Connecticut, Indiana, Michigan, Minnesota, Mississippi, New York, Pennsylvania, Tennessee and Wisconsin. New Jersey has recently restored its capitol and New Mexico is about to begin a restoration project.

Full-Time Legislatures and Legislators

Debates over the amount of time legislatures spend in session often centre on the desire to preserve the "citizen" legislature versus the need to develop "professional" or full-time legislatures similar to the U.S. Congress. Traditionally, it has been argued that legislatures benefit by having members who represent a variety of different vocations, who come to the legislature for a short period of time and then return to their other occupations. In recent years, many have argued that the complexities of the issues being considered and the demands placed on legislatures have increased the need for full-time lawmakers.

Several factors such as the amount of time in session, the level of compensation, the amount of staff and the turnover in membership can be used to measure whether a legislature is considered full-time. In addition, full-time legislatures tend to provide district offices for the members, place a high priority on constituent service and have a large number of members who consider themselves full-time lawmakers.

A 1988 National Conference of State Legislatures (NCSL) study grouped the legislatures into three categories depending on the extent to which they exhibit the characteristics of a full-time legislature. California, Illinois, Massachusetts, Michigan, New York, Ohio, Pennsylvania and Wisconsin are considered to be full-time legislatures. They meet in session longer than the other legislatures, have relatively high salaries, large staffs and stable memberships. At the other end of the spectrum are the seventeen states with clearly part-time legislatures. They meet in short sessions, have low salaries and small staffs and exhibit high turnover among the members. In between are the 25 states whose legislatures may have some of the characteristics of the full-time legislatures but not all. Florida, for example, has a large legislative staff but meets in a short session and ranks in the midrange for legislative pay. New Jersey meets most of the full-time characteristics except for a relatively high turnover rate among its membership. Given the increased demands placed on legislatures, it is likely that states such as Florida, Missouri and New Jersey will move into the full-time category during the coming decade. Others, such as Maine and North Carolina are likely to evolve from being part-time bodies and begin to take on more characteristics of full-time legislatures.

The number of members who consider themselves to be "full-time" legislators is increasing. In a 1986 study conducted by NCSL, eleven percent of all legislators designated the legislature as their sole profession. It can be argued that the actual percentage of full-time legislators is even higher. If the occupational categories "retired", "student" and "homemaker" are included , full-time legislators would exceed twenty percent of all legislators. More than 60% of the members in the Pennsylvania

General Assembly and the New York Legislature consider themselves to be full-time lawmakers and more than half the legislators in the middle Atlantic states serve full-time. Nearly one-fifth (nineteen percent) of all women legislators consider themselves to be full-time lawmakers with an additional thirteen percent indicating that they are homemakers.

The Evolving Legislatures

The legislative modernization movement was successful in strengthening state legislatures. They are currently independent institutions fully capable of devising innovative and imaginative solutions to complex and challenging public policy issues. The new federalism policies of the 1980s, growing federal budget deficits and the legislatures' enhanced capacity combined to propel legislatures into the forefront of the policy debate on a wide range of issues including education, economic development, health care, delivery of social services and environmental protection.

Legislatures will not relinquish the gains they have made since 1965. In fact, they are likely to build on their present strengths, taking on more issues as the federal budget deficit and trend toward federalism continues.

CHAPTER THREE

Legislative Branch Expenditures

Expenditures for Fiscal Year 1990, with rankings by legislative branch expenditure and per capita cost.

Alabama
Gen. Gov't: $7 399 607 000
Leg. Branch: $11 666 000
Rank: 37
Pop. 1990: 4 041 000
Per Capita: $2.89
Rank: 47

Alaska
Gen. Gov't: $4 284 447 000
Leg. Branch: $23 181 000
Rank: 16
Pop. 1990: 550 000
Per Capita: $42.15
Rank: 1

Arizona
Gen. Gov't: $7 534 510 000
Leg. Branch: $15 100 000
Rank: 28
Pop. 1990: 3 665 000
Per Capita: $4.12
Rank: 41

Arkansas
Gen. Gov't: $3 930 129 000
Leg. Branch: $12 549 000
Rank: 32
Pop. 1990: 2 351 000
Per Capita: $5.34
Rank: 29

California
Gen. Gov't: $70 188 885 000
Leg. Branch: $198 598 000
Rank: 1
Pop. 1990: 29 760 000
Per Capita: $6.67
Rank: 18

Colorado
Gen. Gov't: $5 627 017 000
Leg. Branch: $11 566 000
Rank: 38
Pop. 1990: 3 294 000
Per Capita: $3.51
Rank: 43

Connecticut
Gen. Gov't: $8 880 382 000
Leg. Branch: $27 923 000
Rank: 13

Pop. 1990: 3 287 000

Per Capita: $8.49

Rank: 14

Delaware Gen. Gov't: $1 994 332 000

Leg. Branch: $8 266 000

Rank: 44

Pop. 1990: 666 000

Per Capita: $9.41

Rank: 8

Florida Gen. Gov't: $20 557 573 000

Leg. Branch: $76 318 000

Rank: 5

Pop. 1990: 12 938 000

Per Capita: $5.90

Rank: 24

Georgia Gen. Gov't: $11 392 913 000

Leg. Branch: $18 378 000

Rank: 24

Pop. 1990: 6 478 000

Per Capita: $2.84

Rank: 48

Hawaii Gen. Gov't: $3 546 650 000

Leg. Branch: $18 310 000

Rank: 26

Pop. 1990: 1 108 000

Per Capita: $16.53

Rank: 2

Idaho Gen. Gov't: $1 831 124 000

Leg. Branch: $4 599 000

Rank: 47

Pop. 1990: 1 007 000

Per Capita: $4.57

Rank: 35

Illinois Gen. Gov't: $20 054 854 000

Leg. Branch: $49 245 000

Rank: 7

Pop. 1990: 11 431 000

Per Capita: $4.31

Rank: 37

Indiana Gen. Gov't: $9 992 133 000

Leg. Branch: $18 744 000

Rank: 23

Pop. 1990: 5 544 000

Per Capita: $3.39

Rank: 44

Iowa Gen. Gov't: $5 935 452 000

Leg. Branch: $14 823 000

Rank: 29

Pop. 1990: 2 777 000

Per Capita: $5.34

Rank: 28

Kansas Gen. Gov't: $4 329 336 000

Leg. Branch: $11 967 000

Rank: 34

Pop. 1990: 2 478 000

Per Capita: $4.84

Rank: 31

Kentucky Gen. Gov't: $7 101 401 000

Leg. Branch: $20 460 000

Rank: 21

Pop. 1990: 3 685 000

Per Capita: $5.55

Rank: 26

Louisiana Gen. Gov't: $8 523 583 000

Leg. Branch: $19 093 000

Rank: 22

Pop. 1990: 4 220 000

Per Capita: $4.52

Rank: 36

Maine
Gen. Gov't: $2 743 255 000
Leg. Branch: $12 623 000
Rank: 33
Pop. 1990: 1 228 000
Per Capita: $10.20
Rank: 5

Maryland
Gen. Gov't: $9 832 483 000
Leg. Branch: $23 381 000
Rank: 15
Pop. 1990: 4 781 000
Per Capita: $4.89
Rank: 30

Massachusetts
Gen. Gov't: $17 038 958 000
Leg. Branch: $46 630 000
Rank: 9
Pop. 1990: 6 016 000
Per Capita: $7.57
Rank: 15

Michigan
Gen. Gov't: $19 561 154 000
Leg. Branch: $86 814 000
Rank: 4
Pop. 1990: 9 295 000
Per Capita: $9.34
Rank: 9

Minnesota
Gen. Gov't: $10 406 769 000
Leg. Branch: $39 737 000
Rank: 11
Pop. 1990: 4 375 000
Per Capita: $9.08
Rank: 12

Mississippi
Gen. Gov't: $4 393 991 000
Leg. Branch: $11 769 000
Rank: 36
Pop. 1990: 2 573 000
Per Capita: $4.57

Rank: 33
Missouri
Gen. Gov't: $7 703 336 000
Leg. Branch: $21 441 000
Rank: 19
Pop. 1990: 5 117 000
Per Capita: $4.19
Rank: 38

Montana
Gen. Gov't: $1 661 012 000
Leg. Branch: $6 022 000
Rank: 45
Pop. 1990: 799 000
Per Capita: $7.54
Rank: 16

Nebraska
Gen. Gov't: $2 815 040 000
Leg. Branch: $9 402 000
Rank: 39
Pop. 1990: 1 578 000
Per Capita: $5.98
Rank: 23

Nevada
Gen. Gov't: $2 365 783 000
Leg. Branch: $13 327 000
Rank: 31
Pop. 1990: 1 202 000
Per Capita: $11.09
Rank: 4

New Hampshire
Gen. Gov't: $1 678 319 000
Leg. Branch: $6 971 000
Rank: 43
Pop. 1990: 1 109 000
Per Capita: $6.29
Rank: 21

New Jersey
Gen. Gov't: $18 041 262 000
Leg. Branch: $47 337 000
Rank: 8
Pop. 1990: 7 730 000

	Per Capita: $6.12	
	Rank: 22	
New Mexico	Gen. Gov't: $3 891 219 000	
	Leg. Branch: $8 121 000	
	Rank: 42	
	Pop. 1990: 1 515 000	
	Per Capita: $5.36	
	Rank: 27	
New York	Gen. Gov't: $49 697 487 000	
	Leg. Branch: $172 225 000	
	Rank: 2	
	Pop. 1990: 17 990 000	
	Per Capita: $9.57	
	Rank: 7	
North Carolina	Gen. Gov't: $12 555 345 000	
	Leg. Branch: $15 145 000	
	Rank: 27	
	Pop. 1990: 6 629 000	
	Per Capita: $2.28	
	Rank: 50	
North Dakota	Gen. Gov't: $1 596 916 000	
	Leg. Branch: $2 733 000	
	Rank: 50	
	Pop. 1990: 639 000	
	Per Capita: $4.28	
	Rank: 38	
Ohio	Gen. Gov't: $20 489 043 000	
	Leg. Branch: $27 258 000	
	Rank: 14	
	Pop. 1990: 10 847 000	
	Per Capita: $2.51	
	Rank: 49	
Oklahoma	Gen. Gov't: $5 612 348 000	
	Leg. Branch: $20 466 000	
	Rank: 20	

	Pop. 1990: 3 146 000	
	Per Capita: $6.51	
	Rank: 20	
Oregon	Gen. Gov't: $5 562 796 000	
	Leg. Branch: $15 979 000	
	Rank: 26	
	Pop. 1990: 2 842 000	
	Per Capita: $5.62	
	Rank: 25	
Pennsylvania	Gen. Gov't: $21 233 590 000	
	Leg. Branch: $121 100 000	
	Rank: 3	
	Pop. 1990: 11 882 000	
	Per Capita: $10.19	
	Rank: 6	
Rhode Island	Gen. Gov't: $2 667 677 000	
	Leg. Branch: $11 898 000	
	Rank: 35	
	Pop. 1990: 1 003 000	
	Per Capita: $11.86	
	Rank: 3	
South Carolina	Gen. Gov't: $8 774 776 000	
	Leg. Branch: $22 750 000	
	Rank: 17	
	Pop. 1990: 3 487 000	
	Per Capita: $5.52	
	Rank: 19	
South Dakota	Gen. Gov't: $1 281 356 000	
	Leg. Branch: $2 908 000	
	Rank: 49	
	Pop. 1990: 696 000	
	Per Capita: $4.18	
	Rank: 40	
Tennessee	Gen. Gov't: $7 879 053 000	
	Leg. Branch: $14 397 000	

Rank: 30

Pop. 1990: 4 877 000

Per Capita: $2.95

Rank: 46

Texas Gen. Gov't: $23 629 530 000

Leg. Branch: $51 408 000

Rank: 6

Pop. 1990: 16 967 000

Per Capita: $3.03

Rank: 45

Utah Gen. Gov't: $3 470 858 000

Leg. Branch: $8 158 000

Rank: 41

Pop. 1990: 1 723 000

Per Capita: $4.73

Rank: 32

Vermont Gen. Gov't: $1 465 551 000

Leg. Branch: $5 045 000

Rank: 46

Pop. 1990: 563 000

Per Capita: $8.96

Rank: 13

Virginia Gen. Gov't: $11 850 399 000

Leg. Branch: $22 524 000

Rank: 18

Pop. 1990: 6 187 000

Per Capita: $3.64

Rank: 42

Washington Gen. Gov't: $11 389 102 000

Leg. Branch: $44 241 000

Rank: 10

Pop. 1990: 4 867 000

Per Capita: $9.09

Rank: 11

West Virginia Gen. Gov't: $3 530 003 000

Leg. Branch: $8 199 000

Rank: 40

Pop. 1990: 1 793 000

Per Capita: $4.57

Rank: 34

Wisconsin Gen. Gov't: $10 499 148 000

Leg. Branch: $32 882 000

Rank: 12

Pop. 1990: 4 892 000

Per Capita: $6.72

Rank: 17

Wyoming Gen. Gov't: $1 484 748 000

Leg. Branch: $4 181 000

Rank: 48

Pop. 1990: 454 000

Per Capita: $9.21

Rank: 10

Total Gen. Gov't: $507 874 626 000

Leg. Branch: $1 494 700 000

Pop. 1990: 248 103 000

Per Capita: $6.02

Compensation and Living Expenses

State legislators' compensation and living expenses during session, as of January 31, 1991. Salary is annual unless otherwise indicated.

Alabama Salary: $10/day (30 session days regular session)

Living Expenses During Session: $40 per diem (unvouchered), $40 one additional day per week for committee meetings

Alaska Salary: $22 872

Living Expenses During Session: $100 per diem (unvouchered)

Arizona Salary: $15 000

Living Expenses During Session: $35/day for local members, $60/day otherwise (unvouchered)

Arkansas Salary: $7 500

Living Expenses During Session: $74/day (unvouchered)

California Salary: $52 500

Living Expenses During Session: $92/day for members who sign in

Colorado Salary: $17 500

Living Expenses During Session: $99/per diem ($45 for Denver area members) (vouchered)

Connecticut Salary: $16 760

Living Expenses During Session: Senators, $4 500/year; Representatives, $3 500/year (both unvouchered)

Delaware Salary: $24 213

Living Expenses During Session: $5 500/year (unvouchered)

Florida Salary: $22 560

Living Expenses During Session: $60 day session, $3 000 for 43 days actually in capital

Georgia Salary: $10 509.60

Living Expenses During Session: $59/day (unvouchered) + $4 800/year vouchered expense account

Hawaii Salary: $27 000

Living Expenses During Session: $75/day for members not from Oahu Island + $5 000/year expense allowance

Idaho   Salary: $12 000

Living Expenses During Session: $70/day ($40/day for members not establishing a second residence in Boise + $25 daily round trip travel (vouchered)

Illinois   Salary: $35 661

Living Expenses During Session: $74 per diem (vouchered)

Indiana   Salary: $11 600

Living Expenses During Session: $92 per diem (unvouchered)

Iowa   Salary: $18 100

Living Expenses During Session: $50/day ($30 for Polk County members) (unvouchered)

Kansas   Salary: $59/day for approximately 90-95 calendar days in session

Living Expenses During Session: $60 per diem (unvouchered)

Kentucky   Salary: $100/day for approximately 101 calendar days in biennium

Living Expenses During Session: $75/day (unvouchered)

Louisiana   Salary: $16 800

Living Expenses During Session: $75 per diem (unvouchered)

Maine   Salary: $10 500 (1991); $7 500 (1992)

Living Expenses During Session: $70 per diem (vouchered)

Maryland   Salary: $27 000

Living Expenses During Session: $90 per diem (vouchered)

Massachusetts   Salary: $30 000

Living Expenses During Session: $5-$50 per diem depending on distance from capital (unvouchered), $2 400/year (unvouchered)

Michigan   Salary: $45 450

Living Expenses During Session: $8 500/year (unvouchered)

Minnesota   Salary: $27 979

Living Expenses During Session: House, $48 per diem; Senate, $50 per diem (both unvouchered). House, up to $500/month lodging; Senate, up to $450/month lodging

Mississippi   Salary: $10 000

Living Expenses During Session: $76/day (unvouchered)

Missouri   Salary: $22 870.20

Living Expenses During Session: $35 per diem (vouchered)

Montana   Salary: $52.13/day (90 session days per biennium)

Living Expenses During Session: $50/day (unvouchered)

Nebraska   Salary: $12 000

Living Expenses During Session: $67 per diem ($26 for members within 50 miles of Lincoln) (vouchered)

Nevada   Salary: $130/day (for no more than 60 calendar days per biennium)

Living Expenses During Session: $66 per diem (unvouchered)

New Hampshire   Salary: $100/year

Living Expenses During Session: None

New Jersey   Salary: $35 000

Living Expenses During Session: None

New Mexico   Salary: $75/day

Living Expenses During Session: None

New York Salary: $57 500

Living Expenses During Session: $89/day in state, in "upstate counties"; $130/day in N.Y.C., Westchester, Nassau, Suffolk or out of state; $45/day elsewhere (vouchered)

North Carolina Salary: $12 504

Living Expenses During Session: $81/day (unvouchered) $522/month unvouchered expense allowance

North Dakota Salary: $90/day (110-115 calendar days per biennium) + $180/month while in office

Living Expenses During Session: $35 per diem up to $600/month (vouchered)

Ohio Salary: $40 406.57

Living Expenses During Session: None

Oklahoma Salary: $32 000

Living Expenses During Session: $35 per diem (vouchered) + mileage for 1 round trip home

Oregon Salary: $11 868

Living Expenses During Session: $73/week (unvouchered)

Pennsylvania Salary: $47 000

Living Expenses During Session: $88/day (vouchered)

Rhode Island Salary: $5/day (60 session days per year)

Living Expenses During Session: none

South Carolina Salary: $10 400

Living Expenses During Session: $79/day subsistence for actual attendance on session days

South Dakota Salary: $4 267 (1991); $ 3 733 (1992)

Living Expenses During Session: $75/day (unvouchered)

Tennessee Salary: $16 500

Living Expenses During Session: $78/day (unvouchered)

Texas Salary: $7 200

Living Expenses During Session: $30 per diem (unvouchered)

Utah Salary: $65/day (45 calendar days in session)

Living Expenses During Session: $25 per diem (unvouchered) plus $50/day for members outside Davis County

Vermont Salary: $480/week (estimate 17 weeks = $8 160)

Living Expenses During Session: $87/day (or $32/day + mileage for members who commute) (unvouchered)

Virginia Salary: $18 000

Living Expenses During Session: $75/day (vouchered)

Washington Salary: $19 900

Living Expenses During Session: $66 per diem (vouchered)

West Virginia Salary: $6 500

Living Expenses During Session: $30/day meals, $40/day lodging

Wisconsin Salary: $33 622 (some senators at lower rate)

Living Expenses During Session: up to $64/day (unvouchered)

Wyoming Salary: $75/day

Living Expenses During Session: $60/day (unvouchered)

D. C. Salary: $71 885

Living Expenses During Session: $118 per diem when out of town (vouchered)

CHAPTER FIVE

Legislative Allowances for Staff, District Offices and Other Office Expenses

In thirty-three states, some sort of allowance is provided for either district office or capital office expenses. These allowances range from amounts designated specifically for postage (Minnesota, Nevada) to budgets in the tens of thousands of dollars for all office-related expenses (Illinois, Michigan).

Staffing allowances are provided in only seventeen states and vary greatly, from a minimal sum for district staff (Missouri) to six-figure allowances for staff salaries and benefits (Michigan, New York).

Following are descriptions of office and staffing allowances, as of January 31, 1991, in those states that provide them.

Alabama	District Expenses: $1 900/month (unvouchered) for expenses in district. (Some districts do not have offices).
Alaska	Office and Staffing: $4 000/year for stationery, postage, stenographic services and other staffing for district or capital office. Office space and telephone expenses are also provided. (Primary staffing is provided by the legislature).
Arkansas	Office and Staffing: At the option of each member, $485/month, $545/month, or $600/month for office rental, equipment, supplies, postage, communications, travel, meals, lodging and clerical staff salaries. Committee chairs are eligible for an additional $150 per month.
California	Office and Staffing: $279 380/year in assembly for both capital and district office expenses and staffing. In senate, allowance varies based on staffing level and geographic location of district office.
Connecticut	Staffing: The senate Democratic caucus receives approximately $20 000/year for each senator's constituent caseworker; the senate Republican caucus receives approximately $20 000 for every three senators for caseworkers. House caucuses receive approximately $20 000 for every four rank and file members for caseworkers.

Florida	District Office and Staffing: $1 500/month. (The speaker, senate president and senators who have three district employees for 16 or more calendar days in each month receive $1 750).
Georgia	Office: $4 800/year maximum, vouchered, for postage and other office expenses.
Idaho	Office: Office expenses are included in the $200 per year unvouchered expense allowance mentioned in the Compensation and Living Expenses Table. Members are provided with stationery and postage during session.
Illinois	District Office and Staffing: $57 000/year maximum for Senators $47 000/year maximum for Representatives These allowances cover office rental, utilities, stationery, and staffing of district offices.
Indiana	District Office: $25/day, seven days/week for district office—supplies, rent, etc., when not in session. Unvouchered.
Iowa	District Office: $75/month for postage, travel, phone, and other district office costs.
Kansas	Office: $600/month during 9-month interim, for postage, phones, in-district travel etc.
Kentucky	Office and Staffing: $950/month (unvouchered) in interim for secretarial assistance, books and publications, postage, phone, and other expenses. $50 per session stationery allowance.
Louisiana	Office: $325/month (vouchered) for phone, supplies, postage, utilities, and/or rent. Newly elected members: one payment of $1 000 for equipment and furniture. Returning members: $250/term for equipment and furniture.

	Staffing: $1 047 per month for a legislative assistant (or assistants). An increase of 5% per year up to $1 652 per month is provided.
Maine	Office: $500 per year Consituent Service Allowance (unvouchered). Members do not have district offices.
Maryland	District Office: For office rental, supplies, phone, etc., members receive the following: $18 796/year —Senate presiding officer, majority leader, minority leader, and standing committee chairs. $17 395/year—other senators. $17 818/year—House speaker, speaker pro tem, majority leader, minority leader, and standing committee chairs. $17 002/year—House delegation chairs. $16 197/year—other representatives. Staffing: Senators have a fully funded secretary. Representatives allot a portion of their district office allowance (above) toward clerical staff.
Michigan	Capital Office: Senators receive $47 000/year for postage, phone, in-district travel, printing, publications, and temporary staff. (Members do not have district offices.) Representatives do not have their own office budgets. Staffing: Majority senators receive $168 727/year + 5 maximum benefits packages. Minority senators receive $102 883/year + 3 maximum benefits packages. Representatives do not receive a staffing allowance.
Minnesota	Office: For postage, legislators receive allowances as follows: 1 750 first-class stamps — Representatives (Speaker and minority leader have unlimited postage).

6 500 first-class stamps — Senate leaders and committee chairs, each year.

5 500 first-class stamps — other senators, each year.

Mississippi Office: $800/month in interim.

Missouri District Office and Staffing: $600/month for phone, in-district travel, office supplies, district office staff, utilities, etc.

Nevada Office: $60/biennium postage allowance, plus $2 800/biennium communication allowance for phone, etc. (Leaders and committee chairs receive additional $900).

New Jersey District Office: Lease cost up to $12 000. Up to $1 500/year supplies and furniture.

Staffing: $60 000/year.

New York Office: $1 600/year for incidental expenses. (Major office expenses such as rent, telephone, supplies, furniture, and postage are covered by the legislature.

Staffing: Approximately $130 000 (base) to $250 000 for district and capital staff, depending on position of legislator.

North Carolina Office: $1 500/biennium for postage and telephone.

Oklahoma Office: $350/year for office supplies, $750/year postage, and $600/year phone allowance.

Oregon District Office: $400-550/month depending on size of district.

Staffing: $1 491/month for personal secretary (in session). $1 781/month for legislative assistant (in session).

In interim, members receive $1100/month for 18 months for staff.

Pennsylvania District Office: $20 000/year—Senators

$10 000/year—Representatives

Representatives also receive a $2 000/year postage allowance.

South Carolina Office: $300/month in-district expenses.

$400/month session postage.

Tennessee District Office: Senators are reimbursed for district office expenses. (No set limit). Representatives receive $7 000/month in session and $6 000/month in interim for district office, capital office, staffing, and in-state and out-of-state travel.

Staffing: $15 500/month—Senators.

Virginia District Office: $6 000/year (unvouchered) for office expenses and supplies. (Senate president pro tem, senate majority and minority floor leaders, and house majority and minority floor leaders receive $7 200/year).

Staffing: $15 000/year for secretary or administrative assistant. (the five leaders mentioned above receive $22 500/year; house speaker gets $70 000/year).

Washington District Office: $300/month year-round, for office rental, computer, travel, etc.

Wisconsin Office: Senators receive $25 825 per two-year session for postage, in-district mileage, printing, phone, etc. Senators also receive the cost of one district-wide mailing per year (approximate cost $9 924). Representatives don't have district offices, but receive $10 852/biennium for stationery, newsletters, printing, mailing, phone, etc.

Staffing: Senators receive $109 646 for two-year session for administrative staff (salary and benefits for two people, plus others without benefits subject to approval). Representatives' staff are paid out of the general budget.

D. C.

Staffing: Council members receive staffing allowances as follows:

$229 724—Chairman (6 personal staff positions)

$360 140—Chairman (10 committee staff positions)

$176 210—Chairman Pro Tem (5 personal staff positions)

$164 074—Chairman Pro Tem (5 committee staff positions)

$131 999 (approximately)—Eight council members, who each have an average of 5 personal staff

$157 733—Two council members, each with 5 personal staff positions

$153 224—One council member (5 personal staff positions)

CHAPTER SIX

U.S. Legislative Retirement Benefits

Alaska

Participation: Optional

Requirements for Regular Retirement: Age 60, 5 yrs. service. Age 55, 5 yrs. service, if vested before July 1, 1986.

Contrib. Rate: 6.75%

1990 Salary : $22 140

Monthly Benefits Estimates:

4 yrs: Not elig.

8 yrs: $668

12 yrs: $988

16 yrs: $1 337

20 yrs: $1 696

Benefit Formula: 2% x avg. monthly salary x length of service before 7/1/86 to 10 yrs of service; 2.25% x avg. monthly salary x length of service as of 7/1/86, and from 10-20 yrs. of service.

Same as State Employees: Yes.

Arizona

Participation: Mandatory

Requirements for Regular Retirement: age 65, 5 yrs. service; age 62, 10 yrs. service; age 60, 25 yrs. service.

Contrib. Rate: 1.27%

1990 Salary : $15 000

Monthly Benefits Estimates:

4 yrs: Not. elig.

8 yrs: $400

12 yrs: $600

16 yrs: $800

20 yrs: $1 000

Benefit Formula: 4% x yrs. of service x final salary rate (maximum = 80% of salary)

Same as State Employees: No.

Arkansas

Participation: Mandatory (non-contributory plan–after 1978) and Optional (contributory plan - before 1978).

Requirements for Regular Retirement: Non-Contributory Plan: age 65, 10 yrs. service; age 55, 17 1/2 yrs; Contributory Plan: age 60, 10 yrs service; age 55, 14 yrs. service; age 50, 18 yrs. service.

Contrib. Rate: 0% after 1/1/78 for non-contrib. members; 6% berofe 1/1/78 for contrib. members

1990 Salary : $7 500

Monthly Benefits Estimates:

4 yrs: Not elig.

8 yrs: Not elig.

12 yrs: $270 (mandatory plan); $314 (optional plan)

16 yrs: $360 (mandatory plan); $314 (optional plan)

20 yrs: $450 (mandatory plan); $314 (optional plan)

Benefit Formula: Non-contributory: 1.8% x 5-yr. avg. salary x 2 x yrs. of service; Contributory: $314/month.

Same as State Employees: No.

California Participation: Optional

Requirements for Regular Retirement: age 60, 4 yrs. service; any age, 20 yrs. service.

Contrib. Rate: 8%

1990 Salary : $40 816

Monthly Benefits Estimates:

4 yrs: $448

8 yrs: $996

12 yrs: $1 344

16 yrs: $1 782

20 yrs: $2 190

Benefit Formula: 5%/yr. of service x $500 up to 15 yrs. service; plus 3% per yr. x $500 for service in excess of 15 yrs; plus 3% x total yrs. service x (one month's salary at highest level, minus $500). Benefit may not exceed two-thirds of final salary.

Same as State Employees: No.

Colorado Participation: Optional.

Requirements for Regular Retirement: age 65 and over, 5 yrs. service; age 60-65, 20 yrs. service; age 55-59, 30 yrs. service; any age, 35 yrs. service.

Contrib. Rate: 8%

1990 Salary : $17 500

Monthly Benefits Estimates:

4 yrs: Not elig.

8 yrs: $292

12 yrs: $438

16 yrs: $583

20 yrs: $729

Benefit Formula: 2.5 x highest 3-yr. avg. salary x yrs. of service for first 20 yrs; additional 1% per yr. thereafter

Same as State Employees: Yes.

Connecticut Participation: Mandatory.

Requirements for Regular Retirement: Age 65, 10 yrs. service.

Contrib. Rate: 0%

1990 Salary : $16 760

Monthly Benefits Estimates:

4 yrs: Not elig.

8 yrs: Not elig.

12 yrs: $223

16 yrs: $297

20 yrs: $372

Benefit Formula: (.0133 x avg. annual salary) + [.005 x avg. annual salary in excess of "breakpoint" (specific dollar amount for each year)] x yrs. credited service.

Same as State Employees: Yes.

Delaware

Participation: Mandatory.

Requirements for Regular Retirement: age 60, 5 yrs. service; age 55, 10 yrs. service.

Contrib. Rate: 6%

1990 Salary : $23 282

Monthly Benefits Estimates:

4 yrs: Not elig.

8 yrs: $238

12 yrs: $358

16 yrs: $477

20 yrs: $596

Benefit Formula: $29.80/month per yr. of service.

Same as State Employees: No.

Florida

Participation: Optional.

Requirements for Regular Retirement: age 62, 8 yrs. service; any age, 30 yrs. service.

Contrib. Rate: 0%

1990 Salary : $21 684

Monthly Benefits Estimates:

4 yrs: Not elig.

8 yrs: $415

12 yrs: $622

16 yrs: $830

20 yrs: $1 037

Benefit Formula: 3% x yrs. of service x highest 5-yr. avg. salary.

Same as State Employees: Yes.

Georgia

Participation: Optional.

Requirements for Regular Retirement: age 65, 8 yrs. creditable service, incl. military; age 62, 8 yrs. membership service.

Contrib. Rate: 3.75% plus $7/month.

1990 Salary : $10 376

Monthly Benefits Estimates:

4 yrs: $80

8 yrs: $160

12 yrs: $240

16 yrs: $320

20 yrs: $400

Benefit Formula: $20/month x yrs. of service.

Same as State Employees: Yes.

Hawaii

Participation: Mandatory.

Requirements for Regular Retirement: age 55, 5 yrs. service; any age, 10 yrs. service.

Contrib. Rate: 7.80%

1990 Salary : $27 000

Monthly Benefits Estimates:

4 yrs: Not elig.

8 yrs: $630

12 yrs: $945

16 yrs: $1 260

20 yrs: $1 575

Benefit Formula: (3.5% x final avg. salary x yrs. of service) + monthly annuity based on age and member's contribution (maximum 75% of final avg. compensation).

Same as State Employees: Yes. [1]

Idaho

Participation: Mandatory.

Requirements for Regular Retirement: age 65, 5 yrs. service.

Contrib. Rate: 5.30%

1990 Salary : $6 525*

Monthly Benefits Estimates:

4 yrs: Not elig.

8 yrs: $70

12 yrs: $104

16 yrs: $139

20 yrs: $174

Benefit Formula: $8.70/month x yrs. of service.

Same as State Employees: Yes.

Illinois

Participation: Optional.

Requirements for Regular Retirement: age 62, 4 yrs. service; age 55, 8 yrs. service.

Contrib. Rate: 11.5% [2]

1990 Salary : $35 661

Monthly Benefits Estimates:

4 yrs: $357

8 yrs: $802

12 yrs: $1 337

16 yrs: $1 931

20 yrs: $2 525

Benefit Formula: 3% x final salary x first 4 yrs. service; 3.5% next 2 yrs. service; 4% next 2 yrs. service; 4.5% next 4 yrs. service; 5% for each year in excess of 12 yrs. service (limit 85% of final salary).

Same as State Employees: Yes. [3]

Indiana

Participation: Mandatory.

Requirements for Regular Retirement: age 65, 10 yrs. service.

Contrib. Rate: 5%

1990 Salary : $11 600

Monthly Benefits Estimates:

4 yrs: Not elig.

8 yrs: Not elig.

12 yrs: [4]

16 yrs: [4]

20 yrs: [4]

Benefit Formula: lump sum is returned to member at time of retirement; at present salary, benefit would equal $2 900 plus interest per year of service.

Same as State Employees: No.

Iowa

Participation: Optional.

Requirements for Regular Retirement: age 62, 30 yrs. service; or, total of age and yrs. of service = 92.

Contrib. Rate: 3.70%

1990 Salary : $16 600

Monthly Benefits Estimates:

4 yrs: $92

8 yrs: $184

12 yrs: $277

16 yrs: $369

20 yrs: $461

Benefit Formula: 50% x highest 3-yr. avg. salary based on 30 yrs. service. Benefit prorated for less than 30 yrs. service.

Same as State Employees: Yes.

Kansas

Participation: Optional.

Requirements for Regular Retirement: age 65, 8 yrs. service.

Contrib. Rate: Plan 1: 4%; Plan 2: 2.5%

1990 Salary : $21 948 [5]

Monthly Benefits Estimates:

4 yrs: Not elig.

8 yrs: Plan 1: $205; Plan 2: $293

12 yrs: Plan 1: $307; Plan 2: $439

16 yrs: Plan 1: $410; Plan 2: $585

20 yrs: Plan 1: $512; Plan 2: $732

Benefit Formula: Plan 1: 1.4% x highest 4-yr. avg. salary x yrs. of service; Plan 2: 2% x highest 3-yr. avg. salary x yrs. of service.

Kentucky

Same as State Employees: Plan 1: Yes; Plan 2: No.

Participation: Optional.

Requirements for Regular Retirement: age 65, 5 yrs. service.

Contrib. Rate: 5%

1990 Salary : $27 500

Monthly Benefits Estimates:

4 yrs: Not elig.

8 yrs: $504

12 yrs: $756

16 yrs: $1 008

20 yrs: $1 260

Benefit Formula: 2.75% x yrs. of service x final salary.

Louisiana

Same as State Employees: No.

Participation: Optional.

Requirements for Regular Retirement: age 60, 10 yrs. service; age 55, 12 yrs. service; any age, 16 yrs. service.

Contrib. Rate: 11.50%

1990 Salary : $16 800

Monthly Benefits Estimates:

4 yrs: Not elig.

8 yrs: Not elig.

12 yrs: $588

16 yrs: $784

20 yrs: $980

Benefit Formula: highest 3-yr. avg. salary x [(2.5% x yrs. of service as state employee) + (1% x yrs. in legislature)].

Maine

Same as State Employees: No.

Participation: Mandatory.

Requirements for Regular Retirement: age 60, 1 yr. service; any age, 25 yrs. service.

Contrib. Rate: 4%

1990 Salary : $6 600 [6]

Monthly Benefits Estimates:

4 yrs: $59

8 yrs: $118

12 yrs: $176

16 yrs: $235

20 yrs: $294

Benefit Formula: 2% x highest 3-yr. avg. salary x yrs. service.

Maryland

Same as State Employees: Yes (but employee contrib. = 6.5%).

Participation: Optional.

Requirements for Regular Retirement: age 60, 8 yrs. service.

Contrib. Rate: 5%

1990 Salary : $25 000

Monthly Benefits Estimates:

4 yrs: Not elig.

8 yrs: $417

12 yrs: $625

16 yrs: $833

20 yrs: $1 042

Benefit Formula: 2.5% x highest yr. salary x yrs. of service (maximum 24 yrs. or 60%).

Massachusetts

Same as State Employees: No.

Participation: Optional.

Requirements for Regular Retirement: age 65, 6 yrs. service.

Contrib. Rate: Before 1975, 5%; 1975-83, 7%; 1983-1/12/88, 8%; after 1/12/88, 8% of first $30 000 salary and 10% of additional salary.

1990 Salary : $30 000

Monthly Benefits Estimates:

4 yrs: Not elig.

8 yrs: $500

12 yrs: $750

16 yrs: $1 000

20 yrs: $1 250

Benefit Formula: 2.5% x 3-yr. avg. salary x yrs. of service.

Same as State Employees: Yes. [7]

Michigan　Participation: Optional.

Requirements for Regular Retirement: age 55, 5 yrs. service; or age + yrs. service = 70.

Contrib. Rate: 9%

1990 Salary : $45 450

Monthly Benefits Estimates:

4 yrs: Not elig.

8 yrs: $1 212

12 yrs: $1 818

16 yrs: $2 424

20 yrs: $2 576

Benefit Formula: 20% x final salary x yrs. of service after 5 yrs. service; 4% of highest salary per yr. for yrs. 6 through 15; 1% per yr. for yrs. 16 through 20 (maximum 64%).

Same as State Employees: No.

Minnesota　Participation: Mandatory.

Requirements for Regular Retirement: age 62, 6 yrs. service.

Contrib. Rate: 9%

1990 Salary : $26 395

Monthly Benefits Estimates:

4 yrs: Not elig.

8 yrs: $524

12 yrs: $786

16 yrs: $1 048

20 yrs: $1 310

Benefit Formula: 2.5% x yrs. of service x highest 5-yr. avg. salary incl. reg. & special session per diem (maximum 20 yrs. service credit).

Same as State Employees: Yes.

Mississippi　Participation: Optional.

Requirements for Regular Retirement: age 60, 4 yrs. service; age 55, 25 yrs. service; any age, 30 yrs. service.

Contrib. Rate: 6.5% [8]

1990 Salary : $10 000

Monthly Benefits Estimates:

4 yrs: $200

8 yrs: $375

12 yrs: $575

16 yrs: $750

20 yrs: $938

Benefit Formula: (1.875% x highest 4-yr. avg. salary x yrs. service) + 50% of PERS benefit for legislative time.

Same as State Employees: No. [8]

Missouri　Participation: Mandatory.

Requirements for Regular Retirement: age 60, 6 yrs. service.

Contrib. Rate: 0%

1990 Salary : $22 414

Monthly Benefits Estimates:

4 yrs: Not elig.

8 yrs: $320

12 yrs: $630

16 yrs: $840

20 yrs: $1 300

Benefit Formula: $80/month x number of terms served (for first 3-4 terms); $105/month x no. of terms from 5-9; $130/month x no. of terms for 10 or more terms.

Same as State Employees: No.

Montana Participation: Optional.

Requirements for Regular Retirement: age 65; age 60, 5 yrs. service; any age, 30 yrs. service.

Contrib. Rate: 6%

1990 Salary : $13 554*

Monthly Benefits Estimates:

4 yrs: $75 (if age 65)

8 yrs: $151

12 yrs: $226

16 yrs: $301

20 yrs: $377

Benefit Formula: 1.67% x yrs. of service x highest 3-yr. avg. salary.

Same as State Employees: Yes.

Nevada Participation: Mandatory.

Requirements for Regular Retirement: age 60, 10 yrs. service.

Contrib. Rate: 15%

1990 Salary : $3 900

Monthly Benefits Estimates:

4 yrs: Not elig.

8 yrs: Not elig.

12 yrs: $300

16 yrs: $400

20 yrs: $500

Benefit Formula: $25/month per yr. of service up to 30 years.

Same as State Employees: No.

New Jersey Participation: Mandatory.

Requirements for Regular Retirement: age 60.

Contrib. Rate: 5%

1990 Salary : $35 000

Monthly Benefits Estimates:

4 yrs: $350

8 yrs: $700

12 yrs: $1 050

16 yrs: $1 400

20 yrs: $1 750

Benefit Formula: 3% x highest 3-yr. avg. salary x yrs. of service.

Same as State Employees: Yes.

New York [9] Participation: Mandatory.

Requirements for Regular Retirement: age 62, 10 yrs. service.

Contrib. Rate: 3%

1990 Salary : $57 500

Monthly Benefits Estimates:

4 yrs: Not elig.

8 yrs: Not elig.

12 yrs: $955

16 yrs: $1 273

20 yrs: $1 591

Benefit Formula: 1.66% x final avg. salary x yrs. service.

Same as State Employees: Yes.

North Carolina Participation: Mandatory.

Requirements for Regular Retirement: age 65, 5 yrs. service.

Contrib. Rate: 7%

1990 Salary : $11 124

Monthly Benefits Estimates:

4 yrs: Not elig.

8 yrs: $297

12 yrs: $445

16 yrs: $594

20 yrs: $695

Benefit Formula: 4% x final salary x yrs. of service (maximum = 75% of salary).

Same as State Employees: No.

Ohio Participation: Optional.

Requirements for Regular Retirement: age 60, 5 yrs. service; age 55, 25 yrs. service; any age, 30 yrs. service.

Contrib. Rate: 8.50%

1990 Salary: $38 482

Monthly Benefits Estimates:

4 yrs: Not elig.

8 yrs: $539

12 yrs: $808

16 yrs: $1 077

20 yrs: $1 347

Benefit Formula: 2.1% x 3-yr. avg. salary x yrs. of service (maximum 90% of salary) up to 30 yrs. service; 2.5% for each additional yr. thereafter.

Same as State Employees: Yes, but mandatory for state employees.

Oklahoma Participation: Optional.

Requirements for Regular Retirement: age 60, 6 yrs. service.

Contrib. Rate: 4.5% to 10% (member chooses contrib. rate); 10% from $25 000 to $40 000

1990 Salary: $32 000

Monthly Benefits Estimates:

4 yrs: Not elig.

8 yrs: $316-$666 [10]

12 yrs: $480-$1 000 [10]

16 yrs: $633-$1 333 [10]

20 yrs: $792-$1 667 [10]

Benefit Formula: Final salary x yrs. of service x compensation factor based on contrib. rate selected (.019 for 4.5% CR).

Same as State Employees: No.

Oregon Participation: Optional.

Requirements for Regular Retirement: age 58; age 55, 30 yrs. service.

Contrib. Rate: 0%

1990 Salary: $11 868

Monthly Benefits Estimates:

4 yrs: $79

8 yrs: $158

12 yrs: $237

16 yrs: $316

20 yrs: $396

Benefit Formula: 2% x final avg. salary x yrs. service.

Same as State Employees: Yes. [11]

Pennsylvania Participation: Optional.

Requirements for Regular Retirement: age 50, 3 yrs. service; any age, 35 yrs. service. If in system before 3/1/74: age 50, 21 yrs. service.

Contrib. Rate:
Tier 1: before 3/1/74, 18.75%
Tier 2: 3/1/74 - 7/22/83, 5%
Tier 3: after 7/22/83, 6.25%

1990 Salary: $47 000

Monthly Benefits Estimates:

4 yrs: Tier 1: $1 175
Tiers 2 & 3: $313

8 yrs: Tier 1: $2 350
Tier 2: $627

12 yrs: Tier 1: $3 525
Tier 2: $940

16 yrs: Tier 1: $4 700
            Tier 2: $1 253

20 yrs: Tier 1: $5 875
            Tier 2: $1 567

Benefit Formula: Tier 1: 2% x highest 3-yr. avg. salary x yrs. of service x 3.75; Tiers 2 & 3: 2% x highest 3-yr. avg. salary x yrs. service.

Same as State Employees: Yes. [12]

Rhode Island Participation: Optional.

Requirements for Regular Retirement: age 55, 8 yrs. service.

Contrib. Rate: 30% or $90/yr.

1990 Salary : $300

Monthly Benefits Estimates:

4 yrs: Not elig.

8 yrs: $400

12 yrs: $600

16 yrs: $800

20 yrs: $1 000

Benefit Formula: $600/yr. of service (maximum $12 000/yr at 20 yrs. of service).

Same as State Employees: No. [13]

South Carolina Participation: Mandatory.

Requirements for Regular Retirement: age 60; any age, 30 yrs. service.

Contrib. Rate: 10%

1990 Salary : $13 600 [14]

Monthly Benefits Estimates:

4 yrs: $218

8 yrs: $437

12 yrs: $656

16 yrs: $874

20 yrs: $1 093

Benefit Formula: 4.82% x yrs. of service x "normal compensation" (1990 normal comp. = $10 000 salary + $3 600).

Same as State Employees: No.

Tennessee Participation: Optional.

Requirements for Regular Retirement: age 55, 4 yrs. service.

Contrib. Rate: 0%

1990 Salary : $16 500

Monthly Benefits Estimates:

4 yrs: $280

8 yrs: $560

12 yrs: $840

16 yrs: $1 120

20 yrs: $1 400

Benefit Formula: $70/month x yrs. service.

Same as State Employees: No.

Texas Participation: Optional.

Requirements for Regular Retirement: Before 8/31/83: age 60, 8 yrs. service, age 55, 12 yrs. service. After 8/31/83: age 60, 10 yrs. service, age 55, 30 yrs. service.

Contrib. Rate: 8%

1990 Salary : $7 200

Monthly Benefits Estimates:

4 yrs: Not elig.

8 yrs: $1 017

12 yrs: $1 526

16 yrs: $2 035

20 yrs: $2 544

Benefit Formula: 2% x yrs. of service x state district judge's salary (currently $76 308).

Same as State Employees: Yes.

Utah

Participation: Optional.

Requirements for Regular Retirement: Age 65, 4 yrs service

Contrib. Rate: 0%

1990 Salary : $65/day

Monthly Benefits Estimates:

4 yrs: $40

8 yrs: $80

12 yrs: $120

16 yrs: $160

20 yrs: $200

Benefit Formula: $10/month x yrs. service.

Same as State Employees: No.

Virginia

Participation: Mandatory.

Requirements for Regular Retirement: age 65, 5 yrs. service; age 55, 30 yrs. service.

Contrib. Rate: 0%

1990 Salary : $18 000

Monthly Benefits Estimates:

4 yrs: Not elig.

8 yrs: $185

12 yrs: $277

16 yrs: $370

20 yrs: $462

Benefit Formula: If avg. salary is less than $13 200: .015 x highest 3-yr. avg. x yrs. of service. If avg. salary is greater than $13 200: .0165 x (highest 3-yr. avg. salary minus $1200) x yrs. of service.

Same as State Employees: Yes.

Washington

Participation: Optional.

Requirements for Regular Retirement: Plan 1: age 60, 5 yrs. service; age 55, 25 yrs. service; any age, 30 yrs. service; Plan 2: age 65, 5 yrs. service.

Contrib. Rate: Plan 1: before 10/1/77, 6%; Plan 2; after 10/1/77, 4.9%.

1990 Salary : $16 500

Monthly Benefits Estimates:

4 yrs: Plan 1 & 2: Not elig.

8 yrs: Plan 1: $330; Plan 2: $220

12 yrs: Plan 1: $495; Plan 2: $330

16 yrs: Plan 1: $660; Plan 2: $440

20 yrs: Plan 1: $825; Plan 2: $550

Benefit Formula: Plan 1: 3% x highest 2-yr. avg. salary x yrs. of service; Plan 2: 2% x highest 5-yr. avg. salary x yrs. of service.

Same as State Employees: Plans 1 & 2: Yes.

West Virginia

Participation: Optional.

Requirements for Regular Retirement: age 60, 5 yrs. service.

Contrib. Rate: 4.5%

1990 Salary : $6 500

Monthly Benefits Estimates:

4 yrs: Not elig.

8 yrs: $87

12 yrs: $130

16 yrs: $173

20 yrs: $217

Benefit Formula: 2% x yrs. of service x highest consecutive 3-yr. avg. salary.

Same as State Employees: Yes.

Wisconsin

Participation: Mandatory.

Requirements for Regular Retirement: age 62.

Contrib. Rate: 0.5%

1990 Salary : $32 239

Monthly Benefits Estimates:

4 yrs: $226

8 yrs: $451

12 yrs: $677

16 yrs: $903

20 yrs: $1 128

Benefit Formula: 2.1% x statutory salary when leaving office x yrs. of service.

Same as State Employees: Yes. [15]

D. C.	Participation: Mandatory.

Requirements for Regular Retirement: age 62, 5 yrs. service; age 60, 20 yrs. service; age 55, 30 yrs. service.

Contrib. Rate: 7%

1990 Salary : $71 885

Monthly Benefits Estimates:

4 yrs: Not elig.

8 yrs: $764

12 yrs: $1 213

16 yrs: $1 692

20 yrs: $2 172

Benefit Formula: 1.5% x highest 3-yr. avg. salary x first 5 yrs. service; 1.75% x highest 3-yr. avg. salary x yrs. 6-10; 2% x highest 3-yr. avg .salary x all service over 10 yrs.

Same as State Employees: Yes.

* In some cases, an estimated, annualized salary is used here for purposes of computing retirement benefits.

[1] Plans for legislators are the same as for state employees except that state employees have a different benefit formula (2% rather than 3.5%).

[2] Member contribution is 8.5% plus 1% for an automatic annual increase in annuity, plus 2% for a survivor annuity that is refunded if the member is unmarried at time of retirement.

[3] Plans are the same except that the legislators' plan has a higher contribution rate and a higher payout (maximum achieved sooner).

[4] New retirement plan allows members to withdraw entire lump-sum upon retirement and purchase their own annuities, if they wish. State's contribution is 20% of salary. Some members elected to stay in the state's prior legislative retirement plan, but as of April 30, 1989, all new members will enter the new plan.

[5] Members may figure their contribution rate based on base pay alone ($21 948/year); base pay plus interim expense allowance ($27 348/year); or base pay, interim expense allowance, and session expenses ($53 016).

[6] Since even-year salaries are lower for Maine legislators, the highest three-year average salary would be computed based on the 1989 salary of $9 900, the 1987 salary of $9 000, and the 1985 salary of $7 550; thus, the average for purposes of these benefit computations is $8 817.

[7] Plans are the same except that state employees are vested after 10 years.

[8] Legislators are eligible for both regular retirement at 6.5% employee contribution rate, and legislative supplement retirement system at 3% contribution rate.

[9] Represents only Tier 4 of a four-tier system.

[10] Benefit estimates based on the salary cap of $25 000 and contribution range of 4.5% to 10%.

[11] Plans are the same except that state employees' benefits are figured using a factor of 1.67% (rather than 2%).

[12] Plans for legislators are the same as for state employees except that normal retirement for state employees is at age 60, and legislators in the system prior to 1974 receive higher benefits than newer legislators and other state employees.

[13] State employees contribute 7.5% of their annual salaries.

[14] Annual salary plus in-district expenses.

[15] Plan for legislators same as for state employees except retirement age for employees is 65.

Appendix

The House of Commons

Members can be contacted at the House of Commons main reception: 613-992-4793

Allmand, Warren .... Lib. .... Notre-Dame-de Grâce, Quebec

Althouse, Vic .... N.D.P. .. Mackenzie, Saskatchewan

Anawak, Jack Iyerak .... Lib. .... Nunatsiaq, Northwest Territories

Anderson, Edna .... P.C. .... Simcoe Centre, Ontario

Andre, Harvie .... P.C. .... Calgary Centre, Alberta

Angus, Iain .... N.D.P. .. Thunder Bay-Atikokan, Ontario

Arsenault, Guy H. .... Lib. .... Restigouche-Chaleur, New Brunswick

Assad, Mark .... Lib. .... Gatineau-La Lièvre, Quebec

Atkinson, Ken .... P.C. .... St. Catharines, Ontario

Attewell, Bill .... P.C. .... Markham-Whitchurch-Stouffville, Ontario

Axworthy, Chris .... N.D.P. .. Saskatoon-Clark's Crossing, Saskatchewan

Axworthy, Lloyd .... Lib. .... Winnipeg South Centre, Manitoba

Baker, George S. .... Lib. .... Gander-Grand Falls, Newfoundland

Barrett, David .... N.D.P. .. Esquimalt-Juan de Fuca, British Columbia

Beatty, Henry Perrin .... P.C. .... Wellington-Grey-Dufferin-Simcoe, Ontario

Bélair, Réginald .... Lib. .... Cochrane-Superior, Ontario

Bellemare, Eugène .... Lib. .... Carleton-Gloucester, Ontario

Belsher, Ross .... P.C. .... Fraser Valley East, British Columbia

Benjamin, Les .... N.D.P. .. Regina-Lumsden, Saskatchewan

Berger, David .... Lib. .... Saint-Henri-Westmount, Quebec

Bernier, Gilles .... P.C. .... Beauce, Quebec

Bertrand, Gabrielle .... P.C. .... Brome-Missisquoi, Quebec

Bevilacqua, Maurizio .... Lib. .... York North, Ontario

Bird, J.W. Bud .... P.C. .... Fredricton-York-Sunbury, New Brunswick

Bjornson, David .... P.C. .... Selkirk-Red River, Manitoba

Black, Dawn .... N.D.P. .. New Westminster-Burnaby, British Columbia

Blackburn, Derek N. .... N.D.P. .. Brant, Ontario

Blackburn, Jean-Pierre .... P.C. .... Jonquière, Quebec

Blaikie, William .... N.D.P. .. Winnipeg Transcona, Manitoba

Blais, Pierre .... P.C. .... Bellechasse, Quebec

Blenkarn, Don .... P.C. .... Mississauga South, Ontario

Blondin, Ethel .... Lib. .... Western Arctic, Northwest Territories

Bosley, John W. .... P.C. .... Don Valley West, Ontario

Bouchard, Benoît .... P.C. .... Roberval, Quebec

Bouchard, Lucien .... B.Q. ...... Lac-Saint-Jean, Quebec

Boudria, Don .... Lib. .... Glengarry-Prescott-Russell, Ontario

Bourgault, Lise .... P.C. .... Argenteuil-Papineau, Quebec

Boyer, Patrick .... P.C. .... Etobicoke-Lakeshore, Ontario

Breaugh, Mike .... N.D.P. .. Oshawa, Ontario

Brewin, John F. .... N.D.P. .. Victoria, British Columbia

Brightwell, Harry .... P.C. .... Perth-Wellington-Waterloo, Ontario

Browes, Pauline A. .... P.C. .... Scarborough Centre, Ontario

Butland, Steve .... N.D.P. .. Sault Ste. Marie, Ontario

Caccia, Charles .... Lib. .... Davenport, Ontario

Cadieux, Pierre H. .... P.C. .... Vadreuil, Quebec

Callbeck, Catherine .... Lib. .... Malpeque, Prince Edward Island

Campbell, Coline .... Lib. .... South West Nova, Nova Scotia

Campbell, Kim .... P.C. .... Vancouver Centre, British Columbia

Cardiff, Murray .... P.C. .... Huron-Bruce, Ontario

Casey, Bill .... P.C. .... Cumberland-Colchester, Nova Scotia

Catterall, Marlene .... Lib. .... Ottawa West, Ontario

Chadwick, Harry .... P.C. .... Bramalea-Gore-Malton, Ontario

Champagne, Andrée .... P.C. .... Saint-Hyacinthe-Bagot, Quebec

Champagne, Michel .... P.C. .... Champlain, Quebec

Charest, Jean J. .... P.C. .... Sherbrooke, Quebec

Chartrand, Gilbert .... P.C. .... Verdun-Saint-Paul, Quebec

Chrétien, Jean .... Lib. .... Beaséjour, New Brunswick

Clancy, Mary .... Lib. .... Halifax, Nova Scotia

Clark, Charles Joseph .... P.C. .... Yellowhead, Alberta

Clark, Lee .... P.C. .... Brandon-Souris, Manitoba

Clifford, Terry .... P.C. .... London-Middlesex, Ontario

Cole, John E. .... P.C. .... York-Simcoe, Ontario

Collins, Mary .... P.C. .... Capilano-Howe Sound, British Columbia

Comuzzi, Joe .... Lib. .... Thunder Bay-Nipigon, Ontario

Cook, Chuck .... P.C. .... North Vancouver, British Columbia

Cooper, Albert .... P.C. .... Peace River, Alberta

Copps, Shelia .... Lib. .... Hamilton East, Ontario

Corbeil, Jean .... P.C. .... Anjou-Rivière-des-Prairies, Quebec

Corbett, Bob .... P.C. .... Fundy-Royal, New Brunswick

Côté, Yvon .... P.C. .... Richmond-Wolfe, Quebec

Couture, Clément .... P.C. .... Saint-Jean, Quebec

Crawford, Rex .... Lib. .... Kent, Ontario

Crosbie, John Carnell .... P.C. .... St. John's West, Newfoundland

Crosby, Howard E. .... P.C. .... Halifax West, Nova Scotia

Danis, Marcel .... P.C. .... Verchères, Quebec

Darling, Stan .... P.C. .... Parry Sound-Muskoka, Ontario

DeBlois, Charles .... P.C. .... Beauport-Montmorency-Orléans, Quebec

de Cotret, Robert R. .... P.C. .... Berthier-Montcalm, Quebec

de Jong, Simon .... N.D.P. .. Regina-Qu'Qppelle, Saskatchewan

Della Noce, Vincent .... P.C. .... Laval-Est, Quebec

Desjardins, Gabriel .... P.C. .... Témiscamingue, Quebec

Dick, Paul Wyatt .... P.C. .... Lanark-Carleton, Ontario

Dingwall, David C. .... Lib. .... Cape Breton-East Richmond, Nova Scotia

Dionne, Maurice A. .... Lib. .... Miramichi, New Brunswick

Dobbie, Dorothy .... P.C. .... Winnipeg South, Manitoba

Domm, Bill .... P.C. .... Peterborough, Ontario

Dorin, Murray W. .... P.C. .... Edmonton Northwest, Alberta

Duceppe, Gilles .... B.Q. ...... Laurier-Sainte-Marie, Quebec

Duhamel, Ronald J. .... Lib. .... St. Boniface, Manitoba

Duplessis, Suzanne .... P.C. .... Louis-Hébert, Quebec

Edmonston, Phillip .... N.D.P. .. Chambly, Quebec

Edwards, James .... P.C. .... Edmonton Southwest, Alberta

Epp, Arthur Jacob .... P.C. .... Provencher, Manitoba

Fee, Doug .... P.C. .... Red Deer, Alberta

Feltham, Louise .... P.C. .... Wild Rose, Alberta

Ferguson, Ralph .... Lib. .... Lambton-Middlesex, Ontario

Ferland, Marc .... P.C. .... Portneuf, Quebec

Finestone, Shelia .... Lib. .... Mount Royal, Quebec

Fisher, Ron .... N.D.P. .. Saskatoon-Dundurn, Saskatchewan

Flis, Jesse .... Lib. .... Parkdale-High Park, Ontario

Fontaine, Gabriel .... P.C. .... Lévis, Quebec

Fontana, Joe .... Lib. .... London East, Ontario

Foster, Maurice .... Lib. .... Algoma, Ontario

Fraser, John A. .... P.C. .... Vancouver South, British Columbia

Fretz, Girve .... P.C. .... Erie, Ontario

Friesen, Benno .... P.C. .... Surrey-White Rock-South Langley, British Columbia

Fulton, Jim .... N.D.P. .. Skeena, British Columbia

Funk, Ray .... N.D.P. .. Prince Albert-Churchill River, Saskatchewan

Gaffney, Beryl .... Lib. .... Nepean, Ontario

Gagliano, Alfonso .... Lib. .... St. Léonard, Quebec

Gardiner, Brian L. .... N.D.P. .. Prince George-Bulkley Valley, British Columbia

Gauthier, Jean-Robert .... Lib. .... Ottawa-Vanier, Ontario

Gérin, François .... B.Q. ...... Mégantic-Compton-Stanstead, Quebec

Gibeau, Marie .... P.C. .... Bourassa, Quebec

Gray, Darryl .... P.C. .... Bonaventure-Iles-de-la-Madeleine, Quebec

Gray, Herb .... Lib. .... Windsor West, Ontario

Greene, Barbara .... P.C. .... Don Valley North, Ontario

Grey, Deborah .... Ref. .... Beaver River, Alberta

Guarnieri, Albina .... Lib. .... Mississauga East, Ontario

Guilbault, Jean-Guy .... P.C. .... Drummond, Quebec

Gustafson, Leonard .... P.C. .... Souris-Moose Mountain, Saskatchewan

Halliday, Bruce .... P.C. .... Oxford, Ontario

Harb, Mac .... Lib. .... Ottawa Centre, Ontario

Harvard, John .... Lib. .... Winnipeg St. James, Manitoba

Harvey, André .... P.C. .... Chicoutimi, Quebec

Harvey, Ross .... N.D.P. .. Edmonton East, Alberta

Hawkes, Jim .... P.C. .... Calgary West, Alberta

Heap, Dan .... N.D.P. .. Trinity-Spadina, Ontario

Hicks, Bob .... P.C. .... Scarborough East, Ontario

Hockin, Thomas .... P.C. .... London West, Ontario

Hogue, J. Pierre .... P.C. .... Outremont, Quebec

Holtmann, Felix .... P.C. .... Portage-Interlake, Manitoba

Hopkins, Leonard .... Lib. .... Renfrew-Nipissing-Pembroke, Ontario

Horner, Bob .... P.C. .... Mississauga West, Ontario

Horning, Al .... P.C. .... Okanagan Centre, British Columbia

Hovdebo, Stan .... N.D.P. .. Saskatoon-Humboldt, Saskatchewan

Hudon, Jean-Guy .... P.C. .... Beauharnois-Salaberry

Hughes, Ken G. .... P.C. .... Macleod, Alberta

Hunter, Lynn .... N.D.P. .. Saanich-Gulf Islands, British Columbia

Jacques, Carole .... P.C. .... Mercier, Quebec

James, Ken .... P.C. .... Sarnia-London

Jelinek, Otto .... P.C. .... Oakville-Milton

Johnson, Al .... P.C. .... Calgary North, Alberta

Joncas, Jean-Luc .... P.C. .... Matapédia-Matane, Quebec

Jordan, Jim .... Lib. .... Leeds-Grenville, Ontario

Jourdenais, Fernand .... P.C. .... La Prairie, Quebec

Kaplan, Bob .... Lib. .... York Centre, Ontario

Karpoff, Jim .... N.D.P. .. Surrey North, British Columbia

Karygiannis, Jim .... Lib. .... Scarborough-Agincourt, Ontario

Kempling, William .... P.C. .... Burlington, Ontario

Keyes, Stan .... Lib. .... Hamilton West, Ontario

Kilger, Bob .... Lib. .... Stormont-Dundas, Ontario

Kilgour, David .... Lib. .... Edmonton Southeast, Alberta

Kindy, Alex .... P.C. .... Calgary Northeast, Alberta

Koury, Allan .... P.C. .... Hochelaga-Maisonneuve, Quebec

Kristiansen, Lyle .... N.D.P. .. Kootenay West-Revelstoke, British Columbia

Landry, Monique .... P.C. .... Blainville-Deux-Montagnes, Quebec

Langan, Joy .... N.D.P. .. Mission-Coquitlam, British Columbia

Langdon, Steven .... N.D.P. .. Essex-Windsor, Ontario

Langlois, Charles A. .... P.C. .... Manicouagan, Quebec

Lapierre, Jean .... B.Q. ...... Shefford, Quebec

Laporte, Rod .... N.D.P. .. Moose Jaw-Lake Centre, Saskatchewan

Larrivée, Gaby .... P.C. ...... Joliette, Quebec

Layton, Robert E.J. .... P.C. .... Lachine-Lac-Saint-Louis, Quebec

LeBlanc, Francis G. .... Lib. .... Cape Breton Islands-Canso, Nova Scotia

Leblanc, Nic .... B.Q. ...... Longueuil, Quebec

Lee, Derek .... Lib. .... Scarborough-Rouge River, Ontario

Lewis, Douglas .... P.C. .... Simcoe North, Ontario

Littlechild, Willie .... P.C. .... Wetaskiwin, Alberta

Loiselle, Gilles .... P.C. .... Québec, Quebec

Lopez, Ricardo .... P.C. .... Châteauguay, Quebec

MacAulay, Lawrence .... Lib. .... Cardigan, Prince Edward Island

MacDonald, David .... P.C. .... Rosedale, Ontario

MacDonald, Ron .... Lib. .... Dartmouth, Nova Scotia

MacDougall, John A. .... P.C. .... Timiskaming, Ontario

MacKay, Elmer .... P.C. .... Central Nova, Nova Scotia

MacLaren, Roy .... Lib. .... Etobicoke North, Ontario

MacLellan, Russell .... Lib. .... Cape Breton-The Sydneys, Nova Scotia

MacWilliam, Lyle Dean ...... N.D.P. .. Okanagan-Shuswap, British Columbia

Maheu, Shirley .... Lib. .... Saint-Laurent-Cartierville, Quebec

Malone, Arnold .... P.C. .... Crowfoot, Alberta

Manley, John .... Lib. .... Ottawa South, Ontario

Marchi, Sergio .... Lib. .... York West, Ontario

Marin, Charles-Eugène .... P.C. .... Gaspé, Quebec

Marleau, Diane .... Lib. .... Sudbury, Ontario

Martin, Paul .... Lib. .... LaSalle-Émard, Quebec

Martin, Shirley .... P.C. .... Lincoln, Ontario

Masse, Marcel .... P.C. .... Frontenac, Quebec

Mayer, Charles James .... P.C. .... Lisgar-Marquette, Manitoba

Mazankowski, Donald .... P.C. .... Vegreville, Alberta

McCreath, Peter L. .... P.C. .... South Shore, Nova Scotia

McCurdy, Howard .... N.D.P. .. Windsor-St. Clair, Ontario

McDermid, John .... P.C. .... Brampton, Ontario

McDougall, Barbara .... P.C. .... St. Paul's, Ontario

McGuire, Joe .... Lib. .... Egmont, Prince Edward Island

McKnight, William .... P.C. .... Kindersley-Lloydminster, Saskatchewan

McLaughlin, Audrey .... N.D.P. .. Yukon, Yukon

McLean, Walter .... P.C. .... Waterloo, Ontario

Merrithew, Gerald .... P.C. .... Saint John, New Brunswick

Mifflin, Fred J. .... Lib. .... Bonavista-Trinity-Conception, Newfoundland

Milliken, Peter .... Lib. .... Kingston and the Islands

Mills, Denis J. .... Lib. .... Braodview-Greenwood, Ontario

Mitchell, Margaret Anne ..... N.D.P. .. Vancouver East, British Columbia

Mitges, Gus .... P.C. .... Bruce-Grey, Ontario

Monteith, Ken .... P.C. .... Elgin-Norfolk, Ontario

Moore, Barry .... P.C. .... Pntiac-Gatineau-Labelle, Quebec

Mulroney, Martin Brian ...... P.C. .... Charlevoix, Quebec

Murphy, Rod .... N.D.P. .. Churchill, Manitoba

Nault, Robert D. .... Lib. .... Kenor-Rainy River, Ontario

Nicholson, Robert D. .... P.C. .... Niagra Falls, Ontario

Nowlan, Patrick .... Ind.C. .... Annapolis Valley-Hants, Nova Scotia

Nunziata, John .... Lib. .... York South-Weston, Ontario

Nystrom, Lorne .... N.D.P. .. Yorkton-Melville, Saskatchewan

Oberle, Frank .... P.C. .... Price George-Peace River, British Columbia

O'Kurley, Brian .... P.C. .... Elk Island, Alberta

Ouellet, André .... Lib. .... Papineau-Saint-Michel, Quebec

Pagtakhan, Rey .... Lib. .... Winnipeg North, Manitoba

Paproski, Steven .... P.C. .... Edmonton North, Alberta

Parent, Gilbert .... Lib. .... Welland-St. Catarines-Thorold, Ontario

Parker, Sid .... N.D.P. .. Kootenay East, British Columbia

Peterson, Jim .... Lib. .... Willowdale, Ontario

Phinney, Beth .... Lib. .... Hamilton Mountain, Ontario

Pickard, Jerry .... Lib. .... Essex-Kent, Ontario

Plamondon, Louis .... B.Q. ...... Richelieu, Quebec

Plourde, André .... P.C. .... Kamouraska-Riviére-du-Loup, Quebec

Porter, Robert H. .... P.C. .... Medicine Hat, Alberta

Pronovost, Denis .... P.C. .... Saint-Maurice, Quebec

Proud, George .... Lib. .... Hillsborough, Prince Edward Island

Pru'homme, Marcel .... Lib. .... Saint-Denis, Quebec

Redway, Alan .... P.C. .... Don Valley East, Ontario

Reid, Ross .... P.C. .... St. John's East, Newfoundland

Reimer, John H. .... P.C. .... Kitchener, Ontario

Richard, Guy .... P.C. .... Laval-Ouest, Quebec

Richardson, Lee .... P.C. .... Calgary Southeast, Alberta

Rideout, George S. .... Lib. .... Moncton, New Brunswick

Riis, Nelson A. .... N.D.P. .. Kamloops, British Columbia

Robinson, Svend J. .... N.D.P. .. Burnaby-Kingsway, British Columbia

Robitaille, Jean-Marc .... P.C. .... Terrebonne, Quebec

Rocheleau, Gilles .... B.Q. ...... Hull-Aylmer, Quebec

Rodriguez, John R. .... N.D.P. .. Nickel Belt, Ontario

Rompkey, William .... Lib. .... Labrador, Newfoundland

Roy-Arcelin, Nicole .... P.C. .... Ahuntsic, Quebec

Saint-Julien, Guy .... P.C. .... Abitibi, Quebec

Samson, Cid .... N.D.P. .. Timmins-Chapleau, Ontario

Schneider, Larry .... P.C. .... Regina-Wascana, Saskatchewan

Scott, Geoff .... P.C. .... Hamilton-Wentworth, Ontario

Scott, William .... P.C. .... Victoria-Haliburton, Ontario

Shields, Jack .... P.C. .... Athabasca, Alberta

Siddon, Thomas .... P.C. .... Richmond, British Columbia

Simmons, Roger C. .... Lib. .... Burin-St. George's, Newfoundland

Skelly, Ray .... N.D.P. .. North Island-Powell River, British Columbia

Skelly, Robert E. .... N.D.P. .. Comox-Alberni, British Columbia

Sobeski, Pat .... P.C. .... Cambridge, Ontario

Soetens, René .... P.C. .... Ontario, Ontario

Sparrow, Barbara J. .... P.C. .... Calgary Southwest, Alberta

Speller, Bob .... Lib. .... Haldimand-Norfolk, Ontario

Stevenson, Ross .... P.C. .... Durham, Ontario

Stewart, Christine .... Lib. .... Northumberland, Ontario

Stupich, David D. .... N.D.P. .. Nanaimo-Cowichan, British Columbia

Tardif, Monique B. .... P.C. .... Charlesbourg, Quebec

Taylor, Len .... N.D.P. .. The Battlefords-Meadow Lake, Saskatchewan

Tétreault, Jacques .... P.C. .... Laval-Centre, Quebec

Thacker, Blaine .... P.C. .... Lethbridge, Alberta

Thompson, Greg .... P.C. .... Carleton-Charlotte, New Brunswick

Thorkelson, Scott .... P.C. .... Edmonton-Strathcona, Alberta

Tobin, Brian .... Lib. .... Humber-St. Barbe-Baie Verte, Newfoundland

Tremblay, Benoît .... B.Q. ...... Rosemont, Quebec

Tremblay, Marcel R. .... P.C. .... Québec-Est, Quebec

Tremblay, Maurice .... P.C. .... Lotbinière, Quebec

Turner, Garth .... P.C. .... Halton-Peel, Ontario

Turner, John N. .... Lib. .... Vancouver Quadra, British Columbia

Valcourt, Bernard .... P.C. .... Madawaska-Victoria, New Brunswick

Vanclief, Lyle .... Lib. .... Prince Edward-Hastings, Ontario

Van De Walle, Walter .... P.C. .... St. Albert, Alberta

Vankoughnet, Bill .... P.C. .... Hastings-Frontenac-Lennox and Addington, Ontario

Venne, Pierrette .... B.Q. ...... Saint-Hubert, Quebec

Vézina, Monique .... P.C. .... Rimouski-Témiscouata, Quebec

Vien, Jacques .... P.C. .... Laurentides, Quebec

Vincent, Pierre H. .... P.C. .... Trois Rivières, Quebec

Volpe, Joseph .... Lib. .... Eglinton-Lawrence, Ontario

Waddell, Ian .... N.D.P. .. Port Moody-Coquitlam, British Columbia

Walker, David .... Lib. .... Winnipeg North Centre, Manitoba

Wappel, Tom .... Lib. .... Scarborough West, Ontario

Weiner, Gerry .... P.C. .... Pierrefonds-Dollard, Quebec

Wenmen, Robert L. .... P.C. .... Fraser Valley West, British Columbia

White, Brian .... P.C. .... Dauphin-Swan River, Manitoba

Whittaker, Jack .... N.D.P. .. Okanagan-Similkameen-Merritt, British Columbia

Wilbee, Stan .... P.C. .... Delta, British Columbia

Wilson, Geoff .... P.C. .... Swift Current-Maple Creek-Assiniboia, Saskatchewan

Wilson, Michael .... P.C. .... Etobicoke Centre, Ontario

Winegard, William .... P.C. .... Guelph-Wellington, Ontario

Wood, Bob .... Lib. .... Nipissing, Ontario

Worthy, Dave .... P.C. .... Cariboo-Chilcotin, British Columbia

Young, Douglas .... Lib. .... Acadie-Bathurst, New Brunswick

Young, Neil .... N.D.P. .. Beaches-Woodbine, Ontario

The Senate

Senators can be contacted at the
Senate main reception: 613-995-1900

Adams, Willie .... Lib. .... Northwest
    Territories

Atkins, Norman, K. .... P.C. .... Markham, Ontario

Austin, Jack .... Lib. .... Vancouver S.,
    British Columbia

Balfour, James .... P.C. .... Regina,
    Saskatchewan

Barootes, E.W. (Staff) .... P.C. .... Regina-
    Qu'Appelle,
    Saskatchewan

Beaudoin, Gérald .... P.C. .... Rigaud, Quebec

Beaulieu, Mario .... P.C. .... De la Durantaye,
    Quebec

Bélisle, Rhéal .... P.C. .... Sudbury, Ontario

Bernston, Eric Arthur .... P.C. .... West

Bolduc, Roch .... P.C. .... Golfe, Quebec

Bonnell, M. Lorne .... Lib. .... Murray River,
    Prince Edward
    Island

Bosa, Peter .... Lib. .... York-Caboto,
    Ontario

Buchanan, John .... P.C. .... Halifax, Nova
    Scotia

Carney, Pat .... P.C. .... British Columbia

Castonguay, Claude .... P.C. .... Stadacona, Quebec

Chaput-Rolland, Solange .... P.C. .... Mille Isles, Quebec

Charvonneau, Guy .... P.C. .... Kennebec, Quebec

Chochrane, Ethel .... P.C. .... Newfoundland

Cogger, Michel .... P.C. .... Lauzon, Quebec

Comeau, Gérald J. .... P.C. .... Nova Scotia

Cools, Anne C. .... Lib. .... Toronto Centre,
    Ontario

Corbin, Eymard .... Lib. .... Grand-Sault, New
    Brunswick

Davey, Keith .... Lib. .... York, Ontario

David, Paul D. .... P.C. .... Bedford, Quebec

De Bané, Pierre .... Lib. .... De la Vallière,
    Quebec

DeWare, Mabel Margaret ... P.C. .... Moncton, New
    Brunswick

Di Nino, Consiglio .... P.C. .... Ontario

Doody, C. William .... P.C. .... Harbour Main-Bell
    Island,
    Newfoundland

Doyle, Richard J. .... P.C. .... North York,
    Ontario

Everett, Douglas D. .... Ind. .... Fort Rouge,
    Manitoba

Eyton, John Trevor .... P.C. .... Ontario

Fairbairn, Joyce .... Lib. .... Lethbridge,
    Alberta

Forrestall, John Michael ...... P.C. .... Maritimes

Frith, Royce H. .... Lib. .... Lanark, Ontario

Gigantès, Philippe D. .... Lib. .... De Lorimier,
    Quebec

Grafstein, Jerahmiel S. .... Lib. .... The Highlands,
    Nova Scotia

Grimard, Norman .... P.C. .... Quebec

Haidasz, Stanley .... Lib. .... Toronto-Parkdale,
    Ontario

Hastings, Earl A. .... Lib. .... Palliser-Foothills,
    Alberta

Hays, Daniel .... Lib. .... Calgary, Alberta

Hébert, Jacques .... Lib. .... Wellington,
    Quebec

Johnson, Janis .... P.C. .... West

Kelleher, James F. .... P.C. .... Ontario

Kelly, William M. .... P.C. .... Port Severn,
    Ontario

Kenny, Colin .... Lib. .... Rideau, Ontario

Keon, Wilbert Joseph .... P.C. .... Ontario

Kinsella, Noel A. .... P.C. .... Fredericton-York-
    Sunbury, New
    Brunswick

Kirby, Michael .... Lib. .... South Shore, Nova Scotia

Kolber, Leo .... Lib. .... Victoria, Quebec

Lang, Daniel .... Ind. .... South York, Ontario

Lavoie-Roux, Thérèse .... P.C. .... Quebec

Lawson, Edward M. .... Ind. .... Vancouver, British Columbia

Leblanc, Fernand .... Lib. .... Saurel, Quebec

LeBlanc, Roméo .... Lib. .... Beauséjour, New Brunswick

Lefebvre, Thomas .... Lib. .... De Lanaudière, Quebec

Lewis, P. Derek .... Lib. .... St. John's, Newfoundland

Lucier, Paul .... Lib. .... Yukon

Lynch-Staunton, John .... P.C. .... Grandville, Quebec

MacDonald, Finlay .... P.C. .... Halifax, Nova Scotia

Macdonald, John M. .... P.C. .... Cape Breton, Nova Scotia

MacEachen, Allan J. .... Lib. .... Highlands-Canso, Nova Scotia

Macquarrie, Heath .... P.C. .... Hillsborough, Prince Edward Island

Marchand, Len .... Lib. .... Kamloops-Cariboo, British Columbia

Marsden, Lorna .... Lib. .... Toronto-Taddle Creek, Ontario

Marshall, Jack .... P.C. .... Humber-St. George's-St. Barbe Newfoundland

Meighen, Michael Arthur .... P.C. .... Ontario

Molgat, Gildas L. .... Lib. .... Ste. Rose, Manitoba

Molson, Hartland de M. ...... Ind. .... Alma, Quebec

Muir, Robert .... P.C. .... Cape Breton-The Sydneys, Nova Scotia

Murray, Lowell .... P.C. .... Grenville-Carlton, Ontario

Neiman, Joan .... Lib. .... Peel, Ontario

Nurgitz, Nathan .... P.C. .... Winnipeg North, Manitoba

Oliver, Donald H. .... P.C. .... Nova Scotia

Olson, H.A.(Bud) .... Lib. .... Alberta South

Ottenheimer, Gerald R. .... P.C. .... Waterford-Trinity, Newfoundland

Perrault, Raymond J. .... Lib. .... N. Shore-Burnaby, British Columbia

Petten, William J. .... Lib. .... Bonavista, Newfoundland

Phillips, Orville H. .... P.C. .... Prince, Prince Edward Island

Pittfield, P. Michael .... Ind. .... Ottawa-Vanier, Ontario

Poitras, Jean-Marie .... P.C. .... De Salaberry, Quebec

Riel, Maurice .... Lib. .... Shawinegan, Quebec

Rizzuto, Pietro .... Lib. .... Repentigny, Quebec

Robertson, Brenda Mary ..... P.C. .... Riverview, New Brunswick

Robichaud, Louis J. .... Lib. .... Acadia, New Brunswick

Roblin, Duff .... P.C. .... Red River, Manitoba

Ross, James .... P.C. .... Maritimes

Rossiter, Eileen .... P.C. .... Prince Edward Island

Simard, Jean-Maurice .... P.C. .... Edmundston, New Brunswick

Sparrow, Herbert O. .... Lib. .... Saskatchewan

Spivak, Mira .... P.C. .... Manitoba

Stanbury, Richard J. .... Lib. .... York Centre, Ontario

Stewart, John B. .... Lib. .... Antigonish-Guysborough, Nova Scotia

Stollery, Peter A. .... Lib. .... Bloor/Yonge, Toronto, Ontario

Sylvain, John .... P.C. .... Rougemont, Quebec

Teed, Nancy E. .... P.C. .... Saint John, New Brunswick

Thériault, L. Norbert .... Lib. .... Bai du Vin, New Brunswick

Thompson, Andrew E. .... Lib. .... Dovercourt, Ontario

Tremblay, Arthur .... P.C. .... Les Laurentides, Quebec

Twinn, Walter Patrick .... P.C. .... Alberta

Van Roggen, George C. ...... Lib. .... Vancouver-Point Grey, British Columbia

Watt, Charlie .... Lib. .... Inkerman, Quebec

Wood, Dalia .... Lib. .... Montarville, Quebec

Provincial Parliaments

NEWFOUNDLAND

Legislative Assembly: 709-729-3405

Aylward, Kevin .... Lib. .... Stephenville
Aylward, Robert .... P.C. .... Kilbride
Baker, Winston .... Lib. .... Gander
Barrett, Percy .... Lib. .... Bellevue
Carter, Walter C. .... Lib. .... Twillingate
Cowan, Patrcia .... Lib. .... Conception Bay South
Crane, John .... Lib. .... Harbour Grace
Decker, Chris .... Lib. .... Stait of Belle Ilse
Dicks, Paul .... Lib. .... Humber West
Doyle, Norman .... P.C. .... Harbour Main
Dumaresque, Danny .... Lib. .... Eagle River
Efford, John .... Lib. .... Port de Grave
Flight, Graham .... Lib. .... Windsor-Buchans
Furey, Charles .... Lib. .... St. Barbe
Gibbond, Rex .... Lib. .... St. John's West
Gover, Aubrey .... Lib. .... Burgeo-Bay D'Espoir
Greening, Glenn .... P.C. .... Terra Nova
Grimes, Roger .... Lib. .... Exploits
Gullage, Eric .... Lib. .... Waterford-Kenmount
Harris, Jack .... N.D.P. .. St. John's East
Hearn, Loyola .... P.C. .... St. Mary's-The Capes
Hewlett, Alvin .... P.C. .... Green Bay
Hodder, James .... P.C. .... Port au Port
Hogan, Bill .... Lib. .... Placentia
Kelland, O.P.J. .... Lib. .... Naskaupi
Kitchen, Hubert .... Lib. .... St. John's Centre
Langdon, Oliver .... Lib. .... Fortune-Hermitage

Lush, Tom .... Lib. .... Bonavista North
Matthews, Bill .... P.C. .... Grand Bank
Murphy, Tom .... Lib. .... St. John's South
Noel, Walter .... Lib. .... Pleasantville
Oldford, Doug .... Lib. .... Trinity North
Parsons, Kevin .... P.C. .... St. John's East Ext.
Penney, Melvin .... Lib. .... Lewisporte
Power, Charles .... P.C. .... Ferryland
Ramsay, William .... Lib. .... Lapoile
Reid, Art .... Lib. .... Carbonear
Short, Larry .... Lib. .... St. George's
Simms, Len .... P.C. .... Grand Falls
Small, Harold .... Baie Verte-White Bay
Snow, Alec .... P.C. .... Menihek
Snow, Lloyd .... Lib. .... Trinity-Bay de Verde
Tobin, Glenn .... P.C. .... Burin-Placentia West
Verge, Lynn .... P.C. .... Humber East
Walsh, Jim .... Lib. .... Mount Scio-Bell Island
Warren, Garfield .... P.C. .... Torngat Mountains
Warren, Philip .... Lib. .... St. John's North
Wells, Clyde .... Lib. .... Bay of Islands
Windsor, Neil .... P.C. .... Mount Pearl
Winsor, Sam .... P.C. .... Fogo
Woodford, Rick .... P.C. .... Humber Valley

PRINCE EDWARD ISLAND

Government: 902-368-4330
Opposition: 902-368-4360

Bagnall, Leone (C)	P.C.	1st Queens
Bernard, Leonce (A)	Lib.	3rd Prince
Bradley, Walter (C)	Lib.	1st Kings
Brown, Betty Jean (A)	Lib.	3rd Queens
Bruce, Stanley (A)	Lib.	4th Kings
Buchanan, Alan (A)	Lib.	4th Queens
Campbell, Robert E. (C)	Lib.	1st Prince
Carroll, Tim (C)	Lib.	5th Queens
Cheverie, Wayne D. (A)	Lib.	5th Queens
Clark, Edward W. (C)	Lib.	3rd Prince
Clements, Gilbert R. (C)	Lib.	4th Kings
Connolly, Paul (C)	Lib.	6th Queens
Doucette, Peter (A)	Lib.	3rd Kings
Dunphy, Tom (C)	Lib.	3rd Queens
Ellis, Allison (C)	Lib.	2nd Prince
Fogarty, Albert P. (C)	P.C.	1st Kings
Ghiz, Joseph A. (A)	Lib.	6th Queens
Guptill, Nancy (C)	Lib.	5th Prince
Hicken, Barry (C)	Lib.	5th Kings
Hubley, Elizabeth (C)	Lib.	4th Prince
Hubley, Roberta (C)	Lib.	3rd Kings
Huestis, Stavert (A)	Lib.	4th Prince
MacDonald, Rose Marie (A)	Lib.	5th Kings
MacInnis, Gordon E. (A)	Lib.	2nd Queens
MacKinley (C)	Lib.	2nd Queens
MacPherson, Lynwood (C)	Lib.	4th Queens
Matheson, Claude (A)	Lib.	2nd Kings
McEwen, Walter (A)	Lib.	5th Prince
Milligan, Keith W. (A)	Lib.	2nd Prince
Morrissey, Robert J. (A)	Lib.	1st Prince
Murphy, Marion (A)	Lib.	1st Queens
Young, Ross T. (A)	Lib.	1st Kings

NOVA SCOTIA

Clerk's Office: 902-424-5978

Archibald, George G.	P.C.	Kings North
Bacon, Roger S.	P.C.	Cumberland East
Barkhouse, James	Lib.	Lunenburg East
Boudreau, J. Bernard	Lib.	Cape Breton the Lakes
Bragg, D. Ross	Lib.	Cumberland West
Brown, Guy	Lib.	Cumberland Centre
Cameron, Donald W.	P.C.	Pictou East
Casey, Joseph H.	Lib.	Digby
Chisholm, Robert	N.D.P.	Halifax Atlantic
Dechman, Marie P.	P.C.	Lunenburg West
Donahoe, Arthur R.	P.C.	Halifax Citadel
Donahoe, Terence R.B.	P.C.	Halifax Cornwallis
Giffin, Ronald C.	P.C.	Truro-Bible Hill
Gillis, William	Lib.	Antigonish
Graham, Daniel	Lib.	Inverness South
Hawkins, John	Lib.	Hants East
Holm, John	N.D.P.	Sackville
Huskilson, Harold M.	Lib.	Shelburne
Jolly, Sandra L.	Lib.	Dartmouth North
Kerr, Greg	P.C.	Annapolis West
Kimball, Derrick J.	P.C.	Kings South
Lawrence Gerald	P.C.	Halifax St. Margarets
LeBlanc, Guy J.	P.C.	Clare
LeBlanc, Neil J.	P.C.	Argyle
Leele, John G.	P.C.	Queens
Lorraine, Edward F.	Lib.	Colchester North
MacArthur, Charles B.	Lib.	Inverness North
MacAskill, Kenneth	Lib.	Yarmouth
MacEachern, John O.S.	Lib.	Cape Breton East
MacEwan, Paul	Lib.	Cape Breton Nova
Macisaac, J.A.	P.C.	Pictou Centre
MacKinnon, Russell V.	Lib.	Cape Breton West
MacLean, Vincent J.	Lib.	Cape Breton South
MacNeil, C.W.	P.C.	Guysborough
MacNeil, Russell F.	Lib.	Cape Breton Centre
Mann, Richard W.	Lib.	Richmond
Matheson, Joel R.	P.C.	Halifax-Bedford Basin
McDonough, Alexa	N.D.P.	Halifax Chebucto
McInnes, Donald P.	P.C.	Pictou West
McInnis, Thomas J.	P.C.	Halifax Eastern Shore
Moody, George C.	P.C.	Kings West
Mosher, Allan M.	P.C.	Lunenburg Centre
Nantes, G. David	P.C.	Cole Harbour
O'Malley, Gerald J.	Lib.	Halifax Needham
Rayluse, Earle A.	Lib.	Annapolis East
Russell, Ronald S.	P.C.	Hants West
Smith Dr. James	Lib.	Dartmouth East
Stewart, R. Colin D.	P.C.	Colchester South

Streatch, Kenneth .... P.C. .... Bedford-Musquodobit Valley

Thornhill, Rolland J. .... P.C. .... Dartmouth South

Young, Brian A. .... P.C. .... Cape Breton North

NEW BRUNSWICK

Lib.: 506-453-2548
P.C.: 506-453-3456
C.o.R.: 506-457-3515
N.D.P.: 506-453-3305

Allaby, Eric .... Lib. .... Charlotte-Fundy
Allen, Edwin G. .... C.o.R. .... Fredericton North
Barry, Jane .... Lib. .... Saint John West
Bealieu, Rolland .... Lib. .... Edmunston
Blanchard, Edmond .... Lib. .... Campbellton
Blaney, Vaughn .... Lib. .... Queens South
Branch, Frank .... Lib. .... Nepisiguit-Chaleur
Breault, Ann .... Lib. .... St. Stephen-Milltown
Brine, Beverly .... C.o.R. .... Albert
Cameron, Danny .... C.o.R. .... York South
Clavette, Gérald H. .... Lib. .... Madawaska-Centre
Cochrane, Dennis .... P.C. .... Petitcodiac
Corriveau, Georges .... Lib. .... Madawaska-Les-Lacs
Day, Georgie .... Lib. .... Kings Centre
DeLong, Allison .... Lib. .... Carleton Centre
Doucet, Albert .... Lib. .... Nigadoo-Chaleur
Doucett, Rayburn .... Lib. .... Restigouche East
Duffie, Paul .... Lib. .... Grand Falls
Dysart, Shirley .... Lib. .... Saint John-Park
Frenette, J. Raymond .... Lib. .... Moncton East
Gauvin, Jean .... P.C. .... Shippegan-Les-Iles
Gay, Donald .... Lib. .... Miramichi Bay
Graham, Alan .... Lib. .... Kent Centre
Hargrove, Gregory .... C.o.R. .... York North
Harvey, Fred .... Lib. .... Carleton North
Hurley, Reid .... Lib. .... Charlotte West
Jamieson, Stewart .... Lib. .... Saint John Fundy
Jarrett, Laureen .... Lib. .... Kings West
Jenkins, George J. .... Lib. .... East Saint John
Kennedy, Larry .... Lib. .... Victoria-Tobique
King, Russ .... Lib. .... Fredericton South
Landry, Conrad .... Lib. .... Kent North
Lee, Sheldon .... Lib. .... Charlotte Centre

Lockyer, James .... Lib. .... Moncton West
Losier, Denis .... Lib. .... Tracadie
MacDonald, Reginald .... Lib. .... Bay du Vin
Maher, Allan .... Lib. .... Dalhousie
McAdam, Leo A. .... Lib. .... Saint John North
McKay, John .... Lib. .... Miramichi-Newcastle
McKee, Michael .... Lib. .... Moncton North
McKenna, Frank .... Lib. .... Chatham
Mersereau, Marcelle .... Lib. .... Bathurst
Murphy, Louis E. .... Lib. .... Saint John Harbour
Myers, Hazen .... P.C. .... Kings East
O'Donnell, Greg .... Lib. .... Memramcook
Rector, Albert .... C.o.R. .... Oromocto
Richard, Bernard .... Lib. .... Shediac
Ringuette-Maltais, Pierrette Lib. .... Madawaska South
Savoie, Jean-Paul .... Lib. .... Restigouche West
Smith, Bruce .... Lib. .... Carleton South
Taylor, Brent .... C.o.R. .... Southwest Miramichi
Thériault, Bernard .... Lib. .... Caraquet
Thériault, Camille .... Lib. .... Kent South
Trenholme, Marilyn .... Lib. .... Tantramar
Tyler, Douglas .... Lib. .... Queens North
Weir, Elizabeth .... N.D.P. .. Saint John South
White, Max .... C.o.R. .... Sunbury
Willden, Gordon .... C.o.R. .... Riverview

QUEBEC

Assemblée Nationale: 418-643-7239

Atkinson, Gordon .... Eq. .... Notre-Dame-de-Grâce
Audet, Jean .... Lib. .... Beauce-Nord
Bacon, Lise .... Lib. .... Chomedey
Baril, Jacques .... P.Q. .... Arthabaska
Beaudin, André .... Lib. .... Gaspé
Beaulne, François .... P.Q. .... Bertrand
Bégin, Louise .... Lib. .... Bellechasse
Bélanger, Guy .... Lib. .... Laval-des-Rapides
Bélanger, Madeleine .... Lib. .... Mégantic-Compton
Bélisle, Jean-Pierre .... Lib. .... Mille-Iles
Benoit, Robert .... Lib. .... Orford
Bergeron, Jean-Guy .... Lib. .... Deux-Montagnes
Bissonnet, Michel .... Lib. .... Jeanne-Mance

Blackburn, Gaston ....Lib. ....Roberval

Blackburn, Jeanne L. ..........P.Q. ....Chicoutimi

Blais, Yves ............................P.Q. ....Masson

Bleau, Madeleine ....Lib. ....Groulx

Boisclair, André .................P.Q. ....Gouin

Bordeleau, Yvan ....Lib. ....Acadie

Boucher Bacon, Huguette ...Lib. ....Bourget

Boulerice, André .................P.Q. ....Sainte-Marie—
Saint-Jacques

Bourassa, Robert ....Lib. ....Saint-Laurent

Bourbeau, André ....Lib. ....Laporte

Bourdon, Michel .................P.Q. ....Pointe-aux-
Trembles

Bradet, Daniel ....Lib. ....Charlevoix

Brassard, Jacques ................P.Q. ....Lac-Saint-Jean

Brouillette, Pierre A. ....Lib. ....Champlain

Camden, Lewis ....Lib. ....Lotbiniére

Cameron, Neil ....Eq. ....Jacques-Cartier

Cannon, Lawrence ....Lib. ....La Peltrie

Cardinal, Pierrette ....Lib. ....Châteauguay

Caron, Jocelyne .................P.Q. ....Terrebonne

Carrier-Perreault, Denise ....P.Q. ....Chutes-de-la-
Chaudiére

Chagnon, Jacques ....Lib. ....Saint-Louis

Charbonneau, Michel ....Lib. ....Saint-Jean

Chenail, André ....Lib. ....Beauharnois-
Huntingdon

Cherry, Normand ....Lib. ......Sainte-Anne

Chevrette, Guy ...................P.Q. ....Joliette

Ciaccia, John ....Lib. ....Mont-Royal

Claveau, Christian ..............P.Q. ....Ungava

Côté, Albert ....Lib. ....Rivière-du-Loup

Côté, Marc-Yvan ....Lib. ....Charlesbourg

Cusano, William ....Lib. ....Viau

Dauphin, Claude ....Lib. ....Marquette

Després, Michel ....Lib. ....Limoilou

Dionne, France ....Lib. ....Kamouraska-
Témiscouata

Doyon, Réjean ....Lib. ....Louis-Hébert

Dufour, Francis ...................P.Q. ....Jonquiére

Dupuis, Luce ......................P.Q. ....Verchéres

Dutil, Robert ....Lib. ....Beauce-Sud

Elkas, Sam ....Lib. ....Robert-Baldwin

Farrah, Georges ....Lib. ....Iles-de-la-
Madeleine

Filion, Jean .........................P.Q. ....
Montmorency

Forget, Paul-André ....Lib. ....Prévost

Fradet, Benoît ....Lib. ....Vimont

Frulla-Hébert, Liza ....Lib. ....Marguerite-
Bourgeoys

Gagnon-Tremblay, Monique ....Lib.   Saint-
François

Garon, Jean ........................P.Q. ....Lévis

Gautrin, Henri-François ......Lib. ....Verdun

Gauvin, Réal ....Lib. ....Montmagny-
L'Islet

Gendron, François ..............P.Q. ....Abitibi-Ouest

Gobé, Jean-Claude ....Lib. ....LaFontaine

Godin, Gérald ....................P.Q. ....Mercier

Hamel, André J. ....Lib. ....Sherbrooke

Harel, Louise .....................P.Q. ....Hochelaga-
Maisonneuve

Holden, Richard ....Eq. ....Westmount

Houde, Albert ....Lib. ....Berthier

Hovington, Claire-Hélène ...Lib. ....Matane

Johnson, Daniel ....Lib. ....Vaudreuil

Jolivet, Jean-Pierre .............P.Q. ....Laviolette

Joly, Jean A. ....Lib. ....Fabre

Juneau, Carmen ..................P.Q. ....Johnson

Kehoe, John ....Lib. ....Chapleau

Khelfa, Albert ....Lib. ....Richelieu

Lafrance, Yvon ....Lib. ....Iberville

Lafreniére, Réjean ....Lib. ....Gatineau

Lazure, Denis .....................P.Q. ....La Prairie

Leclerc, Jean ....Lib. ....Taschereau

Lefebvre, Roger ....Lib. ....Frontenac

Lemieux, Jean-Guy ....Lib. ....Vanier

Lemire, Yvon ....Lib. ....Saint-Maurice

Léonard, Jacques ................P.Q. ....Labelle

Lesage, Robert ....Lib. ....Hull

Levesque, Gérard D. ....Lib. ....Bonaventure

Libman, Robert ....Eq. ....D'Arcy-McGee

Loiselle, Nicole ....Lib. ....Saint-Henri

Maciocia, Cosmo ....Lib. ....Viger

MacMillan, Norman ....Lib. ....Papineau

Maltais, Ghislain ....Lib. ....Saguenay

Marcil, Serge ....Lib. ....Salaberry-
Soulanges

Marois, Pauline ...................P.Q. ....Taillon

Messier, Charles ....Lib. ....Saint-Hyacinthe

Middlemiss, Robert ....Lib. ....Pontiac

Morin, Gérard R. ................P.Q. ....Dubuc

Pagé, Michel ....Lib. ....Portneuf

Paradis, Henri ....Lib. ....Matapédia

Paradis, Pierre ....Lib. ....Brome-Missisquoi

Paré, Roger ........................P.Q. ....Shefford

Parent, Marcel ....Lib. ....Sauvé

Parizeau, Jacques ................P.Q. ....L'Assomption

Pelchat, Christiane .... Lib. .... Vachon
Perron, Denis .... P.Q. .... Duplessis
Philibert, Paul .... Lib. .... Trois-Rivières
Picotte, Yvon .... Lib. .... Maskinongé
Poulin, Rémy .... Lib. .... Chauveau
Rémillard, Gil .... Lib. .... Jean-Talon
Richard, Maurice .... Lib. .... Nicolet-Yamaska
Rivard, Guy .... Lib. .... Rosemont
Robic, Louise .... Lib. .... Bourassa
Robillard, Lucienne .... Lib. .... Chambly
Ryan, Claude .... Lib. .... Argenteuil
St-Roch, Jean-Guy .... Lib. .... Drummond
Asintonge, Jean-Pierre .... Lib. .... La Pinière
Savoie, Raymond .... Lib. .... Abitibi Est
Sirros, Christos .... Lib. .... Laurier
Thérien, Robert .... Lib. .... Rousseau
Tremblay, Gérald .... Lib. .... Outremont
Tremblay, Michel .... Lib. .... Rimouski
Trépanier, Violette .... Lib. .... Dorion
Trudel, Rémy .... P.Q. .... Rouyn-Noranda—
Témiscamingue
Vallerand, André .... Lib. .... Crémazie
Vallières, Yvon .... Lib. .... Richmond
Vermette, Cécile .... P.Q. .... Marie-Victorin
Williams, Russell .... Lib. .... Nelligan

ONTARIO

General Inquiries: 416-325-7500

Abel, Donald .... N.D.P. .. Wentworth North
Akande, Zanana .... N.D.P. .. St, Andrew-St. Patrick
Allen, Richard .... N.D.P. .. Hamilton West
Arnott, Ted .... P.C. .... Wellington
Beer, Charles .... Lib. .... York North
Bisson, Gilles .... N.D.P. .. Cochrane South
Boyd, Marion .... N.D.P. .. London Centre
Bradley, James .... Lib. .... St. Catherines
Brown, Michael A. .... Lib. .... Algoma-Manitoulin
Buchanan, Elmer .... N.D.P. .. Hastings-Peterborough
Callahan, Robert V. .... Brampton South
Caplan, Elinor .... Lib. .... Oriole
Carr, Gary .... P.C. .... Oakville South
Carter, Jenny .... N.D.P. .. Peterborough

Charlton, Brian .... N.D.P. .. Hamilton Mountain
Chiarelli, Robert .... Lib. .... Ottawa West
Farnan, Mike .... N.D.P. .. Cambridge
Fawcett, Joan .... Lib. .... Northumberland
Ferguson, Will .... N.D.P. .. Kitchener
Fletcher, Derek .... N.D.P. .. Guelph
Frankford, Bob .... N.D.P. .. Scarborough East
Gigantes, Evelyn .... N.D.P. .. Ottawa Centre
Grandmaître, Bernard C. ..... Lib. .... Ottawa East
Grier, Ruth .... N.D.P. .. Etobicoke-Lakeshore
Haeck, Christel .... N.D.P. .. St. Catharines-Brock
Hampton, Howard .... N.D.P. .. Rainy River
Hansen, Ron .... N.D.P. .. Lincoln
Harnick, Charles .... P.C. .... Willowdale
Harrington, Margaret .... N.D.P. .. Niagra Falls
Harris, Michael .... P.C. .... Nipissing
Haslam, Karen .... N.D.P. .. Perth
MacKinnon, Ellen .... N.D.P. .. Lambton
Mahoney, Steven .... Lib. .... Mississauga West
Malkowski, Gary .... N.D.P. .. York East
Mammoliti, George .... N.D.P. .. Yorkview
Mancini, Remo .... Lib. .... Essex South
Marchese, Rosario .... N.D.P. .. Fort York
Marland, Margaret .... P.C. .... Mississauga South
Martel, Shelley .... N.D.P. .. Sudbury East
Martin, Tony .... N.D.P. .. Sault Ste. Marie
Mathyssen, Irene .... N.D.P. .. Middlesex
McClelland, Carman .... Lib. .... Brampton North
McGuinty, Dalton J.P. .... Lib. .... Ottawa South
McLean, Allan .... P.C. .... Simcoe East
McLeod, Lyn .... Lib. .... Fort William
Miclash, Frank .... Lib. .... Kenora
Mills, Gord .... N.D.P. .. Durham East
Morin, Gilles E. .... Lib. .... Carleton East
Rae, Bob .... N.D.P. .. York South
Ramsay, David .... Lib. .... Timikaming
Rizzo, Tony .... IND. ..... Oakwood
Runciman, Robert W. .... P.C. .... Leeds-Grenville
Ruprecht, Tony .... Lib. .... Parkdale
Scott, Ian .... Lib. .... St. George-St. David
Silipo, Tony .... N.D.P. .. Dovercourt
Sola, John .... Lib. .... Mississauga East
Sorbara, Gregory .... Lib. .... York Centre
Sterling, Norman W. .... P.C. .... Carleton
Stockwell, Chris .... P.C. .... Etobicoke West
Sullivan, Barbara .... Lib. .... Halton Centre

Sutherland, Kimble .... N.D.P. .. Oxford
Swarbrick, Anne .... N.D.P. .. Scarborough West
Tilson, David .... P.C. .... Dufferin-Peel
Turnbull, David .... P.C. .... York Mills
Wood, Len .... N.D.P. .. Cochrane North
Ziemba, Elaine .... N.D.P. .. High Park-
Swansea

MANITOBA

Legislative Assembly: 204-945-3636

Alcock, Reg .... Lib. .... Osborne
Ashton, Steve .... N.D.P. .. Thompson
Barrett, Becky .... N.D.P. .. Wellington
Carstairs, Sharon .... Lib. .... River Heights
Cerilli, Marianne .... N.D.P. .. Radisson
Cheema, Gulzar S. .... Lib. .... The Maples
Chomiak, Dave .... N.D.P. .. Kildonan
Connery, Edward .... P.C. .... Portage La Prairie
Cummings, Glen .... P.C. .... Ste. Rose
Dacquay, Louise .... P.C. .... Seine River
Derkach, Leonard .... P.C. .... Roblin-Russell
Dewar, Gregory .... N.D.P. .. Selkirk
Doer, Gary .... N.D.P. .. Concordia
Downey, James E. .... P.C. .... Arthur-Virden
Driedger, Albert .... P.C. .... Steinbach
Ducharme, Gerald .... P.C. .... Riel
Edwards, Paul .... Lib. .... St. James
Enns, Harry .... P.C. .... Lakeside
Ernst, Jim .... P.C. .... Charleswood
Evans, Clif .... N.D.P. .. Interlake
Evans, Leonard S. .... N.D.P. .. Brandon East
Filmon, Gary .... P.C. .... Tuxedo
Findlay, Glen M. .... P.C. .... Springfield
Friesen, Jean .... N.D.P. .. Wolseley
Gaudry, Neil .... Lib. .... St. Boniface
Gilleshammer, Harold .... P.C. .... Minnedosa
Harper, Elijah .... N.D.P. .. Rupertsland
Helwer, Ed .... P.C. .... Gimli
Hickes, George .... N.D.P. .. Point Douglas
Lamoureux, Kevin .... Lib. .... Inkster
Lathlin, Oscar .... N.D.P. .. The Pas
Laurendeau, Marcel .... P.C. .... St. Norbert
Maloway, Jim .... N.D.P. .. Elmwood
Manness, Clayton .... P.C. .... Morris
Martindale, Doug .... N.D.P. .. Burrows
McAlpine, Gerry .... P.C. .... Sturgeon Creek
McCrae, James C. .... P.C. .... Brandon West

McIntosh, Linda .... P.C. .... Assiniboia
Mitchelson, Bonnie .... P.C. .... River East
Neufeld, Harold .... P.C. .... Rossmere
Orchard, Donald .... P.C. .... Pembina
Penner, John .... P.C. .... Emerson
Plohman, John S. .... N.D.P. .. Dauphin
Praznik, Darren .... P.C. .... Lac Du Bonnet
Reid, Daryl .... N.D.P. .. Transcona
Reimer, Jack .... P.C. .... Niakwa
Render, Shirley .... P.C. .... St. Vital
Rocan, Denis .... P.C. .... Gladstone
Rose, Bob .... P.C. .... Turtle Mountain
Santos, Conrad .... N.D.P. .. Broadway
Stefanson, Eric .... P.C. .... Kirkfield Park
Storie, Jerry T. .... N.D.P. .. Flin Flon
Sveinson, Ben .... P.C. .... La Verendrye
Vodrey, Rosemary .... P.C. .... Fort Garry
Waslycia-Leis, Judy .... N.D.P. .. St. Johns
Wowchuk, Rosann .... N.D.P. .. Swan River

SASKATCHEWAN

Legislative Assembly: 306-787-2376

Anguish, D. .... N.D.P. .. The Battlefords
Atkinson, P. .... N.D.P. .. Saskatoon
Broadway
Boyd, William .... P.C. .... Kindersley
Bradley, J. .... N.D.P. .. Bengough-
Milestone
Britton, John .... P.C. .... Wilkie
Calvert, L. .... N.D.P. .. Moose Jaw
Wakamow
Carlson, E. .... N.D.P. .. Melville
Carson, C. .... N.D.P. .. Melfort
Cline E. .... N.D.P. .. Saskatoon Idylwyld
Crofford, J. .... N.D.P. .. Regina Lake
Centre
Cunningham, D. .... N.D.P. .. Canora
D'Autremont, Dan .... P.C. .... Souris-Cannington
Devine, Grant .... P.C. .... Estevan
Draper, L. .... N.D.P. .. Assiniboia-
Gravelbourg
Flavel, D. .... N.D.P. .. Last Mountain-
Touchwood
Goohsen, Jack .... P.C. .... Maple Creek
Goulet, K. .... N.D.P. .. Cumberland
Hagel, G. .... N.D.P. .. Moose Jaw Palliser

Hamilton, D. .......................N.D.P. ..Regina Wascana
Plains

Harper, R. ............................N.D.P. ..Pelly

Haverstock, Lynda ....Lib. ....Saskatoon
Greystone

Keeping, T. ..........................N.D.P. ..Nipawin

Kluz, K. ...............................N.D.P. ..Kelvington
Wadena

Knezacek, R. ........................N.D.P. ..Saltcoats

Koenker, E. ...........................N.D.P. Saskatoon
Sutherland-
University

Koskie, M. ...........................N.D.P. ..Quill Lakes

Kowalsky, P. ........................N.D.P. ..Prince Albert
Carlton

Kujawa, S. ............................N.D.P. ..Regina Albert
South

Langford, J. ..........................N.D.P. ..Shellbrook-Torch
River

Lautermilch, E. ....................N.D.P. ..Prince Albert
Northcote

Lingenfelter, D. ...................N.D.P. ..Regina Elphinstone

Lorje, P. ...............................N.D.P. ..Saskatoon
Wildwood

Lyons, R. .............................N.D.P. ..Regina Rosemont

MacKinnon, J. .....................N.D.P. ..Saskatoon
Westmount

Martens, Harold .................P.C. ....Morse

McPherson, G. ....................N.D.P. ..Shaunavon

Mitchell, R. .........................N.D.P. ..Saskatoon Fairview

Muirhead, Gerald ...............P.C. ....Arm River

Murray, S. ...........................N.D.P. ..Qu'Appelle-
Lumsden

Neudorf, William ................P.C. ....Rosthern

Penner, J. ............................N.D.P. ..Swift Current

Pringle ................................N.D.P. ..Saskatoon
Eastview-Haultain

Renaud, A. ..........................N.D.P. ..Kelsey-Tisdale

Rolfes, H. ............................N.D.P. ..Saskatoon Nutana

Romanow, J. ........................N.D.P. ..Saskatoon
Riversdale

Roy, A. ................................N.D.P. ..Kinistino

Scott, R. ..............................N.D.P. ..Indian Head-
Wolseley

Serby, C. .............................N.D.P. ..Yorkton

Shillington, E. .....................N.D.P. ..Regina Churchill
Downs

Simard, L. ...........................N.D.P. ..Regina Hillsdale

Solomon, J. .........................N.D.P. ..Regina North
West

Sonntag, M. ........................N.D.P. ..Meadow Lake

Stanger, V. ...........................N.D.P. ..CutKnife-
Lloydminster

Swenson, Rick .....................P.C. ....Thunder Creek

Tchorzewski, E. ...................N.D.P. ..Regina Dewdney

Teichrob, C. ........................N.D.P. ..Saskatoon River
Heights

Thompson, F. ......................N.D.P. ..Athabasca

Toth, Don ...........................P.C. ....Moosomin

Trew, K. .............................N.D.P. ..Regina Albert
North

Upshall, E. ..........................N.D.P. ..Humboldt

Van Mulligen, H. .................N.D.P. ..Regina Victoria

Whitmore, G. ......................N.D.P. ..Biggar

Wiens, B. ............................N.D.P. ..Rosetown-Elrose

Wormsbecker, R. .................N.D.P. ..Weyburn

ALBERTA

General Information: 403-427-2826

Adair, Al .............................P.C. ....Peace River

Ady, Jack .............................P.C. ....Cardston

Anderson, Dennis ................P.C. ....Calgary Currie

Barrett, Pam ........................N.D.P. ..Edmonton
Highlands

Betkowski, Nancy ................P.C. ....Edmonton Glenora

Black, Patricia .....................P.C. ....Calgary Foothills

Bogle, Bob ..........................P.C. ....Taber-Warner

Bradley, Fred ......................P.C. ....Pincher Creek-
Crowsnest

Brassard, Roy ......................P.C. ....Olds-Didsbury

Bruseker, Frank ....Lib. ....Calgary North
West

Calahasen, Pearl ..................P.C. ....Lesser Slave Lake

Cardinal, Mike ....................P.C. ....Athabasca-Lac La
Biche

Cherry, Doug ......................P.C. ....Lloydminster

Chumir, Sheldon ....Lib. ....Calgary Buffalo

Clegg, Glen .........................P.C. ....Dunvegan

Day, Stockwell .....................P.C. ....Red Deer North

Decore, Lawrence ....Lib. ....Edmonton
Glengarry

Dinning, Jim .......................P.C. ....Calgary Shaw

Doyle, Jerry ........................N.D.P. ..West Yellowhead

Drobot, John ......................P.C. ....St. Paul

Elliott, Bob .........................P.C. ....Grande Prairie

Elzinga, Peter ......................P.C. ....Sherwood Park

Evans, Brian .........................P.C. ....Banff-Cochrane
Ewasiuk, Ed ........................N.D.P. ..Edmonton Beverly
Fischer, Robert ....................P.C. ....Wainwright
Fjordbotten, LeRoy .............P.C. ....Macleod
Fowler, Dick ........................P.C. ....St. Albert
Fox, Derek ..........................N.D.P. ..Vegreville
Gagnon, Yolande ....Lib. ....Calgary McKnight
Gesell, Kurt .........................P.C. ....Clover Bar
Getty, Don ...........................P.C. ....Stettler
Gibeault, Gerry ...................N.D.P. ..Edmonton Mill Woods
Gogo, John ..........................P.C. ....Lethbridge West
Hawkesworth, Bob .............N.D.P. ..Calgary Mountain View
Hewes, Bettie ....Lib. ....Edmonton Glod Bar
Horsman, Jim ......................P.C. ....Medicine Hat
Hyland, Alan .......................P.C. ....Cypress-Redcliff
Isley, Ernie ..........................P.C. ....Bonnyville
Johnston, Dick ....................P.C. ....Lethbridge East
Jonson, Halvar ....................P.C. ....Ponoka-Rimbey
Klein, Ralph ........................P.C. ....Calgary Elbow
Kowalski, Ken .....................P.C. ....Barrhead
Laing, Bonnie ......................P.C. ....Calgary Bow
Laing, Marie ........................N.D.P. ..Edmonton Avonmore
Lund, Ty..............................P.C. ....Rocky Mountain House
Main, Doug .........................P.C. ....Edmonton Parkallen
Martin, Ray .........................N.D.P. ..Edmonton Norwood
McClellan, Shirley ..............P.C. ....Chinook
McCoy, Elaine .....................P.C. ....Calgary West
McEachern, Alex ................N.D.P. ..Edmonton Kingsway
McInnis, John .....................N.D.P. ..Edmonton Jasper Place
Mirosh, Dianne...................P.C. ....Calgary Glenmore
Mitchell, Grant ....Lib. ....Edmonton Meadowlark
Mjolsness, Christie ..............N.D.P. ..Edmonton Calder
Moore, Ron .........................P.C. ....Lacombe
Musgrove, Tom ...................P.C. ....Bow Valley
Nelson, Stan .......................P.C. ....Calgary McCall
Oldring, John ......................P.C. ....Red Deer South
Orman, Rick ........................P.C. ....Calgary Montrose
Osterman, Connie ...............P.C. ....Three Hills
Pashak, Barry ......................N.D.P. ..Calgary Forest Lawn

Paszkowski, Walter ..............P.C. ....Smoky River
Payne, Bill ...........................P.C. ....Calgary Fish Creek
Roberts, William .................N.D.P. ..Edmonton Centre
Rostad, Ken .........................P.C. ....Camrose
Schumacher, Stan ...............P.C. ....Drumheller
Severtson, Gary ..................P.C. ....Innisfail
Shrake, Gordon ...................P.C. ....Calgary Millican
Sigurdson, Tom ..................N.D.P. ..Edmonton Belmont
Sparrow, Don ......................P.C. ....Wetaskiwin-Leduc
Speaker, Ray ........................P.C. ....Little Bow
Stewart, Fred .......................P.C. ....Calgary North Hill
Tannas, Don ........................P.C. ....Highwood
Taylor, Nick ....Lib. ....Westlock-Sturgeon
Thurber, Tom ......................P.C. ....Drayton Valley
Trynchy, Peter .....................P.C. ....Whitecourt
Weiss, Norm .......................P.C. ....Fort McMurray
West, Steve ..........................P.C. ....Vermilion-Viking
Wickman, Percy ....Lib. ....Edmonton Whitemud
Woloshyn, Stan ...................N.D.P. ..Stony Plain
Wright, Gordon ..................N.D.P. ..Edmonton Strathcona
Zarusky, Steve .....................P.C. ....Redwater-Andrew

BRITISH COLUMBIA

Legislative Assembly: 604-387-3952

Anderson, Val ....Lib. ....Vancouver-Langara
Barlee, Bill ..........................N.D.P. ..Okanagan-Boundary
Barnes, Emery ....................N.D.P. ..Vancouver-Burrard
Beattie, Jim .........................N.D.P. ..Okanagan-Penticton
Blencoe, Robin ...................N.D.P. ..Victoria-Hillside
Boone, Lois .........................N.D.P. ..Prince George-Mount Robson
Brewin, Gretchen ...............N.D.P. ..Victoria-Beacon Hill
Cashore, John .....................N.D.P. ..Coquitlam-Mallardville
Charbonneau, Arthur ..........N.D.P. ..Kamloops
Chisholm, Robert ....Lib. ....Chilliwack
Clark, Glen .........................N.D.P. ..Vancouver-Kingsway
Conroy, Ed .........................N.D.P. ..Rossland-Trail

Copping, Barbra .... N.D.P. .. Port Moody-Burnaby Mountain

Cowie, Art .... Lib. .... Vancouver-Quilchena

Cull, Elizabeth .... N.D.P. .. Oak Bay-Gordon Head

Dalton, Jeremy .... Lib. .... West Vancouver-Capilano

De Jong, Harry .... S.C. .... Abbotsford

Dosanjh, Ujjal .... N.D.P. .. Vancouver-Kensington

Doyle, Jim .... N.D.P. .. Columbia River-Revelstoke

Dueck, Peter .... S.C. .... Matsqui

Edwards, Anne .... N.D.P. .. Kootenay

Evans, Corky .... N.D.P. .. Nelson-Creston

Farnworth, Michael .... N.D.P. .. Port Coquitlam

Farrell-Collins, Gary .... Lib. .... Fort Langley-Aldergrove

Fox, Len .... S.C. .... Prince Georgia-Omineca

Gabelmann, Colin .... N.D.P. .. North Island

Garden, Frank .... N.D.P. .. Cariboo North

Giesbrecht, Helmut .... N.D.P. .. Skeena

Gingell, Fred .... Lib. .... Delta South

Hagen, Anita .... N.D.P. .. New Westminster

Hammell, Sue .... N.D.P. .. Surrey-Green Timbers

Hanson, Lyall .... S.C. .... Okanagan-Vernon

Harcourt, Mike .... N.D.P. .. Vancouver-Mount Pleasant

Hartley, Bill .... N.D.P. .. Maple Redge-Pitt Meadows

Hurd, Wilf .... Lib. .... Surrey-White Rock

Jackson, Fredrick .... N.D.P. .. Kamloops-North Thompson

Janssen, Gerard .... N.D.P. .. Alberni

Jarvis, Daniel .... Lib. .... North Vancouver-Seymour

Jones, Barry .... N.D.P. .. Burnaby North

Jones, Ken .... Lib. .... Surrey-Cloverdale

Kasper, Rick .... N.D.P. .. Malahat-Juan de Fuca

Krog, Leonard .... N.D.P. .. Parksville-Qualicum

Lali, Harry .... N.D.P. .. Yale-Lillooet

Lord, Margaret .... N.D.P. .. Comox Valley

Lortie, Norm .... N.D.P. .. Delta North

Lovick, Dale .... N.D.P. .. Nanaimo

MacPhail, Joy .... N.D.P. .. Vancouver-Hastings

Marzari, Darlene .... N.D.P. .. Vancouver-Point Grey

Miller, Dan .... N.D.P. .. North Coast

Mitchell, David .... Lib. .... West Vancouver-Garibaldi

Neufeld, Richard .... S.C. .... Peace River North

O'Neill, Shannon .... N.D.P. .. Shuswap

Pement, Jackie .... N.D.P. .. Bulkley Valley-Stikine

Perry, Tom .... N.D.P. .. Vancouver-Little Mountain

Petter, Andrew .... N.D.P. .. Saanich South

Priddy, Penny .... N.D.P. .. Surrey-Newton

Pullinger, Jan .... N.D.P. .. Cowichan-Ladysmith

Ramsey, Paul .... N.D.P. .. Prince George South

Randall, Fred .... N.D.P. .. Burnaby-Edmonds

Reid, Linda .... Lib. .... Richmond East

Sawicki, Joan .... N.D.P. .. Burnaby-Willingdon

Schreck, David .... N.D.P. .. North Vancouver-Lonsdale

Serwa, Cliff .... S.C. .... Okanagan West

Sihota, Moe .... N.D.P. .. Esquimalt-Metchosin

Simpson, Bernie .... N.D.P. .. Vancouver-Fraserview

Smallwood, Joan .... N.D.P. .. Surrey-Whalley

Stephens, Lynn .... Lib. .... Langley

Streifel, Dennis .... N.D.P. .. Mission-Kent

Symons, Douglas .... Lib. .... Richmond Centre

Tanner, Clive .... Lib. .... Saanich North & the Islands

Tyabji, Judy .... Lib. .... Okanagan East

Warnke, Allan .... Lib. .... Richmond-Stevenson

Weisgerber, Jack .... S.C. .... Peace River South

Wilson, Gordon .... Lib. .... Powell River-Sunshine Coast

Zirnhelt, David .... N.D.P. .. Cariboo South

YUKON

Legislative Assembly: 403-667-5498

Brewster, Bill	P.C.	Kluane
Byblow, Maurice	N.D.P.	Faro
Devries, John	P.C.	Watson Lake
Firth, Bea	I.A.	
Hayden, Joyce	N.D.P.	Whitehorse South Centre
Joe, Danny	N.D.P.	Tatchun
Joe, Margaret	N.D.P.	Whitehorse North Centre
Johnston, Sam	N.D.P.	Cambell
Kassi, Norma	N.D.P.	Old Crow
Lang, Dan	P.C.	Whitehorse Porter Creek East
McDonald, Piers	N.D.P.	Mayo
Nordling, Alan	I.A.	
Penikett, Tony	N.D.P.	Whitehorse West
Phelps, Willard L.	P.C.	Hootalinqua
Phillips, Doug	P.C.	Whitehorse Riverdale North
Webster, Art	N.D.P.	Klondike

NORTHWEST TERRITORIES

Legislative Assembly: 403-873-7791

Allooloo, Titus	Amittuq
Antoine, Jim	Nahendeh
Arngna'naaq, Silas	Kivallivik
Arvaluk, James	Aivilik
Ballantyne, Michael	Yellowknife North
Bernhardt, Ernie	Kitikmeot
Cournoyea, Nellie	Nunakput
Dent, Charles	Yellowknife Frame Lake
Gargan, Samuel	Deh Cho
Kakfwi, Stephen	Sahtu
Koe, Fred	Inuvik
Lewis, Brain	Yellowknife Centre
Marie-Jewell, Jeannie	Thebacha
Mike, Rebecca	Baffin Central
Morin, Don	Tu Nedhe
Nerysoo, Richard	Mackenzie Delta
Ningark, John	Natilikmiot
Patterson, Dennis	Iqaluit
Pollard, John	Hay River
Pudlat, Kenoayoak	Baffin South
Pudluk, Ludy	High Arctic
Todd, John	Keewatin Central
Whitford, A.W.J.	Yellowknife South
Zoe, Henry	North Slave

Speakers and Clerks

House of Commons

Speaker: John Fraser
Rm. 222-N, House of Commons
Ottawa, Ontario
K1A 0A6
(613) 992-5042

Clerk: Robert Marleau
Parliament Buildings
Ottawa, Ontario
K1A 0A6
(613) 992-2986

The Senate

Speaker: Guy Charbonneau
Rm. 280-F, The Senate
Ottawa, Ontario
K1A 0A4
(613) 992-4416

Clerk: Gordon L. Barnhart
Rm. 289-S, The Senate
Ottawa, Ontario
K1A 0A4
(613) 992-2493

Newfoundland

Speaker: Tom Lush
Confederation Building
St. John's, Newfoundland
A1C 5T7
(709) 729-3403

Clerk: John Noel
Confederation Building
St. John's, Newfoundland
A1C 5T7
(709) 729-2579

Prince Edward Island

Speaker: Edward Clarke
P.P. Box 2000
Charlottetown, P.E.I.
C1A 7N8
(902) 368-4310

Clerk: Douglas B. Boylan
P.P. Box 2000
Charlottetown, P.E.I.
C1A 7N8
(902) 368-5970

Nova Scotia

Speaker: Ronald S. Russell
7th Floor, 1700 Greville Street
1 Government Place
Halifax, Nova Scotia
B3J 2Y3
(902) 424-5707

Clerk: Roderick MacArthur
Province House
Halifax Nova Scotia
B3J 2Y3
(902) 424-5978

New Brunswick

Speaker: Shirley Dysart
Legislative Assembly Building
P.O. Box 6000
Fredericton, New Brunswick
E3B 5H1
(506) 453-2506

Clerk: David Peterson
Legislative Assembly Building
P.O. Box 6000
Fredericton, New Brunswick
E3B 5H1
(506) 453-2506

Quebec

Speaker: Jean-Pierre Saintonge
Hôtel du Parlement
Québec (Québec)
G1A 1A4
(8+1+418) 643-2820

Clerk: Pierre Duchesne
Hôtel du Parlement
Québec (Québec)
G1A 1A4
(8+1+418) 643-2724

Ontario

Speaker: David Warner
Rm. 180, Legislative Building
Queen's Park
Toronto, Ontario
M7A 1A2
(416) 325-7435

Clerk: Claude L. DesRosiers
Rm. 104, Legislative Building
Queen's Park
Toronto, Ontario
M7A 1A2
(416) 325-7431

Manitoba

Speaker: Denis Rocan
Legislative Building
Winnipeg, Manitoba
R3C 0V8
(204) 945-3706

Clerk: William H. Remnant
237 Legislative Building
Winnipeg, Manitoba
R3C 0V8
(204) 945-3707

Saskatchewan

Speaker: Herman Rolfe
Rm. 129, Legislative Building
Regina, Saskatchewan
S4S 0B3
(306) 787-2282

Clerk: Gwenn Ronyk
Rm. 239, Legislative Building
Regina, Saskatchewan
S4S 0B3
(306) 787-2279

Alberta

Speaker: David H. Carter
325 Legislative Building
Edmonton, Alberta
T5K 2B6
(403) 427-2464

Clerk: David McNeil
313 Legislative Building
Edmonton, Alberta
T5K 2B6
(403) 427-2580

British Columbia

Speaker: Joan Sawicki
Parliament Buildings
Victoria, British Columbia
V8V 1X4
(604) 387-3952

Clerk: Ian M. Horne
Rm. 221, Parliament Buildings
Victoria British Columbia
V8V 1X4
(604) 387-3785

Yukon

Speaker: Sam Johnston
P.O. Box 2703
Whitehorse, Yukon
Y1A 2C6
(403) 667-5662

Clerk: Patrick L. Michael
P.O. Box 2703
Whitehorse, Yukon
Y1A 2C6
(403) 667-5498

Northwest Territories

Speaker: Michael A. Ballantyne
5010-49th Street
(P.O. Box 1320)
Yellowknife, Northwest Territories
X1A 2L9
(403) 873-7629

Clerk: David M. Hamilton
5010-49th Street
(P.O. Box 1320)
Yellowknife, Northwest Territories
X1A 2L9
(403) 873-7457
1-800-661-0784